Labor's War at Home

In the series
Labor in Crisis
edited by Stanley Aronowitz

Labor's War at Home
The CIO in World War II

With a New Introduction by the Author

Nelson Lichtenstein

Temple University Press
Philadelphia

For Eileen

Temple University Press, Philadelphia 19122
Copyright © 2003 by Temple University
All rights reserved
Published 2003
Printed in the United States of America
First edition copyright © 1982 Cambridge University Press,
    and published by the Press Syndicate of the University of Cambridge.

⊗ The paper used in this publication meets the requirements of
the American National Standard for Information Sciences—Permanence
of Paper for Printed Library Materials, ANSI z39.48-1984

Library of Congress Cataloging-in-Publication Data

Lichtenstein, Nelson.
    Labor's war at home : the CIO in World War II : with a new introduction
by the author / Nelson Lichtenstein.
        p.   cm. – (Labor in crisis)
    Originally published: Cambridge ; New York : Cambridge University Press, 1982.
    Includes bibliographical references and index.
    ISBN 1-59213-196-4 (cloth : alk. paper) – ISBN 1-59213-197-2 (pbk. : alk. paper)
        1. Congress of Industrial Organizations (U.S.) – History.   2. Labor Policy –
United States – History – 20th century.   I. Title.   II. Series.
    HD8055.C75L5 2003
    331.88′33′097309044–dc21

                                                                    2002041625

2   4   6   8   9   7   5   3   1

Contents

Abbreviations

ACTU	Association of Catholic Trade Unionists
ACWA	Amalgamated Clothing Workers of America
AFL	American Federation of Labor
CIO	Congress of Industrial Organizations
GE	General Electric
GM	General Motors
IAM	International Association of Machinists
ILGWU	International Ladies Garment Workers Union
ILWU	International Longshoremen's and Warehousemen's Union
IUMSWA	Industrial Union of Marine and Shipbuilding Workers of America
NDAC	National Defense Advisory Commission
NDMB	National Defense Mediation Board
NIRA	National Industrial Recovery Administration
NLRB	National Labor Relations Board
NMU	National Maritime Union
NRA	National Recovery Administration
NWLB	National War Labor Board
OPA	Office of Price Administration
OPM	Office of Production Management
OWM	Office of War Mobilization
PAC	Political Action Committee
PWOC	Packinghouse Workers Organizing Committee
SWOC	Steel Workers Organizing Committee
TWOC	Textile Workers Organizing Committee
TWU	Transport Workers Union
TWUA	Textile Workers Union of America
UAW	United Automobile Workers
UE	United Electrical, Radio, and Machine Workers
UMW	United Mine Workers
URW	United Rubber Workers
URWDSE	United Retail, Wholesale, and Department Store Employees
USW	United Steelworkers of America
WMC	War Manpower Commission
WPB	War Production Board

Introduction to the new edition

This book is a product of the political and ideological debate that engaged my New Left generation when, in the early 1970s, so many campus-based radicals inaugurated a remarkable probe into the character, meaning, and history of the working class and its institutions. Two events in particular seemed to crystallize my decision to write a history of unionism and the state during the 1940s. The first came on the evening of September 14, 1970, when a few dozen Berkeley students drove down to Fremont's sprawling General Motors assembly complex to support rank and file workers when the United Automobile Workers struck the company at midnight. Hundreds jumped the gun and rushed out of the factory a couple of hours early. The youthful, boisterous crowd happily waved our hand-painted signs – "GM – Mark of Exploitation," took over the union hall, and cheered militant speeches, both anti-company and anti-union. It was the beginning of the first coordinated, nationwide stoppage at GM since the winter of 1945–46. We didn't know it at the time, but the 1970 GM strike, which would continue for ten weeks, came right in the midst of the last great wave of twentieth-century industrial conflict in the United States.[1]

While all this was going on, the Berkeley branch of the International Socialists, a Trotskyist formation of New Left sensibility and "third camp" (i.e. anti-Stalinist and anti-capitalist) politics, was in the midst of furious debate. Along with others radicalized on the campuses and in the anti–Vietnam War movement, a "turn toward the working class" had begun to propel thousands of student radicals into the nation's factories, warehouses, hospitals, and offices. From Berkeley, friends and comrades took off for Detroit auto plants, Chicago steel mills, Cleveland trucking companies, and all sorts of industrial jobs throughout the Bay Area.[2]

But what were they to do when they got there? If these "industrializers" began to work their way up through the trade union apparatus, they would be helping to build an institution that seemed positively anathema to many of us. The AFL-CIO remained a firm backer of the war in Vietnam; moreover, even the more progressive unions, like the UAW and the Packinghouse Workers, appeared so strapped by bureaucracy, law, contracts, and political allegiances that they hardly seemed an appropriate vehicle to advance the class struggle. C. Wright Mills, Stanley Aronowitz, Harvey Swados, C. L. R. James, and other radicals had taught us that the growth of the union bureaucracy and the government's intrusive labor relations apparatus had robbed labor of its radical heritage. By incorporating the trade unions into the structures of the American state, or at least the two-party system, these institutions were thought to resemble those of Stalinist or fascist regimes, where statist unions and labor fronts had been foisted upon the working class.[3]

Thus in the debates that animated my generation of Berkeley students, older activists, like Hal Draper and Stan Weir, made much of labor's experience during the World War II mobilization era. Then the unions had offered the state and enforced upon their members a "no-strike pledge," even as "wildcat" strikes (i.e., those unauthorized by higher officials), union factionalism, and labor party agitation energized many of the rank-and-filers who had built the industrial unions during the great strikes that electrified the nation between 1934 and 1941. A new generation of working-class radicals must therefore keep a wary eye on the union leadership and build their own independent caucuses within the labor movement.[4] Indeed, I was beginning my research as a wave of spirited strikes, many of them wildcat, shattered the industrial relations routine in Detroit auto factories, Midwest trucking barns, big city post offices, and throughout California agriculture. Between 1967 and 1973 the size and number of strikes reached levels not seen since the immediate post–World War II years.

This was the perspective put forth in my 1974 University of California dissertation, published in 1982 as *Labor's War at Home: The CIO in World War II.*[5] The book was skeptical about the staying power of New Deal liberalism; saw the warfare state as a repressive institution; criticized Congress of Industrial Organization leaders, both "conservative" (i.e. social democratic) and Communist; and celebrated the World War II wildcat strike movement in the auto, rubber, and shipbuilding industries. It saw that the emergence of a stolid, bureaucratically insular postwar labor movement was a product not of some inherent, "job-conscious" parochialism within the union rank and file, nor of McCarthyite repression after the war, but of the bargain struck between the government and cooperative, patriotic union leaders during World War II itself. This kind of argument was anathema to the then dominant set of industrial relations scholars, many themselves trained while serving with the War Labor Board and other labor relations agencies of the wartime era. These influential scholars, some of whom, like John Dunlop, Clark Kerr, Archibald Cox, George Schultz, and James MacGregor Burns, had achieved high visibility posts in government and the academy, saw labor's World War II experience as a gloriously successful one: the unions had matured by demonstrating their patriotism, doubling their membership, and stabilizing their relationship with employers and the state.

To their way of thinking, labor history really had come to an end round about 1941, if not before; what followed was "industrial relations," a policy-oriented research enterprise that sought to fine-tune a depoliticized system of labor-management accommodation and conflict.[6] Their enormous influence blocked efforts to reconfigure a twentieth-century history of class relations. Indeed, the most influential labor historians of the 1970s, Herbert Gutman, David Montgomery, and E. P. Thompson, were all students of society and ideology in the eighteenth and nineteenth centuries. David Brody had written a pioneering social history of the 1919 steel strike, but in the 1970s there were still few conceptual tools at hand by which to examine a history of the working class or its institutions during the mid–twentieth-century decades. The "state" had not yet been "brought back in," to use a phrase coined by Theda Skocpol and her associates; nor had historians begun to deconstruct the twentieth-century working class into those categories, including race, gender, skill, and mentalité, that have subsequently proven so illuminating. During the early 1970s the left, even the academic left, still imagined an undifferentiated rank and file, which was itself the ideological product of a biopolar discourse that dichotomized a powerful set of labor leaders and a bureaucratically repressed or misled mass union membership. Thus, there were more studies written on the Knights of Labor in that decade than on the Congress of Industrial Organizations. For labor historians it seemed a lot easier to find a useable past in the conflicts that divided a late nineteenth-century mill town than among those contractual disputes and internal union fights that structured the production regime in a Detroit factory circa 1945.

Things are different today. Thirty years of union decline and labor–liberal defeat have transformed the questions historians choose to ask about the trajectory of organized labor during the New Deal and World War II years. Contemporary labor and social historians write more about the CIO than the Knights, or even the radical Industrial Workers of the World. In the early twentieth-first century, when the proportion of all union workers hovers just above 13 percent, organized labor's incorporation into a claustrophobic state apparatus seems far less of an issue than survival of those same unions, not to mention the revival of a socially conscious, New Deal impulse within the body politic. The postwar fate of New Deal liberalism has become a highly contentious issue, so an increasingly rich historiography on the "New Deal order" now stands embedded within a reconsideration of the postwar transformation of U.S. capitalism itself. We are becoming as interested in the ideas and institutions of those who fought against labor and the New Deal – the corporations, the various layers of the middle class, the anti–New Deal politicians of the South and West, the traditionalist conservatives within the working class itself – as we are determined to dissect the contradictions inherent in mid–twentieth-century labor liberalism and the Rooseveltian state.[7]

In this re-evaluation, the line that once divided the Depression decade from that of the war and the era of postwar politics now appears increasingly fractured. In part this stems from our understanding that the working class of the 1930s was hardly as radical as once conceived, or rather, that its presumptive militancy cannot be divorced from the state structures and institutions that are dialectically complicit in that advanced level of working-class mobilization. The nature of "militancy" and "conservatism" within the working class has become hugely problematic, as questions of ethnicity, racism, sexism, homophobia, and regionalism have moved to the fore.[8] Thus the warfare state did not instantly make irrelevant the politics, the social ideologies, or the ethnocultural matrix that had structured class relations during the heyday of the New Deal itself. Continuity, not abrupt change, characterizes the political culture of the late 1930s and early 1940s. As I often tell my classes, December 7, 1941 is the most overrated day in U.S. history.[9]

Thus, historians now see that the political economy of World War II is part of a larger New Deal order that stretched from the early 1930s to the 1970s. This was an era characterized by Democratic party dominance, Keynesian statecraft, and a trade union movement whose power and presence was too often taken for granted, not the least by historians of "state development." Industry-wide unions sustained both the dominance of the Democratic party and a quasi-corporatist system of labor-management relations whose impact, far transcending the realm of firm-centered collective bargaining, framed much of the polity's consensus on taxes, social provision, and industry regulation. And finally, the system of production, distribution, and social expectations that characterized both union strength and business enterprise was uniquely stable, resting on both a well-protected continental market and a technologically and ideologically dominant mass-production model.

In this context the economic power wielded by American trade unions was by its very nature political, for the New Deal had thoroughly politicized all relations among the union movement, the business community, and the state. The New Deal provided a set of semi-permanent political structures in which key issues of vital concern to the trade union movement might be accommodated. The National Labor Relations Board established the legal basis of union power and a mechanism for its state sanction; New Deal regulatory bodies stabilized competition in key industries like trucking, coal, air transport, banking, and utilities; and the National War Labor Board provided a tripartite institution that set national wage policy and contributed to the rapid wartime growth of the new trade unions. Corporatism of this sort called for government agencies, composed of capital, labor, and public representatives, to substitute bureaucratic initiative and national economic planning for the chaos and inequities of the market.[10] The successive reappearance of such tripartite governing arrangements during the mid–twentieth-century seemed to signal that in the future as in the past, the fortunes of organized labor would be determined as much by a process of politicized bargaining in Washington as by the give and take of contractual collective bargaining.

This was neither "free collective bargaining" nor the kind of syndicalism that, during the era of the Great War, had informed phrases like "social reconstruction," "industrial democracy," and "workers' control."[11] To insure industrial peace during the Second World War, the state sustained a coercive labor relations apparatus that policed not only recalcitrant corporations, but also radical shop stewards, uncooperative unions, and striking workers. A generation ago the repressive character of this regime came in for much attention. Thus Martin Glaberman celebrated the unstructured spontaneity by which new industrial migrants threw off the contract shackles and Wagner Act procedures forged by the New Deal state. George Lipsitz searched for the link that would unite in song and struggle many of those same working-class rebels, and especially those white Appalachians and African Americans marginal to the New Deal universe. And I condemned as a disastrous bargain the "no-strike pledge" that virtually all union leaders offered the nation. They won "union security" and a rising membership, but advanced the union movement's internal bureaucratic deformities as well as its marriage to the Democratic party and the warfare state.[12]

But in the early years of the twenty-first century, the potential payoff from the corporatist bargain of the World War II era looks much better than it once did. Resistance to union organizing declined dramatically during the war as the union movement nearly doubled in size. In the South the work of the War Labor Board (WLB), not to mention the Fair Employment Practice Commission, generated something close to a social revolution. As Michelle Brattain, Daniel Clark, Michael Honey, and Robert Korstad have demonstrated, the WLB orders that mandated union recognition and collective bargaining opened up the organizational and ideological space that enabled workers, both black and white, to liberate themselves from three generations of paternalism and repression. In his study of Winston-Salem tobacco workers, Korstad rightly calls this the "Daybreak of Freedom."[13] Meanwhile, in the North the WLB socialized much of the labor movement's prewar agenda, thus making union security, grievance arbitration, seniority, vacation pay, sick leave, and night-shift supplements standard entitlements mandated for an increasingly large section of the working class. The Little Steel wage formula, although bitterly resisted by the more highly paid and well organized sections of the working class, had enough loopholes and special dispensations to enable low-paid workers in labor-short industries to bring their wages closer to the national average.[14] Thus black wages rose twice as fast as white, and weekly earnings in cotton textiles and in retail trade increased about 50 percent faster than in high-wage industries like steel and auto. By the onset of postwar reconversion, WLB wage policy was explicitly egalitarian. "It is not desirable to increase hourly earnings in each industry in accordance with the rise of productivity in that industry," declared a July 1945 memorandum. "The proper goal of policy is to increase hourly earnings generally in proportion to the average increase of productivity in the economy as *a whole*."[15]

The capacity of the state to reshape labor relations at the point of production has also been the subject of much debate and reevaluation. *Labor's War at Home* reflected the perspective of those union militants and dissidents who in the 1960s and 1970s saw the codification of routine industrial relations as a disaster for democracy and militancy inside the factory, mine, and mill. The Taft-Hartley era labor law, much of which had been first deployed by the War Labor Board, became an increasingly restrictive straightjacket that constrained and suffocated the union movement's bolder and more progressive spirits. The routinization of industrial relations, the marginalization of shop-floor activism symbolized and embodied in the wartime no-strike pledge, and the rise of a social patriotic ideology all devalued worker militancy and opened the door to the restoration of managerial authority. In the 1980s this perspective generated much support, especially from a new generation of legal scholars animated by the emancipatory spirit of the New Left. Christopher Tomlins thought that the increasingly intrusive character of the New Deal labor law generated little more than a "counterfeit liberty." James Atleson argued that wartime policies, designed to stabilize labor relations and "control rank-and-file militancy" would be "transferred to the peacetime era without any serious questioning of the wisdom of the application of policies originally designed for a quite different time." And in her classic *Yale Law Journal* essay of 1981, Katherine Van Wezel Stone argued that the ideology of "industrial pluralism," which projected a false equality between the power of labor and management, "serves as a vehicle for the manipulation of employee discontent and for the legitimization of existing inequalities of power in the workplace." The elaborate system of grievance handling and arbitration put in place by WLB experts and the postwar courts that followed their lead functioned largely as a therapeutic apparatus of control, not a mechanism designed to achieve industrial justice.[16]

But not all historians have agreed with this doleful perspective. Indeed, if the industrial relations system put in place during the 1940s was so hostile to working-class interests, then why have almost all employers resisted it? Why did company executives see union contracts, seniority systems, and grievance procedures as such a threat to their managerial prerogatives, to the flexibility of their enterprise, to their "right to manage?" And this managerial anti-unionism has been even more the case in the years since 1980, when one has had to search far and wide for any pocket of militant shop-floor unionism.

What seems so clear now, in an era of union defeat and retreat, is that almost any system of "industrial jurisprudence," which was the phrase used by labor economist Sumner Slichter at the time, or "workplace contractualism," a term later coined by historian David Brody, represents a terrain of struggle that is advantageous to most workers in most places. As Steven Tolliday and Jonathan Zeitlin argued shortly after the appearance of *Labor's War at Home*, and in opposition to the perspective put forward in that book, "The contractual system of collective bargaining which emerged from the Second World War placed substantial constraints on management's freedom to deploy labor and to impose arbitrary discipline."[17] This was a judgment that was certainly sustained by those studying the struggle of unions to secure a foothold in the textile industry of the American South, or in industries where women or people of color represented a substantial proportion of the workforce. In his story of two North Carolina textile plants unionized during the war, Daniel Clark hails the grievance procedures and arbitration system as "liberating forces" in the lives of these mill workers.[18] African Americans became staunch unionists, and firm proponents of the grievance procedure, even in unions and workplaces where the seniority system was structured to defend the interests of the white majority. This is because they understood that for those at the bottom of the workplace hierarchy, to those long subject to the capricious exercise of power by petty elites or to an ethnically coded set of discriminations, the very bureaucratization of labor relations had an impact that was liberating in the world of work. Unionism forced the company to pay "the job not the man," asserted a black Birmingham steel worker. "CIO came along and said, well, if you get on a job, from the day you're hired, your seniority starts," remembered a wartime packinghouse worker. "And whoever comes behind you, gets behind you. Color has nothing to do with it."[19]

Some working-class militants may have found this war-era corporatism a poor bargain, but business executives, Southern bourbons, and most of the GOP hated New Dealism of the 1940s even more. In their more recent books, Alan Brinkley and Steven Fraser have sustained my view that the New Deal was very much on the defensive after 1938. The New Deal order did remain intact, but at the policy level, labor–liberals fought a defensive, rearguard battle. In his biography of Sidney Hillman, Fraser entitles his chapter on Hillman's sojourn as a high-level government official, "The Fall to Power." New Deal liberals and Keynesian planners who sought to use the defense-era mobilization crisis to advance a social-democratic perspective found that de facto control of the corporate economy's commanding heights was almost entirely beyond their influence.[20] "The military services were insulated from popular pressures and were not part of the New Deal coalition," writes political scientist Brian Waddell. "They had no agenda for displacing corporate prerogatives through their management of mobilization, as did the New Dealers." FDR's Secretary of War, Henry Stimson, reflected the military-corporate–Wall Street mind-set in a 1941 entry in his diary: "If you are going to try to go to war, or prepare for war, in a capitalist country, you have got to let business make money out of the process or business won't work."[21]

Despite much wishful historiography, no "corporate liberal" bloc ever emerged in the United States, even at the height of union strength and New Deal political hegemony. Twenty years ago Howell Harris demonstrated that even the most "realistic" U.S. firms, like General Motors, U.S. Rubber, and General Electric, were determined to contain, constrain, and marginalize trade unionism. Sanford Jacoby sustains Harris's doleful perspective in the more recent *Modern Manors: Welfare Capitalism Since the New Deal* by rediscovering a cohort of powerful, "progressive" firms that successfully stymied the union impulse, even when this required outright violation of NLRB and WLB directives. Historians of Southern labor and industrialization have never detected much managerial interest there in a postwar accord with the unions. Moreover, Jefferson Cowie's superb *Capital Moves: RCA's 70-Year Quest for Cheap Labor,* demonstrates that even when companies avoided an outright confrontation with labor, corporate liberal firms like RCA systematically relocated production to North American sites thought inhospitable to effective unionism.[22]

Andrew Workman's detailed study of the National Association of Manufactures (NAM) further sustains the view that most American corporations found war-era corporatism intolerable. The participation of NAM leaders in FDR's 1941 labor–management conference setting up the WLB soon generated a backlash that put a new, aggressive set of anti-union, anti–New Deal leaders in charge of the business group. This hardening of management outlook was best exemplified by the famous 1944 photograph of two fully armed soldiers carrying Montgomery Ward's reactionary chairman, Sewell Avery, out of the corporation's Chicago headquarters. Because Avery had defied a WLB order to treat with his unionized employees, Roosevelt took over Montgomery Ward.

But Avery thereby became a hero to the anti–New Deal right. Thus, by 1945 when the Truman administration tried to orchestrate a postwar compact between labor and capital, the NAM skillfully and determinedly sabotaged the high-profile labor–management conference finally held in November of that year. Above all, NAM wanted to eliminate the role of the state in establishing an industry-wide incomes policy, and it sought to discipline union strength at the shop-floor level. This aggressive stance made unavoidable a massive postwar strike wave and thus helped precipitate the anti-labor backlash that saturated American political culture in the years immediately following.[23]

This drift to the right in corporate policy and wartime administrative governance was framed by the consolidation, in Congress and in the national political discourse, of a generation-spanning alliance between Republicans and Southern Democrats. After a careful assessment, Ira Katznelson and his associates have determined that the key element cementing this conservative coalition was the hostility of both factions to the rise of a powerful trade union movement. Until the late 1930s, Southern Democrats supported most New Deal social legislation, albeit with the proviso that such initiatives protect the Southern racial order and the regional advantages of New South agriculture and manufacturing. But this Southern allegiance to the New Deal collapsed after 1938 when organized labor became a more assertive component within the Democratic party. Southern pro-labor voting stopped, and in the war-era Congresses an anti-labor conservative coalition became dominant. The war cemented the Dixiecrat alliance with the Republicans because a labor-backed reform of the South now posed a real threat to the racial oligarchy of the region. Wartime labor shortages and military conscription facilitated union organizing and civil rights agitation. Writes Katznelson: "In this more uncertain moment of rapid economic and central state expansion, the South redrew the line between those aspects of the New Deal it would tolerate and those it could not."[24]

But conservative elites did not get everything they wanted in World War II. Even as they increased their influence within the state's labor-relations apparatus, their social and economic power was challenged by a counter-mobilization from below that sought to take advantage of the unprecedented demand for labor while at the same time actualizing the social patriotic ethos that was the quasi-official ideology of the World War II home front. Indeed, this increasingly contentious juxtaposition, between a rightward drifting state apparatus and an increasingly organized and self-mobilized working class, represents the great paradox of the war, a dichotomy that would be resolved in the postwar years by a rapid, politically brutal divorce between popular aspirations and the state policies needed to fulfill them.

In a shrewd critique of *Labor's War at Home*, Gary Gerstle has argued that the working class of World War II "did not just go to work. It went to war." By this he means that war workers took their patriotism seriously, and their war-era cultural standing and social value to the nation perhaps even more so. In 1940 a majority of industrial workers in the North and West were still immigrants or the sons and daughters of immigrants. The coercive Americanization crusades of the First World War had been directed at these Poles, Hungarians, Jews, Slavs, and Italians, but the ideological thrust of World War II was far more pluralist. In what FDR called the Arsenal of Democracy, the workers became the soldiers of production, and it was now patriotic, not socially demeaning, to take a factory job. Every foxhole movie and war bond campaign celebrated the ethnic heterogeneity of plebian America. Likewise, the new industrial unions were vehicles not only for gaining economic power but also for overcoming cultural discrimination. CIO electoral propaganda in 1944 proclaimed, "All of us in America are foreigners or the children of foreigners. . . . They built the railroads, they built the highways, they built the factories. . . . They all have equal rights to share in America."[25] Working-class agency during the war therefore represented a culmination of the pluralist impulse inaugurated by the New Deal itself. To Gerstle, rising wages and full employment "in conjunction with the wartime celebration of the nation's multicultural character allowed European ethnics to believe that the American dream had finally been placed within their grasp."[26]

All true, yet in the first edition of *Labor's War at Home*, I devalued the social patriotism of the wartime working class, in part because it was hard to do otherwise in an era when "hard hat" hyper-patriotism was so crassly manipulated by the Nixon White House.[27] But during World War II social integration – a belief in the American dream – did not spell social quiescence. Indeed, the very sense of Americanism that Gerstle evokes so well laid the basis for the claims upon their employers and the state that working-class Americans made with such frequency during World War II. Although the character of their aspirations would differ according to their gender, race, age, and occupation, the social-patriotic ethos generated by anti-fascist propaganda and war-era mobilization politicized new aspects of working-class life.

Take the wage issue, for example. While wartime pay was higher than ever, wages represented more than money to most workers. The level of reimbursement symbolized a worker's social worth, and in years past the pay packet had often been an explicit social marker ranking the status of men and women, black and white, Slav and German. Thus, in a war in which patriotic egalitarianism was a pervasive home-front rationale, and in which workers' pay was a product of governmental fiat, inequal-ities of all sorts – in pay, promotions, seniority, and general respect – proved to be among the most vexing and persistent causes of shop-floor discontent.[28] In his study of the "politics of sacrifice" during the war, Mark Leff finds that the War Advertising Council and other business interests feared such a political construction. They therefore worked strenuously to manipulate and constrain an ideology of equal sacrifice, "to curb its subversive potential."[29]

Indeed, a patriotic subversion of the old order took many forms. Ethnic hierarchies lost much of their potency during World War II, al-though we also understand that one overripe fruit of the war era's social patriotism, even of its more liberal brand of cultural pluralism, was the transformation of ethnicity into a sense of entitled whiteness. The white working class became more unified, more militant, and more determined to police its own boundaries, both at work, where seniority rights and skill definitions were highly racialized, and even more so in the working-class neighborhoods where the defense of racial exclusivity consistently trumped laborite liberalism. As Tom Sugrue, Kenneth Durr, John T. McGreevy, and Bruce Nelson have shown in such graphic detail, this white defensive militancy became the submerged rock upon which post-war liberalism would splinter, first at the municipal level, and later on a larger political stage. The degree to which New Deal pluralism and wartime social patriotism had reconstructed white ethnic America re-mained somewhat veiled for nearly two decades, until the rise of an anti-state, Wallacite discourse in the 1960s gave to this insular racism a polit-ical legitimacy it had never before enjoyed, at least outside the South.[30]

By contrast, the legitimacy and visibility of the African-American free-dom struggle, and that of the Mexican-American civil rights movement in the West, took a quantum leap forward during World War II itself. There is not much on this in *Labor's War at Home*, but there should have been because, with some notable exceptions, most labor historians have postulated that mass industrial unionism has more often than not put the citizenship rights of its members and their families high on the socio-political agenda. And this was certainly true during World War II, even taking into account the violent racism of so many in the white rank and file and the hate strikes that periodically exploded in Detroit, Mobile, Los Angeles, and other industrial cities.[31]

There were two reasons for the giant leap forward in civil rights consciousness. First, the war inaugurated a quarter century of African-American migration from farm to city and from the South to the North and West. Compared to the Great Migration of World War I, the African-American proletarianization experience during the era from 1941 to 1946 (and extended in a continuous fashion until the deep recession of 1957–58) was broader, longer, and more massive. Second, this process of class recomposition was accompanied by an ideological transformation which pushed the issue of African-American political and economic rights to near the top of American liberalism's immediate postwar agenda. Just as the New Deal had offered a new kind of pluralist citizenship to immigrant America, so too did World War II engender a vibrant rights-conscious sense of entitlement among African Americans. This was not because the Army or the mobilization agencies or even the newly established Fair Employment Practices Commission (FEPC) were staunch friends of civil rights liberalism. They were not, but the patriotic egalitarianism of the war effort, combined with the creation of a set of state institutions open to grievance and redress, laid the basis for a dialectically powerful relationship – not unlike that of the early 1960s – between social mobilization at the bottom and state building from above. Thus, at the start of the war a reporter for the NAACP's *The Crisis* labeled the CIO a "lamp of democracy" throughout the old Confederate states. The NAACP recruited tens of thousands of unionized workers, increasing its membership nine-fold during World War II, even as it became a foundational pillar of the emergent labor–liberal coalition.[32]

The flagship agency was the FEPC, established by the Roosevelt liberals to fend off A. Philip Randolph's 1941 March on Washington. The FEPC had little institutional power, but its symbolic import was hardly less than that of the Freedman's Bureau in the early Reconstruction era. "It legitimatized black demands and emboldened protest," writes historian Eileen Boris. FEPC hearings, investigations, and grievance procedures gave African Americans a point of leverage with the federal government that proved corrosive to the old racial order. Despite its embattled status within the state apparat – a Southern filibuster would finally kill it early in 1946 – the FEPC's energetic, union-connected, interracial staff served as one of the late New Deal's great mobilizing bureaucracies. As the Atlanta *Journal* sourly put it in 1944, "So adroit are its maneuvers that it is usually out of the picture when any trouble it has started is full-blown. It calls on other government agencies to enforce its decrees and whip dissenters into line."[33]

This kind of mobilization from below, legitimated by government policy from above, also generated a powerful dialectic in the gendered world of consumption politics.[34] Here we find another front in the crucial battle over the relationship between wages and prices that had been so thoroughly politicized during World War II. Indeed, UAW president Walter Reuther would inaugurate the great postwar strike wave with the slogan "Purchasing Power for Prosperity." The key agency in this battle was the Office of Price Administration (OPA). Like the National Labor Relations Board and the FEPC, the OPA's effectiveness depended upon the organized activism of huge numbers of once voiceless individuals. In 1945 OPA employed nearly 75,000 and enlisted the voluntary participation of another 300,000, mainly urban housewives and union activists, who checked the prices and quality of the consumer goods regulated by the government. OPA chief Chester Bowles, a spirited New Deal liberal, called the volunteer price checkers "as American as baseball." Many merchants denounced them as a "kitchen gestapo," but the polls found that more than 80 percent of all citizens backed OPA price-control regulations. In response, the National Association of Manufactures poured as much money into anti-OPA propaganda as it would later spend on agitation for the 1947 Taft-Hartley Act. NAM called OPA an agency leading to "regimented chaos," an oxymoronic phrase which nevertheless captured business fear of a powerful state whose regulatory purposes were implemented by an activist, organized citizenry.[35]

In recent years many historians, policy-makers, and labor partisans have argued for both the existence of and virtue of a "labor–management accord" that governed industrial relations in a generation-long era following World War II. Writing in the early 1980s, economists Samuel Bowles, David Gordon, and Thomas Weisskopf were among the first scholars to identify a "tacit agreement between corporate capitalists and the organized labor movement." Fifteen years later AFL-CIO President John Sweeney himself called for the restoration of the "unwritten social

compact" between capital and labor; while Robert Reich, President
Clinton's first Secretary of Labor, jawboned corporations to restore their
side of the accord.[36]

Although *Labor's War at Home* emphasized the routinization of conflict
in postwar labor–management relations, the book saw this postwar settlement as something quite fragile and hardly a victory for ordinary
workers. Indeed, phrases like "social compact" and "social contract"
were first deployed in the early 1980s by liberals and laborites anxious to
condemn wage cuts, denounce corporate union-busting, and define what
they seemed to be losing in Reagan's America. But such language was
altogether absent in the first decades after the end of World War II.
Most unionists would have thought the very idea of a consensual accord
between themselves and their corporate adversaries a clever piece of
management propaganda. Unionists were well aware that no sector of
American capital had agreed, even under wartime conditions, to an "accord" with labor or the New Deal state. There was no corporatist settlement, either of the hard variety embodied in tripartite mechanisms of
economic regulation, nor in the soft bargaining patterns whereby the
unions sought to regulate wages and working conditions – and even
company pricing policies – in a single industry. A kind of meso-corpo-
ratism did structure a few otherwise highly competitive industries, such
as trucking, airlines, railroads, and municipal transport. There, the extraordinarily high level of unionization reached during the war – above
90 percent – did persist for three decades afterwards. But such corporatist arrangements came flying apart where management in highly competitive industries went on the postwar offensive: first in textiles, where
War Labor Board orders were routinely violated in 1944 and 1945, and
then in retail trade, electrical products, and all along unionism's white
collar frontier.[37]

Though the destruction of trade unionism in the core mid-century industries – auto, steel, rubber, and construction – was not on the corporate agenda, the depoliticization of collective bargaining was an almost
universal goal of these industries' corporate managers. All across the
business spectrum, from brass-hat conservatives on the right to corporate liberal statesmen on the left, postwar executives sought to privatize
and ghettoize bargaining relationships and economic conflict. The abolition or devaluation of the war era's mobilizing bureaucracies – the
War Labor Board, NLRB, OPA, and FEPC – stood near the top of the
postwar Republican–business agenda. Conflict over the degree to which

the unions could still enlist the state in recalibrating the relationship between capital and labor constituted the heart of so many of the celebrated struggles of the postwar era: the 1946 strike wave, the subsequent fight over OPA, enactment of the Taft-Hartley Act in 1947, and the battle over company-paid health insurance and pensions during the 1949–50 collective bargaining round.[38] By the 1950s the divorce between the system of collective bargaining and American politics was far more complete than in any other industrial democracy. Although mid-century strike levels remained comparatively high, the industrial relations system of that era was so "free" that liberal Democratic political victories in 1948, 1958, and 1964 had virtually no impact upon this increasingly insular collective bargaining regime.

So were there any alternative structures that might have emerged from the labor politics of World War II? In *Labor's War at Home*, I saw the wildcat strikers and the militant shop stewards as heroic figures, a vibrant, combative opposition not only to the warfare state, but to management and union bureaucracy alike. But their allure has faded over the years. Labor historians of mid-century America have fragmented point-of-production militancy into a set of competing impulses, not all admirable from a contemporary standpoint. Meanwhile, almost all historians have become more attuned either to formal political and policy initiatives or to the cultural, racial, and gender substructures that have framed the working-class experience. And in recent years trade union leadership, conservative as well as radical, has won a certain appreciation, if only because of its embattled role in American political life.[39]

But the demise of these warfare state rebels remains crucial to understanding the fate of unionism and working-class power in the postwar era. Although the wildcat strikers of World War II never developed the kind of political program, or the kind of leadership, that could make their perspective fully legitimate, their unpredictable militancy did embody a syndicalist current that kept the old "labor question" a focus of unresolved contention. By standing outside the corporatist structures of the wartime state, these industrial radicals brought into question a whole set of policy and political arrangements: WLB wage ceilings, labor's alliance with the Democratic party, even the meaning of patriotism in an era of endemic international tensions. They politicized the emergent system of industrial relations by adding a contingent, ideological dimension to issues that state managers, corporate executives, and not a few union officials sought to routinize and consolidate. Their exit from the postwar stage therefore made the union movement a more insular, de-politicized entity, and therefore one of far less potency and promise.

Notes

1 New Left skepticism toward both the UAW and GM during the 1970 strike is well captured in William Serrin, *The Company and the Union: The "Civilized" Relationship of the General Motors Corporation and the United Automobile Workers* (New York: Knopf, 1973).

2 The International Socialists, which now exists as Solidarity, traced its ideological roots to the 1940 division within the Trotskyist movement. Max Schactman, Irving Howe, Dwight Macdonald, Hal Draper, and others then argued that the Soviet Union was not, as Trotsky held, a "degenerate workers state" worthy of critical support, but a "bureaucratic collectivist" regime, as repressive in its own way as any state in the capitalist world. See Peter Drucker, *Max Shachtman and His Left: A Socialist's Odyssey Through the "American Century"* (Atlantic Highlands, NJ: Humanities Press, 1994). Solidarity is now largely responsible for publication of the widely respected *Labor Notes*.

3 Important influences were C. L. R. James, *State Capitalism and World Revolution* (Detroit: Facing Reality, 1963); C. Wright Mills, *The New Men of Power: America's Labor Leaders* (Urbana: University of Illinois Press, 1948, 2001); and Stanley Aronowitz, *False Promises: The Shaping of American Working Class Consciousness* (New York: McGraw-Hill, 1973); Harvey Swados, "The UAW – Over the Top or Over the Hill?" *Dissent*, Fall 1963, 321–43. The 2001 edition of *The New Men of Power* contains my appreciative introduction.

4 Nelson Lichtenstein, "Industrial Unionism Under the No-Strike Pledge: A Study of the CIO During the Second World War" (Ph.D. diss., University of California, Berkeley, 1974). Richard Abrams was the chair of my dissertation committee, but Michael Rogin (1937–2001) exerted what little real interpretative guidance I accepted from any on the faculty.

5 Hal Draper (1914–1990), a founder of the third camp Worker's Party in 1940, had been a contributor and editor of *Labor Action* and a shipbuilder in Long Beach during World War II. A scholar of Marx and Marxism, his most widely read and influential work was the pamphlet *The Two Souls of Socialism*, first published in 1960. Stan Weir (1921–2001) was a seaman in World War II and a well-known internal union opponent of Harry Bridges in the International Longshoremen's and Warehousemen's Union of the early 1960s. He later published Singlejack Books, which distributed shirt-pocket guides for rank and file militants.

6 See, for example, Joel Seidman, *American Labor: From Defense to Reconversion* (Chicago: University of Chicago Press, 1952); Richard Lester, *As Unions Mature* (Princeton: Princeton University Press, 1958); and Clark Kerr, Frederick Harbison, John Dunlop, and Charles Myers, *Industrialism and Industrial Man* (Cambridge: Harvard University Press, 1960). As a dissertation, my book manuscript was rejected for publication by both Greenwood Press and University of Kentucky Press. The outside readers were from the world of industrial relations. Cambridge University Press decided to publish it because of a fortuitous political–generational shift. Steven Fraser had become

the history editor at Cambridge; one of the readers to whom he sent the manuscript was Peter Friedlander, who had just published the pioneering social history *The Emergence of a UAW Local, 1936–1939: A Study in Class and Culture* (Pittsburgh: University of Pittsburgh Press, 1975).

7 See, in particular, Steven Fraser and Gary Gerstle, *The Rise and Fall of the New Deal Order, 1930–1980* (Princeton: Princeton University Press, 1989); Colin Gordon, *New Deals: Business, Labor, and Politics in America, 1920–1935* (New York: Cambridge University Press, 1994); David Plotke, *Building a Democratic Political Order: Reshaping American Liberalism in the 1930s and 1940s* (New York: Cambridge University Press, 1996); and Michael Brown, *Race, Money, and the American Welfare State* (Ithaca, NY: Cornell University Press, 1999).

8 See Lizabeth Cohen, *Making a New Deal: Industrial Workers in Chicago, 1919–1939* (New York: Cambridge University Press, 1991); Steve Babson, *Building the Union: Skilled Workers and Anglo-Gaelic Immigrants in the Rise of the UAW* (New Brunswick: Rutgers University Press, 1991); Bruce Nelson, *Divided We Stand: American Workers and the Struggle for Black Equality* (Princeton: Princeton University Press, 2000); Eric Arnesen, "Up from Exclusion: Black and White Workers, Race, and the State of Labor History," *Reviews in American History*, 26 (March 1998), 146–74; Gerald Zahavi, "Passionate Commitments: Race, Sex, and Communism at Schenectady General Electric, 1932–1954," *Journal of American History*, 82 (September 1996), 514–48.

9 On this topic see the outstanding work of Gary Gerstle, *Working-Class Americanism: Industrial Unionism in a Textile Town* (New York: Cambridge University Press, 1991); Joshua Freeman, *In Transit: The Transport Workers Union in New York City, 1933–1966* (New York: Oxford University Press, 1989; rpt. Philadelphia: Temple University Press, 2001); and in a different vein, Michael Denning, *The Cultural Front: The Laboring of American Culture in the Twentieth Century* (New York: Verso, 1996).

10 Much of the perspective is summarized in Lichtenstein, "From Corporatism to Collective Bargaining: Organized Labor and the Eclipse of Social Democracy in the Postwar Era," in Fraser and Gerstle, *The Rise and Fall of the New Deal Order*, 122–52. And see more generally Lichtenstein, *State of the Union: A Century of American Labor* (Princeton: Princeton University Press, 2002), 98–140.

11 See especially Joseph A. McCartin, *Labor's Great War: The Struggle for Industrial Democracy and the Origins of Modern American Labor Relations, 1912–1921* (Chapel Hill: University of North Carolina Press, 1997), 94–119; and of course David Montgomery, *The Fall of the House of Labor: The Workplace, the State, and American Labor Activism, 1865–1925* (New York: Cambridge University Press, 1987), 330–410 passim.

12 Martin Glaberman, *Wartime Strikes: The Struggle Against the No-Strike Pledge* (Detroit: Bewick, 1980); George Lipsitz, *Rainbow at Midnight: Labor and Culture in the 1940s* (Urbana: University of Illinois Press, 1981, revised 1994), 69–99, 120–56, 253–334; Lichtenstein, *Labor's War at Home*, 44–81 passim. The introduction and several essays touch on these issues in Sally Miller and Daniel Cornford, *American Labor in the Era of World War II* (Westport, CT: Praeger, 1995).

13 Robert Korstad, *Civil Rights Unionism: Tobacco Workers and the Struggle for Democracy in the Mid-Twentieth-Century South* (Chapel Hill: University of

North Carolina Press, 2003); and see also Michael Honey, *Southern Labor and Black Civil Rights: Organizing Memphis Workers* (Urbana: University of Illinois Press, 1993); Michelle Brattain, *The Politics of Whiteness: Race, Workers, and Culture in the Modern South* (Princeton: Princeton University Press, 2001); and Daniel Clark, *Like Night and Day: Unionization in a Southern Mill Town* (Chapel Hill: University of North Carolina Press, 1997).

14 Recent works that take a relatively favorable view of the union dividend from such war-era labor relations agencies include Robert Zieger, *The CIO, 1935–1955* (Chapel Hill: University of North Carolina Press, 1995), 163–90; and Gilbert Gall, *Pursuing Justice: Lee Pressman, the New Deal, and the CIO* (Albany: SUNY, 1999), 113–91 passim.

15 Lichtenstein, "From Corporatism to Collective Bargaining," 125; WLB quoted in Craufurd Goodwin, *Exhortation and Controls: The Search for a Wage Price Policy, 1945–1971* (Washington, DC: Brookings Institution, 1975), 13 (italics in original).

16 Christopher Tomlins, *The State and the Unions: Labor Relations, Law, and the Organized Labor Movement in America, 1880–1960* (New York: Cambridge University Press, 1985), 328; James B. Atleson, *Labor and the Wartime State: Labor Relations and Law During World War II* (Urbana: University of Illinois Press, 1998), 1–2; Katherine Van Wezel Stone, "The Post-war Paradigm in American Labor Law," *Yale Law Journal*, 90 (June 1981), 1517. I kick myself for not consulting the Stone essay before my book appeared, but in the 1970s when I did most of the research for *Labor's War at Home*, labor law scholarship, especially that involving the history of industrial relations, had become increasingly arid. Today no labor historian can afford to ignore the rich and plentiful work of the current generation of labor law scholars.

17 Nelson Lichtenstein, "Great Expectations: The Promise of Industrial Jurisprudence and Its Demise, 1930–1960," and David Brody, "Workplace Contractualism in Comparative Perspective," both in Nelson Lichtenstein and Howell John Harris, eds., *Industrial Democracy in America: The Ambiguous Promise* (New York: Cambridge University Press, 1993), 113–41, 176–205; and Steven Tolliday and Jonathan Zeitlin, "Shop-Floor Bargaining, Contract Unionism and Job Control: An Anglo-American Comparison," in Tolliday and Zeitlin, eds., *The Automobile Industry and Its Workers* (Cambridge, UK: Polity Press, 1986), quoted on page 112.

18 Clark, *Like Night and Day*, 4.

19 Judith Stein, *Running Steel, Running America: Race, Economic Policy, and the Decline of Liberalism* (Chapel Hill: University of North Carolina Press, 1998), 43; Roger Horowitz, *"Negro and White: Unite and Fight!": A Social History of Industrial Unionism in Meatpacking, 1930–1990* (Urbana: University of Illinois Press, 1997), 96. And see also Honey, *Southern Labor and Black Civil Rights*; Brattain, *The Politics of Whiteness*; and Korstad, *Civil Rights Unionism*.

20 Alan Brinkley, *The End of Reform: New Deal Liberalism in Recession and War* (New York: Alfred A. Knopf, 1995), 175–226 passim; Steven Fraser, *Labor Will Rule: Sidney Hillman and the Rise of American Labor* (New York: The Free Press, 1991), 407–94 passim.

21 Brian Waddell, "Economic Mobilization for World War II and the Transformation of the U.S. State," " *Politics & Society*, 22 (June 1994), 165–94; Waddell quoted on page 170, Secretary of War Stimson quoted on page 173. The pioneering work of Paul A. C. Koistinen sustains Waddell's view. See Koistinen's "Mobilizing the World War II Economy: Labor and the Industrial-

Military Alliance," *Pacific Historical Review*, 42 (November 1973), 443–78. And see the recent biography of Henry Wallace by John C. Culver and John Hyde, *American Dreamer: The Life and Times of Henry A. Wallace* (New York: Norton, 2000), 266–303.

22 Howell Harris, *The Right to Manage: Industrial Relations Policies of American Business in the 1940s* (Madison: University of Wisconsin Press, 1982), 105–27, 177–204; Sanford Jacoby, *Modern Manors: Welfare Capitalism Since the New Deal* (Princeton: Princeton University Press, 1997), 143–92 (on Thompson Product's diabolically successful resistance to the UAW during and just after World War II); Timothy Minchin, *What Do We Need a Union For? The TWUA in the South, 1945–1955* (Chapel Hill: University of North Carolina Press, 1996); James C. Cobb, *The Selling of the South: The Southern Crusade for Industrial Development, 1936–1990* (Urbana: University of Illinois Press, 1993), 96–121; Jefferson Cowie, *Capital Moves: RCA's 70-Year Quest for Cheap Labor* (Ithaca, NY: Cornell University Press, 1999), 1–40.

23 Andrew Workman, "Manufacturing Power: The Organizational Revival of the National Association of Manufacturers, 1941–1945," *Business History Review*, 78 (Summer 1998), 279–317.

24 Ira Katznelson, Kim Geiger, and Daniel Kryder, "Limiting Liberalism: The Southern Veto in Congress, 1933–1950," *Political Science Quarterly*, 108 (Summer 1993), 283–306.

25 As quoted in Joseph Gaer, *The First Round: The Story of the CIO Political Action Committee* (New York: CIO-PAC, 1944), 22. See also Lawrence Samuel, *Pledging Allegiance: American Identity and the Bond Drive of World War II* (Washington, DC: Smithsonian Institution Press, 1997).

26 Gary Gerstle, "The Working Class Goes to War," *Mid-America*, 75 (October 1993), 315. See also the essays by Lary May, Elaine Tyler May, Perry Duis, Reed Ueda, and Gary Gerstle in Lewis Erenberg and Susan E. Hirsch, eds., *The War in American Culture: Society and Consciousness During World War II* (Chicago: University of Chicago Press, 1996).

27 See, for example, Joshua Freeman, "Hardhats: Construction Workers, Manliness, and the 1970 Pro-War Demonstrations," *Journal of Social History*, 26 (Summer 1993), 725–37.

28 I discuss this at greater length in Lichtenstein, "The Making of the Postwar Working Class: Cultural Pluralism and Social Structure in World War II," *The Historian*, 51 (November 1988), 42–63.

29 Mark Leff, "The Politics of Sacrifice on the American Home Front in World War II," *Journal of American History*, 77 (March 1991), 1318.

30 Thomas Sugrue, *The Origins of the Urban Crisis: Race and Inequality in Postwar Detroit* (Princeton: Princeton University Press, 1996), 33–88 passim; John T. McGreevy, *Parish Boundaries: The Catholic Encounter with Race in the Twentieth-Century Urban North* (Chicago: University of Chicago Press, 1996), 55–110 passim; Kenneth Durr, "When Southern Politics Came North: The Roots of White Working-Class Conservatism in Baltimore, 1940–1964," *Labor History*, 37 (Summer 1996), 309–31; and Nelson, *Divided We Stand*, 89–141, 185–218.

31 For the skeptics, see Bruce Nelson, "Class, Race, and Democracy in the CIO: The 'New' Labor History Meets the 'Wages of Whiteness,'" *International Review of Social History*, 41 (Fall 1996), 351–74; Robert Norell, "Cast in Steel: Jim Crow Careers in Birmingham, Alabama," *Journal of American*

History, 73 (December 1986), 669–701; and Herbert Hill, "Black Workers, Organized Labor, and Title VII of the 1964 Civil Rights Act: Legislative Record and Litigation Record," in Herbert Hill and James E. Jones, Jr., eds., *Race in America: The Struggle for Equality* (Madison: University of Wisconsin Press, 1993), 263–341.

32 For an elaboration of this perspective, see Robert Korstad and Nelson Lichtenstein, "Opportunities Found and Lost: Labor, Radicals, and the Early Civil Rights Movement," *Journal of American History,* 75 (December 1988), 786–811; August Meier and Elliott Rudwick, *Black Detroit and the Rise of the UAW* (New York: Oxford University Press, 1979); Gretchen Lemke-Santangelo, *Abiding Courage: African American Migrant Women and the East Bay Community* (Chapel Hill: University of North Carolina Press, 1996); Zaragoza Vargas, *The Union Makes Us Strong: Mexican American Workers, Unionism, and the Struggle for Civil Rights, 1929–1945* (Princeton: Princeton University Press, forthcoming); Honey, *Southern Labor and Black Civil Rights,* 177–213; and Horowitz, *"Negro and White, Unite and Fight!",* 145–74.

33 Eileen Boris, "'You Wouldn't Want One of 'Em Dancing With Your Wife': Racialized Bodies on the Job in World War II," *American Quarterly,* 50 (March 1998), 83; Daniel Kryder, *Divided Arsenal: Race and the American State During World War II* (New York: Cambridge University Press, 2000), 88–132.

34 Of course, the gendered world of *production* politics is another story. Here, the dramatic, massive influx of women into new jobs and new industries during the war has been well studied. But the institutional and social legacy was proportionally tepid because this demographic upheaval was unaccompanied by the kind of ideological legitimization that made the upgrading of black labor such a pivotal development. See Ruth Milkman, *Gender at Work: The Dynamics of Job Segregation by Sex during World War II* (Urbana: University of Illinois Press, 1987); Karen Anderson, *Wartime Women: Sex Roles, Family Relations, and the Status of Women during World War II* (Westport: Greenwood Press, 1981); Nancy Gabin, *Feminism in the Labor Movement: Women and the United Auto Workers, 1935–1975* (Ithaca, NY: Cornell University Press, 1990), 50–51; Alice Kessler-Harris, *A Woman's Wage: Historical Meanings and Social Consequences* (Lexington: University Press of Kentucky, 1990), 81–112. Gunnar Myrdal finished writing *An American Dilemma* by the end of 1942; it would take 21 more years for Betty Friedan, whose feminist politics were heavily influenced by her experiences in the 1940s labor left, to publish the equally influential *The Feminine Mystique.* See Walter Jackson, *Gunnar Myrdal and America's Conscience: Social Engineering and Racial Liberalism, 1938–1987* (Chapel Hill: University of North Carolina Press, 1987); Daniel Horowitz, *Betty Friedan and the Making of the Feminine Mystique: The American Left, the Cold War, and Modern Feminism* (Amherst: University of Massachusetts Press, 1998).

35 Meg Jacobs, "How About Some Meat? The Office of Price Administration, Consumption Politics, and State Building from the Bottom Up, 1941–1946," *Journal of American History,* 84 (December 1997), 910–41; National Association of Manufacturers, "Would You Like Some Butter or a Roast of Beef" (newspaper advertisement), reproduced in Jacobs, "How About Some Meat?" 935; see also Anne Stein, "Post-War Consumer Boycotts," *Radical America,* 9 (July–August 1975), 156–61. In another context Marilynn John-

son captures the war-era flavor of an empowered citizenship in her striking essay, "War as Watershed: The East Bay and World War II," *Pacific Historical Review*, 63 (August 1994), 315–31.

36 Bruce Nissen, "A Post–World War II Social Accord?" in Nissen, ed., *U.S. Labor Relations, 1945–1989: Accommodation and Conflict* (New York: Garland Publishing, 1990), 174–79; John Sweeney, *America Needs a Raise* (Boston: Houghton Mifflin, 1996), 17.

37 Timothy Willard, "Labor and the National War Labor Board, 1942–1945: An experiment in Corporatist Wage Stabilization" (Ph.D. thesis, University of Toledo, 1984); Elizabeth Fones-Wolf, *Selling Free Enterprise: The Business Assault on Labor and Liberalism, 1945–60* (Urbana: University of Illinois Press, 1994); David A. Horowitz, *Beyond Left and Right: Insurgency and the Establishment* (Urbana: University of Illinois Press, 1997).

38 A particularly good discussion of the way in which Taft-Hartley's threat to union security generated a more privatized, interest-group labor movement is found in Brown, *Race, Money, and the American Welfare State*, 135–64.

39 See most recently David Stebenne, *Arthur Goldberg: New Deal Liberal* (New York: Oxford University Press, 1996); and Lichtenstein, *Walter Reuther: The Most Dangerous Man in Detroit* (Urbana: University of Illinois Press, 1997).

Preface

When I began work on this book in the early 1970s, many of us who were active in the student movement concluded that radical social and political change could come only if it were based, at least in part, on a working-class mobilization equal to or greater than that of the 1930s. However, when we looked to those who actually labored in American factories and offices, we found more inertia than activism, and the trade unions seemed sclerotic and increasingly impotent. The old Roosevelt coalition was in its final stages of collapse. In New York City, construction workers on Wall Street only recently had beaten up antiwar demonstrators. George Meany's AFL–CIO seemed a bulwark of the status quo, unconcerned even about the declining proportion of the workforce enrolled in the trade unions. Labor still favored an expansion of the welfare state, but most unions nevertheless remained steadfastly in favor of a vigorous prosecution of the Vietnam War.

Of course, this was also the era in which farm workers and public employees made significant organizational gains, in which an insurgent movement revitalized the United Mine Workers, and in which the young workers at General Motors' Lordstown, Ohio, assembly plant captured the attention of even the mass media. Some ex-students began to "industrialize" in a conscious effort to build a socialist opposition movement within unions such as the Teamsters, the United Automobile Workers, and the United Steelworkers of America. Although I kept largely to academe, I shared their search for a program that could engender a new militancy among American workers and transform the unions once again into the premier progressive force in national life.

A study of the union movement in World War II seemed relevant. During the 1970s, I followed with fascination and a sense of hope the wildcat strikes that flared in the coalfields and auto plants, so my interest was naturally kindled regarding the almost forgotten but far larger wildcat movement of the wartime era. What had happened to that insurgency, and what could be learned from its demise? In the 1940s, an earlier generation of non-Communist militants had unsuccessfully sought to politicize that rebellion, to rescind the no-strike pledge, to smash the wage controls, and to make a start on building the long-delayed labor party; latter-day radicals can learn something from the successes and failures of that experience.

The 1940s were also the years in which business and labor firmly established the industry-wide collective bargaining that would prove routine throughout most of the postwar era. Was this process necessarily counterposed to a more aggressive brand of working-class activism, as some contemporary New Leftists argued, or were there not more specific historical circumstances associated with the war and its legacy that spurred the growth of union bureaucracy and conservatism in the labor movement? Finally, in both the 1940s and 1970s, the state had moved toward a system of wage and price controls that politicized all elements of the collective bargaining regime and brought patriotic union officials onto the various government boards designed to formulate a wage standard. Had this process effectively incorporated the unions in the state apparatus and robbed them of their oppositional potential? If so, what role could the Left play within these institutions? Of course, no historical study can directly provide a political strategy for contemporary struggle, but I hope this work will help to create the larger context necessary for a resolution of these questions.

This text originated as a doctoral dissertation at the University of California, Berkeley. There I found the learning experience the most stimulating of my life, both within and without the walls of the academy. Richard Abrams proved a model thesis director, a probing critic of my endeavor, a forceful advocate of his own historical perspective, and a craftsmanlike editor of the emerging manuscript. Financial support came from two university fellowships and later from an American Council of Learned Societies grant-in-aid. Scores of librarians aided me in my research. Those at Berkeley's Institute of Industrial Relations, at Wayne State University's Walter Reuther Library, at the Catholic University of America, at the Franklin Roosevelt Presidential Library, and at the National Archives proved the most patient.

Various colleagues, comrades, and friends offered advice, argument, and support as this manuscript moved through several stages of revision. I have learned much from Richard Arneson, Richard Boyden, George Cotkin, Joshua Freeman, Ernie Haberkern, Tom Harrison, Bruce Laurie, Mark Levitan, Chris Paige, Michael Rogin, Michael Shute, and Stan

Weir. To Joanne Landy I owe an especially profound debt, for she did more than any to shape my politics and frame this work in its formative stages. David Brody, Howell John Harris, Peter Friedlander, Melvyn Dubofsky, and Steve Fraser read the manuscript with great care, and all offered the sort of constructive criticism that one historian is delighted to take from another. Eileen Boris reworked several versions of this material with me, consistently providing incisive criticism, support, and encouragement. Her collaboration has given to my work both a higher standard and a great joy.

Washington, D.C.   Nelson Lichtenstein
June 1982

1. Introduction

In the summer of 1973, a wave of sit-down strikes swept through the Chrysler Corporation plants in Detroit. The grievances of the men and women employed there – over the pace of work, dangerous conditions, and callous attitude of the supervisors – virtually duplicated those that had troubled and motivated the generation of workers who founded the United Automobile Workers (UAW) in the mid-1930s. Using tactics not dissimilar to those of early union organizers, these largely youthful, sometimes radical strikers of 1973 halted or slowed production, battled security guards, and set up illegal picket lines at plant gates. Although management began to identify and fire the more prominent activists, its efforts to contain the insurgency proved inadequate. The movement was broken decisively only on the morning of August 16, when high officials of the UAW, many veterans of the union's early battles, assembled a "flying squadron" of 1,000 local officials and staff representatives that dispersed the picket lines, manhandled the militants, and persuaded hesitant employees to return to their jobs. [1]

By the early 1980s, the events of 1973 had been overshadowed by the auto industry's most severe economic crisis since the Great Depression. With scores of factories shut down, hundreds of thousands of auto workers unemployed, and billions of dollars of red ink flowing through company account books, the UAW agreed to renegotiate its unexpired contracts and accept an unprecedented rollback of wages and benefits won by the union in better times. These concessions soon spread to many of the plants and companies that the UAW and other industrial unions had organized nearly half a century before. In the economically hard-pressed rubber, packinghouse, agricultural implement, and steel industries, union leaders could find no alternative but to accept the wage reductions and other "givebacks" management demanded.

The suppression of the Chrysler wildcat strikes and the bargaining retreat of the next decade symbolized to many the distance traveled by even the most progressive unions of the old Congress of Industrial Organizations (CIO). By the 1970s and 1980s, their capitulation to a management-dominated industrial order seemed necessarily congruent with their maintenance of an unresponsive and sometimes coercive internal apparatus. Although one can easily overstate the militancy of the mass industrial unions in the 1930s and exaggerate their bureaucratic and conservative nature today, the transformation of these key institutions of American life has never received the systematic historical attention such a major development usually commands. This book about American workers and their unions during World War II seeks to illuminate a key stage in this great change by uncovering the largely neglected history of the industrial union movement during a crucial era of economic regimentation and social upheaval, of growing political conservatism combined with a still powerful tradition of working-class militancy.

The vacuum in historical understanding has been largely filled by the work of an influential generation of social scientists who provided the initial, and still most widely accepted, explanation for the decline of union militancy and democracy in the years after 1940. In their pioneering studies of work process and union structure, social theorists such as Clark Kerr, Richard Lester, Daniel Bell, and Seymour Martin Lipset concluded that, given their mass character and their confrontation with powerful national employers, the new trade unions were virtually destined to develop an oligarchic regime and a set of accommodationist politics.[2] The validity of this perspective rested upon the assumption, held by many ex-radical political intellectuals, that although classes still existed, they did not have to clash in the stable capitalist order that characterized postwar America.

Much of this analysis derived from the work of Robert Michels, who fifty years before had recorded the tendency toward bureaucracy in the German Social Democracy and its allied trade unions. But if Michels, as radical critic, viewed this transformation with horror, Lipset, Kerr, and other liberal ideologues of a pluralist social order maintained that the tendency toward oligarchy in private organizations was a positive good; the fact that leaders did not exclusively represent the interests of their members, but interpreted them in an accommodationist, pragmatically conservative fashion, provided the necessary framework to sustain political democracy in the larger body politic.[3] Although this perspective generated a rich body of empirical data and social insight, it ultimately led to a static, a-historical approach to trade union and working-class history and a fundamentally pessimistic appraisal of the possibility of democratic social change.

The first post–World War II generation of American labor historians largely followed the conceptual guidelines set out by the mainstream industrial sociologists. Writing what have become the standard histories of the early CIO, both Irving Bernstein and Sidney Fine implicitly accepted the modern orthodoxy of industrial relations, to wit, the establishment of collective bargaining on a legal, routine, and unchallenged basis represents the goal toward which all labor history moves. Both Fine and Bernstein wrote as liberal institutionalists, identifying with the struggles of the industrial workers and their leaders but seeing little actual or potential conflict between the needs of the newly organized rank and file and the New Deal ideology of their leadership.[4] In this context, the experience of these institutions during World War II proved a great advance for the CIO because the government's domestic labor policy assured the permanency of the new industrial unions, routinized collective bargaining, and increased union numerical strength by more than half. Joel Seidman, who wrote the only full-fledged study of the labor movement during the war, explicitly advanced this perspective, favorably comparing the seemingly permanent gains of the union movement during World War II with the transitory success the American Federation of Labor (AFL) enjoyed during World War I.[5]

Applause for the political economy of the late New Deal and its collective bargaining arrangements ended abruptly when the generation of younger scholars loosely identified with the New Left began to rewrite the labor history of the 1930s. One group, which might be labeled the "corporate liberal" theorists, emphasized the extent to which the rise of the new industrial unions actually made the old order more secure. Disenchanted with the conservatism of the postwar labor movement and with the domestic political consensus forged by Democratic presidents, scholars such as James Weinstein and Ronald Radosh argued that twentieth-century liberalism represented not the ideology of antibusiness, democratic forces but the movement of the more enlightened capitalists to rationalize and restructure the corporate order. In this context, such seminal New Deal reforms as the Wagner Act and Social Security seemed but clever ruling-class stratagems to defuse social conflict and revitalize the economy. Emphasizing the antiradical ideology of the major CIO leaders, corporate liberal theorists argued that the net effect, if not the purpose, of the massive organizing drives of the decade was to integrate the industrial working class into a midcentury liberal capitalist system, strengthened immensely by the program of military Keynesianism the government adopted during the world war and Cold War eras.[6]

The chief difficulty with this perspective is that the corporate liberal idea vastly oversimplified and distorted the actual relationship between the business community, the growth of the new trade unions, and the exercise of state power. Theorists of this school had postulated an essentially instrumentalist conception of the state, whereby a relatively unified and far-seeing capitalist class exerts its influence directly through a government apparatus it controls. In fact, such an arrangement hardly described political reality during the New Deal years. Although some well-known industrialists such as Gerard Swope and Henry Dennison encouraged the new industrial unions and supported the Wagner Act, the overwhelming majority of American businessmen fiercely resisted most New Deal reforms and fought the new CIO unions with virtually every political and economic weapon at their command.[7] And although World War II did lay the basis for an accommodation between the CIO and the major corporations, this took place only under conditions initially rejected by most business leaders.

A far more fruitful approach has been offered by neo-Marxists such as Nicos Poulantzas and Claus Offe, who have argued that the broad, system-sustaining interests of the capitalist class are advanced through a "relatively autonomous" state apparatus. The state organizes an often divided capitalist class because the bureaucracy alone is capable of transcending the parochial, individual interests of specific capitalists and capitalist class fractions. At the same time, the state itself is not a unified entity; its policy is the product of class conflict in the larger society, mediated through a complex network of state agencies that are themselves the loci of class and interest group conflict. Although often pitched at a level of abstraction historians find difficult to use, the perspective of Poulantzas and other neo-Marxists is helpful because it enables one to understand the way in which the broker-state policies of the Roosevelt administration were designed to maintain social cohesion and at the same time to provide a battleground for divergent forces within the body politic.[8] Thus the National War Labor Board (NWLB), which most businessmen mistrusted as a bastion of New Deal labor liberalism, proved one of the administration's most effective tools in regulating industrial conflict in a way that ultimately strengthened corporate hegemony.

Although their insight into the way the state regulates and channels social conflict has proved extremely important, neo-Marxists have been less helpful in advancing the study of working-class history itself. In their structuralist analysis, the state serves to atomize the working class, destroying its political and social unity through the transformation of workers into individualized citizens. But there is little discussion of the social mechanisms by which the state accomplishes this task, and the structuralist perspective often reduces working-class consciousness to an abstract cipher, virtually dependent on the manipulation of elite state managers. Social reality in the 1930s and 1940s was a good deal more complex, and in this period some state activity designed to contain or weaken and divide the long-range threat from below nevertheless stimulated a working-class mobilization that had far-reaching consequences at the point of production and in the realm of politics. Admittedly, both the National Recovery Administration's famous Section 7a and the Wagner Act were designed to moderate class conflict, but their actual deployment engendered a widespread self-organization of the working class that quickly overflowed the narrow legal channels that had been constructed to contain it.[9]

Historians have only recently begun to explore this "hidden history of the American workplace" that in twentieth-century America proved so crucial to the formation of working-class consciousness. Despite the limitations of their ideology, scholars of the New Left generation did leave a permanent mark on the study of American labor history by shifting its focus from institutional developments within the legal system and the trade unions to the activity and attitudes of the rank and file. In the early 1970s, both Jeremy Brecher and Staughton Lynd emphasized the dimension of depression-era insurgency that sought a fundamental transformation of power relationships in the factory, mill, and office. A few years later, Peter Friedlander and Robert Zieger demonstrated, in two careful local union studies, that unionization functioned as but one step among many that altered the relationship of ordinary workers to their job, family, workmates, and boss.[10] The tension between the immediate fears and aspirations of the workers and the growth and maintenance of an effective union presence is thus a dynamic one that constantly shapes both the activity of the union cadre and the consciousness of the rank and file. Like any social movement, the new CIO unions were not merely the product of the ideology of their leadership or the momentary consciousness of the rank and file, but represented a dialectical combination subject to the often violently changing economic and political crosscurrents of the era.

This text demonstrates how the home-front pressures for social order and political orthodoxy during World War II did much to weaken the independence and shop-floor power that the industrial union movement had won in the late 1930s. When the question of American intervention arose after the fall of France, most CIO unionists – like American liberals generally – came to the conclusion that a military defense had to be built against German fascism. Although many in labor recognized the dangers that a militarized economy might bring to their still incomplete and unstable organizations, the key leadership group in the CIO nevertheless hoped that the collectivist tendencies inherent in the mobilization of the society for total war could be used to forge a quasicorporativist program of social planning and structural reform.

This hope had clearly failed by the time of Pearl Harbor, or shortly thereafter. Given the political conditions of the late New Deal era, the wartime mobilization program was necessarily built on the basis of a thoroughgoing structural accommodation and interpenetration between the resurgent forces of corporate America and a vastly expanded state apparatus. Indeed, planning of an unprecedented sort took place within the War Production Board (WPB) and other wartime agencies, but the economic controls put into effect largely favored those social forces that stood in historic opposition to the industrial union movement. However, the CIO leaders' dependent relationship with the Roosevelt administration was hardly shaken by the new configuration of power in the wartime era. On the contrary, union leaders continued to offer the administration political support, first because they had not rejected those tenets of CIO social unionism that sought to turn the great power of the warfare state toward a program of social democratic reform, and second because they thought a close alliance with the Roosevelt wing of the Democratic party now essential to shield the union movement from the new power of big business and the aggressive anti-union politics of the congressional and entrepreneurial right wing.

Under these conditions, the mobilization effort provided the economic and ideological context required to routinize and channel union activity in such a way as to diminish the legitimacy of rank and file activity while institutionalizing leadership authority and increasing government influence in union affairs. In the first half of the war, a demographic upheaval dramatically expanded the workforce, but reduced the relative weight of the militant union cadre. As a consequence, the direct shop-floor power of many workers increased at the same time that their sense of union consciousness became radically uneven. With wages held in check by government fiat and the right to strike suspended for the duration of the war, the resultant instability generated an internal union crisis that neither the trade union leadership nor the government could long tolerate. In the summer of 1942, the administration resolved much of this dilemma by providing the principal industrial unions with a government-sponsored union security guarantee designed to increase their internal bureaucratic nature. This organizational support reinforced the ideological commitment that most CIO leaders already had to the mobilization policies of the president, but it also trapped them in a Rooseveltian political consensus that soon put them at odds with the immediate interests of their rank and file.

Of course, this process did not take place overnight, nor did it occur without struggle and resistance. The union movement was neither politically nor structurally monolithic, and both the government and the business community contained powerful fragments that dissented from what C. Wright Mills once called the "main drift" of national politics. By 1943, internal opposition to the cross-class *burgfrieden* proclaimed by the national CIO began to bubble up in key unions in the rubber, shipbuilding, auto, and coal mining industries. As a result of dissatisfaction with the NWLB's rigid wage controls and with a renewed managerial offensive on the shop floor, wildcat strikes and other unauthorized job actions increased dramatically in the second half of the war. In the coal industry, United Mine Workers (UMW) President John L. Lewis coopted rank-and-file insurgency in his campaign to break the authority of the NWLB and return collective bargaining to those voluntarist principles the pre–New Deal union movement had once championed. In the UAW and several other industrial unions, a powerful wildcat strike movement exerted significant leftward pressure upon the politicized stratum of secondary union leaders who were the vital cadre of the CIO. The subsequent tension between the control mechanisms of the state, the social pressure from below, and the political requirements of the union leadership became the pivot of labor politics for the remainder of the war. By the late 1940s, the adjustment or suppression of this multi-faceted conflict had reshaped the internal character of the industrial unions and done much to set their course in the increasingly hostile environment of the immediate postwar era.

2. The unfinished struggle

The history of the American working class contains a major paradox. Over the last century, working men and women in this country have repeatedly demonstrated a degree of solidarity that has rivaled or surpassed even that exhibited by the proletariat of Western Europe. The self-conscious collective activity of American workers has normally been hidden, submerged in the day-to-day life of factory, mine, and office, obscured either by an overlay of ethnic culture or by identification with the local community and its social and political values. Still, a latent combativeness has never been far beneath the surface. From the railway upheaval of 1877 to the strike wave of the mid-1930s, almost every decade witnessed a protest movement of remarkable proportions. In an era when the industrial working class was more than half foreign born, when trade unions represented less than a tenth of the nonfarm workforce, when capital exercised its power in direct and unfettered fashion, these national strikes successfully galvanized huge numbers in collective resistance to the harsh, alien work regime fostered by the new industrial system.

Yet, these great movements of the foreign born and the unskilled rarely left an institutional legacy. Most major strikes in the sixty years after 1875 were unsuccessful, and even where workers won substantial concessions from their employers, as in the smaller industrial cities of the Gilded Age or in the coalfields and garment shops early in this century, permanent trade unionism remained insecure and tenuous. Most of these institutions collapsed in the next economic slump or dissolved when management undercut the social basis of the organization by introducing new production methods and new workers into the workplace.[1] Thus, the milestones that mark the course of American labor history are those of heroic failure or great tragedy: the Haymarket riot of 1886, the Homestead and Pullman strikes in the 1890s, the Triangle Shirtwaist fire in 1911, the epochal and climactic mobilization of 1919.

The dilemma of organization

The failure to unionize was rooted in the disparity between the essentially localistic and parochial locus of working-class protest and the increasingly large-scale, industry-wide strength of their opponents. American workers forged strong bonds of solidarity with one another, but their sense of loyalty and organization rarely extended beyond their own place of work, or their own community or ethnic subgroup. Workers frequently stopped production and won the backing of the majority of their fellow citizens in the small towns and cities that were the home of so much industry in the North and West. But the efficacy of their local protest was increasingly undercut by the ability of corporate America to withstand such scattered and episodic resistance and by the willingness of the state legal apparatus to declare such activity illegitimate. Under such conditions, most unions survived only by finding an ecological niche outside of or on the margins of the emerging corporate system.[2] Thus, direct confrontation with oligopolistic industry usually ended in the defeat and destruction of workers' organizations. As the Interchurch World Commission reported in the wake of the 1919 steel strike:

The United States Steel Corporation was too big to be beaten by 300,000 working men. It had too large a cash surplus, too many allies among other businesses, too much support from government officers, local and national, too strong influence with social institutions such as the press and pulpit, it spread over too much of the earth – still retaining absolutely centralized control – to be defeated by widely scattered workers of many minds, many fears, varying states of pocketbook and under a comparatively improvised leadership.[3]

This legacy persisted well into the 1930s. Despite the more favorable legal and political environment, the juxtaposition of locally focused militancy on the one hand and organizational instability on the other did much to shape the character of the industrial unions that finally emerged late in the decade. During the depression era, the greatest surge of purely rank-and-file militancy and political radicalism probably came when unionism had its least influence, in the years 1933 and 1934. Encouraged by what most workers considered a government friendly to their interests, many broke from the apathy and demoralization of the first years of the depression in a remarkably powerful movement of protest and self-organization. Hundreds of thousands of newly hopeful workers breathed life into established unions in coal and clothing, filled hastily

chartered AFL federal locals in the auto, rubber, and electrical industries, created an independent rank-and-file movement in the steel industry, rebelled within and transformed many company-sponsored unions,
and joined Socialist and Communist-led councils of the unemployed that
marched to demand relief funds and prevent evictions. The most spectacular manifestations of this new spirit came in Minneapolis, Toledo,
and San Francisco, where ideologically committed radicals led thousands of workers in quasimilitary, largely successful confrontations with
employers and local government authorities.

For the most part, this remarkable burst of rank-and-file militancy did
not survive long into the year 1935. The activism of the early New Deal
years turned out to be a false start, an episodic and fleeting awakening.
The upheaval probably did much to frighten the left wing of the New
Deal into fighting for passage of the Wagner Act, but the movement
itself left few permanent organizations in its wake. Six hundred AFL
federal locals were discontinued or suspended in 1935 and 1936 as hundreds of thousands of workers in basic industry abandoned the new
unions. Many of these organizations, especially those in auto and rubber, were greatly weakened after their demands for recognition were
taken up and then unrecognizably diluted by National Recovery Administration (NRA) labor boards. The steelworkers' insurgency collapsed when their strike threat was postponed and then canceled at the
behest of President Roosevelt and NRA officials. Meanwhile, the textile
union fell under a barrage of public and private assaults in the South,
where the police and local officials firmly backed open-shop conditions.[4]

Why this rapid collapse? In the NRA era, rank-and-file activists organized well on the local level. But without a larger organizational context
and effective national leadership, they were unable to mobilize the widespread discontent of the time and focus it with sufficient power upon the
government bureaucracy and corporate headquarters, where the crucial
political and economic decisions were made. In an era of centralized
authority, only such large-scale worker organizations could provide an
efficacious vehicle for collective action, a defense against individual vic-
timization, and a basis for lasting victory. In these years, as in others
before and since, militancy and organization were not mutually exclusive. Rather, they were dialectically dependent, building confidence and
hope in a powerful new synthesis. In steel, the popular, broadly based
worker insurgency faltered, concluded sympathetic chronicler Staugh-

ton Lynd, because "The crucial, critical weakness of the rank and file was its inability to organize on a national level."[5]

The failure in 1934 led an important sector of AFL leadership to recognize that unless a concerted national direction was given to these local insurgencies, one of two disasters would befall the trade union movement. In the first instance, a radical alternative leadership might emerge on a national scale to unite, as in Minneapolis or San Francisco, the working-class discontent evident in so many localities. The second alternative, and in the eyes of John L. Lewis and Sidney Hillman the more likely, was that the unparalleled organizational opportunity of the mid-1930s would be simply frittered away while those who could lead such a movement squabbled among themselves. The essential difference between Lewis and the rest of the old-line AFL leadership did not center on the question of industrial versus craft unionism. Rather, it arose over the issue of whether or not a real effort would be made to seize the once-in-a-lifetime organizing opportunities so evident in the mid-1930s. Craft-oriented leaders of the AFL, such as Daniel Tobin, who called the mass-production workers "rubbish," saw in their alternating militancy and resignation an unpredictable quality upon which they thought it foolish to attempt to build solid trade unions. Future leaders of the CIO also recognized the ephemeral union consciousness of these workers, but they hoped that with the friendly neutrality of the federal government, strong trade unions could be built given a sufficient commitment of energy, money, and disciplined leadership. In the pivotal steel industry, John L. Lewis lavished upon the fledgling Steel Workers Organizing Committee (SWOC) 350 paid organizers and a first-year budget of $500,000. SWOC, reported *Fortune* magazine, was a "foe worthy of U.S. Steel."[6]

Although the CIO provided the leadership the rank and file lacked in 1934, the organizational work begun in auto, steel, rubber, and other mass-production industries did not automatically create a large corps of disciplined, union-conscious workers. Most were probably not as actively involved in 1936 and 1937 as they had been three years earlier. In steel, where the CIO placed the bulk of its manpower, money, and hope, the total SWOC membership at the end of 1936 stood at only 82,000 out of some 600,000 in the basic steel industry. "Steel workers continued to be dubious that we could improve their lot and fearful that, if we tried and lost, they would lose everything," recalled then SWOC Secretary-

Treasurer David J. McDonald. Although the CIO had won over the leadership of many of the key company unions by early 1937, SWOC still feared that in a labor board election at a major corporation, the union might well face defeat.[7]

Many of the same conditions prevailed in the auto industry. There, the process of union building rested in the hands of a relatively atypical nucleus of militants who waged shop-floor warfare with management for the allegiance of the large majority of still timid, deferential workers. Much tactical finesse – even outright bluff – was needed in this battle, for the union rarely enrolled more than a committed minority when it came to a showdown with the auto corporations.[8] The sit-down strikes were a brilliantly successful gambit, in large part because they enabled the militant few to stop production and demonstrate union power to those uninvolved in the struggle. To many workers, the formal recognition the UAW finally won at General Motors (GM) and other corporations early in 1937 provided a protective shield that gave them some sense of liberation from older factory hierarchies and a visible link to their more forceful shopmates. It was a powerful symbol of the fact that the supervisor and the foreman were not omnipotent and that the union cadre represented an alternative nexus of legitimate authority in the plant.

Given this social context, it is not surprising that the spectacular growth of the new CIO unions came only after collective bargaining contracts were signed. At B. F. Goodrich and Firestone, the rubber workers increased their membership from 4,000 to 30,000 in one year. In steel, the top-level agreement negotiated by Lewis and U.S. Steel President Myron Taylor early in March 1937 sparked the enrollment of more than 200,000 new unionists by June. The United Electrical, Radio, and Machine Workers (UE) quadrupled its dues-paying membership after the union signed a contract with General Electric (GE) in mid-1937. Most spectacular of all were the auto workers. Triggered by the stirring sit-down victories at GM and Chrysler, over 300 additional strikes affecting almost half a million workers rocked Detroit within the first four months of 1937. UAW leaders proclaimed that the total membership had risen from 30,000 the year before to 400,000 by August 1937.[9]

Unionism surged forward, a powerful stream rushing over the institutions designed to contain it. Few workers accepted the modern distinction between contract negotiation and contract administration, so shop-floor assemblies, confrontations, slowdowns, and stoppages were endemic in the spring of 1937. These demonstrations of collective strength legitimated the union's presence for thousands of heretofore hesitant workers, at the same time offering many their first sense of participation and control. Such job actions extended the meaning of collective bargaining left unresolved in the early, sketchily written, signed contracts. At Chrysler's Dodge Main factory, for example, it was common practice for a grievance to be handled directly by the steward, backed physically by an entire department of workers who might walk off the job to await satisfaction outside the supervisor's office while their representatives argued inside. Through such tactics, the union secured de facto recognition of the shop steward system and a partial veto over production line speeds.[10]

The price of this activism could be high. Given the autonomous, noninstitutional character of the movement, trade union loyalty could dissipate almost as easily as it had blossomed. Pragmatic and often opportunistic in their relation to the unions, American workers often expected an immediate payoff from their union commitment: a resolution of old grievances, a rapid increase in wages, a liberalization of work rules and production standards. As long as the CIO demonstrated its potency on these issues, workers flocked to its ranks, but when the unions stood on the defensive, as most did during the slump that began in late 1937, many new union recruits stepped to the sidelines again to await the outcome of the latest battle between management and the union cadre.[11]

Not surprisingly, membership in the new unions plunged almost as rapidly as it had risen. At Fisher Body in Lansing, 8,027 were enrolled in the UAW local at the height of its power in August 1937. Thirteen months later, after the recession of 1938 had checked union influence, only 1,078 continued to pay any dues. On the West Side of Detroit, the Reuther brothers and their Socialist allies provided some of the ablest local leadership, and there some 14,000 workers paid initiation fees to Amalgamated Local 174. By July 1938, only 4,401 were still fully paid up, out of a potential membership of more than 36,000. The total UAW membership in Michigan dwindled to 57,000 by November 1938. At Goodyear in Akron, Ohio, the story was much the same. Enthusiasm for the large United Rubber Workers (URW) local peaked early in 1937; thereafter the recession and a tough managerial bargaining posture combined to sap union loyalty. By 1940, the Goodyear local's membership had declined to less than a third of the 11,000 enrolled three years earlier.[12]

SWOC encountered still greater difficulties. The failure of the Little Steel strike in June and July graphically demonstrated the limits of union power, and the recession of 1937–38, which cut steel production by 70 percent, enabled managers to regain much of the initiative in their day-to-day contact with the union. Relying on a steward system considerably weaker than the one that existed in auto and rubber, SWOC leaders encountered chronic difficulty in maintaining the everyday structure of their union. Before 1939, the largest dues collection made in any one month indicated a membership of slightly less than one-half the number of men who had signed application cards. A contemporary observer put the union's dilemma this way: "Steel workers will go out and die for the union in the excitement of the picket line, but they'll be damned if they'll pay another dollar to that 'lousy shop steward.'" To remain solvent, SWOC had to resort to monthly dues picket lines that cajoled or threatened delinquent workers to pay up before they could enter the mill. Often steelworkers balked, and absenteeism ran as high as 25 percent on the days dues pickets patrolled mill gates.[13]

Clearly related to the episodic and ephemeral consciousness of the rank and file was the decentralized and local nexus of power in so many of the new industrial unions. This phenomenon was most apparent in the UAW, where the dynamic forces that combined to shape the new unions were most graphically displayed. Created out of an alliance of rebellious AFL federal locals, a former Chrysler corporation company union, and a Communist-led skilled-trades group, the UAW functioned as a coalition of virtually autonomous locals before the war. Even after it won recognition from major auto corporations, its federated character remained intact. Management resisted company-wide bargaining, so each local played a large part in the annual negotiations. The UAW's first contract with GM was a weak document that recognized the union as the exclusive bargaining agent in several key factories but remained vague or silent when it came to seniority, grievance procedures, and wage standards. These issues were fought out on an individual plant basis that, in turn, kept local officers and stewards at the fulcrum of union power and politics.[14]

A key issue measuring local autonomy arose out of the wildcat strikes that racked the union. These frequent work stoppages, involving a department or small group, flowed organically out of the struggles of the immediate preunion era, when organizers had used such tactics to flex the union's muscles and demonstrate the power of collective action to those still uncommitted to the UAW. In large part, auto corporations signed their first collective bargaining contracts with the UAW in the hopes that these numerous small strikes would end. Instead, they escalated as stewards, committeemen, and informal work group leaders used strikes to win concessions from reluctant foremen and supervisors without recourse to the flimsy, untested grievance machinery. Until annual retooling and the 1937 recession slowed their pace, wildcat strikes were legion: GM recorded 270, Chrysler 69, and Briggs 43.[15]

Although these short strikes helped to strengthen the union during the early months, they also posed a major dilemma for the UAW. Uncoordinated and unpredictable – at least to top union officials – these strikes made it difficult for the union as a whole to formulate a general strategy toward management. They proved immediately advantageous to workers who were strategically located in the production process, but they could destroy solidarity among the larger group, especially when a strike in one department produced a layoff in another. Finally, these strikes threatened the union's entire relationship with the company. They undermined the managerial incentive to continue recognizing the union, and during the 1937 recession, when the union stood on the defensive, they were used by management as occasions to eliminate shop-floor militants.

Given the logic of this situation, virtually all wings of the CIO leadership condemned such work stoppages almost from the start. Top officials such as UAW President Homer Martin and SWOC Chairman Philip Murray put their opposition in categorical terms, calling collective bargaining contracts "sacred." Union radicals were more pragmatic: Communists in Flint warned auto workers that the recession had cut deeply into union strength. "Don't be provoked into wildcat strikes or unauthorized actions. This is exactly what management wants."[16]

But the real question faced by the UAW cadre was not whether those strikes should occur, but what to do when they did. During the early summer of 1937, GM complained repeatedly to UAW officials that if they wished the contract renewed in September, they must take decisive action to curb the rash of work stoppages in the company's plants. Under additional pressure from John L. Lewis and Adolph Germer, who worried that the UAW's reputation for irresponsibility would hurt the organizing effort in steel and other industries, President Martin signed an agreement with GM in September assenting to the corporation's sole right to set production standards and granting it the right to fire any employee whom management complained was guilty of provoking an unauthorized strike.[17]

The agreement evoked a howl of protest, and in November a conference of GM delegates overwhelmingly repudiated it. They did so not because they favored or condoned these unauthorized strikes but because they wanted to keep disciplinary action against such strikers either subject to negotiation with the company or firmly in the hands of the local union. Wildcat strike leaders were almost invariably among the key activists in the plants; if they were simply abandoned to the company, the union idea itself would suffer among the mass of new recruits. Moreover, where conditions were favorable, Martin's opponents often favored the post facto authorization of the larger wildcat strikes. Thus in November 1937, Walter Reuther and Wyndham Mortimer, allied against Martin's clique, urged the UAW executive board to throw its support to a six-day-old wildcat strike of Pontiac workers. In contrast, Martin wanted the work stoppage there declared unauthorized because he thought it the result of "professional provocateurs" hostile to his leadership.[18]

The wildcat strike issue remained unresolved until the war. Increasing factionalism destroyed any semblance of centralized authority and further muddled the definition of legitimate strike activity. Taking advantage of the union's disarray, GM and other large corporations suspended their recognition of the UAW. As a result, contending auto union leaders relied with renewed frequency on rank-and-file action to sanction their authority. Often, one group called a strike to demonstrate its influence, whereas another urged workers to ignore the picket lines set up by its rival. By 1939, when the CIO faction finally took firm control of the UAW, real power lay more than ever at the local, even the department, level. In the spring, UAW convention delegates adopted a new constitution, syndicalist in spirit, designed to curb sharply leadership authority in the negotiation and administration of collective bargaining contracts.[19] Then in the summer, key secondary leaders of the UAW led a series of often violent strikes that reestablished a strong union presence in the industry. In characteristically cyclical fashion, rank-and-file activism was renewed with dramatic force at Briggs, Chrysler, and Graham-Paige, and among skilled workers throughout the Detroit area. Although the new international officers sought to defuse hostile political pressures by promulgating an elaborate strike authorization procedure in the fall, the real policy was one of post facto approval of virtually any work stoppage that had a chance of success or that was backed by influential elements in the union. As the new UAW president, R. J. Thomas, later asserted, "When the men are on strike, what can you do? If you don't authorize it, they'll go out anyway."[20]

The internal life of other CIO national unions also contained a large element of the fragmentation that characterized the UAW. Appointed officers with virtually autocratic power ran the organizing committees set up by John L. Lewis and Sidney Hillman, but their authority was often challenged from within by independent-minded local leaders with strong rank-and-file backing. Packinghouse Workers Organizing Committee (PWOC) Director Van Bittner faced such bitter and sustained opposition from a coalition of some thirty dissident locals that he resigned under pressure in the spring of 1941. A leadership split in the newly organized Textile Workers Organizing Committee (TWOC) challenged Sidney Hillman in 1939 and 1940, and he proved helpless to prevent several locals from affiliating with the American Federation of Labor. The autonomous United Rubber Workers kept factionalism under some control, but wildcat strikes were a firmly rooted tradition. The United Electrical, Radio, and Machine Workers long remained an unintegrated coalition that reflected its origins as a federation of Communist, AFL, and independent locals.[21]

An equally important source of institutional insecurity was the CIO's failure to complete the task so dramatically begun in 1936 and 1937: the organization of basic industry. On the eve of World War II, continued resistance of at least one important corporation in its jurisdiction threatened the permanence and power of almost every industrial union affiliate. For all its militancy, the UAW made little headway in the Ford Motor Company's autocratic empire, and managers at General Motors and Chrysler took advantage of factional difficulties to weaken the union. Goodyear, the largest company in the rubber industry, had thus far refused to sign a contract with the URW, nor had Westinghouse been brought to terms by the UE despite a five-year campaign. Bethlehem, Republic, Inland, and other Little Steel companies had successfully smashed organizing efforts during the summer of 1937. Three years later, they still kept more than 30 percent of basic steel employees nonunion, despite numerous labor board and federal court judgments against them.[22]

In certain industries, the CIO maintained only a scattered presence. As late as 1941, the multiplant International Harvester Company effectively resisted organizational inroads from the UAW, SWOC, and the Farm Equipment Workers. In meatpacking the PWOC, severely hampered by the recession, had not yet secured company-wide recognition at any of the industry Big Four, and in 1939 the union lost four of the six strikes it called in the Midwest. The "march inland" of the International Longshoremen's and Warehousemen's Union (ILWU) came to a grinding halt by 1938, broken by a Teamster–warehouse industry alliance that kept the ILWU confined to a series of beachheads along the west coast. Finally, the CIO's drive to unionize the sprawling cotton textile industry ended in virtually complete failure, especially in the South, where almost a million workers remained unorganized.[23]

Recession and conservative backlash

These organizational difficulties were matched by an economic and political environment that grew more adverse as the depression lingered into its second decade. The "Roosevelt recession" that began in late 1937 struck the CIO with devastating force. Production declined by 70 percent in steel, 50 percent in autos, 40 percent in rubber, and 35 percent in electrical manufacturing. Unemployment swelled to one in five, not far below the level of 1932. Hundreds of thousands of newly organized workers were laid off, sapping the collective power of those who remained at work and creating countless problems in the administration of the recently instituted seniority and grievance systems. Most union leaders considered themselves fortunate if they renegotiated major collective bargaining contracts without a cut in pay or erosion of other union conditions.[24]

The recession put an abrupt halt to most organizing work between 1938 and 1940. SWOC dismissed some 250 field representatives, put the rest on nineteen-days-a-month pay, and diverted their attention to building membership in the mills where the union already held bargaining rights. The UAW lost fifty international staff members and abandoned indefinitely any effort to unionize Ford. For lack of funds, the CIO cut sixty-three staff members from its payroll as late as 1940 and pulled organizers out of its fledgling drives in the aircraft, meatpacking, textile, and farm equipment industries. Although John L. Lewis boldly claimed that there were 4 million workers under the CIO banner, the actual dues-paying membership dropped as low as 1.35 million in the late depression era.[25] A year before Pearl Harbor, the CIO remained but a tentative and incomplete structure.

The noticeably more difficult political environment also chilled prospects for an industrial union revival. By 1938, the New Deal was clearly in retreat. In Congress a conservative coalition of Republicans and southern Democrats put an end to the era of legislative advance for liberal–labor forces. The LaFollette Committee no longer captured newspaper headlines with its investigation of industry-sponsored violence and espionage; now, public attention centered on Congressman Martin Dies, whose House Committee on Un-American Activities conducted a sensational hunt for Communists and pro-CIO liberals in New Deal alphabet agencies.[26] On the state and local levels, conservative forces regrouped rapidly after 1937 to counter the new power of organized labor. In the South and West, a variety of new antilabor laws hampered union work. In the North, a UAW slate went down to defeat in the 1937 Detroit municipal elections, and in Pennsylvania, Michigan, and Minnesota, liberal pro-labor governors were defeated the next year.[27]

A master tactician of coalition politics, President Roosevelt both recognized the shifting mood in national politics and did much to shape its rightward drift. The president's close alliance with the new industrial union movement always remained one of calculated convenience, and when it proved embarrassing, as during the Little Steel strike, he did not hesitate to distance himself from the CIO by declaring a plague on the houses of both labor and management in that desperate conflict. After the failure of the president's 1938 effort to purge conservatives from the Democratic party, he relied ever more on the moderate wing of the New Deal coalition for support. And once FDR turned his attention to the European crisis and the need for rearmament, he eschewed new domestic social programs in an effort to win business and conservative backing for his foreign policy initiatives.[28]

The Wagner Act was one of the New Deal's most dramatic, and even radical, legislative initiatives, but it did relatively little to resolve the CIO's immediate problems in the late depression years. Although a generation of unionists would soon declare the National Labor Relations Act organized labor's "magna carta," the actual legal and administrative deployment of the law proved considerably more ambiguous during the years before World War II. Passed in the wake of the 1934 rank-and-file upsurge, the act represented a mixed congressional initiative: a clear concession to the disruptive militancy of the era, but one that also sought to channel worker protest into predictable patterns under a system of state regulation. FDR gave the new law only tepid support, whereas it met fierce and continuing resistance from the bulk of the CIO's business adversaries. For two long years the law remained an operational dead letter, validated by the Supreme Court in April 1937, after the sit-down strikes had already demonstrated the overwhelming power of labor's new offensive. The statute made obsolete much of the AFL's elaborate system of internal governance and established a National Labor Relations Board (NLRB) authorized to determine unit jurisdiction, hold collective-bargaining elections, and certify as representative of the workers those unions that received a majority vote. The law did curb much employer anti-union activity by declaring a whole series of traditional management practices illegal, and it gave the new unions a legal standing that helped shield them from direct employer assault. The Wagner Act asserted the duty of an employer to bargain with a properly certified union, but of course, it did not compel managers to meet union demands or even sign a contract.

The Wagner Act certainly helped institutionalize industrial unions in the late 1930s, but the internally bureaucratic impact of the law remained largely in the future, when the NLRB and the courts responded to the more conservative mood prevalent in the body politic. "The statute was a texture of openness and divergency," writes legal scholar Karl E. Klare, "not a crystallization of consensus or a signpost indicating a solitary direction for future development."[29] In the depression era, the complexity and fluidity of working-class attitudes toward collective bargaining and the hostility of the business community made the interpretation and administration of the Wagner Act sufficiently plastic to afford the new unions a large measure of political and organizational latitude in their internal development.

The quest for union security

The adverse economic and political environment, the episodic militancy of the rank and file, and the local nexus of union power all reinforced the cautious outlook of top CIO officials and generated on their part a powerful drive for routine labor relations and institutional security. Although they had once fought bitterly among themselves in the United Mine Workers, key CIO figures such as Philip Murray, Adolph

Germer, and John Brophy now agreed that stability and leadership authority were essential to the growth and ultimately to the survival of the new unions. Twice in a generation – in the early 1920s and in the NRA years – they had seen industrial organizations with strong rank-and-file support melt away. They knew that militancy and vigor were essential in the early stages of the unionization process, but they mistrusted such sentiments when they shaped union activity after the negotiation of a binding collective-bargaining agreement.

Still unsure of the stability or permanency of their new organizations, most CIO leaders turned to the demand for a union shop as the most feasible solution to their many problems. This contractual device merely provided that all workers in a collective-bargaining unit had to belong to the trade union recognized by their employer. Although a straightforward, traditional bargaining issue, the union shop carried with it far greater organizational and ideological consequences. Most corporate managers rejected this demand when the CIO put it forward in the late 1930s, but the question remained close to the center of labor politics, and in the early days of World War II it would play a crucial role in shaping government labor policy.

In no union was the union shop espoused with greater zeal and political import than in SWOC. The issue had particular significance there because of the skeletal character of the union's internal structure and the tenuous allegiance the SWOC had from many rank-and-file steelworkers. Unlike the locals in auto and rubber, steel lodges were often mere bookkeeping entities, creatures of SWOC headquarters in Pittsburgh, which paid their office expenses and salaries, appointed all district directors, and conducted even routine negotiations with local management. When SWOC suddenly won bargaining rights for several hundred thousand employees of U.S. Steel and 140 other companies in the spring of 1937, it acquired a constituency that this framework could not easily absorb. As *Steel Labor* admitted, "It is a strange situation that steel workers now have a union but do not have an organization. That is what lies ahead. The job of organization will go on to completion in a few short months. This is inevitable."[30]

The disastrous Little Steel strike soon smashed the union's facile optimism. Beginning in late May, more than 90,000 steelworkers struck in an arc extending from the Great Lakes to eastern Pennsylvania. There were daily battles with the police, 970 arrests, and twenty deaths, including ten during the famous Memorial Day Massacre outside Chicago.

Although the work stoppage demonstrated the militancy of the half-organized steelworkers, it also revealed their potential for division and demoralization. SWOC leaders considered a signed contract and union recognition paramount demands of the strike; the Little Steel companies offered to honor all of the wage and hour provisions of the U.S. Steel agreement but refused to put their accord in writing. This tactic probably undermined union solidarity. The steelworker "is hot and bothered about concrete grievances," noted radical journalist Louis Adamic, "and when nothing was said about them by the top leaders, he soon lost interest in the fight, and in most cases, became ready to return to work." In fact, many plants never entirely closed down, and in late June large numbers of workers returned to work. The strike faded away in July when SWOC exhausted its relief fund.[31]

The Roosevelt recession followed closely on the heels of the Little Steel debacle, and together these reverses reinforced the cautious, security-conscious approach of the steel union leadership. SWOC lacked the strength to force the large steel corporations to grant the union shop outright; therefore, its leaders sought to persuade steel management that the contractual device directly served their interest by assuring stable labor relations and increased productivity. SWOC President Philip Murray presided over the campaign, but its real ideologues were two staff intellectuals, Clinton Golden, a close confidant of Murray and former instructor at the social democratic Brookwood Labor School, and Harold Ruttenberg, the SWOC research director who had earlier been a key adviser to the 1934 rank and file movement in the industry.

Golden and Ruttenberg thought labor relations necessarily volatile in the absence of a union shop agreement. Every day, local leaders faced the task of justifying the union's existence to the rank and file to retain their loyalty and collect their dues. Grievance battles were the order of the day, and local officers went about their jobs in an aggressive and energetic manner. Although all SWOC contracts formally prohibited strikes for the duration of the contract, a form of guerrilla warfare nevertheless continued in the mills. Local officers feared that even though management had signed a contract, it still sought the local's disintegration through manipulation of the grievance procedure or some other tactic designed to discredit the union in the eyes of its members or potential recruits.[32]

But once a company had agreed to a union shop contract, the entire relationship between labor and management began anew on a more cooperative basis. For the union shop represented the company's recognition of the union's permanent status in the plant. Immediately, the requirements of local leadership changed dramatically. What were now needed were local officials "capable of administering contracts on a relatively peaceful basis." Instead of fighting for each grievance until they satisfied rank and file members, union committeemen were now expected to process only those grievances supported by the language of the contracts.[33]

"The type of leader who has the courage to fight the company's antiunion activities has a difficult time making this adjustment," reported Harold Ruttenberg, so the responsibility for carrying through on this difficult transition fell to the SWOC apparatus itself. "This is primarily the job of top union leaders," argued Golden and Ruttenberg in their influential *Dynamics of Industrial Democracy*, "since they must show to their followers, on the union staff and in the mines, mills and factories, the way toward industrial peace and fruitful union–management relations."[34] To carry on this work, Golden and Ruttenberg outlined a program designed to transform local SWOC leaders into contract administrators. Most members of the union cadre would gradually adapt to their new responsibilities under the tutelage of SWOC's district directors and their staff, but for those who refused to curb their militancy, the authors justified the use of the full disciplinary power SWOC had acquired under the provision of a union shop contract. With some sympathy, they cite the case of Stanley Orlosky:

On Sunday, March 2, 1941, Stanley Orlosky, a lifelong union worker, a pipe fitter in a steel mill, was expelled from his union after a trial on charges of "violation of obligation to the Steel Workers Organizing Committee." To add to his disgrace, Stanley was tried by union officers whom he had solicited to join the union a few years earlier . . .

The talking for which Stanley was fired consisted of charging the incumbent union officers of "selling the men down the river" since they settled grievances on their merits. His idea of a grievance settlement was to get everything or strike. Stanley's leadership was essential to the establishment of the union against bitter resistance, but after it had been fully accepted by management, such leadership was a handicap to the development of cooperative, union–management relations. His expulsion was sustained by the SWOC national officers.[35]

To managers, SWOC promised not only stable labor relations but union cooperation in making their plants more efficient. The former mineworkers who led SWOC feared that unless they encouraged lower costs in the unionized sector of the industry, they would re-create the same conditions in steel that had earlier hampered unionism in coal, where high-profit nonunion southern mines had long undercut UMW strength in the North. SWOC argued that once the union felt secure, its members and officers would no longer resist those cost-cutting technological innovations that were so characteristic of the steel industry in the twentieth century. In fact, the harmonious and efficient operation of the plant ultimately required the union's full partnership in the management of all phases of the industry. This approach derived in part from the influence exerted on SWOC leadership by an admixture of Catholic social reformism and scientific management theory. Both strains appeared in *Organized Labor and Production*, a 1940 collaboration by Philip Murray and Morris Cooke, the disciple of Frederick Taylor most prominently associated with New Deal social planning and industrial unionism.[36]

SWOC's union shop drive proved a failure in the years before World War II. A few of the smaller, financially marginal companies acquiesced, but major corporations such as U.S. Steel and Jones and Laughlin kept SWOC influence in their mills as low as possible. Like managers throughout basic industry, executives in steel had little desire to strengthen the new industrial unions and to dilute their power any further. Nor did they have much faith in CIO claims that the union shop would help increase productivity in their large, technologically modern facilities.[37]

Management undoubtedly understood that the union shop provided no magic formula to reduce the daily struggle in the mills. The degree of union organization merely determined the relative advantage of the employer over his employees. Many early CIO contracts called for a three- or four-step grievance procedure, but both workers and their supervisors soon learned that these steps did not eliminate shop-floor conflict automatically. No matter how detailed or elaborate the contract – and most SWOC agreements were brief indeed before 1941 – a written accord could never provide a mechanism for the adjustment of disputes in a mutually satisfactory manner in the newly unionized mills and factories. Hence, many stewards and local officials continued to press grievances not covered in the contract or to lead slowdowns and short wildcat strikes if they thought them efficacious.

As steel production and shop-floor union power rose, this conflict influenced politics in the national union itself. During SWOC conventions in the early 1940s, several locals demanded more autonomy: a fifty-fifty distribution of dues income, establishment of locally controlled strike funds, and the contractual right to strike over local issues. Some of the sharpest debate arose over demands of local unions for the election of their own staff organizers who functioned on a day-to-day basis as union business agents. In large measure, the extent of political democracy in the steelworkers' union hinged on the resolution of this issue. Staff men were the direct representatives of the international bureaucracy on the local level; erode their loyalty, and the top union officers would be stripped of one of their most powerful tools. Philip Murray understood the problem well:

If you have an elected field worker responsible only to the group that elects him in a given district, oftentimes that individual does not feel responsible to the president of the union or to the International Executive Board. He takes a certain kind of license unto himself and he may . . . defy even the president of the union, creating internal strife and causing internal political friction.[38]

In the new decade, Murray and the rest of his leadership group easily maintained a formal centralization of authority in the renamed United Steelworkers of America (USW). But they still considered the integrity of their union under a threat as long as the steel corporations resisted their demand for some form of institutional security. In its nearly six years of existence, SWOC had not won a company-wide strike against a major firm, and the union moved into the 1940s still lacking the rank-and-file loyalty that would ensure a dependable flow of dues income during the unpredictable wartime era. Unsuccessful in its efforts to win the union shop in the private collective bargaining arena, the USW leadership would soon turn its attention to the new war mobilization apparatus in Washington, from which it sought a government-dictated union security settlement with the steel corporations.

3. CIO politics on the eve of war

With the outbreak of the war in Europe, the new industrial unions soon found themselves in the midst of a political landscape that reflected issues quite different from those that had defined New Deal politics in the formative years of the CIO. Especially after the fall of France in June 1940, American politics increasingly turned on the degree of intervention in and economic mobilization for World War II. The drift of government policy and public opinion toward support of Great Britain eventually stripped the New Deal of its isolationist wing, increased the weight of southern conservatism, and generated conditions under which important elements in the Republican party and the business community could share control of the burgeoning defense mobilization apparatus.

This conservative shift did not take place without conflict, however, and for at least the next two years, administration defense policy served as an arena for a protracted, multifaceted struggle. At one pole were the representatives of an increasingly aggressive industrial–military alliance that sought to use the wartime emergency as an opportunity to restore business hegemony and firmly contain, if not roll back, the social gains made by the union movement and the liberal community in the previous decade. Opposing this conservative revival, with various degrees of clarity, were those elements in the old Roosevelt coalition that sought to use the collectivist tendencies inherent in the massive conversion to war production to advance the quasidemocratic state planning tradition that had begun to emerge in the late New Deal era.

Exacerbated by the simultaneous debate over American foreign policy, this conflict divided not only the New Deal coalition but the industrial union movement itself, splitting the CIO leadership and generating the organization's most severe internal crisis since its birth. Some unionists, notably John L. Lewis, and for a time the Communists, argued that putting the American economy on a war footing would inevitably strengthen the domestic enemies of the labor movement and reduce the CIO's power to advance a progressive social program at home. The majority of the CIO high command eventually went along with Roosevelt's increasingly interventionist policy, but they differed sharply over the extent to which the trade union movement should subordinate its traditional interests to the defense program and the call for national unity.

Lewis, Roosevelt, and the war

"Talk of war has produced more tons of words than steel to date, and I hope that ratio is maintained, not reversed," wrote SWOC research director Harold Ruttenberg in a 1938 analysis of the lingering depression.[1] Most Americans recognized that a massive preparedness program would somewhat alleviate the chronic unemployment problem, but CIO unionists resisted defense mobilization as a solution to their economic and organizational difficulties. Even after Germany invaded Poland in September 1939, trade union leaders in America were almost unanimous in their opposition to the nation's participation in World War II. Given the unstable nature of industrial unionism, the memories of union collapse in the immediate post–World War I era, and the general antiwar sentiment of the 1930s, most in the CIO high command responded to the deepening European crisis with a vigorous opposition to American intervention or to the transformation of the economy to a wartime status. Instead, they emphasized the necessity for continuing and strengthening the social programs of the New Deal, eliminating unemployment through government work programs, and carrying forward the organizing drives begun in 1936 and 1937.

The former mineworkers who led the CIO in 1939 had all held responsible trade union posts in the years during and immediately after World War I. They shared the belief, widespread in liberal circles, that American belligerency, whatever its merits, led inevitably to a collapse as great as that of the early 1920s or the depression itself. During the Great War, a surge of organization among the unskilled had doubled the total AFL membership, but the gains proved ephemeral. The cooperative arrangements reached between Samuel Gompers and the Wilson administration during World War I merely postponed until the armistice the final accounting, the test of the permanence of the new or expanded unions. Once the wartime truce had ended, the AFL lost about 30 percent of its strength in a few years, and the new, largely industrial organizations virtually collapsed. The most celebrated defeat for the new unionism came in steel, but the packinghouse union fell apart in the early 1920s, and the machinists and boilermakers lost the large gains they had made during the war. Nor could the United Mine Workers, the largest and most powerful union in the nation, escape the economic consequences of the peace: By the early 1930s, it had ceased to exist throughout most of the coalfields of North America.[2]

Would history repeat itself in the next few years? Many CIO leaders obviously feared so. A 1940 CIO economic assessment concluded that "If any nation comes to depend for its prosperity only on increased military expenditures, it becomes chained to a Frankenstein which drags it inevitably toward war . . . the cessation of such a subsidy means depression, the kind of depression that rests most heavily upon the wage earners and farmers."[3]

More than any other major figure, John L. Lewis understood the implications of a war economy for the labor movement as a whole and for the mass industrial unions in particular. Lewis, who turned sixty in 1940, stood at the apogee of a monumental career as a union leader and labor spokesman. Temperamentally cautious when economic and political conditions were adverse, Lewis could be a bold and resourceful leader when he sensed the main chance, as he did in the mid 1930s. When organization and militancy swept the coalfields in 1933, Lewis skillfully used the pressure from below to win concessions from government and business in the broker politics of the early New Deal. Unwilling to see the possibility of a vastly expanded labor movement frittered away by internal AFL bickering and ineptitude, Lewis again acted boldly in 1935 when he poured millions of UMW dollars into organizing campaigns staffed by Communists, Socialists, and his opponents from the fratricidal UMW battles of the 1920s.

Lewis functioned best when he dealt from strength, and in 1936 and 1937 he gave a dazzling performance. In organizing the CIO, he used his sonorous voice and dramatic biblical rhetoric to give transcendent meaning and dignity to the new movement and its mass constituency. Before the fall elections, he led the CIO into full-fledged support for Roosevelt so as to assure the friendly neutrality, if not outright backing, of the federal government in the ensuing conflict. Throughout the winter of 1937, Lewis gave strong moral and organizational support to the General Motors sit-down strikers while secretly negotiating a collective bargaining agreement with U.S. Steel Chairman Myron Taylor.

Ideologically, Lewis remained a sophisticated business unionist, but in the late 1930s his own brand of Gompersian politics drove him toward an increasingly radical and politically independent point of view. Although frequently mawkish and awkward, he acted with a rough consistency, applying the dictum of Samuel Gompers, "reward your friends and punish your enemies," unswayed by the sentimentality of the Roosevelt liberals or the political cynicism of the Communist party's popular front ideology. Lewis's estrangement from the president in the late 1930s was less a result of the undeniable personality differences between the two figures than of their clashing public roles. As a reformer, Roosevelt conserved as much of the status quo as the conditions of depression-era America permitted. Lewis, although profoundly contemptuous of radicals and left-wing ideology, led a broad working-class movement that pressured him to make demands to which the president could not safely yield and still keep intact the New Deal coalition.[4]

Although Lewis had linked CIO fortunes to Roosevelt's reelection in 1936, the alliance was clearly one of convenience. He expected a continuing payoff. When Roosevelt declared a politically expedient neutrality during the waning days of the CIO's desperate Little Steel strike, Lewis replied in a tone of profound remonstrance: "It ill behooves one who has supped at labor's table and who has been sheltered in labor's house to curse with equal fervor and fine impartiality both labor and its adversaries when they become locked in deadly embrace." The CIO, reported Lewis, could not avoid "a political essay of the works and deeds of its so-called beneficiaries. It must determine who are its friends in the arena of politics and elsewhere."[5]

Lewis did not move the CIO into an open break with Roosevelt in 1937, but he became increasingly skeptical of the extent to which CIO interests could be advanced by any form of cooperation with the Democratic administration. He thought that the government had failed to take decisive action to prevent a new surge of unemployment during the Roosevelt recession of 1938. He was not sympathetic to FDR's efforts to accommodate aggressive conservatives after the midterm elections, and he criticized FDR's elimination of the more liberal administrators from the alphabet agencies, the reduction of Works Progress Administration (WPA) appropriations, and the president's greater attention to foreign affairs. Moreover, Lewis, who was not transfixed by the early accomplishments of the New Deal, considered Roosevelt's policies a failure as long as almost a fifth of the workforce remained unemployed in 1939 and 1940.[6]

The president's cautious but determined policy of intervention, begun in 1939 and 1940, precipitated Lewis's outright break with FDR and generated a crisis of authority within the CIO. Lewis opposed the drift to war and to a war economy with a rhetoric often reflective of the antimilitarist pacifism pervasive among liberals in the mid-1930s. "War has always been the device of the politically despairing and intellectually sterile statesman," Lewis observed soon after Nazi armies rolled across Poland. "Labor in America wants no war nor any part of war. Labor wants the right to work and live – not the privilege of dying by gunshot or poison gas to sustain the mental errors of current statesmen."[7] A strong and early opponent of international fascism, Lewis had been among the first leaders of the labor movement to protest Nazi persecution of the Jews and to attribute the rise of fascism to the worldwide economic collapse. Along with others in the labor movement, Lewis pointed out that fascism's first victim, and also its most potent enemy, was a vigorous, progressive union movement. Unlike many conservative isolationists, Lewis did not favor an accommodation with the new German regime. Instead, he proposed that America concentrate upon hemispheric defense with Latin America and strengthen the trade union movement in the Western Hemisphere as the first line of resistance against the rise of fascist or authoritarian movements there.[8]

More importantly still, Lewis argued that the transformation of the American economy to a war footing would inevitably strengthen the domestic enemies of the labor movement and reduce the CIO's power to advance a progressive social program at home. With Cassandra-like foresight, he warned the CIO's 1939 convention of the inevitable wartime difficulties. "The danger is that while prices soar unchecked except by rhetoric, labor will find itself increasingly restrained in its attempts to adjust wages to the cost of living. These restraints would be exercised in the name of national defense, while all restraints upon the rapacity of the profiteers and munition makers would be relaxed under the same excuse that the funds must go for armaments." Lewis thought that if the CIO remained aggressive in its defense of progressive domestic social policies, then the labor federation would inevitably come into open conflict with the administration. In hopes of strengthening what he called the "bulwark" of the union movement, he issued a ringing cry for a massive organizing campaign to bring a total of 10 million workers under the industrial union banner by 1944. Only then would the CIO have sufficient influence in American politics to force the politicians, especially its erstwhile friends in the Democratic party, to do its bidding.[9]

Perhaps because of the cyclical view of history that he held, Lewis more than his colleagues feared a new round of wartime regimentation and postwar collapse as the prelude to another cycle of union decline. Congressional conservatives and anti-union newspaper editorialists had already launched a new offensive against the labor movement, calling for suspension of the new 40-hour week, abridgment of the right to strike in defense industries, and proscription of the union shop. At the War and Navy departments, procurement officers did not hesitate to sign multi-million-dollar contracts with flagrant violators of the Wagner Act. Prominent beneficiaries of this practice were the anti-union Ford Motor Company and Bethlehem Steel, which together accounted for well over 10 percent of all defense orders in 1940.[10] With the military rapidly becoming the largest single customer of business enterprise, this policy might have a disastrous impact upon the CIO's efforts to organize anti-union holdouts in basic industry. In 1939 and 1940, Lewis repeatedly protested this practice to the president, but Roosevelt refused to sign a potentially controversial executive order that might have prohibited its continuation.[11]

Despite his perceptive analysis of the American political economy, the year 1940 turned into one of supreme frustration for the CIO president. Lewis unsuccessfully fought the peacetime draft and the destroyers-for-bases deal, which he thought irreversible steps toward American involvement in the European war. Frantically opposed to FDR's third term, Lewis sought an alternative, first to Roosevelt and then to the Democrats. He vainly encouraged the presidential hopes of isolationist Senator Burton Wheeler in the winter, publicly toyed with the idea of a labor party in the spring, secretly backed Herbert Hoover for the Republican nomination in the summer, and then stunned the nation with his endorsement of Wendell Willkie just before the election.[12]

In his speech backing the Republican candidate, Lewis vowed to resign the CIO presidency if Roosevelt won again. His political gambit proved a spectacular failure. With the exception of those CIO unions heavily influenced by the Communists, Lewis remained isolated in his opposition to the president's reelection. Most of the major industrial unions had already endorsed FDR for a third term at the time of Lewis's speech on October 25; the next week, union leaders by the score took to the airwaves to repudiate the Lewis endorsement and reconfirm their support of the president. On election day, an overwhelming majority of CIO-organized workers cast ballots for Roosevelt.[13]

The repudiation Lewis suffered on election day reached a culmination of sorts at the CIO's third annual convention, held but two weeks after Roosevelt's triumph. Had he chosen to do so, Lewis might still have retained his presidency. He controlled the CIO's organizational apparatus, and most delegates were still willing to split their allegiance between Presidents Roosevelt and Lewis. The mineworkers were unquestionably loyal, and the Communist-led unions supported Lewis as one way of opposing Roosevelt's rearmament program. Leaders of the steel, auto, rubber, and packinghouse unions were only slightly less enthusiastic. The minority of unionists who sought Lewis's resignation came chiefly from the Amalgamated Clothing Workers of America (ACWA), whose leader, Sidney Hillman, maintained a uniquely close political and personal relationship with the president. [14]

Thus Lewis's decision to resign came not from an immediate loss of support by the CIO but from his accurate perception that in an era when the fate of the labor movement largely rested on its relationship to government power, his failure to decisively influence the CIO rank and file on the third-term issue would sorely diminish his effectiveness in any future clash with FDR. Lewis therefore resigned in favor of SWOC Chairman Philip Murray, a supporter of Roosevelt in all three of his campaigns for the White House, but also a long-time lieutenant of the CIO chief whose public critique of the mobilization program was less strident than, but almost as far-reaching as, that of his mentor. Relieved of the political responsibility inherent in the top CIO position, Lewis expected his influence in the organization to diminish only slightly and his maneuverability as head of the powerful UMW to remain unencumbered.

The CIO and the state

What explains the dismal failure of John L. Lewis to swing the CIO against Roosevelt in 1940? There are several interconnected reasons, all growing out of the larger political context of late 1930s America. Most fundamentally, Lewis assumed that the industrial unions could still function in the voluntarist tradition espoused in principle, if not in practice, by Samuel Gompers and the AFL leaders of an earlier generation. But the new political and collective bargaining environment that the CIO itself did so much to create in the 1930s had forever compromised the pre-New Deal autonomy of the unions. When UMW and

SWOC organizers told workers, "The President wants you to join a union," they may have exaggerated FDR's intentions, but they synthesized perfectly the new partnership that they sought to create between government and labor.[15]

By 1940, the CIO had built a dense web of political and emotional connections with the Roosevelt administration that could not be broken by an electoral maneuver, no matter how clever its logic. By politicizing so much of the nation's economic life, the New Deal had undercut the old voluntarist ideology and located the battleground for labor's struggles as much within the apparatus of state policy formulation and administration in Washington as on the factory picket line. Although the Democratic party remained an improbable coalition of reactionary and liberal elements, the vitalization of its urban–liberal wing generated within the executive branch of government a strong social democratic impulse. This gave the bureaucracy a responsiveness that drew the CIO into an intimate relationship with the left-of-center alphabet agencies in the nation's capital.[16]

Among the many new relationships that bound the CIO to Roosevelt and the Democrats, none was more important than those that arose out of the administration of the Wagner Act. Pushed through Congress in response to the wave of working-class militancy that followed the collapse of Section 7a of the NRA, the Wagner Act embodied a radical exercise of state power on behalf of union organization. Although not held constitutional until after the great sit-down strikes of 1937 had already demonstrated labor's independent power, the administration of the labor law nevertheless held enormous consequences for the unions, especially in the late depression slump, when the CIO could no longer count on its strike power to carry all before it. Because the AFL and CIO were bitter rivals, the National Labor Relations Board's determination of what constituted a proper collective bargaining unit for a certification election often decided in advance which union would win and how powerfully that union could represent the interests of its members.[17]

In this era the NLRB, especially its staff, was overwhelmingly in favor of the CIO's brand of industrial unionism. Many of the board's field examiners coordinated their work with LaFollette Committee investigators and CIO organizers to press, at government expense, unfair labor practice suits against anti-union employers. Board member Edwin S. Smith and Chief Executive Officer and Secretary Nathan Witt were probably Communist party members; certainly they were CIO partisans. When House of Representatives conservatives investigated the board in 1938 and 1939, CIO council Lee Pressman, himself a former party member with Witt, recalled that CIO leaders considered it of "profound importance" that the NLRB be kept in hands friendly to the industrial union federation.[18]

The CIO also relied upon the state as an agency that could stabilize economic life. Industrial union leaders had been enthusiastic supporters of the NRA, not only because of the impetus they had hoped it would give to union organization but also because they expected state-supervised coordination of business activity to raise prices, increase employment, and stimulate economic growth. Although the interest group planning of the early New Deal proved a notable failure, the CIO did not give up on state regulation of economic activity. In the late 1930s, the planning idea that grew most directly out of the NRA experience was rooted in the traditionally chaotic coal industry, where the UMW, which feared overproduction and price competition even more than the operators, lobbied hard for the coal stabilization program sponsored by Pennsylvania Senator Joseph Guffey. The assumption underlying the Guffey idea was similar to that of the NRA in that it held competition to be excessive and destructive. A coal commission composed of operators, unionists, and representatives of the public would regulate the industry to create cartels in markets and prices and to assure the maintenance of labor standards.[19]

In most other CIO-organized industries, however, "Guffization" proved impractical and unwanted, because markets were already oligopolistically controlled by a few major producers. From labor's point of view, the problems inherent in industries such as steel and electrical products derived not from too much competition but rather from job-destroying technological change and stabilization of competition among companies at levels insufficient to ensure full employment.[20] By the onset of the Roosevelt recession in late 1937, many CIO leaders called for a system of countercyclical government spending and national economic planning – a liberal Keynesian solution to what many economists now considered a permanently stagnant economy. The CIO argued that "full production in a stable economy can be created only by intelligent direction which has the power and the will to coordinate all economic controls toward that single end."[21]

Exemplifying at the highest levels the working relationship between the New Deal and the CIO were the intimate ties that grew between

Roosevelt and Sidney Hillman, ACWA president for over a quarter of a century and one of the major spokesmen for the new unionism. In the 1920s and early 1930s, Hillman was a leader of the reform current in the labor movement that emphasized the need for order and efficiency in industry as well as social justice and union power. Cooperating closely with advocates of a rational industrial planning system such as Morris Cooke, George Soule, and W. Jett Lauck, Hillman evolved a social vision that soon owed as much to the thought of Thorstein Veblen and the efficiency-minded disciples of Frederick Taylor as it did to the Marx and Debs of his socialist youth. During this same era, Hillman forged close ties to William Leiserson, Felix Frankfurter, Leo Wolman, and other academic liberals who would play a major role in formulating the early labor policy of the Roosevelt administration. Similarly, with liberal clothing manufacturers such as Joseph Schaffner or large retail merchants such as Filene's Louis Kirstein, the ACWA cooperated in the social benefit programs and grievance arbitration techniques that would later become characteristic of unionized industry in the late 1930s and 1940s.

Like Lewis, Hillman headed a union in an industry racked by intense competition, but unlike the UMW leader, his ideas and experience drew him toward a highly statist solution to the problems of industry and labor. During World War I, Hillman had secured the aid of Secretary of War Newton Baker to assure that manufacturers of army uniforms would avoid sweatshop conditions, and in the early 1920s the ACWA fought off the anti-union offensive that decimated other trade unions in that era. In the early depression years, he played a large role in framing the NRA and then negotiated a clothing industry code favorable to his membership. When the NRA was reorganized in 1934, Roosevelt appointed him as labor's representative on the new governing board. After the collapse of the Blue Eagle and the formation of the CIO, Hillman emerged as one of the industrial union federation's most effective representatives in Washington, working tirelessly to secure passage in 1938 of the New Deal's last major piece of social welfare legislation, the Fair Labor Standards Act.[22]

Finally, Hillman's allegiance to the administration derived most of its power from the immense loyalty Roosevelt had won from the urban, immigrant working class. In the 1930s, most ACWA members were Jews, Italians, and other new immigrants. Many were women, and most had but an imperfect knowledge of English. To these men and women, the New Deal was more than a program of economic recovery. It represented a symbolic doorway to the mainstream of American life. To Jewish workers in particular, Roosevelt became an adored figure, with the tangible social reforms of his administration replacing the ideal of socialism many had earlier held.[23] Hillman, a 1907 immigrant from Lithuania, both reflected and encouraged this sentiment. Justifying his union's abandonment of its traditional labor party orientation in 1936, Hillman proudly declared to his executive board, "We have participated in making the labor policy of this Administration."[24]

By the late 1930s, Hillman and his circle were reading the political landscape with a map far different from that used by John L. Lewis. Naturally apprehensive over the expansion of Nazism in Europe, Hillman supported Roosevelt's gradual shift from neutrality to mobilization, and he came to see the labor movement as a defender of the administration against attacks from the right or left. Although the Hillmanites recognized that the president might be "temporizing with the conservative wing of his party," they bristled at the sort of public criticism relished by John L. Lewis.[25] After one of the latter's sharp attacks, Hillman took to the airwaves to deny the presidential retreat from a militant New Deal policy. "There is no man in public life today," he announced, "in whom we can so fully and safely confide for the balance of the journey." Roosevelt responded warmly and shrewdly to such support. He gave Hillman direct access to the White House, invited him for lunch at Hyde Park, and used him as a political sounding board.[26]

Mobilization politics

As American politics became polarized over the domestic consequences of European events, Roosevelt found Sidney Hillman and the wing of the trade union movement he represented valuable allies. In the wake of the German blitzkrieg in the West, American opinion shifted dramatically in favor of defense preparedness, but Roosevelt still faced substantial isolationist sentiment that blocked his efforts to cooperate more closely with the British. On the left, antimilitarism still remained a potent sentiment tapped by both the Communists and the followers of John L. Lewis to oppose Roosevelt's rearmament measures. In the summer of 1940, the CIO attacked the draft as "associated with fascism, totalitarianism and the breakdown of civil liberties." Even the SWOC and the UAW, unions that supported defense mobilization, opposed Roosevelt on this issue in 1940.[27]

On the right, opposition to American involvement in the European war became a major issue among important segments of the Republican party and among old Progressives of the Midwest and West. The reasons for this opposition were quite diverse, ranging from pessimism about the ability of England to hold out against the Nazis to the fear of conservatives such as Robert Taft that a new war would lead inevitably to economic and political regimentation at home and imperialist expansionism abroad. In some respects, Taft's views were not unlike those of Lewis or Norman Thomas, except that the Republican senator from Ohio focused his attention on the impact that an increase in state power would have on the traditional marketplace freedom that small and medium-size business sought to perpetuate.[28]

Pro-intervention forces also reached across the political spectrum. Roosevelt had strong backing among traditionally patriotic southern conservatives, as well as those liberals acutely sensitive to the fascist threat. New Dealers such as Henry Morgenthau, Harry Hopkins, Felix Frankfurter, Harold Ickes, and Archibald MacLeish soon became forceful proponents of greater defense mobilization and all-out aid to England. In the trade union movement, the garment and textile workers unions, with their large Jewish membership, were also militant backers of the defense effort. The ACWA and the International Ladies Garment Workers Union (ILGWU) were among the very few unions that supported the peacetime draft in 1940 and that wholeheartedly backed lend-lease the next year.[29]

Of even greater long-range import was the support Roosevelt won from the eastern, internationalist wing of the Republican party. In July 1940, the president reorganized his cabinet to bring key representatives of this powerful group into his government. To top positions at the War and Navy departments he appointed the conservative but pro-interventionist Republicans Henry Stimson, Secretary of State under Hoover, and Frank Knox, Alf Landon's running mate in 1936. From the corporate law offices and investment banking firms of New York and Boston, Stimson and Knox brought to Washington a corps of civilian managers who would dominate war and postwar politico–military strategy. Among them were John Lord O'Brien, Robert Lovett, John J. McCloy, Robert Patterson, and James Forrestal. "Accustomed to command," observed historian John Morton Blum, "they were at ease with the power they now exercised along familiar lines of personal and business acquaintanceship, lines outside the New Deal's networks."[30]

Just as the debate over American aid to England generated a new political realignment, so too did the protracted conflict over the politics of the defense mobilization program itself. Roosevelt understood that in any rearmament effort, business and financial interests that had once been bitterly hostile to the New Deal would have to be accommodated, but the president was determined to retain as much control as possible in his own hands in order to avoid outright political polarization and to balance interest group and class forces against each other. Rejecting the long-standing plans of the military for an independent mobilization agency dominated by army officers and industrialists, Roosevelt instead reactivated in May 1940 the World War I-era National Defense Advisory Commission (NDAC) to coordinate the defense program. The NDAC was but the first of a series of changing and overlapping mobilization agencies that the president established and then superseded as new problems and political issues emerged.[31]

The makeup of the commission illustrated the New Deal's propensity to resolve difficult problems of political economy using the kind of interest-group planning that had characterized the NRA. The most important post on the new commission went to General Motors President William Knudsen, whose appointment as head of production planning reflected the key role the automobile industry would be expected to play in the mobilization effort. To take charge of industrial materials, Roosevelt installed Edward R. Stettinius, chairman of the board of U.S. Steel. At the head of the transportation division he put Ralph Budd, president of the Burlington Northern Railway. On labor issues, business leaders such as Knudsen and Stettinius represented the dominant "realist" wing of the business establishment. Like Stimson, Knox, and Patterson, they thought union power had grown inordinately strong under the New Deal. When the opportunity arose, they were willing to use their economic leverage to roll back union gains, but in general they thought the political cost too high for any wholesale reduction of union power. Instead, they favored the regularization of labor–management relations on a basis that preserved managerial prerogatives and contained union power.[32]

One of the key issues raised by the vast expansion of military production was the extent to which the mobilization apparatus in Washington would begin a program of national economic planning that might limit the profit potential or curb the autonomy of corporate enterprise. At first glance, there seemed to be little reason for concern. "If you are going to try to go to war, or to prepare for war, in a capitalist country," wrote Henry Stimson, "you have to let business make money out of the process or business won't work."[33] In the summer of 1940, Congress liberalized tax and depreciation schedules for military contracts, and at the NDAC and its successor, the Office of Production Management (OPM), dollar-a-year representatives of the largest corporations occupied the strategic posts. Knudsen, Patterson, and others in charge of procurement for the military thought the large business enterprises best equipped to get production underway rapidly. Companies such as Bethlehem Steel, Ford, and Allis-Chalmers had the staff, experience, and facilities already assembled. Thus in the six months after June 1940, some 60 percent of the $11 billion in prime contracts awarded by the armed services went to but twenty firms, and 87 percent went to only 100 companies.[34]

However, these large businesses sought to take on the burgeoning military production in addition to their regular civilian work; even when material shortages threatened to delay defense orders in early 1941, they proved reluctant to convert or expand their facilities. There were two reasons for this. First, many firms, notably those in the auto and other metal fabrication industries, were enjoying substantial profits for the first time in several years; therefore, they were reluctant to convert their facilities to defense work when a booming market for civilian goods still existed. Second, companies in capital-intensive primary materials, such as steel, aluminum, and petrochemicals, bitterly recalled the costly over-expansion of earlier years and the dwindling markets of the depression decade. As long as debate continued over the likely duration of American involvement in the European war, corporate managers in these firms were hesitant to expand their own capacity, even when the government offered generous loans and subsidies.[35]

The persons whom Roosevelt brought into the defense mobilization apparatus from the labor movement or the New Deal agencies had a larger appreciation of the coordination required in the emerging war economy. Their planning perspective involved greater central discipline than that envisioned by business-oriented elements of the NDAC or the OPM. One such key figure was Leon Henderson, a veteran New Dealer who took charge of the NDAC's price division (later the semi-autonomous Office of Price Administration and Civilian Supply). Henderson had served as director of the NRA's division of research and planning, where he had worked closely with Hillman, and as a member of the Securities and Exchange Commission. An early Keynesian, he believed that the market power of oligopolistic industry introduced rigidities into the economic system that reduced the effective spending power of the masses, and the regenerative potential of the economy. In 1938 and 1939, Henderson had been instrumental in arranging the anti-monopoly Temporary National Economic Committee hearings that probed the price-fixing and market-controlling powers of big business.

Like Hillman and other liberals, Henderson was a strong proponent of aid to the allies and a rapid buildup of military production. During the spring of 1941, he clashed repeatedly with Knudsen and other business-men over the auto industry's failure to curtail civilian production and convert to military work. In general, Knudsen reflected the auto indus-try's desire to continue the simultaneous output of civilian and military goods, whereas Henderson recognized that such a program would gen-erate shortages and distortions in other sectors of the economy. To force conversion of the industry, therefore, he announced a 50 percent reduc-tion in auto production in July 1941. In the ensuing test of wills, Knud-sen and the auto manufacturers delayed full implementation of this order, but Henderson had demonstrated that forceful economic plan-ning had to replace "business as usual." Significantly, New Dealer Hen-derson had the indirect support of many conservative all-outers in this contest with the auto manufacturers. Despite their general orientation toward an accommodation with business interests, Stimson, Patterson, and others in the military recognized that only in a planned economy could the necessary coordination of military and civilian production take place.[36]

Throughout the period before Pearl Harbor, Sidney Hillman also occupied important, highly visible posts in the mobilization apparatus. Without consulting then CIO President John L. Lewis, FDR had ap-pointed Hillman chief of the NDAC's labor division in May 1940. Seven months later, the president gave the ACWA leader even more power and prestige when he made him codirector, with Knudsen, of the more powerful Office of Production Management. Hillman soon recruited a large staff from the trade unions, academia, and government service to coordinate the utilization of skilled manpower, mediate labor disputes, and ensure the maintenance of labor standards. In these highly visible posts, Hillman served a dual political role, acting both as labor's formal representative in the high councils of the defense mobilization apparatus and as FDR's influential voice in the ranks of the industrial union federation. Hillman's success at both these tasks would prove limited, but for many months pro-Roosevelt unionists in the CIO leadership hoped that the ACWA president might play the same important role in America's domestic high command that the British Labour party's Ernest Bevin played in Winston Churchill's war cabinet.[37]

To Hillman and other progressive interventionists, industrial union support for Roosevelt's defense program seemed a politically necessary prerequisite for labor's bid to help shape and administer the wartime economy and lay plans for a liberal postwar order. Like the right-wing Socialists and New Republic Progressives of World War I, pro-Roosevelt unionists hoped that the collectivist tendencies inherent in the mobilization of the society for total war might provide the opportunity to restructure industry so that labor could have a real say. As long as the president needed support for his foreign policy, and as long as business dragged its feet on military conversion, this strategy seemed to have at least a limited chance of success.

In its most advanced form, this perspective unfolded in the industrial council plan put forward by Philip Murray in the fall of 1940. Inspired by the social reformist encyclicals of Pope Leo XIII and by NRA tripartite planning experiments, these quasicorporativist councils would bring together representatives of labor, management, and government to administer jointly those industries that became vital to the defense effort. The Murray proposals were considered abstract and unnecessary until the up-and-coming Walter Reuther of the UAW captured headlines with a program to convert Detroit auto factories into "one great production unit" to fulfill Roosevelt's ambition to manufacture 50,000 aircraft a year. Winning the support of administration liberals such as Henderson, Harry Hopkins, and Jerome Frank, the Reuther "500 planes a day" plan mandated the establishment of a tripartite Aviation Production Board that would have the power to ignore corporate boundaries, markets, and profits as it presided over the conscription of machine tools, working space, and manpower where and when needed. The Murray–Reuther proposals were never put into effect, but while debated in late 1940 and throughout 1941, they held out the promise of a fundamental reform of industry and a powerful labor presence in the administration of the production effort.[38] As we will see in Chapter 6, the fate of the Reuther plan proved an index to the overall complexion of the war-era political economy.

Conclusion

During the defense era, most CIO unionists linked the enhancement of labor's domestic power with the defeat of fascism abroad. After the fall of France, most American trade unionists, like the larger liberal community, shifted rapidly to support of an active defense against European fascism. Unwilling to strain their alliance with the president and the New Deal wing of his administration, few unionists could see any alternative to Roosevelt's defense program or to his increasingly interventionist foreign policy. Lewis had no political strategy other than retreat to a fortresslike Western Hemisphere. The Communists in the CIO opposed the war, but much of their politics was at least temporarily discredited as they zigzagged from a policy of collective security to nonintervention after the Stalin–Hitler pact. Finally, opposition to war on either pacifist or revolutionary grounds seemed virtually nonexistent – in sharp contrast to the World War I era, when large sections of the working class had been influenced by such a vision.

Roosevelt's program, meanwhile, seemed to hold out the promise of a better world. Liberal and labor spokesmen for his policies argued that they defended progressive democracy worldwide. After the British Labour party formed a coalition government with the Conservatives in May 1940, the character of the war changed for the better, asserted Walter Reuther. Aid to England was now to benefit "not the Chamberlains, not the paid imperialists, but the British working class who are struggling today to protect their homes, their institutions and their rights." Later, Communists in the unions also took note of what they considered the changing nature of the war, but they dated the transformation to the moment when Nazi armies headed east in June 1941. Regardless of the forces that transformed the war from one of reaction to one of progress, American belligerency suffused the conflict with a social patriotism that captured the imagination of liberal and labor forces. Certainly, much of the popularity enjoyed by figures such as Wendell Willkie and Henry Wallace stemmed from their sanguine assurance that the war indeed represented a liberal crusade to advance New Deal principles beyond the frontiers of America.[39]

Roosevelt too recognized the importance of this sentiment, especially before Pearl Harbor, when domestic opinion still remained divided. At the Argentia Bay conference with Churchill that produced the Atlantic Charter, FDR insisted upon a clause in the new agreement "securing for all improved labor standards, economic advancement and social security."[40] Given this liberal interpretation of American war aims, most CIO leaders easily rejected the sullen, pessimistic counsel of John L. Lewis and vowed cooperation with Roosevelt and the military in the rapidly expanding mobilization effort.

4. "Responsible unionism"

During the first half of 1941, a series of CIO-organized strikes threatened to disrupt the Roosevelt administration's defense mobilization effort. To counter this threat, the government applied increasing pressure upon the CIO's leadership to curb its strike activity, moderate its economic demands, and refer all industrial disputes to a newly appointed National Defense Mediation Board (NDMB). This government policy culminated in the pivotal North American Aviation strike of June 1941. In this industrial crisis, the Roosevelt administration used military force to break the organizational walkout of a Communist-led UAW aircraft local and uphold the influence of those leaders of the national UAW who were more politically cooperative with the government. The suppression of this strike proved a turning point in defense era labor relations. Thereafter, work stoppages declined and most unions enforced a de facto no-strike pledge. In turn, union leaders demanded some form of government-enforced union security for the duration of the wartime mobilization.

The CIO offensive

Although the CIO had abandoned its president when he directly challenged Franklin Roosevelt, the industrial union federation enthusiastically endorsed the aggressive organizing campaign John L. Lewis had long sought. Immediately after Philip Murray assumed the presidency in November 1940, he convened the CIO executive board to announce plans for the "most vigorous, far-reaching organization drive that has ever been put on." The defense boom was a unique opportunity that would place the CIO on its feet and finally resolve the federation's chronic financial and organizational problems. Although Murray supported the president's foreign policy, he struck a militant note at home: "Personally I tell you frankly and candidly that I don't give a tinker's damn about national defense interfering with our work. I feel that we ought to go ahead just the same as if that kind of situation were not in our midst. Organize and fight and do the job as we originally intended to do the job five years ago."[1]

As Mineworkers union official and then SWOC chairman, the man who gave the CIO these dramatic marching orders had labored for thirty years in the long shadow cast by John L. Lewis. Now in his fifties, Philip Murray, a soft-spoken, Scottish-born Catholic, stepped into the unstable CIO cockpit personally unsure of his capacity to fill the enormous gap left by his mentor. Murray had none of the inner calm of one comfortable with great power. Although he cultivated a dignified and fatherly demeanor, he could not tolerate opposition within the CIO. He took it personally, thought it threatened his manhood, and felt humiliated when other union leaders contradicted him in public or private. Like his predecessor, Murray wanted a strong, powerful industrial union federation, if only to prove his self-worth, but unlike Lewis, he would soon accommodate to forces he felt were greater than those the CIO alone could muster. An insecure man who sought consensus and stability, Murray remained president of the CIO for twelve extraordinary years until his death in 1952.[2]

Supported by all elements of the CIO, the new organizing drive was designed to achieve CIO dominance in the expanding defense sector before government pressure slowed or curbed union activity. The winter and spring of 1941 proved an opportune time for the CIO to flex its muscles. By the fall of 1940, the government had already begun to spend some of the $10.5 billion in defense appropriations that Congress had just authorized. By March 1941, when the lend-lease program finally passed the national legislature, the American government formally took on the responsibility to provide the bulk of the armaments for Britain's land and sea forces as well. Unemployment, which had hovered at around 10 million since the recession of 1937–8, finally began a slow decline in the late winter of 1941. Such defense-related industries as steel, shipbuilding, and aircraft began operating at full capacity. Temporary labor shortages appeared in specialized skills and crafts.[3]

In addition to extending unionization to those sectors of basic industry still unorganized, the CIO sought a substantial wage increase in 1941. Most industrial workers had not received an across-the-board pay boost since the spring of 1937. In the auto industry, new contracts were signed with General Motors and Chrysler in 1940 without a wage increase. In steel, Philip Murray considered SWOC fortunate to survive the Roosevelt recession with no outright reduction in wages at U.S. Steel. Even the powerful UMW had failed to secure a wage increase since 1937, although it did achieve the union shop throughout the independent coal mining industry in April 1939.[4]

The CIO's aggressive organizational program produced a strike wave of historic proportions. During 1941 there were 4,288 strikes involving almost 2.4 million men and women. Work stoppages were more widespread than in 1937, and only 1919 surpassed the year in overall strike statistics. Many of these work stoppages were directed against the section of heavy industry that had fought off the CIO in 1937. Included were companies such as Ford, International Harvester, Remington Rand, Allis-Chalmers, Montgomery Ward, and the Little Steel group, which sought to exclude industrial unions entirely or to weaken and discredit them after they had gained a foothold. Often led personally by conservative "brass hat" entrepreneurs, these firms were militantly hostile to the New Deal and generally isolationist in their foreign affairs outlook.[5]

Great militancy and confidence characterized the strike wave that spread across the United States in the winter and spring of 1941. Almost 70 percent of those on strike were under the leadership of CIO unions. In February and March, steelworkers at Bethlehem's still nonunion Lackawanna, New York, and Bethlehem, Pennsylvania, mills initiated the first successful strikes against any major steel company in the six-year history of the Steel Workers Organizing Committee. The UAW finally organized the Ford Motor Company in early April after a series of work stoppages and sit-downs culminated in a massive walkout from the Ford River Rouge complex. Long, bitter, and violent strikes against such intransigent anti-union companies as Allis-Chalmers, International Harvester, and Weyerhaeuser Timber also characterized the spring labor offensive. In more disciplined fashion, the UMW struck for over a month, beginning April 1, to demolish successfully, for the first time in the union's fifty-year history, the wage differential between northern and southern Appalachian coalfields.

Union militancy brought an increase in real wages as well. In the winter, major corporations such as U.S. Steel and General Motors resisted union demands for a wage increase of ten cents an hour because they feared that the newly established Office of Price Administration would soon impose a rigid ceiling on steel prices. The deadlock was broken when several CIO unions set strike deadlines for early April. The dramatic UAW strike at Ford convinced even the most intransigent industrialists that the CIO unions were a force to be reckoned with. On April 8, T. E. Weir announced a full ten-cent wage increase at Weirton Steel, a tactic presumably designed to undermine SWOC efforts to oust the company union there. Three days later, Ford agreed to National Labor Relations Board elections and an immediate ten-cent wage increase as well. With the wage dike broken, U.S. Steel, General Motors, General Electric, and other major corporations raised their wages to the new level.[6]

The government's search for a labor policy

This CIO offensive and the strike wave upon which it rested soon created a series of difficult political problems for the Roosevelt administration. Many companies that were the targets of the new CIO organizing drive held important defense contracts, and renewed labor militancy threatened what the War Department called "an unpredictable drain on defense production."[7] The investment bankers and corporate lawyers who now staffed the top civilian echelons of the military services were not opposed to union growth per se, but they were sensitive to any disruption of or interference in a smoothly coordinated industrial–military production effort. Along with the industrialists at the OPM, War and Navy Department leaders viewed most defense strikes as selfishly unpatriotic at best, subversive sabotage at worst. Men such as Secretary of War Henry Stimson and John J. McCloy, his assistant for internal security affairs, were quick to advocate legislative or administrative curbs on the unions when they seemed recalcitrant.[8]

The defense strikes also proved an issue upon which elements in Congress hostile to the CIO could seize to roll back the influence of the industrial union federation and discredit the social reforms of the New Deal. Since 1938, the Wagner Act had come under sharp attack, not only from conservative Republicans but also from the American Federation of Labor, which found the NLRB unsympathetic to craft union prerogatives, and from southern Democrats, who feared that the advance of industrial unionism would smash the commercial advantage enjoyed by low-wage industries of the South. After pounding away at the NLRB for more than a year, these forces had failed to amend the Wagner Act, but they did succeed in forcing Roosevelt to appoint a labor board somewhat less sympathetic to the industrial unions. The defense emergency breathed new life into this attack, and under the leadership of Representative Howard Smith, the conservative forces kept up a steady pressure for new legislation curtailing the right to picket, providing for a thirty-day cooling-off period after a strike vote, and implementing compulsory arbitration procedures in many disputes. In Texas, California, and Georgia, state legislatures had already enacted laws that made organizing much more difficult.[9]

Roosevelt and his advisers found such repressive measures politically unpalatable, and they probably thought them unsophisticated and ineffectual as well. So, the administration sought to curb the work stoppages through informal and voluntary means and by appeals to the patriotism of the union members and officials involved. Because the supporters of the administration's defense program had increased their influence in the CIO after Lewis stepped down from its presidency, Roosevelt had reason to expect a relatively sympathetic response to his call for uninterrupted defense production. Even William Knudsen, the former president of General Motors, now director of the Office of Production Management, hoped that a few words from the president about "teamwork and the need for harmony" would have a "tempering effect on the unquestionable [strike] buildup" in the late winter of 1941.[10]

To help carry out this policy, Roosevelt gave Sidney Hillman new power and prestige in December 1940 by elevating him to the new post of associate director of the Office of Production Management. Working with the cooperative and patriotic SWOC leadership, Hillman persuaded Regional Director Van Bittner to call off massive and enthusiastic organizational strikes at Bethlehem Steel before the union had secured a signed collective bargaining agreement. To avoid charges of obstructing the defense program, leaders of the Industrial Union of Marine and Shipbuilding Workers of America (IUMSWA) called off their strike against Federal Shipbuilding and Drydock, a subsidiary of U.S. Steel. The government's policy received the endorsement of the AFL executive council in January 1941, when they declared that they would oppose strikes on defense construction projects. In all, Hillman's OPM labor division claimed to have peacefully mediated 247 disputes during 1940 and 1941.[11]

Even with most national union leaders sympathetic to the idea of avoiding defense strikes, neither Hillman nor the president could maintain labor peace with what we would today call "jawboning tactics."

Industrial unions of the era were still highly decentralized, and local unionists held de facto, if not de jure, strike authority. With skilled labor at a premium and with even unskilled workmen coming into demand, local union officials saw an unparalleled opportunity to settle long-standing grievances, strengthen their contracts, and organize more securely. Several SWOC lodges struck against the counsel of top union officials, the UAW fought its way into the Chicago area for the first time, and an AFL machinists' lodge in San Francisco stopped shipyard defense production for over a month on a local contract issue.[12] Because the Supreme Court had the year before declared sit-down strikes illegal, many of the 1941 work stoppages were enforced with the use of mass picket lines, sometimes a thousand or more strong, that circled the plants, kept scabs and supervisory personnel out, and often battled the police.

The seventy-six-day Allis-Chalmers dispute that began in January 1941 disclosed most dramatically the impotence of Hillman's voluntary mediation efforts when confronted with a militant local and a recalcitrant employer. The Milwaukee-based company was one of the world's leading builders of electrical engines and turbines, and in 1941 it held prime contracts for $40 million in navy orders. Representing most of the 8,000 workers was UAW Local 248, which had tenaciously battled its way into the plant under the leadership of Harold Christoffel, a young, combative militant closely associated with the Communists. Led by Max D. Babb, a brass hat of the old school, the company opposed the local with equal combativeness and tried to undermine the union even after it had won an NLRB election in 1938. Each collective bargaining session was at best a standoff: Because Allis-Chalmers won most of these rounds, UAW activists in the plant felt embattled and were ultrasensitive to company maneuvers against the local.

Management touched off the 1941 work stoppage when it fired six union members who had been particularly zealous in their efforts to collect back dues and fines from anti-UAW workers. Sensing another challenge to the security of the local, Christoffel called for a quick strike vote and received overwhelming sentiment for a walkout. On January 21, the union put up mass picket lines and shut down the plant. Local 248 demanded a union security agreement from the company even though its contract was not due to run out for three months.

After the Labor Department's conciliation service failed to resolve the dispute, Hillman intervened with the suggestion that the union security issue be solved by a "maintenance-of-membership" formula, whereby any Allis-Chalmers worker already a member of Local 248 would be committed to membership for the life of the contract. Both parties reached an agreement on this basis on February 14, but it then broke down when Babb had second thoughts about taking even such a partial step toward what he considered the closed shop. Stalemated, but generating a growing furor among conservatives, the strike dragged on for more than a month. On March 27 the Navy Department abruptly wired the executives of Allis-Chalmers and officers of the UAW that the plant must be reopened at once. Defied by Christoffel and most other Milwaukee area unionists, the military's initiative failed to break the strike but did create a pitched battle outside the plant when 1,200 workers tried to return to work. At this moment of crisis, the national officers of the UAW reaffirmed their support of the work stoppages, and Philip Murray telegraphed OPM Director Knudsen, demanding to know "by what power are you and Secretary Knox authorized to issue ultimatum?" The mass picket lines held firm, and three days of near rioting forced the governor of Wisconsin to call out the National Guard and close the plant once more.[13]

The government's difficulties at Allis-Chalmers were compounded in late March by the possibility of nation-wide strikes at GM, Ford, and in the coal and steel industries. These problems convinced Hillman that the time had come to put into effect a plan for a tripartite mediation board, an idea that he had privately favored since the early fall of 1940. Recommending the mediation plan to the president, Hillman now hoped that the public outcry over defense strikes would make the creation of such a board acceptable to CIO leaders as a means of forestalling congressional passage of antistrike legislation. At the same time, the new mediation machinery might disarm the demands of his military confreres in the war production bureaucracy for more drastic measures that could alienate pro-Roosevelt unionists.

Although AFL and industry spokesmen quickly endorsed the mediation board, Philip Murray held back. The new CIO president certainly supported the defense program, and he normally urged deployment of the strike weapon in a cautious fashion. Moreover, he found defense strikes, especially those led by Communists, an embarrassment to the CIO. But Murray also found himself the leader of a working-class movement that was finally on the move, making up for years of near stagnation. In a private memorandum to Hillman, Murray argued that because the new board would be chiefly concerned with halting or preventing strikes, it would "find its attention directed against labor in order to maintain the status quo as much as possible." The CIO president judged that the board could not long remain a voluntary mediation body but would soon "bring terrific pressure on labor to agree to arbitration in practically all situations."[14]

Murray's critique proved prescient and shrewd, but when President Roosevelt announced the establishment of an eleven-member National Defense Mediation Board late in March 1941, Murray was not about to defy the chief executive. He readily pledged CIO cooperation with the new agency and, at Hillman's behest, agreed to serve as one of its four labor representatives. Still, Murray and other top CIO officials continued to defend labor's autonomy in the face of what they sensed to be a growing mood of government coercion. In April, for example, the CIO published a widely disseminated pamphlet, "The Right to Strike – Keystone of Liberty," which denounced congressional compulsory arbitration proposals as a step toward "involuntary servitude."[15]

The labor board

The NDMB and its successor, the National War Labor Board, were as important as the Wagner Act in shaping the American system of industrial relations. For the next four years, these boards were instrumental in setting for the first time industry-wide wage patterns, fixing a system of "industrial jurisprudence" on the shop floor, and influencing the internal structure of the new industrial unions. They were a powerful force in nationalizing a conception of routine and bureaucratic industrial relations that had been pioneered in the garment trades but that the Wagner Act and the NLRB had thus far failed to implement fully. These boards were remarkably effective, not just because of the scope of their quasi-judicial power but because, as Hillman understood, their legitimacy rested upon their tripartite character. Both labor and business representatives would participate with the government in discussing the issues that arose and in rendering a decision. Although the NWLB would eventually lose much of its autonomy, this tripartite setup, unique among the important wartime agencies, did much to spread the responsibility for even unpopular decisions to the trade union leadership itself. Besides Murray, the other labor members of the NDMB included the secretary-treasurer of the UMW, Thomas Kennedy, who represented the views of John L. Lewis, George Meany, then secretary-treasurer of the AFL, and George M. Harrison, president of the independent Brotherhood of Railway Clerks.[16]

Employer members were less representative than their labor counterparts. They spoke for that minority wing of the business establishment that had favored New Deal efforts to order economic activity in the 1930s and that now thought stable and secure trade unions a further key to industrial rationality and efficiency. Standard Oil Chairman Walter C. Teagle, a founder of the influential Business Advisory Council, had spent many months in Washington as an industry voice in the councils of the National Recovery Administration. Although later estranged from the New Deal during its leftward phase, Teagle supported Social Security and, like General Electric President Gerard Swope, favored the industrial union form of organization as best suited to the stabilization of industrial relations in the large corporation. Teagle was joined on the NDMB by Roger D. Lapham, the sophisticated chairman of the American-Hawaiian Steamship Company, who would later win election as mayor of heavily unionized San Francisco, and by *Washington Post* publisher Eugene Meyer, a Republican party internationalist who strongly backed FDR's foreign policy. U.S. Rubber's Cyrus Ching was perhaps the business community's most well-known progressive in the field of industrial relations policy. Director since 1919 of his company's industrial and public relations, Ching had been a pioneer in personnel management for more than a quarter of a century. In the mid-1930s he had instructed U.S. Rubber plant managers to place no obstacles in the path of the United Rubber Workers in return for a union agreement that its organizing campaign would be a strike-free and orderly one. Before business audiences, Ching defended the Wagner Act, and in numerous articles and speeches, he preached rapprochement between responsible leaders of business and organized labor in order to build a workable union–management relationship on the shop floor and then lay the basis for a new federal policy based on a top-level consensus.[17]

During the next two years – the creative phase of NDMB–NWLB policy formulation – substantial power lay with the full-time public members and their rapidly growing staff. Hillman chose University of Wisconsin President Clarence Dykstra as the first chairman of the NDMB, but he soon resigned in favor of William H. Davis, a leading New York patent attorney, who dominated the board until 1945 as the energetic, highly visible mediator and spokesman in all the board's most important decisions. Davis, a Democrat, had helped write NRA codes for the shipbuilding and retail coal industries and had then taken on the frustrating job of national compliance director during that agency's last year. A friend of Secretary of Labor Frances Perkins and Sidney Hillman, Davis believed that the government could play an active role in resolving social conflict through tripartite mechanisms involving labor, management, and public representatives. He thought strong, stable trade unions essential to this process. From 1937 to 1940, Davis chaired the New York State Mediation Board, where he won the confidence of important sectors of the union movement and built a national reputation as a resourceful labor mediator. After the NLRB came under attack in 1938, Davis chaired the liberal Twentieth Century Fund's Labor Committee, which defended an unamended Wagner Act as effective legislation.

Other public members of the NDMB included Frank P. Graham, the liberal president of the University of North Carolina, who handled many of the difficult race relations issues, and Charles E. Wyzanski, a Massachusetts attorney previously employed in the Labor Department. The latter was replaced in early 1942 by Wayne Morse, the brilliant University of Oregon Law School dean who had won the confidence of both the International Longshoremen's and Warehousemen's Union and the Pacific Maritime Association as a longshore industry arbitrator in 1939 and 1940. Morse was joined on the NWLB by George W. Taylor, a University of Pennsylvania economist who had worked with Hillman for many years as an arbitrator in the men's clothing industry. Taylor had most recently served as grievance umpire under the UAW–GM contract, which mandated the first such post in heavy industry.[18]

Under Davis's vigorous leadership, the NDMB rapidly moved in much the way Philip Murray had foreseen. Davis used the prestige of the board and the president to pressure union leaders to call off strikes as soon as their disputes were certified to the NDMB. This policy soon evolved into one that demanded that a union return to work or refrain from striking before the board would adjudicate the dispute. By the end of June 1941, the NDMB was relying on federal authority to insist upon arbitration of all important union–management conflicts and to enforce a virtual no-strike prohibition.[19]

Strike politics in the UAW

The formation of the NDMB and the development of its strike policy vastly increased the government's pressure upon top union leaders to curb the relative autonomy of their locals and moderate the aggressive character of the national organizing drive. In no other union was the step-by-step unfolding of this process more important or more clearly evident than in the United Auto Workers, where government pressure to curb local militancy reached a climax in June 1941 with the suppression of the North American Aviation Strike.

Three elements governed UAW strike policy in the defense area: the resurgent militancy of the rank and file, the growing government pressure against work stoppages, and the new factional lineup in the union that ranged Walter Reuther and those who supported Roosevelt's foreign policies against a more disparate grouping led by UAW Secretary-Treasurer George Addes. As an early supporter of the defense effort and aid to the allies, Reuther sought to use the pressures generated by the defense buildup and the government's growing demand for internal union discipline as a path to power in the UAW. During the two UAW conventions that took place during the Nazi–Soviet pact era, Reuther had vigorously and successfully pushed anti-Communist resolutions to take advantage of a growing defense era patriotism in UAW ranks. He inaugurated a centralized arbitration system in all GM plants – the first such arrangement in a new CIO union – and he was among the foremost advocates of cooperation with the recently established National Defense Mediation Board.[20] Reuther favored suspension of strike activity where it interfered with defense production.

But Reuther faced two major obstacles in his effort to put this program into effect. First were his factional opponents: followers of John L. Lewis, the Communists and their close followers, and those members of the international union apparatus, such as Addes and, on occasion, President R. J. Thomas, who were largely motivated by the desire to keep "the redhead" in check. Second, and in the defense era far more important, were the key trade union cadres at the local level. They were in no mood to relinquish control of the strike weapon when it proved most efficacious.

A test of strength came in September 1940, when union activists at GM's Fisher Body plant in Flint organized a short wildcat strike to eliminate AFL loyalists from the factory. The work stoppage came in clear violation of a recently enacted UAW executive board "recommendation" that local strikes take place after all steps in the grievance machinery had been taken. Only then would the international consider a strike sanction.[21] Because the walkout appeared unauthorized at either the local or international level, General Motors did not hesitate to fire seventeen secondary leaders of the union. But UAW Local 581 now stood behind the discharged men and began to organize a conference of UAW locals in the Flint area to fight GM and the executive board on the issue. The incident became one of acute political embarrassment for the UAW leadership, especially for Reuther, who was director of the GM department. In order to settle the Flint affair, the UAW had to call upon Philip Murray to negotiate directly with the corporation. General Motors ultimately agreed to accept arbitration on the issue. Most of the discharged men were rehired.

With the Flint incident still churning the factional waters, the UAW executive board formulated its policy on defense strikes in an aggressive manner. "The union," announced George Addes, "is prepared to authorize strikes . . . We must prove to our local unions that this international is not capitulating to the pressure being placed by the government and the management. We must maintain confidence between local union officials and the international union."[22] During the winter, R. J. Thomas publicly defended the right of local unionists to strike over grievances even in defense industries. The UAW international stood behind the embarrassing Allis-Chalmers walkout and sanctioned the huge Ford strike at River Rouge once top union officials had confirmed the massive character of the work stoppage there.[23]

By April, GM locals were gearing up for their first company-wide strike since 1937. The giant auto manufacturer recognized the UAW but fought doggedly to retain managerial prerogatives over working conditions, line speed, and the like. Led by the politically dissident Flint locals, a GM conference in February had demanded a dramatic increase in the number of company-recognized stewards, which in turn would make a union presence on the shop floor more effective. The UAW set a tentative strike date for April 28.

The obvious sentiment of GM local officials for a work stoppage clashed with Reuther's ideological commitment to the defense effort and to the basic outlines of FDR's domestic policies. As the chief proponent of a recently negotiated arbitration system at GM, Reuther emphasized a straight wage increase demand rather than confrontation with the powerful corporation over the steward issue. The GM director also proposed that if a strike did develop, the union should call out only those workers not engaged in defense production.

Reuther was taken off the hook on April 26, when Secretary of Labor Frances Perkins unilaterally certified the GM dispute to the new mediation board. Without consulting other UAW executive officers, Reuther accepted her action as a fait accompli and dispatched telegrams calling off the imminent strike. In an emergency session of the UAW executive board the next day, Reuther came under fierce attack for agreeing to outside mediation so quickly, thereby embarrassing the top officers of the union and reducing the bargaining leverage of the GM negotiating committee. Led by Addes, Reuther's factional opponents also voiced the fear that the GM director had set a dangerous precedent. "Are we to assume," asked Addes, "that when entering negotiations with the corporation in the event our case is certified to the mediation board, our union will follow a 'no-strike' policy?"

Unwilling to reopen the politically explosive strike issue, UAW leaders had little choice but to accept the new situation. They roundly condemned Frances Perkins for what they considered her unwarranted, precipitous intervention in the union's affairs, but they also endorsed Reuther's decision to call off the strike. Reflecting the majority sentiment of the board, Addes concluded the meeting on a note of vague determination: "We must follow an aggressive policy and not one of appeasement."[24]

The ultimate test of this sentiment came not in Detroit but in Southern California, where the UAW had already begun a vigorous organizing campaign among aircraft workers. Since the late 1930s, the union had sought unsuccessfully to organize the airframe manufacturing companies of Southern California. Union efforts had failed because of the anti-union tradition of the Los Angeles area, the loyalty of skilled employees toward paternalistic employers, and the isolation of the California aircraft industry from the main centers of UAW strength. The defense boom changed all this. Aircraft orders from England, France, and the army air force fueled a rapid expansion of the industry. By mid-1941, over 100,000 aircraft workers were employed in the Los Angeles area alone. These were unskilled workers, many in their first industrial job, many attracted by the glamour of the new technology. "Shift change resembled a high school dismissal," recalled one observer. Aircraft wages in the booming industry lagged far behind those of unionized auto and shipyard workers on the west coast. The industry's Aeronautical Chamber of Commerce enforced a fifty-cent-an-hour rate for semiskilled labor, little more than that paid in the southern textile industry.[25]

From the start, Communists were largely in charge of the aircraft drive on the west coast, in part because many UAW activists were "exiled" there from Detroit after party influence began to decline in the defense period but also because the California CIO was more than usually congenial to these radicals. Wyndham Mortimer, a founder of the UAW and a devoted and effective organizer, was unquestionably the key figure in the aircraft drive. Among the other important Communists were Henry and Dorothy Kraus, who had played important roles in the GM sit-down strike, Elmer Freitag, later president of the North American Aviation local, and Lew Michener, UAW Region Six director.[26]

After he arrived in Southern California in the summer of 1939, Mortimer concentrated his efforts upon two important and rapidly expanding companies: Vultee Aircraft and North American Aviation. Organization began slowly, however, because of the UAW's preoccupation with reestablishing its bargaining relationships in Michigan auto centers and because of the continuing factional battle with Homer Martin's forces in California, which did not end until mid-1940. UAW organizing efforts also faced competition from the International Association of Machinists (IAM), which had already signed contracts with Consolidated and Lockheed.

The UAW finally mounted an effective campaign at Vultee in the summer of 1940 and won an NLRB election there in August. Management negotiators proved characteristically dilatory, so Michener and Mortimer called a strike vote that passed overwhelmingly in early November. Mortimer checked briefly by phone with CIO and UAW officials in the East, then authorized a November 15 strike, in the process tying up production of a substantial proportion of the army's trainer planes. Although the work stoppage soon won a reorganization of the company's chaotic wage schedule and a substantial pay increase, the strike also brought down a shrill campaign of denunciation, not only from the usual antilabor conservatives but from Roosevelt administration officials as well. Attorney General Robert Jackson attacked the strike as Communist-inspired. The Federal Bureau of Investigation identified Mortimer and Michener as members of the Communist party. Sidney Hillman denounced the strike and unsuccessfully tried to get Philip Murray and R. J. Thomas to do likewise. In a November 26 news conference, Roosevelt called for uninterrupted production in defense industries, although he refused to endorse antistrike legislation then pending in Congress.[27]

The public outcry soon reverberated within the UAW. Regional Director Michener reported to the union's executive board that the Vultee strike had stimulated organizational sentiment tremendously, but he warned, "*Time* is the essence of the present efforts to bring the benefits of unionism to the aircraft workers. Every indication points to more and more restrictions and obstacles being placed in our way as time goes on and every effort must be made to push organizing *now* while it is still possible to conduct our activities without too much interference."[28]

Philip Murray and the rest of the UAW executive board agreed with Michener that the aircraft organizing drive should be vigorously pursued. But they insisted on greater centralization of control in view of the national uproar over the strike and the charges of Communist influence in the west coast region.

Murray therefore sent Allen Haywood, organizational director of the CIO, to lay down the line to the UAW at the International's December 1940 executive board meeting in Cleveland. Haywood told the UAW officials that from now on the aircraft organizing drive would be conducted under the joint aegis of the CIO and the UAW. He emphasized the importance of defending the CIO against the charges of irresponsibility that followed the Vultee strike. Murray and Hayward used their influence to install Richard Frankensteen, then director of the Chrysler department and not then allied with either UAW faction, as national director of the UAW aviation division. With a treasury of $100,000 contributed jointly by the UAW and the national CIO, and a score or more organizers at his disposal, Frankensteen would now become one of the most powerful figures in the UAW. His jurisdiction extended throughout the nation, and he had complete authority over the new aircraft locals until they won collective bargaining contracts. Frankensteen was to report directly to presidents Thomas and Murray on the progress of the organizing drive.[29]

Frankensteen left day-to-day control of the work in Southern California to Michener, Mortimer, and their assistants. With Frankensteen's encouragement, they poured the UAW's resources into organizing the burgeoning North American Aviation plant at Inglewood, one of the two main producers of fighter aircraft in the country. There they met stiff IAM competition for the loyalty of the 11,000 workers. The first NLRB election, held in February 1941, proved inconclusive. By an uncomfortably slim margin, the UAW defeated the machinists in a second NLRB contest and opened contract negotiations with the company on April 16. The union demanded "seventy-five and ten" – a starting rate of seventy-five cents an hour and a ten-cent blanket raise for higher-paid aircraftsmen. This was far above anything yet won by the IAM. Mortimer and Michener hoped to achieve such a breakthrough at the North American Aviation plant that the AFL would be swept from the field.[30]

By the middle of May, UAW negotiations with North American's management had deadlocked, and Frankensteen turned his attention to the situation. Like any good organizer, he struck a militant note, pledging "all-out-aid" from the international and promising "seventy-five and ten or else" at a mass meeting of North American Aviation workers. He called upon the local, UAW 683, to cast a strike vote so that its bargaining committee would have authority to call a work stoppage "when and if they considered such action necessary." The vote had a twofold purpose: first, to reconfirm UAW support in the plant and thereby put new pressure on management; second, to speed certification of the dispute to the NDMB, which even the Communist leaders of the local in California recognized would inevitably enter the picture. The vote was carried by 5,829 to 210 on May 22; the next day, the Department of Labor mediator in Los Angeles routinely sent the dispute to the mediation board.[31]

At this point, the cumbersome bureaucracy of the board came into play. The NDMB was overwhelmed with disputes and could not immediately set up a panel to hear the North American Aviation case. It took six days to find suitable personnel for such a hearing, an agonizing delay for the inexperienced representatives Local 683 sent to Washington. In the meantime, the union delegation agreed that as long as no strike took place, any wage settlement would be retroactive to May 1.[32] In theory this agreement was not binding, but politically it had the effect of a no-strike pledge, at least from the point of view of the NDMB and some national leaders of the CIO.

Despite the retroactive character of this agreement, time seemed to be working against Local 683's leadership, now split between Washington and Los Angeles. At Inglewood, over 4,000 workers had been hired since the UAW had won an NLRB election in April. The relative handful of UAW activists there feared that they would be unable to consolidate the allegiance of these new thousands. The IAM retained its organization in the plant and pointed to the contracts that it had recently negotiated with Boeing in Seattle and Consolidated in San Diego as examples of its potency. Mortimer feared either undisciplined wildcat strikes within the plant, which would bring a crushing company response, or the development of a cynical, apathetic attitude toward the union. Meanwhile, in Washington the Dies Committee called in Local 683 President Elmer Freitag to answer charges that the Communist party had cooperated with the German-American Bund to foment defense strikes. Informally, NDMB Chairman Clarence Dykstra indicated to union representatives that the board's wage award would be far less than the seventy-five and ten they had so long and insistently demanded.[33]

By early June, preparations for a strike at North American Aviation had reached a fever pitch. There is some evidence that workers on the June 4 night shift actually began the strike as a wildcat, unauthorized even by the leadership still on the scene in Southern California. Henry Kraus, who worked full time with the local, first heard of the work stoppage when he received a phone call at home the next morning:

None of the other organizers had known about it either and it certainly wasn't planned . . . A wildcat strike at that point struck us as foolish, dangerous and unnecessary. When and if the time came to strike, it could be done in orderly fashion. We felt strong enough by this time to know it could be done that way. This wasn't Fisher One or Cleveland of December 1936, when any kind of a strike would have been welcome. Things had indeed changed. Aside from all else, we felt, the national picture required a more careful and certain approach. However, this did not mean that we were going to outlaw the strikers or order them back to work! This was not our approach. Lord knew they had undergone endless delay and provocation. The action had won such evident approval from the workers, besides. Our prompt thought was to accept the strike and help organize and strengthen it.[34]

Without consulting Frankensteen, who was then in Detroit negotiating a new Chrysler contract, Kraus and other UAW organizers established effective picket lines on June 5. Swelling their ranks to some 4,000 strong by noon, they ringed the huge plant and easily repulsed police attempts to break their lines. Aircraft production at North American Aviation ceased. Most of the CIO apparatus in Southern California came to the aid of the work stoppage, which was probably the largest in the state since the San Francisco general strike seven years before.[35]

Bayonets in California

In Washington, news of the North American Aviation events produced alarm, then firm determination to crack down once and for all on defense strikes. Since early in the year, Secretary of War Stimson had urged

Roosevelt to take more forceful steps to prevent these work stoppages. On May 27, Stimson scored a victory when the president issued a "Declaration of Unlimited National Emergency," rhetorically linking defense plant strikes with fifth column activity. Roosevelt called for union adherence to the recommendations of the NDMB and warned that the "government is determined to use all of its power . . . to prevent interference with the production of materials essential to our Nation's security." On June 3, FDR asked Congress to pass legislation to keep plants open that were threatened by strike activity.[36]

When Stimson and McCloy heard of the North American Aviation strike, they were immediately anxious to seize the plant and reopen it with a massive show of military force. They had long sought a politically acceptable use of the military to end a defense strike. The North American Aviation shutdown, which tied up 25 percent of all fighter aircraft production and appeared to be both Communist-led and unauthorized, was the obvious choice for such a display of army strength. But before they could act, William H. Davis persuaded Stimson and McCloy to see if the leaders of the CIO and UAW could end the strike themselves. Davis understood, as the military did not, the crucial importance of making sure that the army did not take over the plant until Richard Frankensteen, director of the joint UAW–CIO aircraft drive, had had time either to settle the dispute himself or to declare the strike unauthorized. If the army acted precipitously, it might find itself in conflict with the CIO. If the government waited, military action would be in support of a UAW–CIO judgment that the strike was unauthorized and in violation of union policy.[37]

In crisis situations of this sort, Murray had little stomach for confrontations with high government officials, especially if his own prerogatives as CIO president were respected, as they had not been during the abortive military intervention at Allis-Chalmers. Accompanied by UAW President R. J. Thomas, he discussed the situation with the mediation board and then dispatched Frankensteen to Los Angeles with the knowledge that if he failed to secure a voluntary end to the strike by June 9, the army would move in and reopen the plant by force. When the majority of the UAW leaders in Southern California refused to call off the strike, Frankensteen lifted the local's charter, suspended the nine-man negotiating committee, and fired five UAW international representatives, including Mortimer, who sided with the strikers.[38]

In a nation-wide radio speech on the night of June 7, Frankensteen advertised the unsanctioned character of the strike, urged a return to work, and attacked the "infamous agitation and vicious underhanded maneuvering of the Communist Party." The next day, he spoke to thousands of North American Aviation workers in a beanfield near the plant. Organized by unionists hostile to Frankensteen, the meeting turned into a demonstration that shouted down the aircraft director and his call to return to work.[39]

News of the beanfield episode convinced Washington officials to take direct action of the sort Stimson and McCloy had originally urged. With the explicit approval of Sidney Hillman and the certain knowledge of Murray and Thomas, Roosevelt signed an executive order that authorized the army to seize the plant and break the strike. On the morning of June 9, 2,500 troops with fixed bayonets moved in, broke up the existing picket lines, and prohibited public assembly within a mile of the plant. Stimson ordered California draft boards to cancel the deferments of those who refused to return to work. When leaders of the strike attempted to organize a march back into the plant, military forces on the scene disrupted this show of solidarity.[40]

Why did the California Communists call the disastrous North American Aviation strike? Even more importantly, why did they think it had a chance of success? The answers lie not only in the politics of those who led the strike but in their mistaken perception of labor politics in the spring of 1941. Although only a few unionists were influenced by the Communist party analysis of the international situation, this stratum struck a responsive chord when they appealed to rank-and-file workers on a program of aggressive trade unionism. Communists in the unions were far less interested in "sabotaging" the defense program, as charged by their pro-Roosevelt opponents, than in taking advantage of the favorable economic circumstances of the defense boom to secure organizational gains against a particularly intransigent set of employers. This strategy was not too different from that pursued by John L. Lewis during the next few years or the one that Philip Murray had outlined in the fall of 1940. Of course, by demonstrating the superiority of a militant strategy in the CIO, the Communists hoped to advance their politics within the union movement. In this sense, their strikes were political.

Throughout most of early 1941, these tactics paid off. The key to their success lay in the fact that aggressive unionists were able to maintain the public support of top CIO officials, who provided a buffer between the increasingly conservative pressures emanating from Washington and the disruptive organizing activities conducted in the field. Murray and

Thomas backed the Vultee and Allis-Chalmers strikes, authorized the Ford walkout, defended free collective bargaining and the right to strike. The NDMB no-strike policy had not yet been solidly cast, nor had important elements in the UAW or the CIO accepted its authority on those terms. John L. Lewis, for example, kept the UMW on strike in April while board hearings on the new coal contract remained in progress; the faction of the UAW led by George Addes had strong misgivings about cooperation with an NDMB no-strike policy. Throughout the spring several small strikes, some Communist-led, continued despite NDMB calls to return to work.[41]

From the point of view of internal trade union practice and tradition, the organizers of the North American Aviation strike were playing by the rules as they had previously existed. Major strikes, especially organizational ones, were often called by union activists on the scene, then authorized by higher officials once they appeared successful. Such was the case in the great Ford strike two months earlier, and Local 683 leaders expected, or at least hoped, that the same pattern would be followed at Inglewood. A successful strike was always its own best recommendation, as even Frankensteen freely recognized. When the local first set a strike deadline in late May, he told its officers, "Don't worry about strike sanction. It's only a scrap of paper: anyway, I can fix that."[42]

Even if the strike remained unauthorized, many of its leaders apparently thought Roosevelt might have hesitated to pay the political cost to break it. Certainly, few on the west coast expected the rapid and forceful deployment of the army.[43] But in the virtual "war hysteria" that gripped Washington in early June, the White House was ready to act, backed in turn by CIO officials who unhesitatingly disowned the strike as the price required to retain their links with the administration and fend off drastic antilabor legislation. This highly charged atmosphere doomed the strike, regardless of the tactical calculations of its organizers or its genuine popularity among North American Aviation workers.

The labor truce

"We met one of our most serious difficulties head-on when we took over the plant," wrote Navy Secretary Frank Knox to a friend on June 13. "It has had a profound psychological effect and from now on I think our troubles from that source will grow less." They did. A CIO conference in July formally condemned the use of troops in labor disputes, and Philip Murray again attacked NDMB "compulsory arbitration."[44] But these grumbles were chiefly for internal union consumption. Trade union officials respected raw power when they saw it, and they soon made it clear throughout their organization that the strike weapon was no longer a legitimate tool in labor's arsenal. Working closely with Hillman at the OPM, CIO and AFL leaders denounced those strikes that continued in defiance of NDMB authority. Murray publicly attacked the Communist leaders of the International Woodworkers of America and insisted that they end a month-long strike in the Puget Sound lumber industry. He pressured Communist-led aluminum plant locals in Detroit and Cleveland to end their work stoppages. Despite a tradition of union autonomy, AFL leaders moved to halt the long-festering IAM shipyard dispute in San Francisco. On June 15, defense-minded leaders of the CIO's Marine and Shipbuilding Workers union agreed to a two-year no-strike pledge contract worked out by Hillman's OPM labor division. The number of workers on strike during 1941, which had reached a peak in early June, declined sharply in the second half of the month, leveled off in July and August, and then dropped rapidly thereafter.[45]

Two other events in June signaled an important decline in the level of union militance and political dissent within the labor movement. On June 22, Germany invaded the Soviet Union. The Communists quickly dropped their unproductive "peace" offensive and moved to advocate U.S. belligerency and a labor policy adamantly opposed to any interruptions in defense production. Their abrupt shift largely checked the growing attack on the Communists within the CIO; by the fall, they were staunch supporters of Philip Murray, allies of Richard Frankensteen, and opponents of John L. Lewis.

Aside from the political maverick who still dominated the UMW, the Communist switch left only one other group of dissident trade unionists unwilling to accommodate to the new policy of labor discipline. These were the Minneapolis teamsters, organized into International Brotherhood of Teamsters Local 544. Under Trotskyist leadership, they were a major force in the upper Midwest and a continual irritant to Teamster President Daniel Tobin and his conservative associates. A close political ally of President Roosevelt, Tobin used the White House's new get-tough policy to crack down on Local 544. In early June he demanded that they accept one of his lieutenants as their administrator. The local rejected his ultimatum and voted to affiliate with a tiny CIO transport union dominated by Lewis forces. The White House condemned the CIO "raid" on June 14. Two weeks later, Justice Department agents descended upon the homes and offices of union radicals in Minneapolis and New York, indicting more than a score on charges of "criminal syndicalism" under the new Smith Act. At the same time, Tobin sent in strong-arm organizers, led by a youthful Jimmy Hoffa, to retake Minneapolis for the AFL. Within a few weeks, the Trotskyist influence there was broken.[46]

The events of June 1941 made strikes illegitimate and suppressed political dissent in the union movement. But this was not fascism. The unions were not destroyed, only tamed. The North American Aviation situation provides a case in point. After the army took over the plant, they installed Colonel Charles Bradshaw, who was instructed to pursue a policy calculated to recognize and strengthen the new leadership of the local appointed by Richard Frankensteen. Hillman assigned a civilian labor adviser from OPM to work with Colonel Bradshaw in administering the plant. The grievance procedure and shop steward system were continued, but the company fired about twenty-five of the workers most active in the strike in accordance with instructions from Under Secretary of War Patterson, as agreed to by Hillman and Frankensteen.[47]

At first, Frankensteen's forces made little progress in reorganizing the local on a basis acceptable to either the army or the CIO. The armed guards who circulated throughout the plant were a constant irritant to the workers. Dues collections dropped to a small fraction of the prestrike amount. The deposed officers of the local continued to command the loyalty of a majority of the employees.[48] On June 19, Colonel Bradshaw reported to the under secretary of war, "The old crowd is in control, and the new crowd does not even dare to call a meeting and go before the workers." When Frankensteen's new assistant director of aircraft, Walter Smethurst, appeared before a group of union stewards, he was nearly thrown out.[49] Bradshaw reported to Patterson that if the army were removed from the plant, there would be a repetition of the strike. He recommended that the NDMB immediately set to work on a new contract, one that had "better be good" if Frankensteen's forces were to retain control of the local after military withdrawal.[50] Patterson agreed, and on June 20 he wrote to Sidney Hillman, "It is my view that if an agreement can be brought about promptly by the mediation board, the better elements in the Union would be strengthened. They would then have proof of their power and ability to get results."[51]

The board soon instructed North American Aviation's management to meet all the union's wage demands, including the famous seventy-five and ten, which represented a pay increase of 50 percent for some job categories. In addition, the NDMB directed the company to include a retroactive maintenance of membership and a dues checkoff clause in the new union contract. This extraordinary decision helped strengthen Frankensteen's new local and enabled the army to withdraw its troops in early July. *The United Auto Worker* greeted news of the award with the headline, "Responsible Unionism Wins at Inglewood."[52]

After June 1941, the NDMB's new authority, the genuine support of defense preparedness by most AFL and CIO leaders, and the shift in the Communist line all seemed to promise a relatively trouble-free labor front as the nation moved toward even greater involvement in the war. But the enforced labor peace soon brought a new series of problems for those leaders who willingly subordinated immediate trade union goals to the overall success of the defense effort. Deprived of the right to strike, and with many of the normal functions of the union leadership now assumed by government agencies, many unionists feared for the stability and integrity of their organizations. To counter this threat, CIO leaders demanded that the government enforce the union shop in all basic industries. In the twelve months following the suppression of the North American Aviation strike, this issue would dominate the labor–management–government debate.

5. Union security and the Little Steel formula

In the year following the suppression of the North American Aviation strike, union security became the most crucial issue facing the industrial unions and one of the key questions of domestic political debate. Of course, the automatic enrollment of employees in a union holding jurisdiction in a workplace had long been a goal of virtually everyone involved in the twentieth-century labor movement. Such enrollment represented a limited form of security against the vicissitudes of the business cycle and the hostility of the employer. CIO leaders keenly recalled the industrial union experience during World War I, when high wages, union growth, and a government-imposed truce with industry were followed by a postwar collapse and repression that destroyed for almost a generation newly formed unions in meatpacking, shipbuilding, steel, and the metal trades. To many unionists, continuing opposition to union shop status by most large employers seemed proof that the titans of industry were merely awaiting another postwar economic downturn to strike a blow at permanent industrial unionism.

Meanwhile, wartime regimentation held its own dangers. Some in the CIO high command realized that the web of loyalties that bound industrial workers to their unions – and to their union leadership – might unravel when labor ceased to exercise the strike weapon and when wages and other working conditions were set by government fiat. Some still vividly remembered the British industrial experience during the last war. Then, patriotic union leaders had also pledged economic and political cooperation with the war effort and had given a no-strike pledge for the duration. But a militant shop stewards' movement had arisen in opposition to these policies and virtually seized control of several major unions from their formal leadership. [1]

The NDMB and the union shop

Reflecting the more conservative tilt of its wartime policy, the Roosevelt administration favored maintenance of the status quo on this issue. The

National Defense Mediation Board accepted the idea, put forward by its industry members, that the federal government would not force individual workers to join a union as a condition of their employment. William H. Davis and other public members of the board thought that the peaceful evolution of labor–management relations would in itself lead directly to membership loyalty and stable, responsible unionism.[2] For example, in the dispute between the United Auto Workers and General Motors in May 1941, the NDMB headed off a strike by offering the union ten cents more an hour in wages, but it turned down the UAW request for the union shop on the grounds that "very real progress has been made in the growth of the union and in its accompanying power to discharge the responsibilities which it had undertaken in the contract." During 1941 the NDMB offered labor a form of union security (usually maintenance of membership) in only seven of the fifty-six disputes in which the issue arose.[3]

Backed by the rest of the Roosevelt administration, the NDMB considered government-imposed union security an artificial device and authorized it only where absolutely necessary to ensure continued defense production. The North American Aviation dispute was one such incident in which the use of troops to break the strike had so disorganized the local that aircraft production sank. "There was an urgent need for reviving the union in order to assure stable labor relations," announced the board, "and the quarrel between local and national leadership made it doubtful whether the national leadership could restore it without the assistance of the maintenance of membership clause."[4]

Another less dramatic dispute involved a New Jersey local of the CIO's Industrial Union of Marine and Shipyard Workers of America (IUMSWA). Under the leadership of John Green and Philip Van Gelder, the rapidly expanding union had been among the first in the CIO to advocate aid to the allies and an end to defense strikes. In June 1941 the IUMSWA agreed to a two-year shipbuilding wage stabilization pact and a virtual no-strike pledge in the industry. In return, the government sponsored a union security clause in the union's Atlantic coast contract. Significantly, one of the largest shipyards, Federal Shipbuilding and Drydock, a U.S. Steel subsidiary, refused to accept the union security clause as part of the steel industry's general resistance to the union shop. As a result, the local there struck to force the government to seize the yard. The navy did so, and the NDMB offered the IUMSWA local maintenance of membership. These decisions provided a hint of the policy the government would apply a year later under new wartime conditions, but in 1941 the mediation board was determined that the grant of union security at North American Aviation and Federal Ship would not set a precedent for the rest of basic industry.[5] The New Deal's taste for left-of-center experimentation had soured; change would come only if it clearly promoted social order and war production.

The government made its overall policy clear in the fall when John L. Lewis demanded extension of the United Mine Workers union shop contract to the "captive mines" owned directly by the giant steel corporations. Although no longer president of the CIO, Lewis still dominated the single most powerful union in the country. His determination to enforce union shop conditions in steel company mines was part of a larger drive he was determined to lead for complete organization and union security throughout basic industry. "The United Mine Workers will not accept the defeatist attitude of some weak-kneed union leaders," trumpeted the *UMW Journal* on Labor Day in 1941. "President Lewis and his co-workers feel, and rightly so, that if there ever was a time in American history when it was imperative for labor to assume the aggressive and complete the job of organizing American working men that time is now."[6] Lewis was anxious to secure a union shop for his miners because he still greatly feared the political and economic consequences of America's impending involvement in the shooting war. Lewis had opposed FDR in 1940 on this issue; now, he was almost certain of a postwar depression and a concerted anti-union offensive. "You wonder why the UMW wants security," Lewis belligerently asked Irving Olds, the chairman of the board of U.S. Steel at a mediation board meeting. "It is because we don't know how long Mr. Grace [president of Bethlehem Steel] will have $1,200,000,000 worth of defense orders as a backlog . . . We don't know when that situation will change . . . We don't know when his managers will recommend the elimination of the union in the mining camps in order that they might produce coal more cheaply, at a lesser wage than the union will negotiate."[7]

The government was more sanguine in its economic and social predictions. Public members of the NDMB were impressed not with the potential vulnerability of the UMW but with the threat of its economic power, its treasury of several million dollars, and its enrollment of over 95 percent of the current workforce in the captive mines. After the UMW had twice struck steel corporation mines, the NDMB, amid rising anti-Lewis sentiment, declared itself against the union shop demand.[8] In the board's majority view, the only threat to the UMW came from the political nonconformity of its leadership. "The security of this union," wrote Frank Graham, "can now be threatened only by an abuse of its power and a loss of public support." Graham thought the question of the union shop in basic industry should be postponed to some future, less troubled era. FDR backed this view three days later when he angrily told a press conference, "I tell you frankly that the government of the United States will not offer, nor will Congress pass legislation, ordering a so-called closed shop."[9]

For a moment in late 1941, the union security issue seemed a shoal upon which administration labor policy would flounder. CIO representatives on the NDMB interpreted the board's rejection of the UMW demand as calculated discrimination against the miners designed to stop the drive for union security in the mass production industries. They resigned on November 11, assuring the NDMB's collapse as an effective strike prevention agency.[10] Into this vacuum moved antilabor conservatives who wanted to use the war emergency as an occasion to crack down on the unions. The House of Representatives passed Howard Smith's antistrike bill banning the union shop in early December, and the Senate seemed likely to do likewise. Sidney Hillman worried that unless a "concrete program to stop interruptions of defense work" was quickly set up, the administration would lose control of labor policy to Congress, thus impairing "the growing consciousness among all workers of labor's stake in this nation's defense of labor's liberties against aggression." Meanwhile, Lewis had called the miners out on strike a third time. Faced with imminent blast furnace closures and a fight with the entire CIO, President Roosevelt now capitulated by appointing a special arbitration panel certain to offer the UMW leader the union shop in the captive mines. This it did on December 7, but the news was buried deep inside the Sunday afternoon special editions announcing the Japanese attack on Hawaii and the Philippines.[11]

Search for a wage policy

Pearl Harbor put an end to the immediate possibility of renewed labor strife. In rapid succession, almost every important labor leader, including Lewis, pledged that his union would not strike for the duration of the war. Urged on by Hillman, Roosevelt seized this opportunity to call a top-level conference of labor and industry spokesmen to set ground rules for a new and more powerful National War Labor Board. Co-chaired by William H. Davis and Elbert D. Thomas, the liberal head of the Senate Education and Labor Committee, the group met in the dignified chambers of the Federal Reserve Board on December 17. The union security issue soon became the chief stumbling block to unanimous agreement. Even the moderate businessmen Roosevelt selected for the conference – men such as Cyrus Ching and Roger Lapham – wished to leave the issue entirely in the hands of Congress and prevent the new board from setting policy on the question. The labor side of the table, fearing that a conservative Congress would impose an outright ban on the union shop, objected to any limitations upon the scope of NWLB authority. Instead, Philip Murray and other top CIO leaders hoped that the reorganized board would now offer the unions genuine security in return for their no-strike pledge. Pushed by Lewis, both the AFL and the CIO also fought for guarantees that a living wage would be maintained and New Deal social legislation preserved.

Although these discussions took place in the shadow of Pearl Harbor, at a time of unparalleled patriotic unity, the conference was deadlocked for five long days. Faced with this impasse, FDR simply informed the conferees that he accepted their recommendations to establish a National War Labor Board and refrain from strikes and lockouts for the duration. The new NWLB would be clothed with formal powers far greater than those of its prewar predecessor, and in an apparent concession to labor, it would retain jurisdiction over the difficult union security problem. [12]

By the time the new labor board began to function in January 1942, the most pressing policy decision faced by the government was no longer union status but wages. The past year had been one of rapid inflation, and most industrial unions demanded a substantial wage increase – about a dollar a day – to compensate for the cost-of-living surge that had eroded wage increases won during the spring of 1941. CIO unions expected a liberal hearing, if only to balance the no-strike pledge they had announced after Pearl Harbor. [13]

But within the Roosevelt administration as well as in the more conservative Congress, the tide moved inexorably against a significant wage boost. Administration policy makers remembered the spiraling inflation of World War I and were determined to avoid a repetition. Working on the theory that an "inflationary gap" would soon exist between disposable income and available consumer goods, economists at the Bureau of the Budget and Office of Price Administration (OPA) advocated a reduction in this inflationary pressure through a sharp cut in expendable income. This meant heavier taxes, compulsory savings, and rigid wage ceilings. OPA's Leon Henderson told FDR that he must freeze wages and prices by April 1, 1942, or face uncontrollable inflation during the balance of the year. Treasury Secretary Henry Morgenthau moved in the same direction, but more cautiously. He thought an immediate wage freeze would be taken as a "slap in the face of labor" and convinced FDR that the NWLB should be left with sufficient latitude to work out a wage program designed to restrain wages in more gradual fashion. This philosophy was embodied in FDR's April 27, 1942, anti-inflation program. His message to Congress called for "stabilization," with the details to be worked out by the NWLB.[14]

The board shaped its wage formula in the months of April, May, and June 1942, during the height of the inflationary surge that spring. Davis and other public members of the board knew that too many inequalities and anomalies existed in the national wage pattern simply to impose a rigid ceiling on income. They tackled the problem by searching for a baseline from which wages could be raised in accordance with increases in the cost of living. Davis first proposed that the date July 1, 1941, be used. Wages prevailing at that time were to be considered standard wages, because they had been negotiated under the relatively unrestrained collective bargaining conditions of early 1941 and before the inflationary surge in the second half of the year. Davis thought the NWLB might increase wages by an amount equal to the cost-of-living increase since July 1 – about 12 percent.[15] This amount generally reflected current CIO wage demands.

The equitable July 1 baseline did not stand for long. Prodded by Leon Henderson and the military services, the NWLB soon moved the standard wage benchmark back to January 1, 1941, a statistical starting point before the general wage increases of April and May 1941. Because the total cost of living had risen by approximately 15 percent after January 1, the NWLB would now be limiting war-time wage increases to less than 3.5 percent in 1942. This formula attained virtual de jure status in the NWLB's famous Little Steel decision of July 1942.[16]

Recomposition of the working class: internal crisis of the unions

Linked to a policy of price control, the government's restrictive wage policy helped dampen inflation, but it also helped create the institutional crisis in the mass production unions that many labor leaders had feared. Part of this crisis was caused by the enormous demographic transformation then taking place in the wartime workforce. Many of the older white male workers, who had become union conscious in prewar years, were moving into new jobs, taking supervisory positions, or enlisting or being drafted into the armed forces. In their place came a flood of new recruits: women, blacks, teenagers, and rural Okies, many from low-wage, unorganized industries or first-time entrants into the factory workforce. To many of these workers, the unions seemed irrelevant because of the comparatively high, steady war industry wages they could now command. The differential between work in agriculture or the urban service trades and in the expanding munitions or shipbuilding industries could be as much as 150 percent. At the same time, the general application of the Little Steel formula gave workers still in low-wage industries even less reason to join unions or pay dues: the 15 percent formula ensured that their wage increases would actually be less than those in higher-paying war work. As a result, the low-wage textile, retail, and aircraft industries suffered chronic labor shortages, large turnover rates, and union instability in 1942 and the remaining years of the war. Moreover, ignorance, apathy, or outright hostility toward the trade unions seemed to characterize many of these workers. Union leaders feared them as superpatriots interested only in military victory and a quick end to the war. [17]

Wartime conditions also promised to exacerbate internal union tensions, even among workers with a comparatively well-founded union tradition. Industrial workers patriotically backed the president, the armed services, and the war itself, but widespread resentment flared when unionists thought that government officials or management industrial engineers were taking advantage of their union's no-strike pledge. In early 1942, a secret government survey found that in Detroit and Pittsburgh, most workers thought that employers would try to use the wartime emergency as a means of destroying labor's recent victories. [18] In Detroit, the conversion of auto factories to war production had temporarily eliminated the jobs of almost 400,000 in the "arsenal of democracy." As these union veterans filtered back to work in 1942, they found their shops bedecked with patriotic posters and placards, but the old disputes over wages and working conditions festered, just as they had in prewar years. Detroit would soon become known as the strike capital of the country, but even in the generally quiescent spring of 1942, CIO leaders thought the city a "keg of powder." After hearing a report on the wartime mood of auto workers, textile union President Emil Rieve reported to the NWLB, "The labor leaders are trying to pacify them, keep them quiet . . . and I don't know how long we . . . will be getting away with that stuff before we have something on our hands."[19]

Apathy toward the unions and disaffection with union leaders were thus dual components of working-class consciousness during the war. The difficulties that arose out of the fusion of these two elements were made abundantly clear to government officials in case after case that came before the National War Labor Board early in 1942. In February the board learned of the near disintegration of a 300-member United Electrical, Radio, and Machine Workers local at Walker-Turner, a small machine tool company in New Jersey. Although organized through an effective and militant strike in late 1940, the Communist-line leadership of the local abandoned efforts to increase the substandard wages paid at the company after the German invasion of Russia in June 1941. Their production-oriented policies soon led to widespread dissaffection among the rank and file. By late 1941, the local had lost 25 percent of its members; over half of those remaining were delinquent in their dues. UE leaders cabled the board in early March that morale was so low that "prompt action of the NWLB is necessary to prevent production delays or complete stoppage of work."[20]

A few weeks later, the board examined another, far larger local in the process of disintegration. Although the old National Defense Mediation Board had ordered maintenance of membership at Federal Shipbuilding and Drydock after the government had seized the Kearny, New Jersey, shipyard in July 1941, the navy officials in charge there had not enforced the union security clause in the local's contract. As a result, the 18,000-member union at Federal Ship began to fall apart in the fall of 1941. Difficulties arose because AFL and independent craft unions refused to accept the Atlantic coast wage standards to which the cooperative and patriotic national leaders of the IUMSWA had agreed. Even though shipyard pay was comparatively high, these craft unions were successful in luring skilled IUMSWA members into their ranks, on occasion sponsoring wildcat work stoppages to test their strength.

The local's decay accelerated in March 1942, when workers there learned of the national CIO's acquiescence in the new government policy eliminating premium pay for holiday and weekend work. Leaders of the local admitted that they were on the verge of losing control; President

Peter J. Flynn complained to the NWLB that many union members felt that "there is no further need to pay dues to the union or to remain in a union because everything was going to be provided . . . by the government anyhow."[21] The NWLB gave such union leaders a sympathetic hearing. West coast shipping magnate Roger Lapham framed the issue in a memorandum to his business colleagues on the board: "Can union leaders be held accountable for labor troubles if because of a falling off in their membership, they find they control a minority rather than a majority in the plants where they are the bargaining agents? If one is realistic, it is hard to reconcile the views of those in management who wish to hold union leaders responsible for more stable labor relations and yet will not help them in some practical way to attain responsibility."[22]

The giant United Steelworkers of America also found the new wartime conditions debilitating. Although the union had won important National Labor Relations Board elections during 1941, USW leaders had not won the membership loyalty that had long eluded them. "We still had the traditional union apathy of the steelworkers to counteract," acknowledged Secretary-Treasurer David J. McDonald. "About one-fifth of the workers were rabidly pro-union, about five percent were strongly anti-union and the remaining three-fourths really didn't give much of a damn one way or the other."[23] In the spring of 1942, a growing disparity appeared between the wages of steelworkers and those of similarly unskilled and semiskilled laborers in other wartime industries. By March, the ten-cent wage increase won by the USW in April 1941 had been entirely eroded by inflation. Real wages were now declining. In many defense-related industries, part of this erosion was offset by an increase in the number of hours worked, but in steel the work week remained constant. Continuous operation of steel mills demanded a three-shift system of eight-hour work days, five days a week. Hence steelworkers averaged about 40 hours a week even when steel mills operated at full capacity. Harold Ruttenberg, the union's research director, estimated that steelworkers were receiving six dollars and forty-one cents less per week than employees of other defense industries who worked 48 and 52 hours per week. As a result, rank-and-file steelworkers felt that they were missing out on the wartime boom. Many left their jobs for higher-paying work in other armament industries. In one USW district, steelworker resignations rose steadily from 280 per month in January to almost double that number in May 1942.[24]

This turnover problem aggravated the union's still unresolved dues collection difficulties. The war boom swelled USW membership to over 660,000 but it had not eliminated the constant problems involved in recruiting steelworkers for the union or collecting their dues. Time and again, the leadership had to resort to embarrassing and disruptive dues picket lines at mill gates in order to collect a dollar a month from reluctant steelworkers. Even in plants where the USW held exclusive jurisdiction, only 70 percent of all eligible workers were formal members. Seventy-nine percent of all payments were individually collected by unrecognized dues committeemen or unpopular dues picket lines. "Wage freezing," Murray told the 1942 United Steelworkers convention, "would definitely discourage membership in unions and the eventual and inevitable effect of national wage freezing would lead to the ultimate destruction of every labor union in America, particularly the labor unions recently created in the powerful mass production industries."[25]

The specter of John L. Lewis

The fear of internal union decomposition in the spring of 1942 was given an even sharper focus by the reemergence of John L. Lewis as a potential rival to Murray and other CIO leaders even within their own trade unions. Although Lewis had stepped down as CIO president in 1940 and had announced his union's no-strike pledge in December 1941, the UMW chief stood clearly apart from other industrial union leaders. To high officials of the Roosevelt administration, to public members of the National War Labor Board, and to his former lieutenants in the CIO, Lewis seemed an unpredictable quantity: autocratic and impetuous, driven by petty rivalries and dangerous ambitions.

Less personally dramatic, but of equal importance, was Lewis's entire attitude toward the mobilization effort. Lewis had opposed the drift toward American belligerency in 1940 and 1941 because he thought that a wartime mobilization would weaken labor's bargaining power and reduce its economic and political influence. Lewis therefore felt uncommitted to Roosevelt's stewardship of the war economy and unwilling to subordinate for long immediate trade union interests to the government's demand for continuous production and stable industrial relations. He thought labor's no-strike pledge part of an implicit bargain with the government, predicated upon the maintenance and, if possible, the improvement of prewar labor standards. To Lewis, the NWLB's emerging wage formula represented a breach of trust on the part of the labor board and the administration. In 1943 he would claim that the board had "fouled its own nest" with the new wage limits and in four massive mine strikes would challenge the government's entire system of wage control machinery.[26]

Lewis's activities in the winter and spring of 1942 already seemed to mark him as a dangerous influence. In January, after conducting secret negotiations with like-minded leaders in the AFL high command, Lewis suddenly announced plans to unite the AFL and CIO on a basis that would shift power decisively in his direction and away from that of Philip Murray and his pro-Roosevelt allies. CIO unionists were furious with their old chieftain for his attempted coup, and the scheme was foiled only at the last minute when FDR personally intervened on behalf of Murray's continued CIO leadership.[27]

Immediately following this unsuccessful gambit, the *UMW Journal* began a series of sharp attacks upon the Roosevelt administration for its intervention in union affairs, indifference to labor's larger interests, and use of dollar-a-year businessmen to administer the production effort. At the same time, the UMW expanded District 50, a catchall organizing vehicle many in the CIO feared Lewis would use to raid their unions by capitalizing upon wartime rank-and-file discontent. In March, UAW and United Rubber Workers officials reported that District 50 organizers were meddling in their affairs. The CIO attacked Lewis's use of the new organization as "dangerous to the security of the nation" because his tactics forced patriotic unions to "divert time and attention from the essential task of organizing the workers of the nation for victory." Lewis, in turn, began withholding UMW dues payments from the CIO and in May humiliated Philip Murray by forcing him to resign his post as vice-president of the mine union.[28]

The break with the still awesome John L. Lewis was profoundly disturbing to Murray and the other CIO leaders who had pledged their all-out cooperation with the war effort. In April 1942, as Roosevelt prepared his wage stabilization program, Murray argued strenuously against the OPA's rigid income limits on the grounds that "it would decrease the prestige of those labor leaders who have supported the President and it would leave the field wide open for the isolationists in the union movement and result in chaotic labor conditions." And after FDR finally announced his restrictive wage program on April 27, Murray denounced it in private and even hinted that he might withdraw from the NWLB. Gardner Jackson, a former CIO official serving in the Roosevelt administration, quickly got word to the president that "an obvious major factor in his resistance . . . is the shadow of John L. Lewis looming over his shoulder."[29]

To calm a skittish Philip Murray and make palatable the initial application of the new wage guidelines in the precedent-setting and politically sensitive Little Steel wage decision, Roosevelt got word to the steel union leader that the NWLB would interpret generously its mandate when dealing with the USW. When the board did make its wage decision public in July 1942, it offered the union five and a half cents more an hour, well below the dollar a day demanded by the USW but about two-thirds more than a strict application of the new Little Steel formula would warrant. Still, Murray was again alarmed, and regional leaders meeting in Pittsburgh reported that it would be difficult to hold the men in line. When White House Assistant Anna Rosenberg reported all this to the president, Roosevelt called Murray to Washington and told him confidentially that the wage award would be applied on an industry-wide basis retroactive to February 1942 even though the USW already held legally binding contracts with U.S. Steel and other producers. Most importantly, FDR assured Murray that the forty-four cents a day offered by the NWLB to the USW in the Little Steel case gave his union more over two years than John L. Lewis could win for his miners in the same period. Mollified by these presidential assurances, the CIO president returned to Pittsburgh on July 17 and successfully urged the USW's wage policy committee to accept the NWLB edict.[30]

Union security

Aware of the increasing fragility of the industrial unions and the potentially disruptive influence of John L. Lewis, the National War Labor Board also grappled decisively with the thorny union security issue. By late spring, public members of the board understood in a very practical way the centrifugal forces at work within the mass industrial unions: "Too often members of unions do not maintain their membership because they resent the discipline of a responsible leadership," observed Frank Graham. "A rival but less responsible leadership feels the pull of temptation to obtain and maintain leadership by relaxing discipline, by refusing to cooperate with the company, and sometimes by unfair and demagogic agitation." With Graham and William H. Davis taking the lead, and with business representatives on the NWLB increasingly formalistic in their objections, the labor board reached the conclusion that only a general union security clause in every contract would give labor officials the "self-confidence" and "firmness" to deal with their members and enforce their contracts.[31]

The national leadership of the CIO reinforced the board's favorable attitude by declaring that they needed union security, not merely to protect their unions against members' disaffection but rather as an aid in transforming these institutions from agencies of collective bargaining into agencies of production. At the NWLB Little Steel hearings, USW counsel Lee Pressman vigorously expounded this political perspective. Enjoying his most influential period of association with Philip Murray, Pressman adopted for the CIO the trade union theory then being advanced by ILWU President Harry Bridges and other unionists close to the Communist party: The war against fascism abroad put at least a temporary halt to the class struggle at home; therefore, the unions could abandon for the duration their traditional raison d'être. They must "reorient their approach to all problems," argued Pressman, "so that the prosecution of the war becomes the sole and major objective." On the shop floor, the USW would not "continue the presentation of the same grievances that it had in the past, but [is] anxious to turn the entire machinery, to turn all the energy of the union and of the members toward increasing production." The USW held out the hope that the quarter of a million man-days per year spent by its staffers on shop problems and dues collection would now be used to make steel. "To do that, for the union to reorient itself," concluded Pressman, "it must have today a clause in the contract . . . that protects it against the need of having to continue unionism as usual."[32]

After experimenting with a series of legal devices, each one stronger than the last, the board announced a standard maintenance-of-membership formula in June 1942 that automatically applied to any union whose leaders agreed to enforce the no-strike pledge and otherwise cooperate with the production effort. The board's policy included a fifteen-day "escape" period during which a new union member (or old member under a new contract) could withdraw from the union. Employer members of the NWLB had insisted upon this clause in the name of an employee's freedom of association, but few workers took the initiative to withdraw from the union in their first hectic weeks on the job. Once enrolled under a maintenance-of-membership contract, war workers

Table 1. *Membership of the ten largest CIO affiliates (thousands)*

	1939	1941	1944	1946	1953	1962
UAW (auto)	165	461	1,065	673	1,417	1,073
USW (steel)	225	373	708	733	1,101	878
UMW (coal)[a]	495	563				
UE/IUE (electrical)[b]	48	133	432	365	266	269
ACWA (clothing)	240	237	224	244	288	268
TWUA (textiles)	83	153	216	301	242	133
URW (rubber)	40	64	124	147	174	158
Packinghouse	39	53	100	102	138	84
IUMSWA (shipbuilding)[c]	35		209	77		
Mine, Mill (copper)[d]		38	98	87		
URWDSE (wholesale)	44	48	60	91	68	139
CWA (telephone)[e]					253	277
OCAW (oil, chemical)[f]					170	140
Total top five	1,208	1,787	2,645	2,316	3,325	2,765
	(66%)	(67%)	(67%)	(60%)	(69%)	(70%)
Total top ten	1,414	2,123	3,820	2,820	4,217	3,419
	(77%)	(80%)	(82%)	(73%)	(87%)	(86%)
Other CIO	424	536	701	1,027	621	439
Total CIO	1,838	2,659	3,937	3,847	4,838	3,958

[a]The UMW left the CIO in 1942. Its membership remained above 500,000 throughout the 1940s.
[b]The UE left the CIO in 1949. The figures for 1953 and 1962 are for the CIO-sponsored rival, the International Union of Electrical Workers. UE membership was 203,000 in 1953 and 55,000 in 1962.
[c]The IUMSWA dropped from the CIO top ten after the end of the wartime shipbuilding boom. Its membership was only 39,000 in 1953 and 19,000 in 1962.
[d]Expelled from the CIO in 1950. Its membership dropped to 39,000 by 1962.
[e]The Communications Workers of America (CWA) joined the CIO in 1948.
[f]The Oil, Chemical and Atomic Workers (OCAW). Figures are for 1955 and 1962.
Source: Data taken from Leo Troy, *Trade Union Membership, 1897–1962* (New York, 1962), A-20–A-43.

were bound to pay their dues, usually under a checkoff arrangement, and abide by all union regulations. Otherwise they could be expelled from the union and then fired by the company.[33]

The practical impact of this government policy dramatically increased the size and financial stability of wartime industrial unions. Lee Pressman later described the NWLB decision as the single most important reason for CIO growth during the war. In the USW, the dues picket lines came down and the union's net worth grew sevenfold between May 1942 and November 1943 despite a slight falling off in total steel employment. Years later, the USW's accountant described the NWLB's dues checkoff policy as "manna from heaven" that finally resolved the union's chronic financial problems. Meanwhile, as factories and mills expanded, new workers were automatically enrolled, increasing the steady flow of dues. With a rising wartime income large industrial unions had the financial resources to organize the new defense plants being built in Texas, Southern California, and other areas far removed from the traditional centers of union strength. Excluding the UMW, which left in 1942, CIO membership almost doubled during the war (Table 1). Overall, the unionized sector of the workforce increased by about 50 percent, from 9.5 to 14.8 million. Most new union members were covered by government-sponsored maintenance-of-membership contracts.[34]

But this institutional growth and security had its price. The conditions of wartime unionism accelerated those bureaucratic tendencies that had been inherent in the new CIO unions from their moment of birth. Many of the new members who flooded into the unions were, as one veteran UAW official put it, "mere labor conscripts" who lacked the "do or die" spirit of the union's formative years. Meanwhile, National War Labor Board deliberations were long and complicated, and the large industrial unions sent their best representatives to the capital, where they acquired the legal and political skills necessary to negotiate and administer collective bargaining contracts under a constantly changing series of government directives, executive orders, and administrative guidelines. Thus, with membership growth virtually assured and with their eyes focused on Washington, union leaders felt less keenly the pressures generated within their own organizations, the grievances and complaints that inevitably arose out of the rapidly changing wartime work environment.[35]

6. "Equality of sacrifice"

As World War II became one of total mobilization on the home front, the state apparatus became a crucial arena of political conflict. With one-half of the Gross National Product committed directly to military production and the entire economy subject to a thicket of controls, the struggle for influence in Washington became almost synonymous with class and interest group conflict over the shape of society itself. Key government agencies such as the National War Labor Board, the Office of Production Management and the War Production Board were the scene of endemic conflict among labor, corporate, military, agricultural, and small business interests. Although a powerful military–industrial alliance came to play the dominant role in setting the national political agenda, the Roosevelt administration and the rest of the state bureaucracy always retained a certain autonomy that made it more than a mere mirror of the power wielded by the large corporations and their allies in the armed services. There were at least two reasons for this. First, the business community was not a unified entity. Major conflicts emerged during the war over the role of small business, the pace of conversion, corporate policy toward organized labor, and the degree of state planning necessary to mobilize the economy and avoid a postwar recession. Second, and of equal importance, the military–corporate outlook was often a narrowly parochial one that could prove socially and politically disruptive. State action opposed to the immediate interests of the major corporations was sometimes necessary to ensure the maintenance of social peace and an ideological consensus that would placate, if not incorporate, the most important elements of a sometimes estranged liberal and labor Left.

During the defense era and the war itself, CIO leaders sought to use the state apparatus to advance the interests of their organizations and, more indirectly, of their broad working-class constituency. The NWLB's maintenance-of-membership compromise provided the unions with a defensive organizational shield against the vicissitudes of wartime social upheaval. But the CIO also thought in terms of a pro-

gram that would use the mobilization experience to shift the entire political economy in a broadly social democratic direction. Thus the
industrial unions sought to assure themselves of genuine functional participation in planning the mobilization program and the reconversion
that would follow. In pushing for the Murray Industrial Council Plan,
the CIO demanded direct participation in the administration of basic
industry; when this effort was blocked, industrial union officials directed their attention to a defensive alliance with those elements in
government and business who still favored a broad program of economic
planning different from that undertaken by the military and the major
corporations. In general, both these efforts were failures. The Roosevelt
administration rejected the Industrial Council Plan shortly after Pearl
Harbor, and although the conflict within the production agencies over
the extent to which the military–industrial alliance would prevail continued throughout the war, civilian advocates of a liberal planning perspective lost most of the key battles. In this context, the CIO retreated to
an ideologically defensive "Victory through Equality of Sacrifice" program designed to make palatable to its membership the steady erosion of
labor's effective power during the remainder of the war.

The Reuther Plan and its demise

During the second half of the defense era, the CIO became increasingly
dissatisfied with its lack of influence in the existing mobilization apparatus. Once the pressure against the use of the strike weapon had begun to
grow, most CIO leaders came to recognize that labor's interests could be
protected only by participation in the administration of the war economy itself. Key decision making lay within the industrial divisions of the
Office of Production Management and its successor agency, the War
Production Board. There, almost 800 of the top posts were held by
dollar-a-year executives on loan from their corporations. Along with
like-minded procurement officers in the military, the men who staffed
the industrial divisions soon presided over a virtual command economy
– deciding on the distribution of contracts, the allocation of scarce raw
materials, and the general coordination of industrial capacity and military requirements. As military spending spiraled upward, even politically cooperative unionists such as Philip Murray recognized that unless
a fundamental reorganization of the mobilization program took place,
the enormous centralization of economic and political power in this

military–industrial alliance would soon put organized labor on in-creasingly unfavorable terrain.[1]

A telling index of CIO sentiment came with its declining assessment of Sidney Hillman's ability to represent industrial union interests effec-tively in Washington. Although Hillman seemed to stand at the apex of the OPM bureaucracy, he had little power to influence the industrial mobilization process itself. The major role played by his labor division was that of a service organization that sought to resolve labor problems created by the production boom. Hillman partially recognized this diffi-culty and therefore advocated AFL and CIO participation on special labor advisory committees attached to the chief OPM commodity divi-sions. But dollar-a-year corporate executives never took these labor rep-resentatives seriously, and they remained, in the words of one critic, "undigested lumps in the stomachs of the management people."[2] As early as July 1941, the CIO denounced the labor advisory committees as "mere tinsel, mere window dressing unable to affect basic policy."[3]

Hillman and his labor division had proven effective in the mediation of some labor disputes, but for all his effort and goodwill, he failed to win men such as Knudsen and Stimson to a policy that would put the govern-ment's enormous contracting power behind a program designed to en-force industry adherence to the Wagner Act. Hillman was also isolated in his effort to plan defense production in such a way as to minimize temporary conversion unemployment or secure small business a larger share of military contracts. Finally, Hillman's close identification with the government's decision to use the army at North American Aviation further sapped his influence in the trade unions and ultimately eroded his power at the OPM.[4]

As the CIO's faith in Sidney Hillman declined, industrial union lead-ers such as James Carey, John Brophy, and Philip Murray put increasing pressure on the Roosevelt administration to adopt some form of their industrial council idea, which they proposed to institute in the steel, copper, aluminum, and auto industries. Many in the CIO's heavily Catholic leadership had long been influenced by the corporativist social reformism then prevalent within church circles. The 1931 papal encycli-cal *Quadragesimo Anno* had condemned unfettered industrial capitalism and called for collaboration between workers and employers in state-sponsored industrial corporations. In the American context, fulfillment of this program meant a partial return to government-supported private planning of the sort first glimpsed during the National Recovery Administration era. But unlike the NRA itself, the labor representatives on the new industrial councils would participate on an equal footing with those of industry. Moreover, the Industry Council Plan heartily endorsed the idea of industry-wide planning, first to carry out the military production program and ultimately to ameliorate, if not avoid, the postwar downturn that most expected.

With these industry councils in place, the administration of both procurement and production would take place under the guidance of a management–labor–government committee functioning, in CIO President Murray's term, as a "top scheduling clerk" for an entire industry. In what came to be called the Murray Plan, these industrial councils would have the power to distribute production orders and direct manpower in the most rational way possible, regardless of corporate tradition or usual marketing arrangements. The Murray Plan, reported the *CIO News*, would regard "each industry, not as a series of corporations, but as a series of plants." They would ensure that small business received its share of the defense contracts and would make certain that labor's organizational and economic interests were fully protected.[5]

Walter Reuther's 500-planes-a-day proposal proved to be the application of the Industrial Council Plan that the CIO adopted most enthusiastically and that came closest to halting the drift toward a business-dominated mobilization effort. In contrast to the often abstract quality of the original Murray proposals, the Reuther Plan provided a detailed blueprint for speeding defense production and advancing a practical social democratic reorganization of the auto industry. Reuther's idea had its genesis in the problems faced by Detroit auto workers during the conversion of automobile factories to military production. Shortly after the fall of France, the government had begun financing the construction of massive new aircraft production facilities far outside Detroit, the center of UAW strength. Because of the auto industry's reluctance to begin voluntary conversion of their facilities, union leaders feared that when raw material shortages diverted production to these new plants, hundreds of thousands of auto workers would be laid off for up to a year. In the ensuing confusion, defense production would be delayed and the auto union weakened.

The Reuther Plan promised to avoid these difficulties. Proposed late in 1940, it was a guns-and-butter program that foresaw the continued production of some 5 million cars a year, while at the same time the industry pooled and integrated its excess capacity to build the thousands of airplanes that Roosevelt demanded after the fall of France. "Normal methods can build all the planes we need – if we can wait until 1942 or 1943," Reuther explained, but the nation could not afford the delay. Reuther proposed a much faster schedule, accomplished by a six-month postponement in retooling for the 1942 model year, freeing thousands of otherwise unemployed skilled workers for the adaptation of existing machine tools to fighter aircraft production. A standard mass production plane could then roll off Detroit assembly lines quickly, long before giant new plants were completed and equipped at Willow Run or Wichita.[6]

The excitement generated by the Reuther Plan reflected the dynamic political energy of its author. Tutored by his father, a Socialist brewery worker and leader of unionism in the Ohio Valley, Walter Reuther and his brothers, Victor and Roy, were Debsian Socialists by the time they were adolescents. Walter mastered tool and die making while still in his teens, and in the late 1920s he had little trouble securing a job as a highly paid die leader at Ford's River Rouge plant. All three brothers were active Socialists in the early depression years. Victor and Walter became active in the Socialist party's 1932 campaign for Norman Thomas, and brother Roy shortly afterward became a lecturer for the left–Socialist Brookwood Labor School. Like other Socialists of this era, the Reuther brothers were favorably disposed toward the Soviet Union, especially its state planning experiments, and in 1933 Victor and Walter signed up for a year-long sojourn at the Gorki auto factory that Henry Ford had equipped with machine tools and skilled workers. There, Walter taught Russian peasants the rudiments of tool and die making and, with a vision of efficiency and social rationality that would later win him fame in the United States, bombarded the authorities in Moscow and Gorki with suggestions for scheduling the flow of work more smoothly and increasing production.[7]

When the Reuthers returned to the States in 1935, they joined brother Roy in virtually full-time work organizing the fledgling UAW. Within little more than a year, Walter and Victor had helped organize more than 30,000 workers on the West Side of Detroit, in the process becoming major figures in the new union. Their attention absorbed by the UAW, all three of them drifted away from the Socialist party by 1940.[8] Outspokenly interventionist, Walter Reuther and his brothers soon sought to use the extraordinary productive requirements generated by the war crisis to forge a social democratic program for American industry.

In 1940 and 1941, the Reuther Plan's promise to speed up vital aircraft production won a sympathetic hearing among a broad section of the liberal interventionist public. During the next year, the proposal's attractiveness increased among prowar liberals as it became clear that the plan represented a practical start at national planning and a democratically controlled rationalization of a major war industry. With management and government, labor would have a seat on a new Aviation Production Board that would have the authority to ignore corporate boundaries, markets, and profits as it presided over the conscription of machine tools, working space, and manpower where and when needed. The joint committee would decide which plants could continue to produce for the civilian market and which ones would be converted most effectively to military production.[9]

Within the Roosevelt administration, the Reuther Plan won support both for its patriotic efficiency and for its social reformism. The proposal complemented Leon Henderson's effort to force the auto corporations to cut production for the civilian market, and it promised a way out of the production bind that bedeviled ardent interventionists such as Secretary of the Treasury Henry Morgenthau. New Deal planning advocates such as Jerome Frank and Mordecai Ezekiel were, of course, in favor of giving the Reuther Plan a try, and even conservatives such as Under Secretary of War Robert Patterson were willing to accept a bold initiative if it dramatically increased defense production.[10] Journalist I. F. Stone spoke for the growing body of liberal interventionists when he endorsed the Murray–Reuther proposals: "Our full potential capacity can be mobilized only by enlisting in the effort the widest participation of American enterprise, engineering ability, and labor. Defense must be democratic if it is to be efficient; only a democratic defense can be a total defense in a total war. This is what the monopolists do not understand, dare not understand, for though a democratic defense would protect our country it would undermine their power."[11]

The Reuther Plan naturally proved anathema to Detroit auto executives and their allies in the military and the defense procurement agencies. Military procurement officers found it most convenient to contract out a program with a large corporation such as Ford or Chrysler and then to let the management of these organizations handle the subcontracting in normal business fashion. Implementation of the Reuther Plan would require a thorough reorganization of this system and ensure much closer government coordination of the entire production process. The plan threatened to disrupt the auto industry's often delicate competitive arrangements, undercut managerial prerogatives, and give the UAW a major voice in shaping the postwar structure of the industry.[12]

Of course, Detroit could not denounce the plan directly; outright opposition on purely ideological grounds might seem unpatriotic. "They wanted to come into the shop as a union committee and try to design fixtures for the present machinery," OPM chief Knudsen remarked in March 1941. "We had to stall on that one and say that it couldn't be handled." Hence the year-long attack on the Reuther Plan as technically unfeasible: Auto machine tools were too imprecise for aircraft production; pooling arrangements were difficult and cumbersome; the American government wanted to emphasize production of bombers, not fighters. But behind these objections was management's fear that the plan represented yet another labor assault on the industrial relations status quo. "There is only one thing wrong with the program," a sympathetic Treasury Secretary Morgenthau told Reuther. "It comes from the 'wrong' source."[13]

Pearl Harbor brought the Reuther Plan not its most promising opportunity for implementation but its demise. All at once, the government banned civilian auto production and poured billions of dollars in production contracts into Detroit. The first argument for the Reuther Plan collapsed when it became apparent that the auto industry would convert entirely to military production – to tanks, truck and aircraft engines, if not complete airplanes. Thus the difficulties of partial conversion, which would have disrupted competitive relationships in the civilian market, were postponed for the duration of the war. The second argument for the plan fell away as well when the auto industry began to pool and convert its tools, its manpower, and even its factory space in a fashion not even Reuther and the UAW had dreamed possible.

Of course, this conversion was firmly under the control of the WPB's Auto Industry Advisory Committee and management-oriented military procurement officers, not Reuther's tripartite committee. The Big Three auto makers, along with hundreds of smaller firms, became tied together by a maze of subcontracts and joint production arrangements. By 1943, moreover, about 66 percent of all prewar machine tools had been converted to aircraft engine production. The Reuther Plan no longer seemed quite as technically innovative or necessary as it had been before Pearl Harbor. In the headlong rush to convert the industry to military production, the rationale for labor participation in the management of the auto industry lost its punch. As Reuther himself put it in a conference with Charles Wilson and Edsel Ford, "We have no argument on what we are trying to achieve. We are discussing the question of how we get at it." By the end of January 1942, government policymakers had rejected the Murray–Reuther industry council plans wherever labor had presented them for serious consideration.[14]

War Production Board politics

After Pearl Harbor, President Roosevelt once again seized an opportunity to restaff the defense production bureaucracy. The year-old Office of Production Management had outlived whatever political usefulness it had once possessed. Saddled with a reputation for sluggish action on the production front and with the politically awkward Knudsen–Hillman leadership, the decline of OPM power had been underway for several months. In January, Roosevelt finally abolished the agency and replaced it with a new and more powerful War Production Board, headed by Donald Nelson, a former Sears, Roebuck executive. Nelson, who had taken part in defense planning since 1940, was a businessman, not a New Dealer, which made him acceptable to the large corporations and the military. At the same time, Nelson represented that wing of the business establishment most sensitive to the war's impact on the civilian economy. He was oriented to distributors and consumers rather than to big producers; thus, Nelson was most attuned to the particular needs of labor and small business. As head of the prewar Supply Priorities and Allocations Board, Nelson had been something of an all-outer, and thus an ally of Leon Henderson and Walter Reuther in their separate efforts to accelerate the conversion of the auto industry to military production. His choice as chairman of the WPB therefore represented at least a symbolic accommodation to those labor–liberal forces that feared big business domination of the wartime economy.[15]

However, Nelson had neither the will nor the resources to reorganize the mobilization program in a fashion likely to reduce its acceptability to big business. His administrative style emphasized negotiation and compromise; thus he proved reluctant to confront directly the powerful industrial interests that had dominated the OPM. For example, in early 1942 Nelson sought to accommodate the CIO's demand for greater participation in the production program by having the WPB sponsor a campaign to establish thousands of labor–management production com-

mittees in individual war plants. Although the CIO hoped that these
patriotic teams might be a step in the direction of the Murray Plan,
Nelson made it clear that their activities would in no way alter the
industrial relations status quo. Under pressure from industry representatives anxious to preserve managerial prerogatives, Nelson soon announced that these factory committees were designed solely to increase
morale and boost production and not to "put labor into management
or . . . management into labor."[16] Eventually, about 1,700 such committees were set up, far fewer than the 10,000 or so originally projected.
But even these, admitted one labor official serving with the WPB, "exist
more on paper than in actuality."[17]

Nelson carried over existing arrangements from the OPM as well. In
the immediate aftermath of Pearl Harbor, he refused to eliminate the use
of dollar-a-year business executives in the industry divisions of the
WPB. High-salaried executives would not serve in the government, he
told a Senate investigating committee in January 1942, unless they retained their corporate salaries and connections. As for military procurement, Nelson thought the WPB did not have time to set up its own
purchasing organization; moreover, logistics and military strategy were
so closely meshed that no civilian agency could take over procurement
without encroaching on the military responsibility for conducting the
war.[18]

Entrusting the power of procurement to the armed forces had broad
repercussions. In the spring of 1942, the army and navy requirements
were increasing to levels far beyond the economy's potential. In six
months, the two services released over $100 billion in new contracts
without a workable priorities system and without proper regard to the
availability of facilities, power, transportation, workforce, and the like.
Economic dislocation to the point of paralysis faced the nation unless the
demand functions of the military were coordinated with the supply
functions of the WPB. Production priorities would have to be set: The
question was, who would set them? Under the leadership of driving
officers such as army supply chief Brehon Somervell, the military services sought an effective veto power over all aspects of the economy,
civilian as well as military, to assure the services unqualified priority for
their orders.

The subsequent conflict between the WPB and the armed forces was
as much a struggle within the WPB as it was a clash between civilians and
the military for control of the wartime economy. The large corporations

that dominated the WPB industry divisions were happy to see the military set priorities because as prime contractors, they would certainly help frame and then serve as major beneficiaries of any such procedure. A military-dominated priorities system would naturally benefit those economic groups with which the armed services had long cooperated. Opposition came not from the WPB civilians but from labor and liberal forces, small businessmen who felt shut out of war contracts, and the New Deal economists in the WPB's Planning Committee and Office of Civilian Requirements. Liberal planners such as Robert Nathan, Simon Kuznets, and Leon Henderson argued that military control of materials priorities was socially inefficient where it was not economically unworkable. In the so-called feasibility dispute during the summer of 1942, Nelson backed civilian planners, who argued that the WPB had to place definite limits on the total level of military purchases lest the entire economy crack under the strain. Moreover, the WPB Planning Committee favored the distribution of military contracts in such a fashion as to minimize the need to build new facilities and to take advantage of unused capacity in labor surplus areas. For example, they wanted to use the priorities power to concentrate civilian production in a selected group of small manufacturers, thus offsetting part of the wartime centralization of economic activity in the largest producers. A lingering hint of the Reuther Plan was unmistakable.[19]

After a series of bitter encounters between August and December 1942, the military accepted the need for production controls and priority ceilings, but it made certain that it would henceforth have an influential say in determining the shape of wartime economic planning. The army and navy continued to determine their requirements and to conduct procurement, whereas the WPB set ceilings for military demands and guided military procurement through the allocation of materials and the scheduling of production. However, the military services or their corporate allies soon came to dominate most of the important posts in the WPB. Civilian and military personnel from the services' procurement system moved over to the board to occupy key positions there. By early 1943, Nelson had given up much of his day-to-day power to General Electric Chairman Charles Wilson, who headed the powerful Production Executive Committee.[20] Meanwhile, the WPB Planning Committee was downgraded and the small business-oriented concentration proposal reduced to insignificance. Henderson, Nathan, and many from their staffs soon left the government. In his angry postwar report, *The*

War Lords of Washington, Bruce Catton, a liberal press aide to Nelson, concluded, "The most striking thing about the whole war production program was not that there were so many controls, but that all of them fell within the established patterns of industry."[21]

The same conservative drift that was apparent on the production front soon manifested itself in the area of manpower policy as well. By the spring of 1942, depression-era levels of unemployment had finally begun to decline even as the emerging Little Steel formula made recruitment of workers in labor-short factories more difficult. In April, therefore, President Roosevelt established the War Manpower Commission (WMC) under the chairmanship of the Indiana Democrat, Paul McNutt. Although Sidney Hillman had angled for this job, McNutt balanced wartime political allegiances more easily; like Donald Nelson, he was identified directly with neither labor nor big business groups. Trade unionists generally welcomed the formation of the WMC because, like the National War Labor Board, it provided for union representation in the framing and administration of its policies. Moreover, given the increasing importance of manpower policy in the middle years of the war, the commission promised to serve as an effective counterweight to the military–industrial alliance that had taken control of the WPB. Under its presidential mandate, the WMC would supervise the Selective Service System, regulate manpower in labor shortage areas, and, most importantly, determine policies to maximize labor utilization that other agencies and departments would implement. At the same time, McNutt was a strong advocate of a voluntary manpower mobilization program that eschewed outright coercion in the transfer or retention of American workers on specific jobs.

But McNutt and the WMC simply lacked the political and economic muscle for winning any contest with the military and the WPB industrialists. By mid-1943, Selective Service Director Lewis Hershey had skillfully used the widespread sentiment against drafting fathers to thwart WMC efforts to win control of the vital deferment power. Nor would military planners heed WMC advice to slow the rapid buildup of the armed services or take into account existing employment or housing patterns in the construction of new production facilities and the distribution of contracts. Most WPB industrialists resisted WMC efforts to measure labor utilization within individual factories, arguing that such employment surveys threatened managerial prerogatives. WMC efforts to end employment discrimination against blacks, women, and retired persons proved effective only when labor shortages had reached crisis dimensions.[22]

By this time, the CIO leadership was seeking a thorough reorganization of all the government offices involved in the war effort and their incorporation in a superagency modeled on the British Ministry of Supply. Civilians serving as civil servants would replace industry dollar-a-year men, and all interest groups, including labor, would have a strong advisory role. Overall planning would safeguard working-class interests during the war and provide the basis for a socially equitable reconversion to peacetime production. Labor wanted to concentrate needed civilian production in plants outside labor shortage areas while assigning military contracts and building new facilities in areas that would minimize migration and social dislocation. As the CIO officially complained, "national mobilization requires centralized administrative control of all the resources and economic policies of the nation. The confusion and conflict now raging . . . must be ended immediately. A single administrative body should be established incorporating the activities of war supply, of war manpower and of economic stabilization."[23]

This concept was embodied in the bill introduced by Congressman John Tolan and Senators Harvey Kilgore and Claude Pepper, which called for the creation of a new Office of War Mobilization (OWM) to oversee the entire domestic war effort. Along with Senators Harry Truman and James E. Murray, who also backed the bill, Tolan, Pepper, and Kilgore had all chaired congressional investigating committees that uncovered waste, inefficiency, and corporate favoritism in the war production program. The Truman Committee, to which the CIO regularly fed information on production difficulties affecting its members, blamed the army and navy for a tendency to multiply the capacity of plants and companies with which contracts were already established, rather than seeking additional sources of supply. After a sensational investigation of faulty aircraft engine production at the Curtiss-Wright Aircraft Company, the second largest holder of military contracts, the Truman Committee challenged the contention of the armed services that "they and they alone were capable of procuring safe and satisfactory material for the fighting forces and that for that reason no civilian agency should ever have anything to say with reference to such matters."[24]

The Tolan–Kilgore–Pepper bill was championed by labor and the left-center of the Democratic party, but it also picked up support from many of those whose political constituencies felt their interests unrepresented in the system of political decision making dominated by the military and its large corporate clients. In this fight, the defense of small businesses (defined as those employing less than 500 persons, usually in the civilian economy) became a rallying point for both liberals and conservatives who opposed the growing concentration of economic power in the WPB. However, small-business spokesmen, such as Robert Taft, were at best ambivalent about the adoption of state planning even if, in a wartime economy, it proved the only way to defend the interests of their constituency. In this context, the CIO leadership and many liberals, such as Maury Maverick and Chester Bowles, became staunch defenders of small business, not because of any political affinity with this group, which was often bitterly antilabor and hostile to the maintenance of New Deal social programs, but because the interests of the small entrepreneur could be protected only under an administrative regime that mandated overall economic and social planning and provided for at least a minimal veto over the military's procurement policy.[25]

As legislative pressure mounted, the administration felt that some action was necessary to forestall unilateral congressional action on the OWM idea. Although both the military and the WPB opposed a new coordinating agency, Roosevelt issued an executive order setting up an Office of War Mobilization in May 1943. To take charge, he appointed James Byrnes, a former Supreme Court justice and Democratic senator from South Carolina, who had most recently served as head of the interim Office of Economic Stabilization in the White House. Often dubbed by the press "assistant president," Byrnes disappointed those who hoped the OWM would undertake a program of overall economic planning. His office had a minuscule staff, and Byrnes operated as a referee, seeking to accommodate the existing centers of economic and political power in such a way as to avoid disruption of the home front. In practice, this involved a skillful holding action against those who favored major structural changes. Byrnes generally backed agricultural and business interests, worked closely with the military, and grew increasingly estranged from labor and other advocates of a liberal planning perspective. Byrnes was a bitter foe of Henry Wallace, and during the reconversion controversy of 1944 he proved an ally of the military in their successful drive to undercut Donald Nelson's effort to increase production for the civilian market. The OWM provided the long-sought civilian control of the war economy, but the Byrnes receivership demonstrated that the obstacles to a centralized restructuring of the political economy were rooted deeply in the conservative drift of domestic politics and in the concurrent immobilization of the labor movement itself.[26]

Attack on labor standards

The failure of the CIO to secure an effective voice in the production program came as part of a general rightward shift in political sentiment in the nation as a whole. The influence of the pro-interventionist liberals had begun to decline even before Pearl Harbor ended the debate over American involvement. Now, military necessity and full production were the deities before which all must bow. "If we devote our every thought and effort to more and more production, and more and more support to our armed forces, we shall turn the tide of battle," announced Philip Murray in a typical speech early in 1942. "Let our slogan be WORK, WORK, WORK, PRODUCE, PRODUCE, PRODUCE."[27] This productionist ethic not only mandated longer hours, harder work, and a cessation of strike activity but also put on the defensive those who still favored structural reform. "Progressives should understand that programs which do not forward the war must be given up or drastically curtailed," wrote Tennessee Valley Authority head David Lilienthal. *Business Week* accurately gauged the new mood when it reported in April that "GM sees the war, its role as the government's biggest supplier and a rising tide of public sentiment that is anti-union as an opportunity not only for rebuffing the UAW's current ambitions – but for actually cutting down on the union's power."[28]

This conservative mood gave renewed life to those elements of the body politic that had long been hostile to New Deal social welfare reforms and to the new industrial unions. Included were those sections of the midwestern business community, represented most vociferously by National Steel's E. T. Weir and Montgomery Ward's Sewell Avery, who had resisted unionization in the late 1930s and who hoped to use the wartime emergency to keep the unions at bay indefinitely. Equally important were the newly mobilized forces of southern conservatism, which found the growing alliance between the black community and the CIO the most serious challenge to southern racial mores in a generation. In Congress, this antilabor coalition made its weight felt with increasing force. On December 3, 1941, during the height of the furor over the captive mine strikes, the House passed a bill introduced by Representatives Howard Smith and Carl Vinson that barred new closed shop agreements, denied Wagner Act benefits to unions with Communist officers, provided for the long-sought thirty-day cooling-off period, and prohibited strikes unless approved by a government-sponsored vote. The administration's opposition, the attack on Pearl Harbor, and labor's announcement of an unconditional no-strike pledge caused the more liberal Senate to shelve the bill, but antilabor conservatives were now clearly on the offensive, seeking at every opportunity to use the war emergency to roll back the institutional power the unions had won in previous years.[29]

In this context, the military and the WPB industrialists not only turned aside the Reuther Plan and other structural initiatives backed by the CIO but began their own offensive against the social and economic conquests of the New Deal era's union movement. On labor relations issues, most executives of the large corporations who came to control the WPB represented the dominant "realist" wing of the business establishment. They favored the regularization of labor–management relations on a basis that preserved management's prerogatives and contained labor's political power. Unlike Avery or Weir, they did not seek to eliminate the new trade unions, and they opposed business or congressional reactionaries whose activities served to mobilize working-class activity. However, when the opportunity arose, these sophisticated conservatives were quite willing to use their economic leverage and political muscle to reshape the industrial relations status quo. The ideological legitimacy and government influence generated by the wartime crisis provided such an occasion, and in early 1942 the WPB began a campaign first to eliminate premium pay for holiday and weekend work and then to inaugurate incentive wage plans designed to increase labor productivity.

The incentive wage program did not gain momentum until 1943, but the government's proposals to eliminate premium pay were pushed through in the winter and spring of 1942. Two days after Pearl Harbor, President Roosevelt called for 168-hour-a-week operation for all defense plants, and the WPB soon put pressure on the unions to eliminate the premium pay provisions of existing contracts. These clauses, mandating time-and-a-half pay for work on Saturday and double time on Sunday, were depression-era victories of the industrial unions designed to discourage weekend operation and to spread existing work. Business now claimed that such premium pay retarded seven-day-a-week operation of defense plants, and in January and February, congressional conservatives led by Howard Smith and Carl Vinson gained substantial support for legislation that would suspend for the duration not only premium pay but other federal labor standards as well, including ordinary time-and-a-half pay for any work beyond 40 hours a week.[30]

The CIO's initial response to this pressure was a cool one, and the steel, rubber, textile, and auto unions opposed unilateral concessions on the premium pay issue. Such pay for weekend work had become part of the national wage structure in the industries where it prevailed and was now as much a part of the pay envelope as simple overtime beyond 40 hours per week. Its elimination would cut pay by 15 percent in some plants. More ominously, CIO leaders feared that this was but a first step in a general conservative assault on all forms of overtime, including time and a half after 40 hours. In a series of conferences with federal officials, James Carey and other CIO officers argued that retention of premium pay would hardly increase the cost to the government of munitions produced on a 168-hour-a-week basis. The higher labor costs involved in large-scale premium payments could be easily absorbed by the proportionally much larger wartime profits earned with a full production schedule in place.[31]

Although opposed to the antilabor Vinson–Smith amendments, both the Roosevelt administration and the WPB leadership wanted labor to abandon premium pay on a voluntary basis in order to undercut the initiatives won by the antilabor conservatives and to keep union problems out of the hands of Congress. Decision making in the wartime economy no longer took place primarily in a legislative context but instead emerged out of the accommodation of conflicting interests within in a highly bureacratic state apparatus. From the administration's point of view, therefore, congressional initiatives, whether liberal or conservative, represented disruptive political constraints that complicated this process, especially when union problems required subtle manipulation rather than a polarizing confrontation. Thus, WPB Chairman Donald Nelson told Congress that repeal of the 40-hour law itself would "create a widespread demand for increase in wage rates, throw the entire wage structure out of adjustment, and remove an important incentive for labor to shift from nonessential industries into war production jobs."[32]

At the same time, the administration was not above making its own accommodation to the growing anti-union sentiment, deploying it as a reserve weapon ready for use if the more usual control mechanisms proved ineffective. Thus Roosevelt told Philip Murray in March 1942 that the CIO's voluntary relinquishment of premium pay would have "a salutary effect upon the public state of mind." More bluntly, Donald Nelson announced to a Washington conference of the industrial unions that if they did not agree within thirty days to give up such pay, the government would press for a law to compel surrender. As one New York daily put it, this represented a "velvet-gloved ultimatum" to labor.[33]

The administration's strategy proved most effective. Throughout the winter of 1942, the CIO had looked upon Roosevelt as a bulwark against what Murray called the "blitzkreig" of antilabor sentiment. Now the CIO feared that administration-sponsored congressional action would open the floodgates to the conservatives and subject industrial unions to a tide of antilabor laws and regulations. Moreover, if they failed to relinquish premium pay, Roosevelt might retaliate by promulgating harsh wage guidelines for the WLB to follow in the Little Steel case. Under this pressure, a conference of five hundred CIO officials agreed to capitulate to the administration on March 24.[34] Remarkably, the CIO advertised its retreat on premium pay as a challenge to and defense against those conservatives who had attacked the labor movement in recent weeks. The industrial union federation justified its action "in the light of the same single touchstone which has guided all its policies – the necessity for maximum war production . . . The CIO in this as in all matters is prepared to make all sacrifices which in the judgment of competent authorities acting without anti-labor bias and without the motivation of personal gain are necessary for war production."[35]

The executive boards of most CIO unions put into effect their organization's national policy with little consultation of local union leaders or a representative assembly of the rank and file. The Steel Workers Organizing Committee and the United Rubber Workers began the immediate renegotiation of their contracts. Communist-led unions such as the United Electrical, Radio and Machine Workers and the International Longshoremen's and Warehousemen's Union took the occasion to publicize their plans for greater use of incentive wage schemes and speedup efforts. UE officers declared a union campaign to increase production output by 15 percent "by the direct additional expenditure of energy and effort over and above such increases as will be effected through improved methods or techniques."[36]

"Equality of Sacrifice"

In contrast to the rest of the CIO, the elimination of premium pay in the UAW encountered stiff resistance. This form of pay had been won only in 1939 and 1940, and several UAW locals had already petitioned their executive board to hold fast to its retention. With some 250,000 auto workers unemployed in early 1942 during the conversion of their plants to military production, the industry demand for the elimination of premium pay seemed entirely premature, if not simply arrogant. Rank and file indignation was reinforced in early March, when the UAW–GM arbitrator ruled that the corporation should indeed continue to pay production workers extra money for weekend work.[37]

Because even the now united UAW leadership did not feel politically secure enough simply to end premium pay, they called a hastily assembled War Emergency Conference in early April to explain and vote through the unpopular concession. In preparing for the conference, the elimination of premium pay was made part of a larger "Victory through Equality of Sacrifice" program. Walter Reuther and George Addes designed this set of UAW proposals to meet the criticism of those in the union who attacked the CIO's forfeiture of premium pay as an example of the general wartime retreat by the labor movement. In return for labor's no-strike pledge, premium pay concessions, swing shift scheduling, and an all-out production effort, the Reuther–Addes program called for sacrifice by industry and management as well. The UAW asked the government to institute a rigid ceiling on profits and executive salaries ($25,000), along with democratically controlled rationing and price control. For workers, they proposed wage increases to meet the cost of living, a moratorium on debts, and a guaranteed living wage for dependents of those in the armed services. The Equality of Sacrifice program also recommended a somewhat scaled-down version of the Murray Industry Council Plan that would provide labor representation on the WPB for war and postwar planning. Upon adoption of all the foregoing measures, the UAW would agree that all wages for time over 40 hours a week be paid in the form of nonnegotiable war bonds.[38]

A major flaw in the Equality of Sacrifice program was that the concessions called for by industry were made merely in the form of recommendations to the president and Congress, whereas labor's sacrifices were to be put into effect without preconditions. Through Philip Murray, UAW President R. J. Thomas contacted Roosevelt aide Wayne Coy, informing him of the ticklish situation in the auto union and the possibility of widespread opposition to the ending of premium pay for weekend work. At Murray's request, Coy drafted a letter for FDR to send to the UAW's emergency conference. It contained assurances that much of the Equality of Sacrifice program had the president's blessing. This included a presidential promise to seek legislation renegotiating contracts with employers wherever necessary to ensure that the savings from the elimination of double time went not to the employer but to the government treasury. When FDR's message was dramatically read at the UAW conference, it strengthened the leadership by advancing the prospect that at least part of the Equality of Sacrifice program would be put into effect.[39]

Despite their careful preparations, UAW leaders encountered widespread and articulate opposition at the conference. Some delegates, especially those from the GM plants in Detroit and Flint, vigorously opposed the Equality of Sacrifice idea because they remained skeptical of the extent to which the government could force the corporations to make real concessions. John McGill, president of the Flint Buick local, said, "we are not convinced that giving up double time is vital to winning the war. Labor is making sacrifices everywhere . . . Can anyone show any sign that the men who sign checks have made any sacrifices?" Michael Manning, of Detroit's West Side Local 174, Reuther's home base, feared that elimination of premium pay would be only the beginning of a general retreat by labor that would not end with the close of the war.

Although they had been bitterly divided less than a year before, Reuther, Frankensteen, Addes, and Thomas now united to push through the wartime program against the local union dissidents. They were supported from the floor by Communist party spokesmen Nat Ganly and John Anderson, officers of Detroit's big tool and die Local 155. After a long debate, opponents of the Equality of Sacrifice program went down before this solid leadership phalanx, but they garnered 150 votes, representing some of the UAW's largest and most strategic locals, out of some 1,200 cast.[40]

The UAW initially attempted to portray the Equality of Sacrifice idea as a labor thrust against the corporations, but even Reuther, who usually sought to advertise his current proposals as militant advances for the union, admitted that the new program was an exercise in appeasement: "I say the surest way to see that a tidal wave is launched in Washington that will engulf all of us is to refuse to recognize the double time issue as something we cannot fight on at this time, but we can fight on the 40 hour week." As usual, Frankensteen put the matter much more bluntly. He challenged the delegates: "Are you going to tell the President to go to hell?"[41]

Despite their lopsided victory at the War Emergency Conference, UAW leaders recognized that the decision to relinquish premium pay might be unpopular with much of the union's membership. Thus the task of local union leaders, declared Walter Reuther, was to "educate your rank and file to the new realities of wartime unionism." To ensure this understanding among their own membership and the general public, the UAW appropriated $50,000 to publicize the Equality of Sacrifice program. The union purchased radio time and took out full-page newspaper ads in the major metropolitan dailies. *The United Auto Worker* and most of the important local UAW papers pushed the new program.[42]

The UAW sought to use the Equality of Sacrifice idea as part of an ultrapatriotic wartime organizing strategy, especially in the booming aircraft plants, where the union was locked in fierce competition with the International Association of Machinists. During the War Emergency Conference, Reuther had asserted that Equality of Sacrifice was "the kind of program you can rally around and make the fight for in the shops." Richard Frankensteen, in charge of the massive UAW aircraft drive, endorsed this perspective because he thought the several hundred thousand new recruits to the wartime airframe industry more concerned with winning the war than with maintaining prewar labor standards. A large proportion held an anti-union bias common to the less industrialized sections of the country from which they were recruited. They were "patriots and superpatriots," argued Frankensteen; they would not understand the union's desire to quibble over premium pay.[43]

The net effect of this approach was to accommodate to the existing "backward" consciousness of the tens of thousands of new war workers who flooded the airframe factories. Instead of the usual education and agitation on work-related issues, leaders of the organizational effort at Douglas Aircraft in Southern California played up General Douglas MacArthur's recent message of praise for the CIO and relegated to an infrequent leaflet the UAW's standing demand for a wage increase and an equitable job promotion ladder. In a union-sponsored radio broadcast directed toward still unorganized Douglas workers, the UAW announcer summed up what the union considered its main appeal:

Contributions which the CIO has made [to the war effort] have profoundly impressed the Douglas Aircraft workers. They are beginning to realize that the best way they can speed up war production and contribute even more to the war effort is to join the CIO, which has made this business of winning the war its main objective.[44]

Aircraft drive leaders in California devoted much of their attention to war bond sales and blood campaigns in a further effort to impress aircraft workers with the cooperative, patriotic character of the CIO. In part, this approach reflected the extensive influence of the Communists in the California UAW, but the organizing strategy was not very different in the Midwest and the East, where Richard Frankensteen put non-Communists in charge of the aircraft drive.[45]

Although the UAW expanded rapidly during 1942, enrolling almost a million members by the end of the year, its Equality of Sacrifice program proved notably unsuccessful. The UAW media blitz on behalf of its program won the favorable attention of liberals such as Eleanor Roosevelt and William O. Douglas, but the hard-nosed conservatives in Congress who controlled the union's fate were less impressed. They soon gutted an executive salary limitation proposed by the president, eroded the administration's price control program, and opened loopholes in the rationing schedules. Other progressive elements in the Equality of Sacrifice program were ignored, defeated, or watered down, and the entire idea suffered much the same fate as the 500-planes-a-day proposal put forward a few months earlier.[46]

The UAW also misjudged the temper of rank and file workers, for the Equality of Sacrifice program, and especially the union's abandonment of premium pay, proved a burden rather than an incentive in wartime organizing efforts. Many small companies that hoped to remain non-union refused to stop paying their employees double time for Sunday work. This put the UAW at a disadvantage in organizing these plants because during a National Labor Relations Board election, the employer could truthfully argue that unionization would mean an actual pay cut. In June the UAW went down to defeat at the Victor Manufacturing Company in Detroit after local organizers reported that 80 percent of the plant's employees had already signed union cards. Frankensteen blamed the UAW's loss to a company-dominated union on one issue, the UAW's forfeiture of premium pay.[47]

The union's most jarring reverse on the overtime pay issue took place in July at the huge Buffalo plant of the Curtiss-Wright Aircraft Company. There the IAM soundly defeated the UAW by some 2,000 votes out of more than 17,000 cast. The defeat was an extraordinary setback because the UAW considered Curtiss-Wright one of the "Fords" of the aircraft industry and had made organization of the company its top priority in the East. In the final days of the NLRB election, Frankensteen sent more than a score of organizers into the Buffalo area, climaxing the campaign with a mass rally that brought George Addes and Allen

Haywood to the lakefront city. Added to the sting of the machinists' victory was the fact that the CIO dominated the industrial union scene in Buffalo, with such major plants as Bethlehem Steel and Bell Aircraft already under contract.

The machinists defeated the UAW at Buffalo because they directly attacked the auto union's sacrifice of premium pay and its commitment to wartime social unionism. Since World War I, the IAM had been a conservative and opportunistic union, oriented toward the interests of skilled craftsmen. Like many other AFL unions rooted in this craft tradition, the IAM staunchly defended its contractual rights during the war and took a more parochial view of the extent to which labor should subordinate its interests to the total war effort. Many of the IAM's powerful, virtually autonomous lodges simply refused to relinquish premium pay even after the government requested it. Thus the IAM proved aggressive in its bargaining strategy and recruitment propaganda, emphasizing wages and hours and the maintenance of overtime pay standards. As the NLRB election at Curtiss-Wright approached, the IAM attacked the UAW: "Can the CIO's masterminds tell you why they know what's good for the worker better than he knows himself? . . . the CIO sacrifices worker's pay, worker's overtime as the CIO's contribution to the war effort. Big of them, huh?" To this, the machinists counterposed pure and simple trade unionism: "While the AFL has been loyal to the country it has also been loyal to its members. IT HAS NOT FELT CALLED UPON TO MAKE SACRIFICES OF WORKERS' PAY OR OF LABOR'S GAINS."[48]

Executive Order 9240

In defeat, the UAW's Buffalo local petitioned the NLRB to void the election on the grounds that the IAM had "deliberately spread confusion and disruption with subversive propaganda against the government's war policies on overtime pay." The UAW further charged that IAM propaganda "sought to create the impression that employees of the company could disregard the need for unity and sacrifice requested by the President of the United States and could safely concern themselves solely with their own selfish interests isolated from the welfare of the country at war." The CIO's top leadership carried these complaints to the president and the War Labor Board. In a joint letter to FDR, Murray, Thomas, and Frankensteen indignantly asked, "Is this to be tolerated? Is the CIO to be expected to make sacrifices which may result in its own destruction to the aggrandizement of those who are lending aid and comfort to the enemies of the country?"[49]

In what was to become a characteristic wartime response to rank-and-file agitation, these labor leaders appealed to the president to reinforce their authority. They demanded that Roosevelt force all labor organizations to accept the concessions that the CIO had already made and warned that if something was not done quickly, unrest would spread, especially within the UAW. As in April, Murray and Thomas wanted FDR to reassure the UAW rank and file that the government would see to it that fair treatment prevailed if they followed the policies laid down by their leaders.[50]

When the UAW met for its first wartime convention in August 1942, harmony of purpose again prevailed among the union's top officers, but rank-and-file delegates reflected an unfocused but real dissatisfaction with the conduct of the home front. They complained that grievance procedures were ignored by management, that the Little Steel formula was unfair, and that price and profit controls were rigged in favor of the rich. Spurred on by maverick radicals such as Briggs Local 212 President Emil Mazey, the delegates sharply cut the salary increase proposed for union officers, defeated an increase in union dues, and forced the executive board to call its next convention in 1943 rather than 1944.[51]

As the convention opened, CIO leaders hoped that FDR and WPB chief Nelson would send a special message to the UAW assuring the union that AFL unions would be legally required to yield their double-time standards for holiday and Sunday work. But FDR was not willing to make such a commitment at this time, chiefly because Labor Secretary Perkins still hoped to solve the problem through a series of voluntary agreements worked out between AFL affiliates and the War Production Board. In the absence of a presidential commitment, UAW leaders sought to deflect rank and file anger over this touchy issue without repudiating their Equality of Sacrifice gambit. Under Victor Reuther's guidance, the union's War Policy Committee proposed that the UAW rescind its premium pay sacrifice in thirty days unless the government took action to force uncooperative AFL unions to relinquish the extra pay provisions in their contracts as well. To many convention delegates dissatisfied with the elimination of extra weekend pay, the War Policy Committee resolution contained an implied threat by the union to fight for its restoration. To the leadership, chiefly concerned with the prospect of more NLRB election defeats at the hands of the AFL, passage of the proposal would give them a mandate to insist that the president issue an executive order ending premium pay in all union contracts.[52]

The convention debate over the premium pay resolution served as the focus of a more far-reaching discussion concerning the union's role in the war. Although the leadership once again stood shoulder to shoulder in support of Equality of Sacrifice, some local union leaders for the first time questioned the international's no-strike policy, its cooperation with the NWLB, and its reliance upon FDR as guardian of labor's wartime interests. The first standing vote on the premium pay resolution reflected the auto workers' generalized discontent; half, perhaps a majority were opposed, and the executive board was forced to rewrite the resolution. When they introduced it again the next day, their proposal more closely tied the UAW's sacrifice of labor standards to a renegotiation of defense contracts. This vote passed handily.[53]

Following the convention, which President Thomas labeled "the most demoralizing sight I have ever experienced," UAW leaders stepped up their pressure on FDR to issue an executive order banning premium pay from all trade union contracts. On August 28, Reuther, Frankensteen, and Thomas met with Roosevelt and reached a tentative agreement that the president would issue the long-sought executive order before the thirty-day deadline expired. They expected FDR to establish this new policy in his Labor Day speech of September 7. The issue was complicated, however, by the fact that although many AFL unions were willing to forego premium pay, they insisted that the proper time to end such pay would be when their existing contracts expired. The AFL had an ally in Frances Perkins, who had already reached such an understanding with the AFL metal trades department on July 16. She opposed an executive order on this subject and urged that the president give the AFL more time to renegotiate its contracts and enforce the government's policy on the labor federation's international affiliates and federal locals.

Perkins realized the immense difficulty of applying a uniform premium pay rule to the thousands of wage relationships and work schedules that had evolved in American industry. In many plants, premium pay policies had become part of the wage structure of the industry, and employees would insist on an across-the-board wage increase to compensate for the loss of weekend premium pay. In the building trades, the

Department of Labor had already agreed that the relinquishment of premium pay would be impractical in some circumstances because of long-standing work practices. Because any agreement on this issue would require the cooperation of the trade unions for its application and enforcement, Perkins hoped to carry out the national policy on premium pay through a series of piecemeal agreements worked out over the next few months between the unions and industries involved.[54]

These problems delayed the issuance of an executive order beyond the date of the president's Labor Day address. With the UAW's self-imposed deadline literally hours away, Thomas contacted FDR's secretary, Marvin McIntyre, in a state of near panic and insisted that unless the president issued an executive order immediately, several Detroit area locals were prepared to strike for a restoration of their extra pay at the start of the coming weekend. At Thomas's suggestion, FDR sent the UAW a telegram informing the union that compliance with national policy on premium pay would soon be enforced in all industries. Two days later, on September 10, Roosevelt issued a hastily prepared executive order, Number 9240. In addition to banning premium pay for work on Saturdays and Sundays, as the UAW had demanded, the order provided that if an employee was required to work for seven consecutive days of any regularly scheduled work week, double-time compensation would be paid for work on the seventh day. The order also designated six holidays throughout the year upon which the time-and-a-half pay was in order. The secretary of labor was vested with the authority to interpret the order as the need arose.[55]

Executive Order 9240 failed to end the CIO's difficulties with premium pay; instead, it merely turned the controversy into a dispute over the interpretation of the new guidelines. Initially, the CIO expected 9240 to solve many of their problems with this vexing issue and to produce a few added benefits as well. Not only did 9240 end the AFL threat to their organizing efforts, but in some continuous-operation industries, such as steel, smelting, and glass, the executive order was expected to represent a small wage increase. Before the war, the basic steel industry had not paid premium wages for weekend work because the traditional work schedule rotated the onerous weekend workdays among all employees. But with 9240 mandating double time for the seventh consecutive day of work, steel unionists now expected premium pay for at least one and sometimes two days a week. The steel corporations, however, backed by the procurement agencies of the military, balked at this provision of 9240. In late September, they secured a reinterpretation of the executive order from the secretary of labor. Perkins ruled that double time need not be paid for the seventh consecutive work day if the employer and his employees had previously arranged a mutually satisfactory work schedule that accorded a day of rest in each regular work week.[56]

The ruling set the stage for extended bickering in the steel plants. Employers argued that the pre-Pearl Harbor work rules and the existing union contract represented "mutually satisfactory work schedules"; hence, premium pay need not be paid for the seventh consecutive day. Employees disagreed. Because the secretary of labor designated the military's procurement agencies to enforce 9240, employers usually won the dispute (because the company's point of view would entail lower total production costs to the military). This confusion generated steelworker discontent over the issue that culminated in a two-day December walkout of 3,000 workers at Bethlehem Steel's Johnstown, Pennsylvania, facility. A similar controversy raised tempers at Ford's River Rouge complex, and 20,000 auto workers staged a short wildcat strike for a few days later.[57]

While this controversy simmered, the secretary of labor exempted several industries, including transportation, agriculture, and the building trades, from the provisions of 9240. These exemptions were made for the same reasons that Perkins had been opposed to the entire executive order in the first place: the difficulty of applying an administrative order to myriad, complex labor–management relationships. In trucking and railroads, for example, wage structures had long been adjusted to an around-the-clock schedule; an attempt to apply 9240 would have meant a wholesale revision of existing wage schedules. In agriculture, on the other hand, the nonunion character of the industry and its seasonal nature proved an obstacle to enforcement of the order without large-scale social changes that the federal government was unwilling to sponsor. The CIO, of course, considered the announcement of these exemptions a direct act of discrimination against its unions, and Philip Murray complained bitterly to the president of the secretary's action.[58] In fact, these exemptions and their later extension to such fields as printing, warehousing, and utilities simply confirmed the failure of the CIO's attempt to rely upon administrative fiat, rather than collective bargaining, to enforce uniform and equitable wages and working conditions in wartime industries.

After prodding by the military and the maritime commission, Perkins ended the confusion over 9240 in January 1943 by once again reinterpreting the order, but this time in a manner even more unfavorable to industrial union labor. She ruled that regardless of past practices, so long as a worker received one day off in a calendar week, he was not entitled to any double-time pay. Consequently, an employee could have Monday of one week off, work twelve full days, and then have Sunday of the next week off without receiving double-time compensation. Perkins's new interpretation derived from the military's wish to remove any obstacles to the flexible scheduling of wartime production, especially in such critical industries as nonferrous mining and shipbuilding.[59]

The CIO strenuously but unsuccessfully demanded revocation of the new interpretation. Omitting any mention of the UAW's frantic efforts to secure adoption of Executive Order 9240 as a bulwark against IAM competition, the CIO executive council now condemned the government edict as an intrusion into "the entire field of collective bargaining contracts and work schedules in a manner as to practically disrupt American industry." Not surprisingly, Philip Murray and other CIO leaders now charged that the elimination of premium pay had worked to reduce overall wage standards. In a spirit far removed from the days of March 1942, the CIO demanded that where prewar contracts providing premium pay for Sundays and holidays had been abrogated, an overall wage increase should be instituted to avoid an effective wage cut.[60]

The National War Labor Board ultimately resolved much of the premium pay imbroglio. A complicated series of decisions established the principle that where premium pay had been part of the prewar wage structure of an industry or plant and its elimination had reduced total take-home pay, the NWLB would approve a wage increase in order to make up the difference.[61] These decisions nullified, for the most part, the CIO's original patriotic sacrifice of premium pay as a contribution to the war effort in the form of lower production costs to the military.

Conclusion

The administrative history of the Reuther Plan and of Executive Order 9240 has been chronicled in some detail because it illuminates the CIO's political and ideological relationship to the pressures generated by the war economy. In the eighteen months before Pearl Harbor, pro-Roosevelt interventionists such as Philip Murray and Walter Reuther had hoped to use the production crisis to remold the entire structure of capitalist enterprise into a more pliable social democratic form. They recognized that state planning of a sort never attempted, even during the NRA era, would be necessary both to inaugurate a successful mobilization program and to advance its democratic character. Hence, they seized the political opportunity presented by the conversion difficulties of the large corporations to build an alliance with Roosevelt administration technocrats and business elements whose interests were damaged by the military takeover of the economy. The Reuther Plan and the wartime effort to foster civilian control of the WPB represented the unsuccessful attempt to implement this program.

After Pearl Harbor, CIO hopes for major structural changes rapidly waned. The WPB did plan, but the locus of power was now the military and the large prime contractors, who structured the booming economy largely in their own interest. The loss of CIO power became clear with its defeat on the highly symbolic premium pay issue. Ironically, it was the UAW's tradition of political liberalism and social unionism that provided the ideological rationale for its capitulation. To win a restless membership to this unilateral concession, the UAW leadership packaged this hidden wage reduction as part of an all-class Equality of Sacrifice program. Recognizing the thorough politicization of all trade union activity during the war, UAW leaders hoped to parlay their union's premium pay concession into a general social program on the home front. Although this idea undoubtedly appealed to some elements of the working class and to much of the liberal community, the fate of the Equality of Sacrifice idea revealed the extent to which the rightward shift of institutional power made it possible for the WPB, Congress, and the administration safely to ignore the economic demands of the industrial union movement.

In July, aircraft workers at Buffalo-Curtiss delivered another blow to the illusory promise of the UAW's wartime program by choosing the IAM's pure and simple trade unionism over the UAW's brand of social democratic patriotism. The CIO's policy of voluntary sacrifice fell in a shambles, but instead of generating a program of political opposition, such as John L. Lewis would adopt during a similar crisis in 1943, the CIO leadership called upon the administration to intervene further in union–management affairs. Increasing statism protected the CIO from short-term embarrassment at the hands of internal critics and AFL rivals, but administrative difficulties inevitably arose, involving the CIO in an ever more complicated bureaucratic tangle that was not finally resolved until the end of the war.

7. The social ecology of shop-floor conflict

The failure of the Equality of Sacrifice idea by early 1943 coincided with the growth of an elemental frustration that touched large sectors of the unionized working class. The social disruption associated with the transformation of the economy to a war footing, the increasingly rigid and cumbersome government wage policy, and the growing volume of shop-floor grievances all provided the social and economic context for the structural crisis that gripped the mass industrial unions in the second half of the war. In this chapter and the next, we examine the social psychology of the wartime workforce, the character of the growing wildcat strike phenomenon, and the impact of both upon the internal politics of the United Automobile Workers, in which a wave of rank-and-file militancy shattered the wartime solidarity of the union leadership.

The wages of war

During World War II, American workers never lived so well, and yet their sense of personal security, even prosperity, laid the basis for the restless militancy that characterized so many highly paid, steadily employed war workers. By mid-1943, virtually anyone who wished to find a job could do so at real wages higher than those prevailing at any previous time. With the military taking more than 15 million persons, the reserve army of unemployed, retired, and part-time workers now provided some 10 million additional recruits for the American labor force. Housewives, teenagers, and underemployed farm laborers were drawn by patriotism and pay to the ranks of the fully employed. By 1943, the jobless rate stood at a socially insignificant 1.3 percent, less than a tenth of what it had been during 1937, the most prosperous year of the previous decade.[1] Naturally, the new demand for labor enhanced the individual worker's bargaining power, which was soon reflected in absentee and labor turnover rates more than double those of prewar years. Another statistic records even more dramatically the newly favorable situation of the average worker: In 1939, layoffs accounted for 71 percent of worker separations from the job; in 1943, by contrast, voluntary resignations, usually by employees in search of better work, produced 72 percent of the turnover.[2]

Despite the general regimentation of the economy, real income also increased for most workers during the war. The nation's wage bill more than doubled between 1940 and 1944, and average weekly earnings in manufacturing leaped 65 percent after December 1941, rising from $32.18 to $47.12 in the subsequent forty months. Corrected for inflation, real earnings rose substantially: at least 26 percent in steel, 36 percent in coal, 20 percent in autos, and 27 percent in all manufacturing. There were two reasons for this significant rise in real pay. First, almost everyone worked some overtime at time-and-a-half pay, and the average length of the work week rose from 40.6 hours in 1941 to 45.2 in 1944. Kept up for months, this schedule proved exhausting, but it meant high and steady pay for many who had never known such security.[3]

Second, the tight labor market enabled millions to change and upgrade their jobs. Fifteen million Americans – a third of the prewar workforce – used their new labor power to move into higher-paying or more pleasant occupations.[4] To plant supervisors, the maintenance of the new and unfamiliar production schedules established by the military was now all important, the necessity for low-cost production greatly reduced. Because no one in top management or government really knew the cost of a piece of war material rushed into production, costs were relatively uncontrolled in both Washington and the field. Promotions and reclassifications came easily in situations in which employers feared that strict National War Labor Board wage guidelines would prove a barrier to the recruitment or retention of a vital group of employees. There was much employer "hoarding" of labor and much use by employees of company time, material, and tools for their own so-called government work. Likewise, piece-rate standards and bonus schedules were often loosely set, especially in the early years of the war, so that workers on incentive pay could easily make their quota and earn extra money.[5]

But the full pay and steady work of these years did not come without their social and psychological vexations. Most workers feared that the wartime prosperity was a temporary phenomenon that might end before they enjoyed its full rewards, yet they also resented those who seemed to take obvious advantage of the wartime boom. Veteran industrial unionists often perceived the newly arrived Okies, blacks, and women as socially disruptive elements who effortlessly reaped the rewards and benefited from the sacrifices of others.[6] Workers, new and old, proved sensitive to the usual exercise of managerial authority when they had a patriotic stake in efficient military production, and little infuriated them more than overstaffing or enforced idleness in the factory. Union periodicals and the liberal press continuously reported such cost-plus abuses, but Harriette Arnow best captured the popular blend of cynicism and resentment in *The Dollmaker*, her sympathetic novel of Appalachian migrants in wartime Detroit. As one of her characters put it: "These big men that owns these factories, th' gover'mint gives em profits on what things cost – six cents on th' dollar I've heard say. So every time they can make a thing cost two dollars stid a one . . . they're six cents ahead, an everybody's happy. Th' more men, th' more plus fer th' owners, th' more money an more men fer them unions. I figger."[7]

As millions of workers streamed into the booming war plants, many experienced abrupt and disruptive changes in their quality of life. Most of the new jobs were located either in congested, older urban areas such as Buffalo or Baltimore, or in raw new plant site cities such as Wichita, Kansas, or Richmond, California. Community services and facilities were usually inadequate. Busses, trains, and highways were frequently overcrowded, housing was in short supply, and meat was difficult to find. Major consumer goods that most workers had not purchased for a decade were nowhere to be seen, except at black market prices or in shoddy quality.[8]

Meanwhile, two deductions not present in the prewar era shrunk most defense workers' paychecks. In 1942 came a nearly compulsory 10 percent war bond purchase; the next year, a 5 percent victory tax for the first time in U.S. history withheld money directly from 35 million working-class paychecks. Combined with the ever-present inflation, which affected food, clothing, and other necessities purchased by urban wage earners hardest, the new wartime levies reduced significantly the average factory worker's real spendable income (see Figure 1). For a work week 20 percent longer, estimated an AFL economist, most workers received additional real income only 5 percent over their prewar earnings in the same job.[9] Late in 1942, a *Fortune* reporter in Pittsburgh accurately assessed the disquiet that lingered among longtime steelworkers in the booming city: "To the workers its a Tantalus situation: the luscious

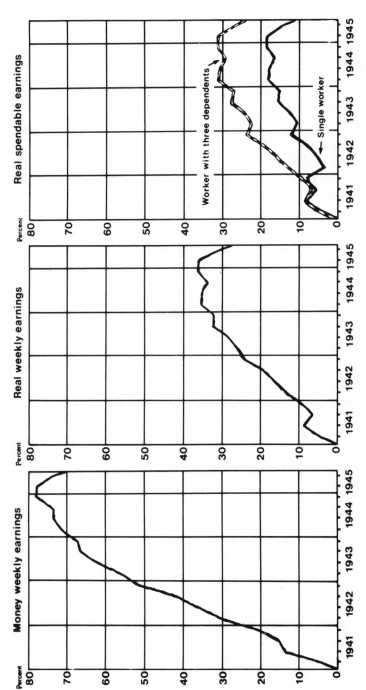

Figure 1. Changes in money and in real and spendable earnings in manufacturing industries, 1941–5. (Department of Labor, *The Termination Report of the National War Labor Board*, vol. 1, Washington, D.C., 1947, 552).

fruits of prosperity above their heads – receding as they try to pick them."[10]

The inadequate social infrastructure of the new war industry centers annoyed workers, who often sorely felt the bite taken by taxes and bonds ($25 war bond redemptions doubled between 1942 and 1944). But the most vexing irritations encountered by wartime industrial workers were those found in the factory itself, often in the form of wage and job inequities that revealed how those who presided over the newly mobilized economy had failed to ensure that equality of sacrifice – or benefit – prevailed in the American workplace. The trend of wartime wages resembled a rising tide on a rocky coast. The water surged inward, not smoothly, as on a sandy beach, but unevenly among the coves and inlets carved or broken by the existing system of production. Although the industrial unions had made some progress in standardizing industry-wide wage schedules in the late 1930s, the conversion of the civilian economy to war production did nothing to rationalize automatically these often chaotic wage rate differences; in fact, the conversion process frequently highlighted the problem, especially when separate plants began to produce standard military items. Late in 1943, labor journalist Mary Heaton Vorse reported, "The chaotic state of [the Pacific coast aircraft] industry finds two people working with identical tools on the same job, one paid twenty cents an hour more than the other. Parts made at the Ford plant in San Diego at $1.00 an hour minimum are shipped to Douglas in Los Angeles and paid 65 cents an hour in assembly. Multiply these instances by hundreds of thousands and add the many more complex upgrading and ingrading problems, and a situation of unimaginable confusion is created."[11]

Unionists soon took such difficulties to the National War Labor Board, but they found the national tribunal unwilling or unable to set uniform national pay standards. In theory, the board had immense authority in this area, for in September 1942 the president had delegated to the NWLB the formal responsibility to "correct inequalities and inequities" in existing wage structures. Anxious to routinize collective bargaining and rationalize the labor market, the administrative liberals who presided over the board acted swiftly and unanimously to strike down de jure racial and sexual wage differentials and abolish formal barriers to occupational upgrading for blacks and women. The NWLB also proved sensitive to what it called "substandard" rates of pay, and in November 1942 it gave employers the authority to raise wages immedi-

ately to fifty cents an hour, thus narrowing somewhat the historic
North–South wage gap in textiles and other low-wage industries. [12]

But the National War Labor Board chose not to tamper with the basic
structure of the American labor market. "Differences in rates are not
necessarily inequalities in rates," explained NWLB economist George
Taylor. "On the contrary, the wages paid in American industry are
normally characterized by all sorts of differentials created for different
reasons." Thus the board rejected a UAW request that wages in
Chrysler Corporation plants be equalized regardless of the factory's
location or previous wage schedule, and the NWLB turned down union
demands that the historic and discriminatory wage pattern that characterized the packinghouse industry be abolished. Although diminished,
the North–South wage differential in textiles remained intact, and new
regional inequalities emerged after the board set west coast aircraft
wages in March 1943. [13]

However, the board could not ignore entirely inequitable wage rates
within the same geographical labor market. Here, such inequities created immense pressure for migration from lower-paying jobs to those
with higher scales, creating acute labor shortages and high rates of turnover in the less favorable occupations. In the Seattle area, for example,
the 40 percent wage rate inequality between shipyards and the huge
Boeing Aircraft plant caused a chronic labor deficit in the latter facility.
Production lagged, the International Association of Machinists lodge
there staged a demonstration strike, the army became alarmed. Although NWLB policy forbade the use of direct wage incentives to solve
such manpower problems, in this case the crisis ended only after the
military prodded the board to boost regional aircraft pay at the same time
the Maritime Commission cut back shipyard employment. [14]

Wage rate inequalities within a single plant or department proved an
even more vexing and persistent cause of working-class discontent. Each
employee knew well the wages paid his or her coworkers, and because no
general pay increase seemed in the offing to take the sting out of such
differentials, those that remained were particularly irksome. In the steel
industry, for example, U.S. Steel maintained more than 26,000 different rates, most of them purposely designed to fragment and divide the
workforce. "A man at the blast furnace does the same work another
fellow does at the open hearth, but gets a few cents an hour less,"
reported a United Steel Workers of America district official in 1942.
"Now frankly it's not a question of starving, much as he could use the

money. It's just not right. A man does not see any sense in it and gets pretty mad. Who wouldn't?"[15] As a result, local unions came under direct pressure from the rank and file to equalize such wages, and local leaders soon flooded the NWLB with intraplant wage inequality cases, some covering but a handful of workers, others involving thousands. Although its work was slow, the NWLB could not resist accommodating to this pressure, if only because it recognized the "adverse effect upon employee morale and productive efficiency" of such internal inequalities. By the spring of 1943, the upward equalization of wages had become one of the union movement's most promising ways of circumventing the Little Steel formula.[16]

President Roosevelt soon dropped a bombshell on this process. On April 8, 1943, he issued a sweeping executive order ending the NWLB's authority to correct wage inequalities. "The only way to hold the line [against inflation]," stated the president in his speech announcing Executive Order 9328, "is to stop trying to find justification for not holding it here or not holding it there." Prepared secretly in the office of the "assistant president," James Byrnes, the new order centralized economic decision making as part of a general administration strategy to keep the farm bloc in check, stop John L. Lewis's current drive to break the Little Steel formula, and curb the upward wage drift allowed by the NWLB. The hold-the-line order gave Byrnes's Office of Economic Stabilization (OES) final authority to review all National War Labor Board decisions, thus destroying once and for all the legal fiction that the board was an independent and voluntary government agency.[17]

The NWLB immediately threw out some 10,000 pending inequality cases, representing approximately three-fifths of its entire backlog. The new order stood for a "freezing of chaos," charged Philip Murray; the CIO argued that "the most dangerous confusion" would result on factory floors unless the board rewon the power to ameliorate the wage inequity situation. Public members of the NWLB agreed, and after a month of hard bargaining with Byrnes – during which Wayne Morse and George Taylor hinted at resignation – the labor board gained a "clarifying order" from the economic stabilizer that restored some of its authority to eliminate wage rate inequalities.[18]

Byrnes accepted a board proposal that it develop a set of standard "wage brackets" that established a system of "sound and tested" regional rates to which inequitably low wages could be increased. Under this system, small wage raises were authorized for large numbers of workers who had received the maximum under the Little Steel formula, but instead of simply exercising its independent judgment in this field, the NWLB was required to rely on time-consuming wage surveys to determine the minimum going rates in a particular geographical region. This bracket system – the "bracket racket," some unionists called it – perpetuated numerous regional wage variations and put in effect an elaborate set of wage guidelines and an unduly cumbersome administrative structure. By 1944, unionists such as Walter Reuther complained that the delay and inequity inherent in the system were "unstabilizing the industry pattern established through years of collective bargaining."[19]

Shop-floor conflict

Working-class sensitivity to chronic wage inequality problems was symptomatic of a larger disruption of workplace discipline and a decline in managerial authority that characterized the factory environment in the war era. The alienation of the foreman from the ranks of factory supervision proved another key element in this process. By the end of the depression, this front-line lieutenant of management had already undergone a generation-long decline in power and prestige. Since 1900, corporate personnel and engineering departments had steadily assumed more and more of the foreman's traditional control of hiring, wages, and production. Then in the late 1930s, the new unions further restricted the foreman's authority as grievance procedures and seniority rules limited and regulated his unilateral disciplinary power.[20]

The war itself produced a final major decline in the status and managerial power of this crucial figure in the factory hierarchy. The dramatic expansion and internal transformation of the wartime labor pool forced managers quickly to recruit thousands of ordinary workers into the supervisory ranks. At General Motors, for example, 42 percent of its 19,000 foremen in 1943 had been on the job for less than a year.[21] These new foremen complained that without overtime pay for themselves, but with overtime aplenty for production workers, their average wage was little above the rate of those they supervised. Moreover, because foremen ceased accumulating seniority when promoted from the ranks, they feared that without their own grievance procedure they would be unemployed when the postwar layoffs began. In short, foremen grew increasingly disaffected throughout the war. "They have not been properly trained or instructed in order to function efficiently," complained a middle-level supervisor at Packard, "nor have they the proper viewpoint of management toward their jobs."[22]

The Foreman's Association of America (FAA) built its spectacular wartime growth on their disenchantment. Beginning with veteran foremen at Ford's River Rouge complex shortly after the UAW success there in May 1941, the FAA signed up more than 33,000 by mid-1944. About 80 percent of its membership lay in Detroit area auto–aircraft plants, but the organization made inroads in the rubber, metal fabrication, and electrical industries. In some industries, such as coal mining, construction, and lake transport, foremen joined established unions directly.[23] In the face of adamant opposition from management and ambiguous administrative rulings from the NWLB and the NLRB, the ability of foremen to maintain their organization, independent or union affiliated, depended upon the active goodwill of the rank-and-file workers they supervised. The impact of this problem was hardly lost on management. "Picture if you can the confusion of an army in the field," asserted a Vinco Corporation executive, "if the non-commissioned officers were forced to listen to the demands of the men in the ranks as well as those of their superior officers."[24]

Taken together, then, the conversion of the factories to high-cost military production, the new demand for labor, and the alienation of the foreman created an environment on the shop floor that contributed to the erosion of factory discipline and the rise of worker power, even control of the production process. At Dodge Main in Detroit, aggressive stewards turned the union's formal right to observe company time-study procedures into the power to set jointly all new rates. At Packard, union committeemen prevented managers from making any new time studies in the naval engine department and reached an agreement with foremen in the overstaffed aircraft division that once the work quota for the day had been fulfilled, the men could doze or play cards until quitting time. At Brewster Aeronautical on Long Island, New York, where an inept management, a poorly designed plant, and a rush order for Buffalo fighters gave the militant union there extraordinary power, stewards held a veto over the discharge of any employee. In the turbine buildings at General Electric's Erie, Pennsylvania, complex, management virtually abandoned control of piecework standards to the workers.[25] Auto industry executives complained in early 1945 that such conditions had generated as much as a 39 percent decline in the productivity of factory workers. To cite but one example, at the Briggs Manufacturing Company the prewar production quota for fender stampings was 150 per hour for a gang of four. After conversion to war production, the company conceded to shop stewards the right to time production jointly. Now the same gang used the same press to turn out jettison fuel tanks, but they produced only seventy stampings per hour.[26]

As long as production remained paramount and labor scarce, there was little factory managers could do about their loss of shop control. Depending on the company, however, the opportunity for tightening up on discipline and abandoning the policy of making concessions to guarantee uninterrupted production came somewhere between mid-1942, when conversion problems were generally resolved, and the end of 1943, when output peaked and layoffs began at certain factories. At General Motors, top management quickly recognized that the war put them on a more favorable ideological ground in their effort to preserve and reassert managerial prerogatives. In prewar contract negotiations, the corporation had merely sought to stem the tide of union demands, but as early as 1942, GM called on the UAW to reduce by half the number and curtail the duties of union grievance committeemen, permit larger wage differentials among individual employees, and allow management more discretion to introduce incentive pay and change shop-floor work rules. GM expressed management's new vigor by repeatedly demanding that UAW locals "discontinue in official union papers, handbills and other literature attacks and accusations of 'speed up' on management's efforts to increase production of war materials."[27]

From the perspective of the shop floor and the lower ranks of the union infrastructure, this managerial effort took the form of an increase in the arbitrary character of supervisory decisionmaking and a breakdown in the grievance procedure. In prewar years, the strike weapon often backstopped a local's handling of grievances and provided an incentive for management to resolve disputes at the lowest possible level. But with the adoption of the no-strike pledge, this incentive evaporated. Thus, with seeming unpredictability, informal shop routines worked out over months and even years were abruptly violated and broken by higher-level management. Local unions found themselves "plagued by a malady of unsettled grievances," reported one veteran unionist, who observed that "expert committeemen, with five years' experience, are unable to any longer obtain the success they once scored in winning settlements." And novelist John Dos Passos reported from Detroit early in 1943, "The gist of it was that the men couldn't get over the suspicion that the great automobile concerns were using the war emergency for their own purposes: when it was over they were the ones who would come out on top."[28]

Grievances left unresolved were shuttled upward to an impartial umpire, or, if they involved a wage increase or set an important precedent, were dumped in the lap of an already overburdened National War Labor Board. In theory, that agency served as a court of last resort for all problems that might lead to a work stoppage, but to local union leaders, the NWLB proved a "sort of box canyon" that was administratively incapable of dealing with the tens of thousands of disputes arising out of the collapse of local grievance procedures and other forms of inplant collective bargaining.[29] By the winter of 1943, the board received 10,000 to 15,000 new cases each month, whereas it was incapable of reviewing one-third that number. Even after its operations were decentralized in late 1943, delays of up to a year were routine, especially if the dispute was complicated or unique. And when it finally acted, the NWLB normally sided with the employer when the latter could show that "managerial prerogatives" were clearly at stake.[30]

Factory managers never publicly spelled out their newly aggressive policies, but at companies such as Chrysler and Ford, where labor relations were often conducted in an erratic and opportunistic fashion, efforts to maintain discipline and managerial authority increased noticeably in 1943. Confident that any strikes would merely isolate and politically embarrass the union, individual managers at Chrysler began to enforce nuisance smoking and dress code rules and to resist settling grievances that could have equalized individual wage rates within and between Chrysler factories. By the early summer of 1943 an NWLB panel concluded that collective bargaining between the Chrysler Corporation and the UAW had broken down after the parties could not reach agreement on some fifty contract issues, chiefly concerned with union status in the shops.[31] Much the same pattern prevailed at Ford, where management reorganized and centralized its labor relations late in 1943. "Clearly defined policies were set out," reported one of the company's key industrial relations executives, "particularly with reference to meting out of disciplinary action and enforcement of company rules, handling of unauthorized work stoppages, enforcement of production standards and other similar items." Leaders of UAW Local 600 at the Rouge found evidence that mid-level managers there consciously procrastinated on handling grievances to discipline strike ringleaders and blacken the union's image with a patriotic public.[32] Similarly, at Briggs, a super-visor raised the production of fuel tanks to the prewar level after firing two workers for not making a greater effort. "Reasonable output was reached only after successful application of disciplinary action and after a strike," he concluded.[33]

The ecology of wildcat strikes

Workers responded to this new managerial toughness with a dramatic increase in the number of protests, slowdowns, and work stoppages over production standards and workplace discipline. Beginning in the spring of 1943 and accelerating with the nation-wide coal strikes launched by John L. Lewis, a wave of unauthorized strikes swept through heavy industry. In unionized industries such as rubber, steel, and shipbuild-ing, the number of work stoppages rose steadily until the end of the war, when they equaled or exceeded the number in such tumultuous years as 1937 and 1941. In the auto industry, the unquestioned center of this phenomenon, over half of all workers took part in some form of work stoppage in 1944, up from one in twelve in 1942 and one in four in 1943.[34]

Most of these strikes were "quickie" stoppages, involving from half a dozen to a few hundred employees who halted work for a shift or less. They typically began when management retimed an operation or changed a job assignment and then insisted that the employees meet the new standard or perform the task. If they refused or proved sluggish, managers took disciplinary action by either firing or suspending those who failed to meet their new duties. At this point, the strike issue became less the original grievance than the discipline itself, and an entire department might go out in defense of those penalized. The record of a couple of Chrysler quickies gives a hint of the character of these work stoppages: "Ten machine operators were sent home for refusal to operate two machines as instructed: 23 others walked out in sympathy, neces-sitating sending home 99 others." And in another instance: "Seven em-ployees stopped work in protest of discharge of employee for refusing to perform his operation: five of seven were discharged when they refused to return to work: 320 employees then stopped work and left the plant." Both these strikes lasted for only one shift.[35]

Thus the issue in these strikes was chiefly the control of production and maintenance of discipline. A GM vice-president reported that most of the 1944 strikes in the corporation's plants were "caused by the refusal of small groups of workers to meet production standards." That year, GM reported that about 52 percent of all strikes were a result of "necessary disciplinary action," up from 15 percent in 1940, when wage and recognition issues predominated. Of man-hours lost, almost 83 percent involved disputes over discipline, compared to 4 percent in 1940.[36] The Bureau of Labor Statistics figures for the auto industry, which capture only the larger and longer strikes (at least a shift in duration), show the same trend. Work stoppages to protest discipline, work assignments, and working conditions increased from 205 to 452 between 1943 and 1944 and rose as a percentage of all stoppages from 31 to 43 percent.[37]

In strikes such as those described above, the wage issue was not of paramount concern, except insofar as in-plant wage inequalities exacerbated an already difficult situation. Conversely, when production standards were not a pressing issue but wages were considered unsatisfactory, wildcat strikes were infrequent. In the relatively low-wage airframe plants of California and the Midwest, there were few quickie walkouts over production standards or shop discipline, chiefly because aircraft assembly work was, for the most part, individually paced, task oriented, and physically well spread out. Because of a complex pay scale imposed by the National War Labor Board, all airframe plants generated an enormous number of wage grievances, but these disputes usually involved individual skill reclassifications that provided little basis for collective action. In short, the response of this workforce to the low rate of pay was to move up or move out. Because relatively few could do the former, the turnover rate in these factories was enormous.[38]

A second group of workers who struck infrequently were the highly skilled tool, die, and maintenance workers. Like the aircraft assemblers, they generally controlled the pace of their own labor in an autonomous work environment, but unlike the workers in airframe manufacturing, these skilled workers were among the most union-conscious in the UAW. Their chief grievance was the wage inequalities that the war economy generated in their trade: Tool and die workers found their wages in the major "captive" tool and die shops such as Fisher Body and Ford well below those commanded in the scattered "job" shops of Detroit. Likewise, maintenance men found their pay below that of AFL craftsmen who were sometimes assigned to their work. However, tool and die makers rarely took part in quickie strikes; instead, they sought to move to higher-paying job shops or, after manpower controls were imposed, to use union channels aggressively to win a wage increase from the War Labor Board. Maintenance workers did conduct a city-wide strike in October 1944, but it was basically a political demonstration directed against the War Labor Board, with few of the characteristics of the production standard quickie strikes discussed above.[39]

The quickie strikes that did flare up in the auto industry reveal the extent to which wartime conditions threw auto workers back to a more primitive level of the working-class struggle. The massive social changes associated with the mobilization effort seemed to turn back the clock to the mid-1920s, before stable unionism appeared in the industry. A major demographic convulsion shook Detroit's workforce in the first half of the war, and its social composition came to resemble that of the nonunion era when a "suitcase brigade" of transient workers from the rural South and upper Midwest had been attracted to Detroit by its high wages and urban excitement. About 30 percent of the half million predominantly male factory workers in 1940 had left the area, chiefly for military service; they were more than replaced by some 400,000 new workers. Half of these were from outside the metropolitan area, and about a third were women or youths entering the labor force for the first time. Meanwhile, as the draft took its toll of veteran unionists, the UAW cadre became, like the Wobblies of old, a thin stratum, somewhat older and more skilled than the mass of raw recruits who had not experienced the deeply transforming process of building the unions to which they now paid dues.[40] As a frustrated officer of the UAW's 42,000-member Willow Run local put it, "At the bomber local the majority are paying $1 a month for the privilege of working. They have no understanding at all of the union and are probably a little mystified as to how they ever got into it."[41]

Among the most notable features of this wartime employment surge was the substantial increase in the number of white women and blacks in the industry. Unlike the regional auto boom of the 1920s, the nationwide labor shortage in World War II ultimately forced the major corporations to recruit and upgrade workers who had heretofore been automatically excluded from most sections of the industry. Women's employment in the Detroit–Willow Run area more than doubled during the war, and in some of the newer plants – chiefly in aircraft assembly – they reached 40 percent of the workforce. Of these women, about 90 percent had never before belonged to a union. In Detroit, as elsewhere, World War II proved a watershed in the history of women's work. Before the conflict, the typical woman worker had been young and single; the well-paying jobs available during the war drew into the workforce large numbers of older married women who had worked only intermittently or not at all.[42]

Of course, the new demand for women workers did not fundamentally alter the sexual division of labor in either the factory or the home. To most employers and male workers, and to many women themselves, the new job openings of the 1940s came not as part of a general feminist advance but rather as women's opportunity to aid the war effort and as a more effective way to contribute to the family economy. The economic mobilization led to a shift in the location of the boundaries between men's and women's work, not to the elimination of those boundaries. Thus, many of the jobs women war workers took over were now informally redefined as part of the new realm of "women's work." Aircraft riveting and wiring became predominantly female occupations at Willow Run, although the more highly skilled workers and the foremen in these departments were almost exclusively male. When they were considered an alien intrusion into formerly all-male departments, women suffered a good deal of petty harassment, but except for occasional protests over sexist clothing regulations, women participated in relatively few job actions as a group. Outside of work, severe housing, transportation, and child-care shortages in the Detroit area made the traditional responsibilities of women at home even more difficult. In general, women workers responded to the discrimination they found on the job and the problems they encountered in the wartime household economy on an individual basis. Absenteeism among women was about 50 percent higher than that of men, and their rate of labor turnover more than double.[43]

Black participation in the Detroit labor force increased as rapidly as that of women, growing by almost 100,000, from 8 to 14.5 percent in the five years after 1940. Like white women, blacks began to move out of traditional occupational categories, in their case janitorial and foundry work, and into departments heretofore reserved for white men. But the upgrading of black workers proved far more explosive than that of white women, because it came as part of a larger program of aggressive civil rights action that had begun to sweep the northern black community in the late 1930s and early 1940s. During the war, most blacks adopted the ideology of the "Double V" campaign: victory over the nation's enemies abroad, victory over discrimination and segregation at home. The movement of blacks into new and better jobs would represent, therefore, not a temporary expedient to win the war but the clear start of a fundamental change in social relations.[44]

As blacks sought to move into white jobs, they encountered resistance from many workers and a policy of continued segregation or mere tokenism from key employers in the shipbuilding, aircraft, and transport industries, as well as in auto companies such as Ford, Chrysler, and Packard. As historians August Meier and Elliott Rudwick have recently shown, the UAW's well-known commitment to interracial solidarity at the leadership level often dissipated in the locals, where seniority rules and informal agreements sustained a pattern of white discrimination against black workers. Interracial conflict proved most intense in 1942 and 1943, when a well-coordinated effort by black UAW leaders, the local National Association for the Advancement of Colored People, and liberal elements of the federal bureaucracy and the UAW's top leadership pushed for implementation of President Roosevelt's 1941 executive order banning discrimination in defense industries. This effort was backed by the mobilization of thousands of black workers who took part in numerous protest demonstrations and strike actions. One of the largest came at the foundry unit of the Rouge, a center of black militancy in the auto industry, when 12,000 workers walked off the job in April 1943 to demand that Ford's management accelerate the transfer and hiring of black workers to the corporation's expanded wartime facilities.[45]

Black mobility ushered in the era of Detroit's "hate" strikes that erupted when whites quit work to protest black integration of previously segregated departments. These work stoppages reflected the racism endemic to large sections of the Detroit working class, but that racism was exacerbated by the perception of many whites that factory managers would use the influx of black workers to erode work standards and lessen their job security. Most of these strikes were quickly organized job actions taken by small groups of workers in a single department, although some of the larger stoppages seem to have been either condoned or led by local union officials, possibly in league with fundamentalist "worker–preachers" or Ku Klux Klan members in the plants. Such strikes reached a climax in June 1943, when 25,000 Packard workers walked off the job for a week after two blacks had been promoted to a grinding machine department.[46]

Such racially motivated strikes subsided thereafter, both because of increasingly firm opposition by UAW and government officials and because, after an initial tense integration period, many white workers did accept blacks as part of the factory work environment. Although the number of wildcat strikes over other issues increased after the spring of 1943, hate strikes almost vanished. At the Timken-Detroit Axle Company, for example, three wildcat strikes over racial issues accounted for almost half of all man-hours lost in the eleven work stoppages recorded before September 1943. Thereafter, the number of strikes more than tripled to thirty-six, but only one very minor department protest involved a racial dispute. Detroit remained a city of racial antagonism, but for the next twenty years, such conflicts no longer exploded primarily at the workplace.[47]

Struck by the dramatic demographic changes in the auto–aircraft industry, some observers have argued that the very absence of a union tradition among these several hundred thousand new workers caused the breakdown of factory discipline so evident in these walkouts.[48] The influx of these raw industrial recruits certainly disrupted the usual pattern of factory life, diluted union influence, and generated new racial and sexual conflicts within the workforce. These new workers increased the level of tension within the factory, but their presence alone hardly explains the intensity or the location of the shop-floor conflict that grew during the war. Of greater long-range import was an oppositional infrastructure and a preexisting tradition of struggle into which these new recruits could be acculturated. Thus working-class militancy during World War II was centered not in the "cornfield factories" erected far from the oldest centers of UAW strength, but rather in the unionized shops of Detroit and other industrial centers.

As the workforce at factories such as Briggs, Packard, Dodge, and Ford Highland Park doubled and tripled, the influx of workers untutored in collective action disrupted the tradition of department militancy and the pattern of steward–foreman accommodation. Often, this confusion gave management the opportunity to restructure production and introduce higher output norms. It then fell to the relatively thin line of stewards and union militants to integrate these new workers into the shop-floor culture they hoped to sustain. Normally, this acculturation took place in the day-to-day life of the factory, but sometimes tradition was renewed in a more dramatic fashion. Two sociologists who visited Detroit factories late in the war reported that "we were struck by the fact that several of the most paralyzing strikes were set off by the discharge of men who had been with companies for a long time. In one case a company had set an output standard in an operation on which a large number of inexperienced workers were employed, and that the workers were about to make the standard. Whereupon an old-timer who was also important in the union had come to the youngsters and told them that they ought to stick together and turn out a good deal less. Then the old-timer and some of the new men were fired and the strike was on."[49]

Such job actions represented the class struggle at a fundamental level, but these same disputes over production standards and factory discipline were among the most difficult grievances to define or resolve. Also, given the unequal and imprecise distribution of work and authority in a factory, shop-floor problems might be intensely felt by some workers and not at all by others. Like the work stoppages that flared up in the rubber, auto, electrical, and packinghouse industries during the non-union era, the wartime stoppages were often uncoordinated except on a department or shift level, brief, and led by a changing and sometimes unrepresentative leadership. Their timing and organization could prove awkward, thus providing management with an opportunity to take re-taliatory action.[50]

Although usually led by stewards or popular union militants, these job actions lacked the overall union-building context that had given such prewar strikes a more consistently progressive character. The presence of a large group of inexperienced workers had already diluted union consciousness in the workforce; the CIO's formal no-strike pledge, and the increasingly heavy-handed efforts the leadership took to enforce it, also gave many of these work stoppages a debilitating anti-union flavor. Although an increasing number of shop-floor leaders defended these actions as part of a larger rank-and-file insurgency, the Communists in several unions threw their considerable weight against the coordination of these shop-floor eruptions, arguing instead for the maintenance of the cross-class unity the party thought necessary to win the war against fascism. Under such social and political conditions, a union-organized factory could degenerate into a balkanized set of rival work groups, each seeking to make the best deal possible with management that reflected its importance in the production cycle or its degree of ethnic or occupational combativeness and solidarity.[51]

The union cadre in action

Disaffection of this sort put the secondary leadership of unions such as the UAW under enormous pressure. These were the experienced and committed union cadre – the stewards, committeemen, department chairmen, and local officials – who had built the UAW in the 1930s and who composed its essential organizational infrastructure for many years thereafter. Given the heterogeneous character of the new wartime workforce and the growing management offensive, many of these unionists recognized that without some accommodation to the pressure from below, they might lose the confidence of the rank and file, leading either to their ouster from office or to disintegration of the local. From the point of view of this stratum, the no-strike pledge and, to a lesser extent, the government wage and manpower controls robbed them of much of their effectiveness in the complicated game of thrust and parry, militancy, and accommodation that composed so much of their day-to-day relationship with mid-level plant management. As a GM unionist in Flint put it, "the company took advantage of this situation. The fact that we had pledged that we would not strike meant that when we went in to negotiate something, a mere 'no' was enough. There was nothing much that we could do about it. We had government agencies, of course, and long drawn-out procedures to seek relief but they were so time consuming and so detailed and very, very difficult."[52] As a result, wrote a Briggs local official in a similar quandary, "workers began to ask each other, 'What good is our union? What are we paying dues for, anyway? Why do our leaders let us down like this?'"[53] The Association of Catholic Trade Unionists (ACTU), which generally spoke for the nonradical segment of this leadership group, analyzed the situation with some precision: "Workers may remain loyal to their unions even when no wage increase can be obtained. They may accept wage freezing of unsatisfactory conditions. But if the union loses its capacity to represent its members effectively when they get into trouble with management, it has lost its primary reason for being."[54]

Beginning in 1943, a growing number of secondary leaders sought to restore meaningful unionism to the shop floor. They did this not by championing quickie strikes, although these were sometimes endorsed when they generated mass support, but by channeling the unrest they represented into a more unified and powerful movement. Especially when key union activists were fired, the local leadership might "adopt" a department stoppage and authorize a plant-wide closure. They did so to aggregate grievances, reintegrate their local unions, and close "the gap between the rank and file and their elected leaders."[55] Certainly this was the motivation of Local 91's President Lawrence Wilkey, who told an international executive board committee investigating a four-day wildcat strike at Ohio Crankshaft: "The only time I have ever had respect from the membership is when I finally had guts enough to stand up and face the people we had directing things in Region 2A and tell them I didn't give a damn what they done, I was sticking with my membership."[56]

Such factory-wide, even company-wide, walkouts were often well-led affairs conducted with the apparatus of the traditional strike: picket lines, mass meetings, and a clear set of bargaining demands often directed simultaneously at the international UAW, the plant management, and the National War Labor Board. At the Brewster Aeronautical Corporation in Long Island City, New York, for example, shop-floor tensions reached a climax late in 1942 after the rapidly expanding factory became a part of Henry Kaiser's growing wartime munitions empire. Determined to increase productive efficiency by curbing union power, the new Kaiser management refused to sanction informal shop practices that had given the union a large measure of control over work processes and wage payments without regard to the written contract. In turn, the company's hard line brought to a head plant-wide dissatisfaction with an antiquated and inequitable wage-scale classification system, exacerbated a few months earlier when the new management rejected a job reclassification schedule worked out by a foreman–steward committee. By December 1942, Local 365's appeal to the NWLB had languished in the files of the board's Washington office for eight months, and many of the 14,000 workers at the plant had gone for a full fourteen months without a wage-rate reclassification, although work processes had been radically altered in the meantime. By this point, employee absenteeism and turnover were enormous, slowdowns and shop-floor fights were frequent, and a lagging production schedule had brought the plant to the attention of both the War Department and a congressional committee investigating the defense program.[57]

In the face of this crisis, Local 365's leadership took offensive action. In part because of its unusual location near New York City, the local contained a large number of sophisticated, politically aware workers, students, intellectuals, and others who had "industrialized" during the war both to escape the draft and to attempt to project their politics into the working class. In alliance with Thomas DeLorenzo, the charismatic, politically adroit president of the local, these radicals organized a week-long work-to-rule demonstration late in 1942 to protest the NWLB's delay in adjudicating their case. The slowdown paralyzed production –

management called it a strike – but the well-disciplined job action prodded the board into quickly handing down a directive order that set up a
special panel as final arbiter for all wage classification disputes in the
plant. In those departments where militancy and union organization
remained high, the new panel voted in relatively liberal wage schedules
in the weeks that followed; where workers were less active, the panel
kept wage increases to a minimum.

The incident proved a turning point in the local's political history.
Thereafter, DeLorenzo and others from the local led the opposition to
the CIO's national policies in the UAW's eastern region. They publicly
attacked the no-strike pledge and labor participation on the National
War Labor Board. The local's newspaper, *Aero Notes*, provided non-
Communist radicals, including Trotskyists, with a platform to attack the
national CIO's automatic support of the Roosevelt administration. With
Briggs Local 212 in Detroit, the Brewster local won a reputation as the
most oppositional and politically sophisticated in the entire UAW, pos-
ing a constant irritation to the international's top leadership.[58]

Perhaps a more typical, because a less overtly political, response to
shop-floor dissidence came from the leadership of the several Chrysler
locals centered in Detroit. There, a city-wide strike in May 1943 swept
through all the corporation's major factories when management at the
Dodge Main plant assigned high-paying jobs to newly hired employees
without regard to the seniority list. To protest this contract violation and
break a grievance logjam that had kept the plants in turmoil for several
months, the elected leaders of locals 3 and 7 called mass meetings on May
20 to explain the issues, shut down the plants, and organize effective
picket lines. "It was just like old times," reported one worker. "The
stewards walked through the plant and announced the meeting, and in
five minutes the plant was dead."[59] Other Chrysler plants followed suit,
and soon 24,000 workers were on strike in the Detroit region. Despite
appeals by the head of the UAW's Chrysler department and other high
union officials, the strikers stayed out for four days, returning to work
only after the NWLB offered assurances of a quick hearing on the grievance problem and a rapid decision in the long-pending Chrysler–UAW
contract dispute.[60]

"Official" wildcat strikes such as these did much to restore local union
leadership authority. In fact, there is considerable evidence that where a
strong, union-conscious leadership conducted these work stoppages, the
number of quickie strikes dropped off dramatically. At the Chrysler

Corporation, for example, scores of short stoppages plagued the new war-born defense plants. In the older and more militantly led Detroit locals, however, more experienced and sophisticated leaders forcefully demonstrated the union's power and unity by conducting less frequent but larger and better-organized wildcat strikes during the last two years of the war.[61]

Even where local union leaders fully supported the no-strike pledge, they sometimes condoned industrial action, or its threat, in order to prod their employers and the NWLB. In the summer and fall of 1943, a series of sit-ins, slowdowns, and walkouts at an important east coast shipyard demonstrated the complex relationships that could develop between the grievances of rank-and-file workers, the tactics of the local union leaders, and the administrative response of the NWLB. Shipyard labor was among the highest paid in the nation, but at Federal Shipbuilding and Drydock Company's Kearny, N.J., yard, as along the east coast in general, a complex wage classification scheme greatly exacerbated the grievances of the nearly 25,000 workers represented by Local 16 of the Industrial Union of Marine and Shipbuilding Workers of America. In theory, jobs were classified according to the skill and experience needed, but constant changes in construction methods altered the value and character of much shipyard work, thus generating numerous grievances among several of the yard's traditionally well-defined and cohesive oc-cupational groups. Hookers-on and welders demanded large wage in-creases, and craft-minded building trades workers, who had been re-cruited to the yard in great numbers, objected to the lower industrial pay they received in ship construction. Moreover, among shipyard workers, a tradition of autonomous and independent work prevailed, as it had in peacetime. Supervision was always difficult in a segmented hull, and many foremen were actually working leaders who, despite company objections, considered themselves members of Local 16.[62]

After their first contract expired on June 23, 1943, Local 16 leaders knew that a general wage reclassification would take the NWLB's new Shipbuilding Commission many months to complete. In the meantime, they thought wildcat strikes within the yard might be forestalled if the NWLB offered shipyard workers two things: first, an improved vacation plan, clearly needed because of the yard's long hours and high accident rate, and second, assurance that any wage adjustment would be made retroactive to June 1943, when the contract expired. In addition, Local 16 officers sought greater institutional security: a dues checkoff to complement the maintenance-of-membership clause they had won from the NWLB in 1942 and company-paid release time for shop stewards to handle grievances.

Throughout the summer of 1943, Local 16 leaders shuttled to Washington to prod the NWLB into action. They got a cool reception from the overburdened board until they enlisted the help of Jersey City's powerful mayor, Frank Hague, who secured a personal assurance from NWLB Chairman William Davis that their case would soon be adjudicated. As the weeks dragged on, however, some workers baited the local leadership for "being afraid to strike." Slowdowns and short stoppages increased in frequency as the slogan "No dues until we get action" appeared around the yard. After one particularly large sit-down strike by the hookers-on, IUMSWA President William Green had to fly to Kearney to plead for a return to work.[63]

By this time, Local 16's leaders had begun a subtle accommodation to the temper of their members. Mass meetings to report on negotiations with the NWLB were moved from a downtown auditorium to the yard itself, where they necessarily halted production. President John Dempsey and other Local 16 officials were still vocally opposed to strike action, but a tacit alliance had been made with the more militant groups. As one union activist recounted, "Though no open threat was made in the politely worded telegram sent to the NWLB, Washington could draw its own conclusion. Unless there was action in the capital, there was going to be action in the shipyards – plenty of it."[64]

In mid-September 1943, the NWLB's Shipbuilding Commission finally came through with a directive that granted the local the union security provisions its leadership wanted, instituted a vacation plan, and offered retroactivity to a large but annoyingly indeterminate number of workers. As expected, reclassification was put off for more study. Knowledgeable observers considered the decision to be the minimum that would keep the shipyard workers from striking, but Federal Shipbuilding's management, worried about postwar competitiveness in a shrinking market, nevertheless appealed the commission order to the full NWLB. With the case again in limbo, shipyard tensions mounted, and on October 13, 13,000 walked out for two days. Again, IUMSWA President Green ordered a return to work, and Local 16 leaders, fearful of losing their newly won dues checkoff and recognizing that any strike could be little more than a demonstration, started a back-to-work movement that successfully returned the men to the yards with the local's

Table 2. *Work stoppages in the United States, 1932–47*

Year	Number	Average duration (days)	Workers involved (thousands)
1932	841	19.6	324
1933	1,695	16.9	1,170
1934	1,856	19.5	1,470
1935	2,014	23.8	1,120
1936	2,172	23.3	789
1937	4,740	20.3	1,860
1938	2,772	23.6	688
1939	2,613	23.4	1,170
1940	2,508	20.9	577
1941	4,288	18.3	2,360
1942	2,968	11.7	840
1943	3,752	5.0	1,980
1944	4,956	5.6	2,120
1945	4,750	9.9	3,470
1946	4,985	24.2	4,600
1947	3,693	25.6	2,170

Source: U.S. Department of Labor, *Handbook of Labor Statistics, 1974, Bulletin 1825,* (Washington, D.C., 1974), 367.

authority intact. The strike proved effective, however, in bringing a rapid NWLB confirmation of the Shipbuilding Commission's order.[65] Of course, work-site agitation and job actions did not cease, especially as it became apparent that the long-delayed reclassification would bring only minor wage increases. In 1944, man-hours lost to stoppages were about five times greater than they had been in 1943, and in early 1945 a Rank-and-File caucus pledged to independent political action and revocation of the no-strike pledge nearly won control of Local 16.[66]

Throughout American industry, wildcat strike activity increased steadily until the fall of 1945, when these stoppages merged, in a statistical sense, with the general postwar strike wave. The number of strikes and the number of workers on strike in 1942 were on a par with most of the peacetime depression years. In 1943, the number of workers on strike more than doubled, chiefly because of the four official Mine Workers' strikes of that year, but in 1944 and 1945 the number of walkouts and the number of workers on strike continued to increase even while the United Mine Workers remained at work (see Table 2). These strikes were quite short. The five- or ten-day average reported by the Bureau of Labor Statistics probably overstates their length because

Table 3. *Workers involved in strikes as a percentage of industry workforce*

Industry	1941	1942	1943	1944	1945	1946	Workforce in 1944 (thousands)
All industry	8.4	2.8	6.9	7.0	12.1	14.5	41,883
Manufacturing	12.2	NA	NA	11.3	19.2	16.7	17,328
Textiles	7.9	7.2	4.4	4.6	9.3	3.8	1,197
Printing	NA	2.4	0.6	0.7	3.7	3.2	558
Rubber	27.1	10.1	46.8	18.5	127.3	39.1	285
Iron and steel	20.4	6.0	20.4	20.3	26.4	54.1	1,279[b]
Auto/aircraft	39.0	8.4	26.8	50.5	75.9	21.7	3,682
Mining	105.6[a]	10.5	86.2	34.3	89.8	120.1	892
Construction	11.2	1.9	3.4	3.5	5.8	10.3	1,094
Electrical machinery	8.7	3.6	4.7	4.4	18.4	40.1	1,087

[a]More than 100 percent indicates that some workers struck more than once.
[b]The 1946 figure for "primary metal industry."
Source: Data compiled from *Monthly Labor Review* (May issues), 1942–7, and U.S. Department of Labor, *Handbook of Labor Statistics, 1974*, Bulletin 1825 (Washington, D.C., 1974), 103–5.

many of the smaller quickie stoppages remained unreported. In the auto industry, where strikes were quite large and therefore highly visible, the stoppages averaged three and a half days in length in 1944.[67]

The size of these stoppages grew as well, and by the second half of the war they had become as large as those of prewar years, despite the formal no-strike pledge maintained by almost all unions. The average number of workers involved in the 4,956 reported strikes in 1944 was 427. About 43 percent of the strikes involved fewer than 100 workers, and 8 percent involved over 1,000 workers each. There were eighty-two stoppages involving 1,000 or more workers each in the iron and steel industry, seventy-six in plants manufacturing transportation equipment (except automobiles), and sixty-eight in the converted-automobile industry. In all, the Bureau of Labor Statistics recorded forty-one strikes involving more than 5,000 workers each in 1944 and 106 strikes involving more than that number in 1945.[68]

The proportion of all American workers who participated in wartime strikes quadrupled after 1942, reaching about an eighth of the workforce by the time of the surrender of Japan in September 1945 (see Table 3). Wildcat strikes were centered in the highly integrated mass-production rubber and converted automobile factories, where half or more of all

Table 4. *Proportion of all strikes by labor union affiliation*

	CIO		AFL		Unaffiliated[a]		Unorganized	
	Strikes	Workers	Strikes	Workers	Strikes	Workers	Strikes	Workers
1941	36.6	69.5	54.3	24.7	1.6	1.1	3.0	0.9
1942	34.1	45.1	53.3	39.9	3.7	6.3	4.7	1.9
1943	36.6	44.3	37.3	19.6	15.7	32.5	7.3	1.6
1944	39.2	52.2	34.2	21.5	20.1	19.2	4.2	1.2
1945	40.3	49.3	37.2	19.8	17.2	27.3	2.8	0.4
1946	33.3	41.8	54.8	33.9	6.4	13.1	1.9	0.3

[a]Includes the United Mine Workers after 1942.
Source: Data compiled from *Monthly Labor Review* (May issues), 1942–7.

workers took part in wartime strikes in 1944 and 1945. Of the sixteen strikes involving over 10,000 workers each in 1944, eleven took place in the auto–aircraft industry. About a fifth of the workers struck each year in steel and shipbuilding, but only about 5 percent in textiles and electrical machinery. In crafts such as printing and construction, wartime stoppages were rare; when they did take place, they were small. As a consequence, workers in CIO-organized industries made up about half of all wartime strikers, even though the AFL and independent unions such as the United Mine Workers enrolled at least 2 million more workers than the industrial union federation (see Table 4). And because the mass-production industries had been largely converted to military production, CIO strikes were among the most publicized and politically sensitive of the war. In a typical two-week period in late March 1943, the army found that of all workers engaged in stoppages that halted war production, 87 percent were organized in CIO affiliates.[69] Although such strikes had only a minuscule impact on the nation's overall production effort, their reverberations within union and national politics proved far-reaching in the second half of the war.

8. Incentive pay politics

The union movement's relative political impotence, the government's increasingly restrictive wage guidelines, and the growing unrest symbolized by the wildcat strikes all provided the context for a bitter factional conflict that divided many CIO unions, above all the United Automobile Workers, the key trade union in the nation during the 1940s. Although such factional warfare sometimes degenerated into a mere quest for office by rival groups of union leaders, many of the actual issues that divided these men rose directly out of the dilemma the organized working class faced during the era of political retreat and wartime economic regimentation. As a consequence, those unionists who had a larger vision of the strategy the unions should pursue – the Communists on one side, the Trotskyists and socialists on the other – played a considerably larger role in focusing and enlarging the debate than their numerical strength would suggest.

The government-sponsored incentive pay program

The unrest pervading the UAW ranks burst into union-wide debate early in 1943, when General Motors and the War Production Board sought to enlist the union leadership's support for the introduction of a widespread system of incentive pay in the auto–aircraft industry. In its 1942 negotiations with the UAW's GM department, the corporation demanded that as part of the union's contribution to the war effort, the UAW agree to negotiate an incentive pay system that would establish differentials in wage rates to reward employees who produced more and better work. Initially, UAW negotiators vetoed the idea, backed shortly thereafter by the National War Labor Board, which probably felt that the union and the government would have enough difficulty in putting over the newly minted Little Steel formula.[1] Undeterred by this setback, GM executives took their idea to the War Production Board as a means of boosting production during a period of increasing manpower shortages. Not unexpectedly, the dollar-a-year businessmen who staffed the WPB proved more receptive, and in October 1942 they convinced the NWLB to exempt from the Little Steel formula "any adjustments that might be made for increased productivity under piecework or incentive plans." The WPB plan called for the pay of everyone in a plant to rise in partial proportion to the increase in production. WPB specialists considered such group piecework programs more efficient and equitable than older individual piecework schedules, because now all employees in a plant, including nonproduction workers, could benefit. And the WPB hoped to allay union fears by introducing incentive pay only after such wage plans had met a series of NWLB guidelines, and only after these schemes had passed inspection by the individual unions involved. [2]

The WPB incentive pay proposal itself was not radically innovative. Union-negotiated piecework standards were already decades old in the clothing and coal mining industries, where a tradition of skilled, autonomous manual work made for wide variations in employee productivity. Piecework enabled the relatively strong unions to standardize unit labor costs, thus stabilizing their collective bargaining relationships with numerous small competing employers and enabling the unions to enforce work-sharing schemes during slack time. In other more recently organized industries such as steel, electrical equipment, and rubber, piecework or group bonus plans still covered about half of the workforce. Skilled production workers such as tire builders or steel rollers, who enjoyed a high level of small-group control of production, were especially able to manipulate the incentive system to their advantage, often doubling, sometimes even tripling their pay, in comparison to other less advantageously situated workers. Because elimination of piecework would mean a reduction in pay for these workers, many locals jealously defended such incentive pay schemes in the interests of those who held the good jobs. [3]

Despite its deep entrenchment in these industries, incentive pay remained in disrepute among the more sophisticated leaders of the union movement. Trade union officials had traditionally opposed these pay schemes because of the arbitrary fashion in which management had imposed them, the often incomprehensible pay calculations they entailed, and the temptation they offered supervisors to reduce periodically the rate per unit to keep the general wage level constant while output soared. The AFL had campaigned against time studies and piecework since Frederick Taylor and his followers had popularized the idea early in the century, and the federation had kept the plan out of military arsenals and most shipyards since World War I. Strong craft unions in the printing and building trades prohibited any form of incentive pay by contractual agreement. In the 1930s, industrial union organizers made an attack on piecework and speedup a central part of their appeal to unskilled production workers. Even before the UAW became a powerful institution, auto worker resistance to the system had become so pronounced that most of the large companies in the industry had reduced substantially their reliance on the pay scheme.[4]

The War Production Board's push for wage incentives might have remained a dead letter if not for the growing crisis faced by UAW leaders in the spring of 1943. By this time, the virtual wage freeze imposed by the War Labor Board had begun to generate enormous counterpressures from the industrial union rank and file, and no UAW leader seemed in greater difficulty than Richard Frankensteen, the conservative, often opportunistic UAW vice-president in charge of the union's sprawling aircraft division. As director of the organizing campaign in the giant new industry, Frankensteen had just been dealt two stunning blows. First, in a referendum vote, the union's increasingly disaffected membership had turned down an executive board proposal for a dues increase, the money from which would have gone to defray organizational expenses in California, Texas, and other states where the new aircraft plants were being built.[5] Factories there were located in regions remote from older centers of UAW strength, and many paid staffers were necessary to organize the new industrial workers in these plants.

Second, and more importantly, the NWLB had delivered a body blow to organizational efforts in aircraft by turning down an across-the-board wage increase for several hundred thousand California aircraft workers. Ever since the North American Aviation strike, Frankensteen had relied upon the government to upgrade and standardize wages in the industry, which the aircraft director hoped to make an important power base for his advancement to the UAW presidency. Now, this policy seemed in a shambles.[6] A few days after the NWLB issued its unexpectedly tough wage order in early March, scattered wildcat strikes broke out in west coast aircraft plants, but most of this protest centered in International Association of Machinists-organized factories, especially in the giant Boeing facility in Seattle and the Consolidated Aircraft plants of San Diego. Frankensteen did not fear a general strike or a rank-and-file revolt; rather, he worried that low wage ceilings would generate an exodus of workers from the industry, a rejection of unionism by those who remained, and a failure of the UAW aircraft organizational drive.[7]

This unionization effort already suffered from a multitude of difficulties. Among the thousands of teenagers, rural migrants, and women – by mid-1943 more than 60 percent of all new employees – who poured into the plants, few had any previous industrial work experience, let alone contact with organized trade unionism. Even where the UAW held collective bargaining rights, rapid turnover among the lowest-paid workers kept union organizers scrambling continuously for new recruits. A visiting Detroit-based UAW staffer reported that the west coast locals appeared "flimsy" and "ready to be blown into the ocean by the first big storm."[8] At North American Aviation, the labor turnover rate stood at 110 percent a year. Because union activists could not keep up with the revolving workforce, membership in the local declined steadily after 1942. A month after the NWLB wage edict, the UAW formally withdrew its petition for a corporation-wide National Labor Relations Board election in the four giant plants of the Southern California-based Douglas Aircraft Corporation.[9] "We no longer have the approach we once had of telling these workers that if they join up with us, we have a very tangible something to put into their hands," complained Frankensteen, "that we can get them a wage increase, that we will get them five, ten or fifteen cents an hour and their retroactive pay."[10]

After the NWLB's wage freeze decision in March, Frankensteen became convinced that introduction of incentive pay remained the only method left by which to circumvent the Little Steel formula and revive the lagging aircraft drive without a disruptive political confrontation with the Roosevelt administration. His perspective coincided neatly with that of incentive pay advocates in government and management, who also worried that excessive labor turnover on the west coast threatened to limit war production in the vital aircraft industry. By early 1943, labor time per pound of aircraft produced had already dropped some 50 percent and promised to decline still further as the industry refined its manufacturing techniques. A War Production Board Advisory Committee, of which Frankensteen was a member, concluded that the general adoption of group incentives in aircraft would have the effect of raising wages there substantially and stabilizing the workforce. Inexperienced aircraft workers seemed unconcerned with labor's traditional opposition to incentive pay, and Frankensteen feared that they would become further disenchanted with the union if his organization seemed to stand in the way of a fatter wage envelope. UAW organizers already felt compelled to support continuation of a preexisting incentive pay plan at a Missouri aircraft plant because of its popularity with the workers there.[11]

Frankensteen brought the WPB proposals to the UAW executive board on March 10, 1943. He urged the union to take the initiative in negotiating new incentive pay schemes; otherwise, Frankensteen feared, the WPB would go ahead anyway, and employers would be free to coerce their workers into accepting unsatisfactory incentive pay plans detrimental to the union. Although the UAW executive board unanimously reaffirmed the union's "traditional opposition to incentive payment plans," the aircraft director actually made progress at the meeting. Local unions were given the right to negotiate for wage incentives if their plans were approved by the international and if such schemes met a detailed set of UAW guidelines designed to avoid erosion of labor standards or wage rates.[12] The push for wage incentives in the UAW thus might have been quietly compromised had it not been for two additional political developments that made the question a high-profile controversy; first, the strong support given the scheme by the Communists and their allies in the UAW, and second, Roosevelt's promulgation of the hold-the-line order in early April, which made incentive pay part of the political debate over the government's entire labor policy.

The Communists

The Communists' identification with the wartime incentive pay issue proved important because of the party's significance in shaping the politics of the liberal wing of the New Deal coalition and because of the influence the party exerted within several of the industrial unions. Scholars as different in their approach as Bert Cochran and Roger Keeran have recently demonstrated that the legitimacy of the Communists within the CIO rested upon their vital role in the formation of the new unions during the 1930s. Unlike the Socialists, whose fortunes were but temporarily revived in the early depression years, the Communists were able to give their trade union work a strategic coherence that won them recruits and influence throughout this period. By the mid-1930s, they were the largest single ideological group from which the CIO drew its shop-floor cadre and union organizers. In the maritime, electrical, and auto industries, Communist dual unions merged into the CIO, and party members easily moved into influential posts as the new institutions grew in size and power. In the steel and packinghouse drives, the Communists were for a time virtually indispensable to the success of the day-to-day struggle in the field.[13]

In the late 1930s and early 1940s, membership in the Communist party fluctuated between 60,000 and 80,000, but its influence easily extended to a periphery of "fellow travelers" and ex-members perhaps ten times that size. The core of party strength within the industrial working class consisted of skilled workers who combined a tradition of militant job control and craft pride with a vision of social transformation. Communist influence among English and Scottish tool and die makers in Detroit, Finnish lumbermen and iron ore miners in Minnesota, skilled craftsmen at Allis-Chalmers, General Electric and Westinghouse, and Jewish furriers and the worldly seamen and longshoremen of New York and San Francisco rested upon this stratum. A relatively stable component of the party, this layer of the working class gave the Communists much of the continuity of their shop-floor leadership.[14]

During the late 1930s and early 1940s, this stratum was of declining weight within both the party and its industrial base. The majority of the party's growth after 1935 had come from an influx of second-generation Jewish white-collar and professional workers, who helped boost the nonblue-collar component of its membership from about 5 percent to almost 45 percent. In effect, the party transformed itself from a predominantly foreign-born, largely working-class organization to one that was more Americanized and half middle class. At the same time, a recomposition of its industrial base began to take place in the 1940s as workers of considerably less skill and factory experience began to join the party. Middle-class elements in white-collar occupations or temporary heavy-industry war work were important in this group, but so too were blacks and working-class ethnics in autos, meatpacking, and steel. During the war, the loosening of party structures and the easing of its membership requirements facilitated the recruitment of such workers. After enrolling 15,000 new members in 1943, party organizational secretary John Williamson took note of the character of these recruits: "We cannot expect to be the same well-knit organization that we were when we were smaller and composed of a group of conscious and tested Communists."[15]

Many of the party's new wartime members found in the patriotic and

populist orientation of the Communists a means by which groups excluded from the mainstream of civic and cultural life could affirm their
own Americanism in a progressive pluralist fashion. The party's record
in the fight against racism made it particularly attractive to American
blacks; to this overwhelmingly working-class minority, the party served
as a cultural and political bridge between the insular world of the racial
ghetto and active participation in the politics of the labor movement and
the larger community. During the war, about one-third of the industrial
workers joining the party were black. Of course, the turnover among
such wartime recruits was enormous, and the allegiance of the party's
industrial base remained less than that of its other adherents. For example, in Michigan, where the party had its greatest factory concentration,
two-thirds of the membership had been on party rolls for less than a year
in the mid-1940s.[16]

Despite the instability of its industrial enrollment, Communist influence within the CIO remained significant during the wartime era. In
part, this reflected the fact that in the crucial ten years after 1935,
Communist goals in the new unions largely coincided with those of CIO
leaders such as John L. Lewis and Philip Murray, as well as with the
militant union-building sentiment of many thousands of rank-and-file
activists on the shop floor. Although the Communist commitment to the
Soviet Union as the symbol of the socialist ideal remained inviolable and
provided the essential ideological element that engendered loyalty in the
party cadre, the actual trade union activities of the party came to differ
little from those of unionists in the CIO mainstream. As vocal supporters
of the New Deal and the war effort, the Communists moved easily
within the social democratic current of the late 1930s and the social
patriotic enthusiasm of the wartime mobilization.[17] And as we have
seen, even during the era of the Nazi–Soviet pact, when the party stood
most strongly opposed to the Roosevelt administration and the CIO on
international issues, the militant trade union tactics of party activists
more often coincided than clashed with those of the national CIO.

Thus, by 1943 the Communists were a powerful force in unions
representing between a quarter and a third of all CIO union members.
They held top posts in the CIO's third largest affiliate, the 600,000-
member United Electrical, Radio and Machine Workers, and maintained a sizable following and occupied leading offices in such strategically important smaller unions as the International Longshoremen's
and Warehousemen's Union, the National Maritime Union, the Trans-

port Workers Union, the International Fur and Leather Workers, and in the United Farm Equipment and Metal Workers. They played a significant role within the internal life of both the United Packinghouse Workers and the UAW. The Communists controlled outright a number of international unions, such as the American Communications Association, and United Office and Professional Employees, and the United Furniture Workers, which were little more than organizing committees; nevertheless, these posts helped give them a considerable presence within the CIO hierarchy. James Carey, the anti-Communist secretary-treasurer of the CIO, once estimated that nineteen of forty-one union representatives on the CIO's executive board were part of a "left-progressive" Communist-influenced group.[18] The party's legitimacy in the high councils of the organization was such that both CIO attorney Lee Pressman and *CIO News* editor Len DeCaux were both open fellow travelers. Meanwhile, the party itself cultivated a national presence, calling frequently upon such well-known figures as singer Paul Robeson, Congressman Vito Marcantonio, and ILWU President Harry Bridges to help project its viewpoint. *The Daily Worker* covered the labor movement closely and maintained a circulation of about 100,000 during the war.

It is important to recognize, however, that Communist organizational influence was far from monolithic. The decentralized character of the new industrial unions and the local nexus of power in the CIO precluded tight control by any political group. At both the national and local levels, trade union leaders and shop-floor activists functioned in a complicated social milieu that limited their power and often reshaped their politics. Certainly, the Communists and those who chose fellow traveler status in the 1940s were the most coherent and distinct political entity within the CIO (with the possible exception of the Trotskyist groups), but a gap could often exist between the promulgation of a political line in New York and its translation into party activity at the base. Some party cadres in heavy industry more or less abstained when it came to a vocal defense of the no-strike pledge in a grievance-plagued factory, and Communist incentive pay proposals proved unpopular among many skilled craft workers in the party.[19] Moreover, party influence rarely pervaded an entire international union, even when Communists occupied the top posts and controlled the newspaper and field staff. Thus a coalition of Communist and nonparty allies ousted James Carey from the UE presidency in September 1941, but they never dominated all the important locals and districts in the organization. Similarly, Reid Robinson and others close to the party held the chief posts in the Mine, Mill and Smelter Workers International throughout the war, but their power proved insufficient to eliminate vigorous union opposition among New England brass foundry workers.[20]

Both the Communists and their opponents saw the UAW as the crucial arena of political conflict within the CIO. By organizing new workers in the booming munitions, tank, truck transport, aircraft engine, and airframe factories, the UAW had more than doubled its membership after 1941, reaching a wartime peak of 1,250,000 by early 1944. With a secondary leadership described by Dwight Macdonald as "articulate, aggressive and infinitely disrespectful to its top officers," the UAW's factional conflict achieved a level of sophistication and democratic participation unparalleled in any CIO union.[21] The Communist party's weight in the UAW had probably reached its peak in 1938 and 1939 as a consequence of the key role it had played in the fight against Homer Martin's disastrous leadership of the union. Although its power declined during the last year of the Stalin–Hitler pact, the German invasion of the Soviet Union and American entry into the war renewed its legitimacy among many workers in the auto/aircraft industry. In the year following Pearl Harbor, the Communists rebuilt and doubled the size of their UAW membership; by early 1943, the party probably numbered about 1,200 active members in the industry, with a periphery several times that size.

None of the top officers of the UAW were Communists, but the party provided much of the leadership that gave the internal union caucus, led by George Addes and Richard Frankensteen, its political coherence. This did not mean that either Addes or Frankensteen consciously functioned within a Communist world view; rather, their relationship to the party represented an alliance of mutual support whose overriding objective was to deny the aggressive Reuther caucus full control of the union. Among the important figures of this caucus were UAW regional directors Leo LaMotte and Charles Kerrigan, who stood near the Communist party on many questions. James Wishart, the UAW research director, and Maurice Sugar, the union attorney, were among the more prominent of the several UAW staff members who were active in the Addes–Frankensteen group. UAW Communists were either the local officers or key figures in several important locals in Detroit, Cleveland, Milwaukee, and on the west coast. In the motor city, Communists held top posts in Plymouth Local 51, Packard Local 190, Bohn Aluminum

Local 208, and Amalgamated Local 155 representing the tool and die workers. They were a strong force at the River Rouge, where they had built a presence among black foundrymen and among the skilled tradesmen of the maintenance and tool and die units.[22]

Despite this extensive organizational influence, the main impact of the Communists – in both the UAW and the CIO – stemmed less from the offices they held than from the ideology they advanced. The persistent theme of the Communists during the war was the need for the unity of all "progressive win-the-war forces." They defended the no-strike pledge with passion and prided themselves on their support of Philip Murray and the official CIO line. Communist spokesmen urged the labor movement to agree to all concessions demanded by the government, not so much as a necessary tactical retreat, which was often the perspective of leaders such as Philip Murray and Richard Frankensteen, but as a progressive step in itself, one that mirrored on the home front the Big Three unity that Churchill, Roosevelt, and Stalin would forge at the Teheran Conference in mid-1943. "In the United States we have to win this war under the capitalist system," declared Communist leader Earl Browder in his *Victory and After*. "Therefore we have to make the capitalist system work . . . we have to help the capitalists to learn how to run their own system under war conditions."[23] Blunter still was Harry Bridges at a CIO executive board meeting in 1942: "You have to get down to brass tacks in your own union . . . We will talk speedup, because you know what speedup means. Production involves management, machinery and everything, but speedup involves the workers: and we talked action, speedup and we are going to keep it up and get more of it, we are not ashamed of it."[24]

The appeal of this ideology during the war should not be underestimated. For the mass of new workers who had not come out of a syndicalist or craft tradition, incentive pay and the speedup idea carried relatively little negative meaning. On the contrary, they paralleled the CIO's own productionist propaganda and seemed to affirm the patriotic sentiment of many Americans. Moreover, by giving the world conflict an uncritically progressive quality, by forecasting a postwar era of class peace and social progress, the Communists provided a rationale for those in the union movement and the progressive community who sought to reconcile the waning power of domestic labor–liberalism with their own radical and anticapitalist sensibilities. Otherwise reactionary programs, such as advocacy of incentive pay or imposition of undemocratic forms of internal union discipline, were justified because they strengthened the left–center bloc within the CIO and the win-the-war forces in the world battle against fascism. In turn, this attitude rationalized to the CIO rank and file the conservative politics of such union leaders as Murray, Thomas, and Hillman by defending their unchallenged leadership as vital to the unity of progressive pro-Roosevelt forces in America.

Given this political perspective, the Communists welcomed the War Production Board's incentive pay proposals and favored widespread application of the system. The *California Labor Herald*, controlled by Bridges, reported with enthusiasm the success of several such plans on the west coast. UE leaders announced the full cooperation of their union with NWLB incentive pay advocates. Several UAW local papers publicized the idea early in 1943.[25] In a widely distributed pamphlet, "Production for Victory," Earl Browder forecast that all wartime wages would soon be tied to increased productivity. With characteristic over-enthusiasm, the party leader commented, "If we still have any prejudices that make it impossible to talk to anyone who works for Bedaux [a management consultant and time study company] let us get rid of them. The Bedaux production experts, in alliance with the labor movement, will help smash Nazism everywhere in the world."[26]

Reuther and the UAW militants

Frankensteen's incentive pay proposals won more restrained, but perhaps more significant, support from the national CIO itself after Roosevelt issued his jarring hold-the-line order in early April. Although traditional-minded unionists such as George Meany and John L. Lewis vigorously denounced the new edict as a unilateral breach of the promises made to labor when they agreed to join the National War Labor Board in 1941, the CIO responded more cautiously, even after public members of the NWLB itself nearly threw up their hands in despair. A circular to all international union affiliates, prepared by Lee Pressman but sent out over Murray's signature, welcomed Executive Order 9328's ostensible promise to roll back the price line but made no mention of the CIO's campaign to revise upward the Little Steel formula. Instead the CIO announced, "Today we must accept the basic principle of stabilization of wages," of which a growing element was the institution of NWLB-approved incentive wage programs. "This general category," wrote Murray, "is one that promises to be of extreme importance to labor and should be examined very closely." When queried as to whether this represented endorsement of incentive pay, Murray replied, "The CIO is neutral."[27] Of course, when linked with an accommodation to a rigid Little Steel formula, such neutrality proved a green light to those who favored implementation of the government-sponsored incentive pay proposals.

This rather supine acquiescence in the government's most rigid wage edict occurred as CIO leaders braced for the battle between John L. Lewis and the government over the United Mine Workers' demand for a two-dollar-a-day wage increase. The conflict and its impact on CIO politics in the spring of 1943 are closely examined in Chapter 9. Suffice it to say that much of the top CIO leadership, backed strongly by Communist elements within the unions, feared that if Lewis successfully used the strike weapon to break the Little Steel formula and destroy the authority of the NWLB, then they would find their entire policy of cooperation with the government in disrepute. An open revolt of their rank and file, led by a dissident secondary leadership, would then be a real possibility, especially in such volatile unions as the UAW or the United Rubber Workers where Lewis's militant tactics enjoyed much support. This fear impelled Murray to actually welcome much of the thrust behind the harsh hold-the-line executive order as a means of strengthening the NWLB in its forthcoming struggle with Lewis and the miners. Incentive wages seemed a legitimate means of circumventing the strict wage ceiling imposed by Executive Order 9328 and might relieve some of the pressure generated from the ranks. "There is now manifest a change in the attitude of organized labor," reported an NWLB observer in the West. "Although the American Federation of Labor still appears non-committal, it is noted that the CIO is not only showing an active interest in the problems, but has more or less committed itself to the principles underlying wage incentive systems."[28]

But the last word on incentive pay came from the union rank and file, or rather from that politically alert stratum that provided the real leadership in the shops and local union halls. In Flint, Detroit, and Toledo, long experience with such plans in the auto industry's preunion era had convinced UAW activists that incentive pay meant speedup, stretchout, and a complicated wage rate schedule incomprehensible to the average worker. Although the WPB's group incentives were based on increased pay for a collective rise in production, the impact on the elementary solidarity of the union could be as disastrous as old-fashioned piecework. "I never saw anything that . . . would separate us into a number of quarreling backbiting groups so easy," asserted one union veteran. "The luckier physically fit would'ride the unlucky man, causing arguments and hard feelings."[29]

Of course, midwestern workers felt inadequate wartime pay to be as great a problem as those in California, but the main difficulty these more union-conscious workers faced was the erosion of the grievance procedure and the growing managerial challenge to union power on the shop floor. Complaining that "collective bargaining has broken down," they doubted whether any of the incentive pay guidelines proposed by the NWLB, the CIO, or the UAW itself promised safety if foremen and supervisors regained the raw authority to manipulate production and pay schedules as they wished.[30] Finally, incentive pay had powerful symbolic qualities linked to the meaning of unionism itself. "We fought nine years to eliminate piecework and haven't been able to do it yet," argued Toledo UAW leader Richard Gosser in the 1943 UAW convention. "You put it up now and by God our children's children won't eliminate it."[31]

By mid-April, letters and telegrams opposed to the Frankensteen incentive pay proposals had poured into the UAW national office. Late in the month, a delegation of eleven Detroit area union presidents organized by Emil Mazey, the socialist president of Briggs Local 212, descended upon a Cleveland meeting of the UAW executive board to demand not only a formal denunciation of incentive pay but also rejection of Roosevelt's new wage guidelines. Mazey and a slate of like-minded unionists had just swept the local elections at Briggs, regaining control of that traditionally militant local on a program of opposition to the no-strike pledge, hostility to the Communists, and support of independent political action for labor. Another equally significant indication of rank-and-file sentiment came at Ford Local 600, where incentive pay became such an explosive and unpopular issue that a Communist-backed group running in a hard-fought election found it expedient to dissociate themselves from the idea.[32] In fact, opposition to incentive production schemes also arose among veteran unionists in trade unions well within the Communist orbit. In 1942 Harry Bridges had met a storm of opposition when he tried to convince a meeting of 3,000 Los Angeles longshoremen to increase their slingloads. And in Schenectady, New York, Communist party organizer Max Gordon found equal resistance to UE incentive pay proposals among the skilled workers at General Electric.

"The guys in the shop said to me, 'For Christ's sake, Max, if we go all out and quadruple our production, what happens after the war?' They wouldn't do it."[33]

Alone among the top leaders of the UAW, Walter Reuther recognized the implications of the growing rank-and-file revolt on incentive pay. Reuther was an open-minded opportunist in this era, supremely ambitious for power but always keenly sensitive to the moods and anxieties of the decisive secondary leadership in his union. Since 1940, he had worked to build a broad constituency within the UAW based on a policy of political liberalism and support of a progressive-minded mobilization effort. Reuther won a national reputation for imaginative labor leadership on the basis of his 500-planes-a-day proposal in 1941 and his Equality of Sacrifice program in early 1942. As recently as March 1943, he had led 250 local union officials on a morale-building junket to Camp Atterbury, Indiana, for three days of training as foot soldiers.[34] But the grand effort to link a progressive social program to the wartime mobilization effort had proved unsuccessful by 1943, and Reuther had the political intelligence to recognize this failure earlier than most CIO leaders. The growing rank-and-file revolt on incentive pay provided him with the opportunity to champion internal union discontent, consolidate his loose-knit caucus, and carve for himself a new and more militant image sharply distinguished from that of other UAW leaders, who clung tenaciously to the increasingly tarnished Rooseveltian mobilization effort.

In championing the popular opposition to incentive pay, Reuther came into political alliance with elements far more radical than he: opponents of the no-strike pledge, supporters of John L. Lewis, advocates of independent political action for labor, Socialists, and Trotskyists. The last were certainly the smallest numerically, but they were not without influence in the fluid politics of the UAW faction fight. Divided into two groups, the "orthodox" Socialist Workers party and Max Schachtman's "third camp" Workers party, they together had about 200 members in the auto industry, many in such war baby locals as Brewster 365 and Willow Run 50, where young, ideological radicals taking their first industrial job could win influence in the unstructured political and social climate of these large factories. They cooperated with the Reutherites on many questions but attempted to give a consistently radical focus and organizational direction to the quasi-rebellious mood of the UAW rank and file. They defended the wildcat strikes and provided much of the impetus for the Rank and File caucus that challenged the no-strike pledge outright in 1944 and 1945.[35] With the Trotskyists and others to his left, Reuther could successfully unite in opposition to WPB piecework proposals and the government's more audacious efforts at labor regimentation. Anything beyond such a tactical coalition promised to strain the radical–Reuther alliance. In the next few years, the success or failure of Walter Reuther's politics in the UAW would rest upon the difficult attempt to balance his relationship with the radical left against the more conservative demands of a union officer and loyal CIO adherent.

Although Reuther had been willing to allow Frankensteen to use incentive pay in the aircraft industry when the latter first proposed adoption of the WPB plan in March, the GM director's rejection of the scheme hardened in April after widespread opposition grew among the locals and after the Communists became even more forcefully identified with the idea. Reuther helped to politicize the question further and at an April 19 UAW executive board meeting won a bare majority to table Frankensteen's proposal. Reuther argued that the widespread use of incentive pay would defeat the UAW's long-standing efforts to equalize wages throughout the aircraft industry and to secure industry-wide collective bargaining. Incentive pay plans would raise wages among aircraft workers, but these schemes would also introduce myriad wage rate variables among the partially equalized auto–aircraft plants of the Detroit, Ohio, and eastern UAW regions. Because the WPB proposed to use present wage and production standards as a base from which to calculate incentive payments, efficient plants would be penalized but inefficient ones rewarded when managers reorganized production or secured a more favorable contract that increased output.[36]

Finally, Reuther attacked the WPB–Frankensteen proposals on political grounds. Agreement to the government's incentive pay idea represented "defeatism" in labor's drive to break the Little Steel formula, he told a conference of 200 GM union delegates in early May. Those who supported the NWLB scheme saw "the so-called incentive plans as the only way to get wage raises. If labor even indicates that it is considering piece work, such an attitude will be used to make the labor and wage freeze stick."[37]

Reuther's perspective put him in conflict not only with the Communists and the Frankensteen–Addes faction of the UAW but with Philip Murray as well, who accepted the wage freeze embodied in Executive Order 9328 as a means of heading off Lewis's assault on the NWLB and maintaining the CIO's cooperative alliance with the Roosevelt administration. Thus, when George Addes proposed that the UAW issue a statement on the president's hold-the-line order that echoed Murray's acquiescence, Reuther countered with a demand that the union leadership reject outright the new executive order. If the union condemned 9328, did that mean that the UAW repudiated the president himself? asked George Addes in a heated UAW executive board debate that April. Reuther hesitated to take this step, but he insisted that the labor movement must pressure FDR to counter the increasingly conservative thrust of his administration of the war economy. Although Murray strongly backed Addes and Frankensteen in this contretemps, Reuther had the votes, and the UAW issued a resolution on April 21 denouncing wage and manpower restrictions of Executive Order 9328 as a "menace" to the labor movement and the "national mobilization for victory."[38]

The extent to which the Reuther brothers forcefully opposed 9328 became apparent with their reaction to the manpower section of the order, which drastically tightened the wartime regulations that bound the workers to their jobs. Victor Reuther had been the UAW's chief representative on the Detroit Regional Manpower Commission, a semivoluntary government authority upon which labor (the UAW in Detroit) held effective veto power. Victor worked assiduously during the early months of 1943 to develop liberal manpower controls that protected individual seniority rights and union status.

With the promulgation of 9328, however, War Manpower Commissioner Paul McNutt altered the composition of the regional boards so as to reduce drastically labor's influence in their deliberations. McNutt also issued national guidelines that made labor transfers to higher-paying jobs more difficult, thus destroying much of the work Victor Reuther had painfully accomplished during the previous six months. Although no other CIO leader favored such drastic action, the Reuther brothers now insisted that the UAW counter these unfavorable arrangements by removing its representatives from all war manpower regional commissions. Pushing their proposal through the UAW executive board, they soon scored a notable victory over the manpower commission. Without labor representation, the Detroit regional board collapsed, and in early June, McNutt capitulated to the union by reorganizing the agency along lines that the Reuthers had earlier demanded. UAW representatives then returned to their seats.[39]

Reuther's new militancy proved popular with the union membership.

"As of today," wrote the labor reporter for the *Detroit News*, "Reuther is the fair-haired boy of the rank and file."[40] At regional UAW conferences in New York and Detroit, delegates applauded Reuther's attacks on the Communists, on incentive pay, and on the government wage freeze. By overwhelming votes – 98 percent in Detroit – they rejected the War Production Board's wage scheme endorsed by Frankensteen and Addes. By the end of May, public proponents of incentive pay were reduced to little more than the Communist party cadre in the union. The issue would again come under debate at the UAW's Buffalo convention in September 1943, but by then the Reutherites used it merely as a bludgeon with which to batter the Communists and their allies in the union. Years later, UAW Communist party leader Nat Ganley conceded that Reuther's "most effective slogan was 'Down with Earl Browder's piecework.'"[41]

But Reuther's leadership in this fight moved him only cautiously toward a more militant and independent approach to the problems facing the wartime CIO. The incentive pay debate had taken place just as the national furor over the UMW mine strikes reached a climax, and many of Reuther's partisans in the UAW were also warm supporters of John L. Lewis, opponents of the no-strike pledge, and leaders of the wildcat strikes that flared in Detroit and other industrial centers. Naturally, they linked the UAW movement against incentive pay with the growing wildcat strike phenomenon and with the miners' effort to smash the Little Steel formula. But Reuther shrank from any such association and stood shoulder to shoulder with conservative UAW unionists in condemnation of the mine strikes and the "mis-leadership" of John L. Lewis. Moreover, Reuther forcefully opposed wildcat strikes throughout this period.[42] Such timidity earned the GM director a barrage of criticism from all sides. Earl Browder thought Reuther "less bold but more hypocritical than Lewis." Militant incentive pay opponent John Lucas of Pontiac Local 653 attacked Reuther's "straddling position" on the mine strike; top CIO officials such as Philip Murray and Sidney Hillman marked the UAW leader as untrustworthy.[43]

The Michigan CIO convention

The course of the Michigan CIO convention late in June 1943 registered the growth of UAW rank-and-file radicalism and revealed the extent to which the union's secondary leadership had transcended the issues that had sparked the faction fight two months before. A substantial majority of the 1,800 delegates to this most powerful and representative of all industrial union councils found themselves in opposition to their national leaders and the policies pursued by the CIO. August Scholle, longtime president of the Michigan CIO, and Victor Reuther controlled the right wing of this group, whereas leadership of the militant left went to Emil Mazey and several local union officers, many affiliated with the Association of Catholic Trade Unionists, an anti-Marxist but independent group sponsored by the liberal wing of the Catholic hierarchy. Mazey chaired the convention's resolution committee and commanded a majority of its members for his oppositional program: repeal of the no-strike pledge, support of the coal strike, and advocacy of independent political action. (Incentive pay was hardly an issue.)[44] When on the last day of the convention elections were held for officers of the Michigan Industrial Union Council, the Reutherite–socialist–ACTU slate took every position that it contested by majorities of almost two to one. For the first time in the council's history, no candidates even remotely associated with the Communist faction won election to the state executive board.[45]

The militant thrust at the Michigan convention arose out of what many assembled there considered the virtual collapse of domestic liberalism in recent months. Republicans had scored large gains in the 1942 elections, and many unionists considered the president's recent hold-the-line order intolerable. Meanwhile, the mine strikes had opened an enormous reservoir of sentiment hostile to all the unions that swept the Smith–Connally War Labor Disputes Act through Congress on June 24. Although it would prove ineffective as an antistrike weapon, the new law gave the government enhanced power to curb union political and economic rights. It represented a major defeat for the union movement, the first rollback on the national level of the legislative gains embodied in the Wagner Act of 1935.[46]

In this tense political atmosphere, the regional CIO convention meeting in Grand Rapids began a rare intraunion debate over labor's role in the wartime domestic order. Emil Mazey's resolutions committee condemned the Smith–Connally Act and asserted that it "makes a mockery out of the avowed claims that this is a war for democracy. The passage of this bill should bring home to every lover of democracy that we have a real fight on our hands." To which UAW Communist spokesman Nat Ganley replied, "Now, my opinion is that regardless of what reactionary legislation is passed by big business agents or agents of Hitler, that this war . . . still remains a just progressive war against Fascism." But this was too much for Victor Reuther, who lashed out at the Communists: "I don't agree with those who say that no matter what happens on the home front, this is automatically a war for democracy . . . This is a war against fascism and all that it symbolizes, not against German fascism and Italian fascists, but against all brands of fascists, foreign and domestic."[47]

The oppositional and militant character of the Michigan convention came to a climax on June 30 and July 1, when delegates there overwhelmingly carried resolutions calling on the national CIO to consider rescinding its no-strike pledge and then joining with other progressive groups in the formation of a labor-based third party to fight the rightward drift in domestic politics. The motion on the no-strike pledge recounted labor's familiar disappointments with the government's wage, price, and manpower policies and then recommended the following:

Unless the assurances that were made to labor at the time we gave up our right to strike are immediately and effectively put into operation, that we consider our "no-strike" pledge no longer binding and that labor will settle its problems in the future in the only manner left open to it by the use of its economic strength.[48]

Of course, the Communists and the conservative CIO loyalists fought this proposal, but the real political debate took place among the majority who favored it. Many of the local union leaders who argued for an end to the no-strike pledge found it a means to a simple assertion of union power on the shop floor. For example, Earl Reynolds, president of the 16,000-member Dodge Local 3, long remained a firm backer of Richard Frankensteen in UAW affairs, yet Reynolds had also helped lead the massive Chrysler walkout in May. Since that strike, the NWLB had remained as dilatory as ever in its adjudication of the UAW–Chrysler contract dispute. But actual conditions inside the Dodge plant had improved immensely after the local's show of raw power. "The corporation that I work for knows only one language," reported Reynolds, "and that is the language of strike." His pragmatic conclusion: strikes work; therefore "let's give it to them."[49] Although not present in Grand Rapids, another tough-minded union president, Tom DeLorenzo of Brewster Local 365 in New York, offered the same perspective in an even larger political context: "The policy of our local union is to win the war without sacrificing too many of the rights which we have at the present time . . . If I had brothers at the front who needed the 10 or 12 planes that were sacrificed [during a recent strike] I'd let them die, if necessary, to preserve our way of life or rights or whatever you want to call it."[50]

The Reutherites were unwilling to go this far. Instead, they hoped to use the strike threat implied in the resolution urging revocation of the pledge as a tactic to pressure the NWLB and the Roosevelt administration into adopting policies more acceptable to organized labor. Victor Reuther argued that such a posture would strengthen Philip Murray's hand and that of other labor members of the National War Labor Board in their periodic negotiations with the government.[51] The conservative minority at the convention rejected such backing, for they correctly feared that any equivocation on the no-strike policy would legitimize oppositional and wildcat strike currents within the labor movement itself. UAW President R. J. Thomas and USW District Director Thomas Shane, Murray's personal representative at the convention, therefore fought the no-strike pledge resolution to the end. "This desire to straddle the fence seems to be the motivating force of nine out of ten labor leaders in Michigan," wrote Shane in a bitter letter to Murray a few days later. "Need I say that to me it is very disgustful [sic]."[52]

The divergent tendencies within the Mazey–Reuther forces approached an open split when the convention debated formation of a labor party in Michigan. Such a political grouping had long been part of the political program of the left, and even many in the top leadership of the CIO talked of the creation of a party of labor, farm, and liberal groups, although always at some distant and propitious time. By June 1943, many in the Mazey group had already begun the spadework for such a party, but the Scholle–Reuther forces balked. The latter were willing to set up a state labor party on the model of the American Labor party in New York, but they insisted that such a formation support President Roosevelt on the national level.[53] Although Victor and Walter Reuther opposed the craven fawning before the name of FDR exemplified by the wartime Communists, they were unwilling to repudiate the Democratic president. Instead, they sought to use the threat of nonendorsement as a tool to move Roosevelt's politics to the left. In the fall of 1943 Addes, Frankensteen, and the Communists wanted the UAW to endorse Roosevelt for a fourth term immediately, but the Reuther forces insisted that the UAW delay action until the summer of 1944, when the union could see more clearly the political shape of Roosevelt's fourth term.[54]

By then, the faction fight in the UAW had far transcended the simple issue of incentive pay with which it had begun, for the debate over this problem embodied the entire dilemma posed by labor's commitment to a war effort in which it had little influence and less control. Squeezed between the powerful millstones of an increasingly rigid government wage control apparatus and growing rank-and-file unrest, some union leaders, such as Richard Frankensteen, adopted incentive pay as an adroit means to escape their wartime dilemma. The Reuther brothers understood the deleterious consequences this policy entailed, but in order to rally the UAW ranks in resistance, they were forced to rely upon elements far to their left: Socialists, Trotskyists, and militant local leaders whom they had opposed only a year before when they helped Frankensteen, Addes, and other leaders put over the union's ill-fated Equality of Sacrifice program.

The Reuther brothers sought to limit the radical drift of this realignment, but the Communists correctly understood the logical trajectory of their politics and hammered away at the necessary connection between opposition to incentive pay and the Reuthers' increasing estrangement from the Roosevelt administration and the CIO leadership of Philip Murray. Although Reuther did not move as far or as fast as the Communists had forecast, his adherents and supporters surely did. Spurred on by the powerful stimulus flowing from unresolved grievances in their shops and the militant example set by the UMW's battle with Roosevelt and the NWLB, UAW rank-and-file leaders broke the bounds of Reuther's limited political and trade union program. During the two remaining war years, left-wing Reutherites grappled with fundamental issues involving labor's role in the war itself: the meaning of the wildcat strike wave, the question of independent political action, and the character of democracy in a mobilized society.

9. Holding the line

As dissidence grew within the United Automobile Workers, the Roosevelt administration faced a challenge from an old nemesis, John L. Lewis. The subsequent interplay between the UMW leader's bold attack on the government wage ceiling and the threatening insurgencies within their own unions is an important key in explaining the politics of the CIO leadership during the crisis-filled spring and summer of 1943. Faced with Lewis's audacious effort to break the Little Steel formula and legitimize the wartime strike weapon, officers of the CIO clung ever more tenaciously to their alliance with Roosevelt and relied with redoubled steadfastness upon the policies and procedures of the National War Labor Board. In turn, government strategists understood the importance of stopping Lewis at all costs, for his victory in the 1943 coal dispute could only weaken the prestige and political leadership of those union officials who loyally backed the no-strike pledge and the government's wage stabilization program.

Miners versus the Little Steel formula

The restlessness that plagued the auto workers at the end of the first full year of the war infected the ranks of the United Mine Workers as well. Beginning in December 1942, upward of 20,000 Eastern Pennsylvania Anthracite coal miners downed their tools in a work stoppage initially engendered by their opposition to a recent 50 percent hike in UMW dues, but then directed at the Little Steel formula itself. Led by an insurgent anti-Lewis Tri-District Mining Committee, the Anthracite wildcatters demanded that Lewis cut dues payments and reopen their contract to secure a two-dollar-a-day pay increase. Strike leaders commanded extraordinary support. For almost a month, the miners remained out, first in defiance of UMW orders, then despite a NWLB back-to-work directive, and finally in the face of a presidential appeal to return to the pits.[1]

Lewis shrewdly used the strike to his own advantage. Although he had quickly declared it unauthorized, he emphasized that the work stoppage had to end, not so much because of its breach of the no-strike pledge but because it violated the union's Appalachian Wage Agreement, due to expire on March 31. Furthermore, Lewis carefully remained in the background during the early stages of the dispute, first because the Anthracite ranks were solidly united behind the strike, and second because he sought to avoid identification with the increasingly unpopular National War Labor Board effort to end the strike. Not until the morning of January 15 – only hours before he was to testify before the NWLB on the stoppage – did Lewis send telegrams to the locals ordering their members to return to work. Lewis's aloofness alarmed the government almost as much as the work stoppage itself. NWLB public officials asked Lewis why he had not gone immediately to the Anthracite region to put his prestige on the line against the strike. Van Bittner, once a loyal UMW district director but now a CIO labor member of the board, contrasted Lewis's attitude to that of Philip Murray, who did not hesitate to "dirty his hands" in the suppression of even minor work stoppages at obscure mills and mines.[2]

The Anthracite miners finally returned to work in late January after Lewis threatened to expel the protest leaders, but by this time he had succeeded in steering their attention, and that of the public, away from the politically embarrassing dues protest and toward the demand for a two-dollar-a-day wage increase as the UMW's formal bargaining request when contract negotiations for all 600,000 union members reopened in March. This was cooptation in a classic and brilliant form.[3] Its effectiveness became apparent throughout the course of the four mine strikes that Lewis led during the balance of 1943. Despite his often high-handed, sometimes maladroit conduct of the protracted conflict and the ceaseless opposition of the government, the press, and former union allies, Lewis's rank and file never wavered in their allegiance to his leadership. He championed their cause, and the miners gave him rocklike solidarity in return.

The Anthracite discontent reinforced Lewis's own disenchantment with the Roosevelt administration's conduct of the home front. As he had forecast in 1939 and 1940, labor had little influence in the higher councils of the new war economy, whereas Roosevelt, preoccupied with foreign affairs, relied upon conservative politicians such as James Byrnes and Paul McNutt to preside over the powerful domestic regulatory agencies. In the coalfields, injustice seemed rife. The Office of Price

Administration (OPA) granted the operators a substantial price increase in the fall of 1942 (to allow production on a six-day-a-week basis), but under the government's wage stabilization policy the coal miners were ineligible for any wage increase despite a 20 percent rise in the cost of living since their last pay boost in April 1941.[4]

Like the good business unionist that he was, Lewis thought the no-strike pledge part of a negotiated bargain that bound both labor and government to full production and maintenance of labor standards for the duration of the war. At the 1941 Christmas eve White House conference that had originally set up the National War Labor Board, Lewis had fought hard, and he thought successfully, to ensure that the new agency had sufficient power to "hand down in every wage controversy a decision based upon a judicial determination of the issues." Because Lewis had little faith in the government's effort to halt inflation under wartime conditions, he expected the NWLB to grant periodic wage adjustments sufficient to keep labor's standard of living abreast of the ever-advancing price rise.[5] But to Lewis's way of thinking, Roosevelt unilaterally broke this agreement when the NWLB promulgated the Little Steel formula in July 1942. And the UMW, which already enjoyed the union shop, did not even gain a benefit from maintenance of membership as a consolation prize. "The WLB violates the government agreement with labor each day that it operates," declared the *UMW Journal* in February 1943. "Under its arbitrary and miserably stupid formula, it chains labor to the wheels of industry without compensation for increased costs, while other agencies of government reward and fatten industry by charging its increased costs to the public purse."[6]

The implications of this perspective were far-reaching. If the government and the NWLB had violated their understanding with organized labor, then not only was the Little Steel formula unjust and illegal, but labor's no-strike pledge need no longer be honored. Lewis proposed to reopen collective bargaining on a laissez-faire basis, backed, of course, by labor's unfettered right to strike. By March, he had linked his demand for a two-dollar-per-day wage increase to a call for the dissolution of the National War Labor Board itself. The agency had fouled its own nest, he charged, and Lewis shortly thereafter began a UMW boycott of the board that lasted until the end of the summer.[7] In this fight, the mine chief self-consciously placed himself again at the head of all American workers. Their current leadership remained "weak and vacillating," but Lewis thought that, just like a decade before, the rank and file would follow his leadership. "We are always breaking new ground for someone else to follow in some other industry and we are glad to be able to render that service again."[8]

From April to November 1943, Lewis marched more than half a million union miners forward and back in a daring, tension-filled game of maneuver with his adversaries among the mine owners, on the National War Labor Board, and in the White House itself. In the spring he called the miners out on strike three times (May 1–2, June 1–2, June 18–23), generating an enormous storm of opposition and precipitating a five-month seizure of the mines. In July, August, and September, Lewis tried to reach a new contract settlement in a less confrontationist and sensational fashion, but in October as the UMW's latest contract extension neared its end, the union's rank and file took the initiative once again, this time shutting down the entire industry. At this point, Roosevelt himself capitulated, and the UMW won a substantial wage increase. This protracted and complicated conflict has been well recorded by Melvyn Dubofsky and Warren Van Tine in their biography of the UMW leader. Our purpose is not to chronicle it again, but to examine how this epic struggle threatened the authority of the National War Labor Board, generated a rank-and-file response among thousands of industrial workers, and sharpened the growing political crisis within the CIO itself.

In fighting for a new mine contract, Lewis intended to circumvent and thereby render impotent the machinery of the National War Labor Board. He found a powerful ally in Harold Ickes, who as Secretary of the Interior and Solid Fuels Administrator came to operate the mines after the government took control on May 1. The old New Dealer recognized that Lewis and his union could neither be split nor defeated without the risk of a prolonged and chaotic disruption of coal production. "Bayonets cannot mine coal," repeated Ickes on more than one occasion. Ickes respected Lewis as a responsible, even conservative, labor leader, and he wanted a quick accommodation with the UMW to assure stable coal production for the remainder of the war. He was sympathetic to the mine union's wage request and considered the reactionary southern coal operators responsible for much of the current impasse. Although Lewis knew that the NWLB had to approve formally any contract he worked out with Ickes, he calculated that once an agreement had been reached and another coal strike averted, the labor board would be under immense pressure to approve it, even if it breached the sacred Little Steel formula.[9]

Lewis sought another ally when he announced his application for readmission to the AFL on May 20, a request immediately greeted as "wonderful" by President William Green. His decision to affiliate undoubtedly represented an effort to avoid the political isolation into which the Roosevelt administration and the CIO increasingly sought to maneuver him. It reflected an accurate calculation that the AFL now stood considerably further from and more independent of the administration than did the CIO. Although Lewis's greatest rank-and-file support clearly lay in the mass industrial unions, he found that the trade union program actually pursued by the AFL's business union leadership now paralleled more closely the course that he had marked for the UMW. Such crusty AFL executive council members as Matthew Woll and William Hutcheson, who sponsored Lewis's reaffiliation, did not hesitate to criticize FDR and the stabilization program, if only from a Republican point of view. Slightly more liberal AFL officials such as Secretary-Treasurer George Meany and International Association of Machinists President Harvey Brown thought the NWLB virtually bankrupt and were anxious, like Lewis, to return the labor movement to an environment of "free" collective bargaining.[10] Because AFL officials did not fear rank-and-file insurgency as a threat to their leadership, the craft-dominated federation actually condoned, sometimes even sponsored, more militant wartime tactics than did the CIO. For example, IAM lodges in the aircraft industry conducted several one-day demonstration work stoppages in early 1943 to prod the NWLB into taking action on their grievances. Local affiliates of the International Brotherhood of Electrical Workers, the Teamsters, and the Boilermakers often used the strike weapon in wartime jurisdiction disputes with the CIO.[11]

John L. Lewis versus the CIO

In the CIO itself, Lewis's strategy took two forms: the expansion of District 50, the UMW's catchall industrial union affiliate, and even more importantly, the rise of his influence among the rank and file in key industrial unions such as the UAW and the United Rubber Workers. Under the direction of his daughter Kathryn, District 50 had been notably unsuccessful in organizing probes of such disparate industries as nonunion construction, the railroad shops, and midwestern dairy farming. The district had made some inroads among chemical workers but was often used as a mere sinecure for burnt-out UMW staffers. Still, Lewis viewed the district as a potential third labor federation whose success would once again win him prestige and glory. Opportunity seemed to knock in early 1943, so Lewis increased the district's budget to $500,000 a year, added more than 200 new organizers to its staff, and appointed Michael Widman, who had directed the successful unionization drive at Ford, as head of organization.[12]

District 50 flexed its muscles against the CIO in the early spring, when the union took control of a New Jersey textile local in a spectacular raid that seemed indicative of Lewis's growing strength among the CIO rank and file. For almost a year, the Textile Workers Union of America local at the Celanese Corporation's northern New Jersey plastics division had vainly sought NWLB adjudication of its contract. After a series of tumultuous protest meetings in the winter, leaders of the 1,500 plant workers began serious discussions with District 50 organizers. National officials of the TWUA, a relatively weak international in a low-wage, partially unionized industry, feared a massive raid by the powerful UMW. In a wire to William Davis, a New Jersey textile union leader directed the organization's ire at the National War Labor Board itself: "Lewis' invasion of our ranks at Celanese is typical of what will happen throughout the country unless the board speedily fulfills its obligations to the American people."[13] Responding quickly, the labor board granted Celanese workers the maximum pay raise allowable under the Little Steel formula – 4½ percent. The NWLB also mandated maintenance of membership without the usual fifteen-day escape clause in an effort to freeze Celanese employees in their textile local and prevent District 50 from recruiting in the plant. But the labor board's long-delayed directive failed to undercut UMW influence; soon the entire leadership of the local had switched to District 50.[14]

A test of strength came in April after a UMW activist had been fired for handing out District 50 propaganda on company property. Most workers walked out on April 12 and demanded recognition as a UMW local. Recognizing the importance of the contest, both the CIO and District 50 poured organizers into the struggle. After a number of clashes outside the plant, decisive victory went to the UMW, which retained the allegiance of the workers and kept the plant closed. Celanese workers later voted to continue their strike until a special tribunal, not associated with the NWLB, determined who actually held bargaining rights at the factory.[15] Their strategy paralleled that of John L. Lewis, who sought to circumvent the NWLB in his dispute with the nation's coal-mine owners.

In this fight against District 50, the NWLB and the CIO were of one mind. Both thought the strike merely part of Lewis's larger design to smash the labor board and raid the CIO. And both the NWLB and the CIO wanted the strike broken at almost any cost. Thus, on April 23, a unanimous labor board referred the dispute to FDR, who in turn warned the Celanese strikers that if they did not return to work immediately, he would use troops to open the plant. With the prospect of mass arrests and military occupation in the offing, District 50 leaders capitulated. They called off the strike on April 27 just before the UMW itself began its first nation-wide work stoppage.[16]

Pro-Lewis sentiment grew in the UAW as well. As Chapter 8 showed, support for the mine workers became linked to the drive by UAW militants to repeal the no-strike pledge, resist incentive pay, and reassert union power on the shop floor. With Lewis now in an epic battle with the NWLB, many secondary officials of the UAW, some former mine workers, saw the UMW president as an alternative champion of their own struggle. John McGill, president of Flint Local 599, stayed in frequent communication with the UMW, and the local at Ford's Lincoln factory in Detroit resolved that if their own international officers could not secure a wage increase for the rank and file, the local would petition John L. Lewis to take on their fight instead. "Many workers in the plant say to me John Lewis has the right program," admitted UAW President R. J. Thomas in May; veteran labor journalist Mary Heaton Vorse, back from a two-month tour of industrial America, reported a "Lewis groundswell," especially in Detroit, where the "boys there say they would leave the CIO and join Lewis if he asked them to."[17]

Workers began to emulate Lewis's strike militancy as well. Coinciding with the nation-wide coal strikes, a wave of major wildcats swept through Detroit, Akron, and the east coast shipyards, a movement that the commissioner of labor statistics labeled a "fundamental swell of industrial unrest."[18] In one of the largest unauthorized strikes of the war, rubber workers dramatically demonstrated the extent to which Lewis's tactics had influenced the CIO rank and file. For an entire year, workers at the Big Four Akron locals – Goodyear, Goodrich, Firestone, and General – had waited for the NWLB to revise their wages in accordance with the Little Steel formula. In April a labor board panel recommended an eight-cent increase, but weeks passed with no word from the NWLB itself. Finally, the Akron Industrial Union Council called for a demonstration work stoppage to prod the government agency along. On May 21, the board finally handed down its wage order, slashing the panel's eight-cent recommendation to but three cents an hour. In effect, the NWLB had credited the large general wage boosts it offered in low-wage plants outside Akron to the higher-earning workers in the rubber capital. Industry-wide collective bargaining, long a hard-fought goal of the URW's leadership, had been used by the NWLB to cut dramatically the expected wage increase of the union's most militant and important locals.[19]

In protest, leaders of three of the Big Four locals called a city-wide strike on May 22 that involved over 50,000 workers and quickly shut down most plants. At Goodyear, where a Communist-allied local leadership opposed the strike, rank-and-file workers stayed out anyway. Led by union oppositionists such as George Bass, president of Goodrich Local 5, the strikers demanded NWLB reconsideration of their case and ignored pleas by URW President Sherman Dalrymple to return to work. Bass announced that the workers had lost their "confidence in the fairness and impartiality of the WLB."[20]

Convinced that the rubber strikes had been inspired by John L. Lewis, the NWLB counterattacked on two fronts. First, it put its weight behind President Dalrymple so that he might regain effective control of the union. In private conferences with the URW president, board members Wayne Morse and William Davis agreed to reopen the rubber case – an unprecedented decision – but only after all strikers had returned to work. On May 26, while virtually all of Akron remained on strike against Dalrymple and the NWLB, Chairman Davis issued an extraordinary press release reaffirming the "WLB's confidence in the good faith and patriotism of Mr. Sherman Dalrymple . . . even though he has strongly challenged the soundness of the Board's decision" in the URW wage case.[21]

The labor board also moved to squash the strike in Akron. Wayne Morse, the brilliant, combative organizer of the NWLB's compliance strategy, recognized the larger implications of the work stoppage. To FDR he wrote, "the time has come for you to hit and hit hard in regard to the rapidly increasing violations of the 'no-strike' pledge. Strikes are spreading at an alarming rate and unless they are checked immediately, the 'no-strike–no-lockout' agreement will become meaningless." Morse drafted for the president a strongly worded telegram demanding that the rubber workers return to their jobs. He also prepared an executive order authorizing army seizure of the plants, to be implemented if the commander-in-chief's verbal command had no effect.[22]

Faced with this government ultimatum, the Akron strikers ended their work stoppage, although when the Goodrich local finally voted to return on May 29, it did so merely for a three-week "truce." Unlike the situation in the coalfields, where the miners were scattered among thousands of pits, army occupation of the four Akron factories probably would have broken the strike outright. (A similar army seizure and occupation did so in 1945.) Although George Bass and others hoped that the pressure generated by the massive strike would prod the NWLB into revising its May 21 wage order, the board waited until the situation had calmed and then reaffirmed its initial decision. Thus burned, the Big Four rubber locals were soon welded into a solid opposition bloc in the union, hostile to the no-strike pledge, the NWLB, and Dalrymple's continuing leadership of the international. Representing about a third of the URW's swollen wartime membership, they supported George Bass's unsuccessful 1944 effort to win the union presidency.[23]

Holding the line

Throughout this crisis, the leadership of the CIO clung tenaciously to the authority of the NWLB. Although the CIO formally supported the UMW's two-dollar-a-day wage demand, the federation reaffirmed its devotion to the no-strike pledge in the boldest terms and with unbending consistency insisted that only the labor board held the authority to review and approve the UMW's next contract. Despite some public and much private criticism of its policies and procedures, CIO leaders felt politically comfortable with the National War Labor Board and its apparatus. Staffed largely by academic liberals and old New Dealers, it was the only agency in which labor had a strong voice in both policymaking and operations, and it represented the tripartite model that most union leaders sought for the administration of the war economy as a whole.[24]

CIO leaders also feared that if John L. Lewis succeeded in circumventing the National War Labor Board, he would legitimize the wildcat strike movement in their own organizations and unleash a wave of rank-and-file militancy and opposition. Hence, the CIO condemned their rival in the harshest terms: "this man has consistently schemed to undermine duly established war-time agencies. . . . In times of emotional stress the labor movement of this country must be particularly wary of any person or element which seeks to substitute for sane and democratic processes willful and revengeful dictation."[25] Of course, this strategy entailed muting the CIO's own home front criticism. Thus Philip Murray consistently played down the impact of the hold-the-line order and allowed the AFL to bear the brunt of the effort to modify its terms. The CIO dropped its request for an upward revision of the Little Steel formula during the height of the fight with Lewis, relying instead upon a Roosevelt promise to lower food prices to the level of September 15, 1942.[26] (A system of cash subsidy payments to farmers and middlemen dampened food price increases for a few months, but inadequate congressional funding crippled the program by the fall of 1943. For his part, Lewis considered the price rollback effort an exercise in futility, and he sneered at "these intellectual pint pots who thought that the waves of the sea could be brushed back by the passage of a resolution or a petition to the Great White Father.")[27]

The combined NWLB–CIO fight against Lewis came to a searing climax in June and July, when he seemed on the verge of reaching a settlement with the mine owners that would substantially increase wages in the coalfields. Ickes favored such an out-of-court agreement, even if it came about while the miners still remained out on one of the UMW's periodic strikes. The operators, especially those in the North, who had had two or three decades of experience with the union, now recognized that no contract dictated by the NWLB could be made to stick and that only one freely negotiated with Lewis himself could assure peace in the coalfields and the return of their properties from government hands.[28]

To the NWLB, Lewis's ability to involve Ickes and the mine owners in public negotiations during a time of strike posed a supreme threat to that agency's authority, and if continued, it promised to legitimize the strike weapon. The labor board would then be unable to apply its leverage, as in the rubber wildcat, to force strikers to return to work before reconsidering the merits of their case. Van Bittner feared that if a group of operators agreed to the UMW's wage demands, then Ickes would certainly approve and Lewis could hail his victory as a vindication of the UMW's strike policy. When the labor board then rejected the Ickes–Lewis agreement, it would "put us in a terrible position with

American labor." Bittner actually lobbied some of the mine owners in an attempt to strengthen their resolve to resist the Lewis–Ickes combination. There was irony aplenty here in the efforts of a former UMW district director to quarterback management's fight against his old chief, but to Bittner the situation was merely grim: "We have just simply got to decide here . . . whether or not we are going to be part of this vacillating, palavering, inconsistent, go-nowhere policy or whether or not we are going to act as Americans and meet the enemy head on."[29]

Backed by its CIO members and led with single-minded determination by Wayne Morse, the NWLB made what its officers considered a last-ditch effort to stop Lewis and retain supreme government authority in the coal dispute. In a high-level conference in early June, Morse persuaded Roosevelt and Byrnes that unless they forced Ickes and the Interior Department to stay out of the wage negotiations, the effort to stop Lewis would fail and the board might as well resign. In what Morse later called "the greatest single victory I have ever been a party to," the president reconfirmed the NWLB's sole authority to adjudicate the UMW contract.[30]

Still, the labor board had yet to bring Lewis himself to terms, and as long as he boycotted the agency and described its directive orders as "yellow dog" contracts not binding on the UMW, the task remained bogged down in a frustrating stalemate. As Morse and other administration liberals saw it, the NWLB needed new powers that could be used against Lewis and other maverick unionists without generating a backlash from loyal supporters of the NWLB and the no-strike pledge. To this end, the solicitor general had begun to draft legislation in April that would have enabled the government legally to enjoin wartime work stoppages, conscript strikers, and fine or imprison their leaders.[31]

Congressional conservatives took the initiative from the administration in mid-June, when they overrode FDR's veto to pass the long-simmering Smith–Connally War Labor Disputes Act. Rushed through an angry Senate in the immediate aftermath of the UMW's third strike in six weeks, the new law was above all the hard slap at the union movement that the Dixiecrat–Republican forces had sought to deliver since the late 1930s. Based on the right-wing theory that unscrupulous labor bosses such as Lewis single-handedly instigated strikes and manipulated politicians, the act gave the NWLB power to subpoena witnesses, banned direct union contributions to political candidates, and mandated that unions issue written strike notices followed by a thirty-day cooling-off period and a National Labor Relations Board supervised secret strike vote. It also provided for federal seizure of a struck facility (a power the government already had) and fines or jail terms for strike leaders.[32]

FDR had vetoed the bill, not because he or his advisers opposed its punitive sections – many thought them inadequate and maladroit – but because this particular effort to curb the unions promised only instability and disaffection within labor ranks. Ickes told FDR that the bill would make Lewis a martyr, and William Davis feared that if Roosevelt signed the measure, it would drive "responsible and loyal labor leaders into Lewis' corner."[33] The section of the bill mandating rank-and-file strike votes forecast even more trouble. After talking to Philip Murray, domestic affairs aide Wayne Coy warned FDR that the Smith–Connally Act would "encourage local leaders to submit strike notices on their own responsibility. . . . Such a tendency can only weaken the authority and influence of responsible international officers over their constituencies, thereby increasing rather than diminishing the danger of widespread stoppages."[34]

Although enactment of the Smith–Connally Act gave the NWLB few additional powers with which to bring Lewis to terms, the UMW chief recognized that the great public outcry against the mine strikes could not be defied indefinitely. He therefore shifted tactics once again and announced on June 23 that his miners would return to work until at least October 31, provided only that the operation of the coal mines remain in government hands. Lewis thought that time would work in his favor. So long as he refused to sign an NWLB-imposed contract, the Little Steel formula stayed under attack, support for his cause grew in other unions, and at least some of the mine operators remained his allies in their mutual effort to negotiate an acceptable contract.[35]

The UMW's strategy put the NWLB in an intolerable position. They could not force Lewis to sign a contract, but he insisted that his miners would strike if the government returned the mines to private ownership before a satisfactory agreement was worked out with the mine owners. Wayne Morse reported that the NWLB was bogged down with a backlog of cases and a series of defiance problems upon which the board could not act until it resolved the UMW question. As compliance officer, Morse feared that the board could not survive the summer unless the government took drastic action. In mid-July, Morse outlined a program for the Roosevelt administration designed to break any strike that Lewis might call in the future and, if necessary, destroy his organization at the same time. Morse proposed that the government sponsor a new and vigorous propaganda campaign against the UMW's leader in order to weaken his hold on the rank-and-file mine workers. As part of this campaign, Attorney General Francis Biddle looked into the possibility of prosecuting John L. Lewis for tax evasion, and other administration officials quietly pressured the American Federation of Labor to repudiate Lewis's tactics and reject the UMW's bid for affiliation.[36]

In August, Morse also won for the NWLB new disciplinary authority from the president. If the UMW threatened a coal strike in the fall, a new executive order gave the agency power to impound union funds, seize its property, and suspend the union shop. Another order provided the Selective Service with the authority to cancel draft deferments of striking workers up to age 65.[37] When Frances Perkins objected to the use of these powers as tantamount to the destruction of the UMW, Morse unhesitatingly replied: "That is exactly what it amounts to . . . in time of war, when a union seeks to defy the government of the U.S., I am all in favor of breaking that union . . . because that is not the type of union that I think is helpful to the American labor movement; and I don't think that union is worth saving."[38]

These additional powers seemed to give the NWLB the upper hand in its continuing struggle with John L. Lewis. He abandoned his boycott of the NWLB's proceedings and did nothing when Ickes, under pressure from hard-liners in the Roosevelt administration, began to return the coal mines to private hands. In August and again in October, the labor board rejected contracts Lewis had negotiated and renegotiated with a group of cooperative Illinois mine owners. Fearful of the new penalties that threatened his union, Lewis complied with the government's request to order his men back to work when wildcat strikes spread across the coalfields in October.[39]

But the UMW rank and file were not to be thwarted. As their contract neared its October 31 expiration date, thousands of miners in hundreds of locals stayed out in a genuine surge of militancy from below. On November 1, all 530,000 bituminous miners were on strike.[40] By then, administration policy had reached an impasse. The NWLB's single-minded commitment to the Little Steel formula had only plunged the nation into yet another coal strike, this one seemingly beyond the control of even the UMW's powerful leader. The president again seized the mines, but this time he directed Harold Ickes to negotiate a contract that Lewis would accept. Ignoring the NWLB's policy of refusing to talk with a striking union, Ickes quickly got down to business. Two days later, on November 3, Lewis and Ickes reached an agreement that closely approximated the wage of eight and a half dollars per day that the Illinois contract originally provided, but that the NWLB had earlier rejected. (The total was achieved by juggling the time for which the miners were paid for portal-to-portal travel time below ground, reducing their lunch break to 15 minutes, and increasing the overall number of work hours.) Although a good deal of litigation and hard bargaining continued on contract details, the final agreement with Ickes, later approved by a reluctant NWLB, increased the mine workers' weekly wages by about 25 percent above the rate nine months before, when Lewis launched his campaign to break the Little Steel formula.[41]

Lewis had won the epic battle of his career, and the victory immediately reverberated within the CIO itself. Until November, the industrial union federation leadership had still backed the Little Steel formula, although by now most doubted the efficacy of the president's price reduction program and the accuracy of the Bureau of Labor Statistics cost-of-living index. In preparing for the CIO's 1943 convention, the issue of wage policy had been carefully ignored, both by Murray's hand-picked resolutions committee and in his own cautiously worded *Presidential Report*.[42] But as the CIO delegates assembled in Philadelphia late in October, the UMW's fourth mine strike neared its climax. To a precon-vention executive board meeting, Murray now declared: "the situation has reached such proportions – I mean as the clamour of the membership is concerned, the membership of my union particularly – that it seems to me the time has come for the Executive Board to provide guidance . . . Unless we provide guidance for our people, I am afraid that our people will provide guidance for us."[43]

The CIO's guidance was cautious indeed. Within hours of FDR's announcement that Harold Ickes would finally be permitted to work out an interim wage agreement with the UMW, Murray reconvened his executive board in a hurriedly assembled "extraordinary session" to frame a new CIO wage policy. Individual CIO unions were authorized to make demands for a general wage increase – later set at about seventeen cents an hour – strictly in accordance with the cumbersome administrative procedures of the NWLB. Ritualistically, they reaffirmed "unconditional" CIO support for the no-strike pledge.[44]

To such minimal pressure, the administration responded with minimal action. Murray's own United Steelworkers of America, demanding a wage increase and a guaranteed annual income, provided the CIO's pacesetting case in this "drive" to break the Little Steel formula. Yet, the NWLB took well over a year even to reject decisively the basic USW wage proposal.[45]

Although Murray had definitely rejected the strike weapon in the CIO's fight for higher wages, the USW itself demonstrated the efficacy of this tool less than two months after Lewis had secured his Little Steel formula breakthrough. When the union called upon the NWLB to increase steelworker wages, the USW necessarily reopened the several hundred contracts that it held in the steel industry. Pressman and Murray then argued that any wage increase granted the union should be retroactive to the date of contract termination. They did so in order to protect themselves against the charge that their cautious, drawn-out approach to the NWLB would cost steelworkers months of increased pay if a wage award was finally made.[46]

The NWLB foolishly and legalistically rejected the USW request for retroactive pay. This put the USW leadership in an intolerable position, for they could no longer take their time in winning a sorely needed wage boost for the steelworker rank and file. Murray now took a leaf from Lewis's book of tactics by announcing that the NWLB was provoking a possible strike when USW contracts formally expired on December 24, 1943. Sure enough, walkouts involving at least 150,000 men spread on Christmas eve.[47]

To stop the strikes and restore USW leadership confidence, Roosevelt intervened directly in the dispute to order the NWLB to grant the steelworkers retroactive benefits when the board handed down its ultimate decision in the steel case. With this presidential assurance, the USW high command never again deviated in its adherence to NWLB procedures or the no-strike pledge. Steelworkers waited until February 1945 to receive a retroactive "fringe benefit" wage increase worth about two cents an hour. The Little Steel formula itself remained in force until the end of the war.[48]

The CIO's Political Action Committee

The CIO's desperate alliance with the NWLB against the disruptive threat posed by John L. Lewis in 1943 proved but one element in a larger pattern of political rigidity that characterized the industrial union federation in the war era. The renewed association the CIO forged with the Democratic party through the formation in July 1943 of a powerful Political Action Committee (PAC) solidified a relationship of even greater long-range import. CIO leaders designed the new political organization to meet a twofold challenge to their authority. Ostensibly, they formed the PAC simply to counter the conservative drift in domestic politics that had culminated in the passage of the Smith–Connally Act. In a massive show of apathy and disaffection, millions of working-class Democrats had failed to vote in the 1942 congressional elections. As a result, labor faced its most hostile Congress since the 1920s. A reforged conservative coalition there soon thwarted liberal efforts to pass progressive tax legislation, enforce price controls, and roll back food prices. Old New Deal agencies were mercilessly cut back or eliminated. Accommodating to the new mood, Roosevelt later made his famous announcement that "Dr. New Deal" had been replaced for the duration by "Dr. Win-the-War."[49] CIO leaders naturally feared that the liberal doctor might never be seen again unless they offered like-minded souls in the Democratic party the organization, energy, and support of which a mobilized labor movement was capable. The PAC would reelect Roosevelt in 1944 on a liberal platform and lay the basis for a progressive postwar order.

But the PAC had an equally important, purely organizational rationale: to deflect or coopt the growing internal agitation for some form of independent political action in the 1944 election. As we have seen, in Michigan a group of radical UAW leaders linked support for the mine strikes and opposition to the no-strike pledge with a grass-roots movement for a CIO-based Labor party. Joining forces with the more moderate group headed by Victor Reuther and August Scholle, the UAW insurgents had already laid the basis for a state third party modeled after the Canadian Commonwealth Federation, the growing labor–liberal political group in nearby Ontario.

Meanwhile, on the east coast, a section of the CIO and AFL union leadership in the retail trade, garment, and textile industries advocated more aggressive electoral tactics for labor. The International Ladies Garment Workers Union paper, *Justice*, editorialized, "The present Congress is the best argument for independent political action the country has had in years." Proponents of this tendency in the CIO included old social democrats such as the TWUA's Emil Rieve and George Baldanzi, and United Retail, Wholesale and Department Store Employees Union leader Samuel Wolchok. Their still shaky unions battled some of the most unreconstructed employers in the nation, notably Montgomery Ward's recalcitrant Sewell Avery, who defied with impunity even the NWLB and the NLRB. Led by the ILGWU's David Dubinsky, these New York and New Jersey-based unionists hoped to link up with the Reuther wing of the Michigan radicals and spread their American Labor party to other industrial states. Although neither Dubinsky nor the Reuther–Scholle group favored opposition to Roosevelt on the national level, they did support direct labor party challenges to state and local Democratic machines, thereby undercutting FDR's conservative base and forcing him (they hoped) to the left.[50]

The idea of such a political regrouping was also part of a counter-offensive by the so-called right wing of the CIO against Communist influence in the unions and the accommodation of labor's top leadership to that ideology. For example, in March 1943, Dubinsky had organized a successful mass rally in New York to protest the Soviet execution of Henryk Erlich and Victor Alter, Polish social democrats who had fled to the USSR after the Nazi invasion of their homeland. CIO anti-Communists such as James Carey and Emil Rieve appeared on the platform. Later, the publications of the Reuther wing of the UAW offered a full account of the meeting.[51] But Hillman and Murray kept their distance, not even allowing a mention of the protest in the *CIO News, Steel Labor*, or the Amalgamated Clothing Workers of America's *Advance*.[51] The same division reappeared in the CIO's handling of its fight with John L. Lewis. Murray, Hillman, and the Communists solidly defended the NWLB and denounced as subversive the idea that their no-strike pledge was not a unilateral sacrifice but part of a bargain with the government. Reuther, Rieve, and Wolchok represented a minority in the CIO who favored at least a rhetorically more aggressive attack on home front inequalities.[52]

As the CIO executive board assembled in Washington's sticky heat on July 7 and 8, 1943, Murray and Hillman wrung their hands over the recently enacted Smith–Connally Act but reserved their real animus for the presumptuous UAW radicals, whom they repeatedly denounced as "sideline mugwumps," "meddlers," and "enemies" defying official CIO policy.[53] In launching the new Political Action Committee, the CIO leadership specifically rejected any "ultraliberal political party in the name of the workingman." Instead, they sought to discipline the unruly left wing by channeling its energy into a firmly controlled political action group that could function safely within the two-party system.[54] "The

issue is not that of 'liberalism vs. reaction,'" argued the *CIO News.*
"Defeatists like John L. Lewis, Senator Wheeler and Norman Thomas
are still classed as 'liberals' by some people who in the same breath talk
about President Roosevelt 'losing his liberalism.' To place this issue as
'liberalism vs. reaction' means to call off national unity and to notify
everybody that the time has come to resume the internal fights on the
homefront."[55]

The most conservative and pro-Roosevelt elements in the CIO dominated the PAC from the start. As chairman, Sidney Hillman headed a
top committee consisting of USW officers Bittner and McDonald, embattled loyalists Dalrymple and R. J. Thomas, and United Electrical,
Radio and Machine Workers President Albert J. Fitzgerald. Although
Hillman kept the organization under his firm personal control, he staffed
the PAC with Communist-oriented progressives and popular front liberals such as ACWA counsel John Abt, C. B. (Beanie) Baldwin, and
former Congressman Thomas Amlie. And on the local level, the Communists, who had been the staunchest supporters of the CIO in its fight
with Lewis, now became the hard-working, day-to-day partisans of the
PAC.[56]

Under Hillman's leadership, the PAC sought an accommodation with
the Democratic party in a wartime popular front whose right wing
would include the most conservative elements in the Roosevelt coalition.
The Political Action Committee did force some Democratic reactionaries out of the running in the 1944 primaries – notably the House Un-
American Activities Committee's (HUAC) Martin Dies in east Texas.[57]
But the basic program of the national PAC encouraged its state units not
to challenge local Democratic organizations, but to reach an accord with
them in order to "weld the unity of all forces who support the Commander-in-Chief behind a single progressive win-the-war candidate for
each office." Obviously, this precluded a precise liberal standard. As
PAC propagandist Joseph Gaer admitted after the campaign, "It was not
possible to support only ideal candidates. The choice was sometimes
between   the   none-too-good   and   the   outright   labor-baiting
isolationist."[58]

Where labor sentiment for an independent political voice remained
strong and threatened to disrupt the alliance with the Democrats, Hillman mobilized PAC forces to defeat it. In New York, he linked his still
anti-Communist Amalgamated Clothing Workers with the Communist

unions of the city to win control of the American Labor party from the Dubinsky forces and make the state labor party an uncritical adjunct of the Democratic party there.[59] In Minnesota he presided over the merger of the Democrats with the once radical Farmer–Labor party. And in Michigan, where a viable Democratic party hardly existed, Thomas, Frankensteen, and the Communists successfully fought efforts by some UAW radicals to put political backbone in the PAC by supporting only those candidates pledged to work for a guaranteed annual wage, an upward revision of the Little Steel formula, and other well-publicized CIO bargaining demands.[60]

Under the PAC's direction, the CIO trade union apparatus mobilized its forces as an important adjunct to – in some cases, as a substitute for – the Democratic party's electoral effort. Since its formation in the 1930s, the industrial union federation had supported Roosevelt and most local Democrats, but in 1944 the CIO for the first time organized down to the precinct level, with union membership lists indexed by city block for registration and education.[61] In many industrial cities of the North, the PAC filled the political vacuum left by aging Democratic machines. Local unions were told to make political action "a primary concern for 1944 around which your normal trade union activities revolve." Between August and November, all UAW staffers devoted at least half their time to the campaign, and in the UE and the USW the proportion probably rose even higher. In a typical industrial city such as Buffalo, the PAC recruited more than 500 canvassers to register potential working-class voters and "plug the gaps in the Democratic machine."[62] All this activity was skillfully coordinated on the national level, where hundreds of enthusiastic PAC professionals turned out millions of slickly produced pamphlets, posters, and radio programs. The most remarkable were undoubtedly Ben Shahn's stirring series of color posters, which in 1944 produced the emotional impact of the best thirty-second TV campaign spots a quarter of a century later.[63]

Although the PAC helped to revitalize the Democratic party campaign, among industrial workers themselves the new political effort failed to "rekindle the spirit of 36" or reverse their growing estrangement from the union bureaucracy. Treasurer David J. McDonald reported that contributions "trickled in" from the rank and file despite Hillman's high-powered fund-raising operation. In all, less than 5 percent gave the dollar apiece that the PAC wanted. Seventy percent of the organization's financial support came from the CIO's satellite middle-class group, the National Citizen's PAC, and directly from international union treasuries.[64]

In the final tally, the PAC impact on the working-class vote proved only marginal, even among CIO voters. The president's relative standing in those heavily CIO counties where the PAC conducted its most vigorous campaigns remained virtually identical to that in 1940, although in 1944 the CIO was larger, better organized, and more unified, at least at the top. Moreover, in congressional districts in these same labor counties, the Democratic vote was no higher than in a series of northern and western districts where the PAC made no campaign effort at all. Concluded one close student of the vote returns, "Seemingly, whatever bait the PAC had set out to lure labor voters into the Democratic fold had worked no more effectively than traditional political methods."[65]

As in its struggle with Lewis in 1943, the CIO fought the 1944 campaign in defense of the Rooseveltian status quo, and this fact may explain part of the reason for its relative electoral failure. The PAC's propaganda called for a glowing postwar order of full employment, world peace, and racial egalitarianism but made everything dependent upon the reelection of Roosevelt and the preservation of the increasingly fragile and right-ward-drifting political coalition over which the president still presided. In effect, the CIO leaders relied upon FDR to protect their unions from many of the same elements in the Democratic party that were responsible for the president's own political survival. As a consequence, the PAC had little leverage with Roosevelt or his party. The remarkable organizational support that the industrial unions offered the president in 1944 did not even earn for the CIO the vice-presidential renomination of its favorite, Henry Wallace, or an upward revision of the Little Steel formula. In both instances, Roosevelt merely toyed with the CIO to retain its enthusiastic loyalty. As historians now know, FDR had decided to dump Wallace well before the Democratic National Convention. The president's purported instructions to "clear it with Sidney" in Chicago made Hillman and the PAC feel at the center of things, but few people outside the CIO took them seriously in any functional sense.[66] Likewise, Roosevelt hinted in September that the government might make more flexible the NWLB wage ceiling, and in October, when a steel industry panel recommended a twelve-cent pay boost, Murray assured CIO unionists that the formula would soon crack. But a month later, after the elections, the NWLB formally rejected any significant change in wage policy, and Roosevelt, who had the power, did nothing to alter its decision.[67]

Conclusion

In 1943 and 1944, the CIO moved firmly into the filial-dependent relationship with the government that would characterize its politics for many years to come. Challenged by John L. Lewis, by a growing wildcat strike movement, and by resurgent right wing forces, CIO leaders were caught in an apparent quandary. The economic restraints imposed by the conservatively administered war economy eroded the loyalty of the industrial union rank and file and curbed the institutional power of the trade unions in American politics. One strategy of reconsolidation and revival would have been to make an aggressive assault on the government's system of economic controls, as Lewis himself began after the Anthracite wildcat strike in early 1943. But Murray, Hillman, and other top CIO officials feared the disorder and confrontation such a course entailed. Without a conduit to the prestige and power of the administration, the CIO would open a Pandora's box of rank-and-file militancy and third party experimentation. Hence, they saw little alternative but to link themselves with the authority of the National War Labor Board and put their faith in the reelection of the president, although the policy of both offered few rewards as the war neared its end. The net result was an increasingly bureaucratic and politically timid industrial union federation. Dissidence within many unions continued to grow, but the shape of American labor politics remained rigidly unchanged, and the CIO entered the difficult postwar era with many of the same handicaps under which it had labored during the war itself.

10. The bureaucratic imperative

While they campaigned vigorously for FDR's reelection, leaders of the industrial union federation also redoubled their efforts to maintain discipline and order within their own institutions. With military victory now certain and the inequalities of the home front more apparent, American workers, especially those organized in the CIO, demonstrated an increasing propensity to ignore the no-strike pledge and lay down their tools. In 1944 and 1945, more strikes took place and more workers stopped work than in any similar period since 1919, and well over half of the wildcat strikers were CIO union members.[1] Yet the industrial union federation's formal commitment to the no-strike pledge remained steadfast, continually reforged by the powerfully symbolic quality the pledge assumed in an election year, by the National War Labor Board's use of its disciplinary powers, and by the fear that any wavering on this issue would provoke a new antilabor onslaught in the form of crippling national service legislation. In this political context, industrial union leaders took unprecedented steps to ensure the maintenance of order in their ranks, steps that forced these officials to rely upon increasingly bureaucratic and undemocratic methods of institutional control.

"Union responsibility"

Faced with the working-class challenge to industrial order and internal union discipline, the NWLB used its power and prestige to uphold the authority of management over its employees and that of cooperative union leaders over their often rebellious rank and file. At the core of the NWLB industrial relations philosophy was the idea that a system of industrial jurisprudence could resolve shop-floor conflict and harmonize worker–manager interests. This idea, however, was embedded within an equally strong commitment to the prerogatives of management and the necessity of continuous production. Associate board member Harry Shulman, while serving as impartial umpire under the Ford–United Automobile Workers contract, framed the issue in virtually metahistori-

178

cal terms: "Any enterprise in a capitalist or socialist economy requires persons with authority and responsibility to keep the enterprise running . . . That authority is vested in Supervision. It must be vested there because the responsibility for production is vested there; and responsibility must be accompanied by authority."[2]

Of course, the NWLB understood that innumerable grievances would arise in the day-to-day life of the workplace, but the board sought to build a system of shop governance that would settle these disputes and at the same time prevent them from either interfering with production or challenging wholesale the necessary authority of shop management. To this end, the board elaborated a system, first worked out in the prewar garment and needle trades, that removed industrial disputes from the shop floor and then provided a set of formal, bureaucratic procedures to resolve them. The system rested upon an elaborate four-step grievance procedure, capped in most industries by an impartial umpire who adjudicated those grievances that were not settled at lower levels. Immensely influential in setting a national postwar pattern, the NWLB came "to regard an appropriate grievance procedure, with its terminal point in an impartial umpire, as indispensable to the establishment of justice within the industry community."[3]

So universal became the adoption of this system that its deployment seemed a natural and inevitable evolution of a mature system of industrial relations. In part, its rapid acceptance derived from the genuine usefulness such a procedure held for the union. Stewards and local leaders used the grievance procedure to consolidate a union consciousness among the workers whose complaints they handled, and trade union officials found the system useful for policing the contract without frequent, debilitating confrontations with management.[4] CIO intellectuals such as Clinton Golden and Harold Ruttenberg thought that the progressive evolution of the grievance procedure and collective bargaining might lay the basis for a democratic, civil society in the workplace, certainly for a system of judicial restraint upon the unfettered power of management. In 1942, therefore, the CIO formally reversed its long-standing opposition to grievance arbitration and adopted the NWLB philosophy in this realm.[5]

Despite its concrete advantages and hopeful potentiality, the grievance procedure worked to defuse union power and legitimate managerial authority. The system shifted disputes from the shop floor, where the stewards and work groups held the greatest leverage, to the realm of contractual interpretation, where the authority of management and the value of orderly procedure weighed more heavily. In the meantime – possibly several weeks – the discipline and authority of management remained intact. As long as production continued on management's terms, workers with grievances were, in effect, guilty until proven innocent. Arbitration finally came into play for those grievances still unresolved after the fourth step, but the judicial authority here steadily shrank in the 1940s and soon extended only to an interpretation of the written contract itself and to an increasingly complex set of case law precedents.[6]

To make this system work, the NWLB insisted that production stoppages could not be tolerated when grievances were being processed. The board would not review a case if there was a strike in progress. More importantly, the National War Labor Board demanded "union responsibility" and threatened to withdraw or deny maintenance of membership and dues checkoff to any union whose leadership led or condoned wartime work stoppages. In fact, union leaders were expected to take a direct hand in disciplining wildcat strikers. In 1943 the NWLB denied Chrysler locals of the UAW maintenance of membership because the board felt that local leaders had been insufficiently vigorous in their opposition to recent wildcat strikes. And in another strike incident, the NWLB instructed UAW international officers to "investigate" a General Motors local president and impose five-dollar fines on each of 179 members of his union who had participated in wildcat disturbances.[7]

The NWLB's wartime union responsibility doctrine was part of a subtle redefinition of the meaning of industrial democracy that enabled top union officials to discipline rank-and-file dissidents and reshape their organizations in a more conservative and bureaucratic mold. The board defined its mandate as one advancing democratic trade unionism in the context of a larger battle between democracy and fascism. But the public members of the NWLB interpreted their duty exclusively in terms of the development of routine and peaceful labor–management relations and the increase in war production. Hence the board called the United Steelworkers of America "one of the most democratic, responsible and efficient unions" but thought the United Mine Workers "coercive" and "irresponsible," not because of any distinction in the way they were run – both autocratically – but because the president of one union cooperated with the government and the president of the other did not.[8] Administratively, the NWLB did oppose race and sex discrimination, but it was blind to the democratic rights of internal union rebels. For example, in 1943 the American Civil Liberties Union's Roger Baldwin asked William Davis if the board recognized the right of union members to organize against the policy of their union leadership. Davis replied that the board did not. He viewed the internal trade union structure as essentially analogous to that of a business corporation, and he saw the duties of lower-level union officials as equivalent to those of foremen and middle-level management.[9]

Significantly, the NWLB did not automatically deny a local union maintenance of membership just because a strike had occurred. Instead, the political attitude of the union leadership on the scene became the key to the board's decision. During the spring and summer of 1942, for example, workers in a small steel fabrication plant in New England conducted several unauthorized strikes against the advice of their local USW leadership. Because the NWLB was convinced that these work stoppages were "a spontaneous and unplanned demonstration of the rank and file," the board did not hesitate to grant the local union its now standard security clause. In justification, the NWLB argued, "If this union is to become a responsible organization acting through its leaders, it is necessary that it have some power over its members . . . The inclusion of a maintenance of membership provision in the contract between the parties will have that result because an employee who elects to be bound by the maintenance clause must remain a member in good standing in order to keep his job."[10]

The NWLB demonstrated its attitude on an even larger scale in the rubber industry, where the government and United Rubber Workers President Sherman Dalrymple cooperated closely to maintain labor discipline. In Akron the independent power of shop stewards, committeemen, and local leaders had been built and tested in several years of daily struggle with the city's Big Four rubber companies. A tradition of shop-floor militancy, born in the 1930s, continued well into the war years. Recognizing that "the elimination of habits, nurtured in successful practice, from thousands of workers is no overnight task," the NWLB encouraged the URW's international leadership to curb the power of secondary leaders and eliminate the use of such direct action techniques. "The practical and symbolic value of union security," declared the labor board in April 1943, "will further this process." Little more than a year later, the NWLB proved the "practical" advantage of its policy when Dalrymple's union seemed in open revolt. Then the NWLB threw the full weight of its own machinery and that of the military behind his leadership, and, as we shall see later in this chapter, helped enforce his discipline by upholding the expulsion of seventy-two unionists in one instance and the unchecked authority to fine several hundred others in another.[11]

Although not so spectacular, the organizational advantages that a politically cooperative union leadership derived from the NWLB policy were often equally profound. Once a trade union had won bargaining rights in its jurisdiction, it could count on a relatively secure existence so long as it preserved industrial peace. When UAW Local 904 sought a union security clause in its contract with Southern California's Vultee Aircraft, its leaders did so almost entirely in terms of the local union's work on behalf of the war effort. Although officials of the local admitted that morale was low and interest in the union spotty, they easily persuaded the NWLB to grant them maintenance of membership because of the cooperation that local officers had given the company in its production drive, their active participation in Red Cross and war bond campaigns, and the fact that Vultee Aircraft had recently won an army–navy E award.[12]

Such activities were a far cry from those of the prewar era, when the fight for almost any form of union security required mobilization of the union's membership for a long and bitter fight. But now the wartime expansion of the labor force, coupled with the NWLB maintenance-of-membership policy, enabled American unions to increase their dues-paying numbers from 9 to 14 million with relatively little effort. Some older militants complained that many of the new unionists were but temporary "conscripts" who lacked the "do-or-die" spirit of the 1930s, but the international leadership of most unions proudly hailed each numerical advance. The CIO alone doubled its dues-paying membership under Roosevelt's wartime labor program, of which Philip Murray and other top leaders of the organization never ceased to remind those who doubted their cautious stewardship.[13]

The drive for national service

If the NWLB's maintenance-of-membership policy represented a carrot held out to CIO leaders to enforce the no-strike pledge, the growing government effort to enact national service legislation proved a weighty and coercive stick. With a perverse logic all its own, this movement for greater regimentation of labor actually grew in strength as military victory in the war became certain and as production requirements declined. Such a "labor draft" would give the government power to assign civilian workers to essential industries under threat of criminal penalty. The armed services considered labor supply the main bottleneck to full wartime production, but a lack of reconversion planning for the postwar era merely exacerbated labor problems by creating temporary pools of unemployment where military contracts were canceled but new civilian production was prohibited. Because the government refused to allow the NWLB to use increased wage rates as a means of inducing workers to move into critical but low-wage industries, there were labor shortages in some industries and a growing specter of unemployment in others. This anomalous situation naturally produced still more labor unrest, coupled with a widespread sense of job insecurity among large numbers of war workers. The military supply services compounded these difficulties by keeping their prime contractors in the dark as to when programs would be canceled. They feared that if workers knew in advance when a production quota had been fulfilled, they would slacken their pace of work in order to stretch out the remaining weeks of employment. Hence, rigid labor controls accompanied by intensified wartime propaganda became the military's alternative to a planned and full-employment reconversion program.[14]

Urged on by the patrician, well-connected Grenville Clark and his influential "Citizens' Committee for a National Service Act," the Roosevelt administration began a steady accommodation to military and conservative pressure for such a labor draft, especially when government officials projected its use as an antistrike measure. Thus, after the coal strikes of spring 1943, Roosevelt and Secretary of War Stimson shifted to a stance favoring national service legislation.[15] Both often emphasized what they considered the democratic and egalitarian features of such a law, but the democracy of national service was always akin to that of the barracks and the regiment, where all shared equally in their unfreedom. Thus Stimson told the Senate Military Affairs Committee in 1944 that the nation faced a "situation of anarchy" on the labor front. "The purpose of a National Service Law is to get at this basic evil which produces the irresponsibility out of which stem strikes, threats of strikes, excessive turnover, absenteeism, and other manifestations of irresponsibility with which we are now plagued." Without national service legislation, Stimson and the military forecast growing antilabor sentiment in the armed services that they could not control and would not discourage.[16]

FDR's unexpected endorsement of national service legislation in his 1944 State of the Union Address caught the CIO off guard, for the president now favored a bill that the labor movement had consistently denounced as a "slave labor" measure. If enacted, it would weaken union security provisions and make inoperative much of the seniority system painfully built over the last several years. Furthermore, it would subject individual unionists to criminal penalties for either quitting work, engaging in collective strike action, or refusing to work where assigned. Philip Murray feared that once such a law was on the books, it would linger well into the postwar era, crippling the CIO's postwar strike power, just as the World War I era Lever Act had helped break the UMW's postwar wage offensive late in 1919. Thus the CIO president greeted FDR's endorsement of the Austin–Wadsworth bill with the quip that Dr. Win-the-War had obviously prescribed "quack medicine."[17]

Naturally, the CIO found it difficult to fight directly the president and his proposal in the months before the 1944 elections. Because FDR initially linked his call for national service to a progressive tax, rationing, and price control package, the CIO rhetorically emphasized its support for these liberal measures and characteristically blamed "defeatist" and "reactionary" elements in Congress and the war production agencies for the labor draft proposal.[18] But all this merely put a rose-colored light on a bad situation. Murray and other top CIO leaders knew from private conversations with the president that he would sign virtually any national service law passed by Congress. And, of course, the conservatives in the national legislature made it clear in 1944 that they would emasculate any prolabor proposals left in FDR's arsenal – a circumstance that Roosevelt himself publicly acknowledged early in 1945, when he capitulated entirely to the military demand that national service be enacted with no legislative strings attached.[19]

Because Roosevelt could not be relied upon to head off a repressive legislative onslaught, CIO leaders determined early in 1944 that the only way to avoid national service was by firmly reasserting their authority within their own organizations. They feared that unless they enforced the no-strike pledge on the local union level, hostile forces in Congress and the armed services would dominate government policy, creating an even more bitterly antilabor climate of opinion and jeopardizing FDR's chances in November. The way would then be open for a vicious anti-labor reaction in the immediate postwar era.

These fears mounted throughout the spring of 1944. Philip Murray warned dissident delegates to the USW's second convention in May that if the union rescinded its no-strike pledge "its leaders would be required to rush to Washington and combat the influence of a powerful anti-labor group."[20] Two weeks later, R. J. Thomas gave the UAW's rebellious membership a nearly apocalyptic vision. With the Detroit press full of wildcat strike news and the impending invasion of France, the UAW president pleaded for restraint: "Public opinion has become inflamed against our union. Our union cannot survive if the nation and our soldiers believe that we are obstructing the war effort." Thomas admitted that management took advantage of the no-strike pledge, that the NWLB dragged its feet, and that government labor policies were unfair. Nevertheless, the burden of winning the war fell upon labor's shoulders. "We may have to take it on the chin here and there for a time, but if we can present the nation and the returning soldier with a clean record, we will gain after the war for the sacrifices we are making today."[21]

Such were the bleak alternatives that leaders of even the CIO's most powerful unions seemed to face in the third year of the war. Either the rank and file adhered to the no-strike pledge, or organized labor faced destruction at the hands of its enemies, now brandishing the multiple threat of national service legislation, NWLB discipline, and a growth of anti-union sentiment, both at home and among the millions of young servicemen who would soon be veterans in the unpredictable postwar world.

By 1944, of course, the maintenance of industrial discipline in CIO unions proved a difficult matter. In one guise or another, the no-strike pledge had become the central internal issue in many of the largest internationals. In volatile unions such as the URW and UAW, well-organized factions opposed to the pledge challenged the union leadership time and again. In less politically well developed organizations, such as the USW and the Industrial Union of Marine and Shipyard Workers of America, the issue sparked a strong debate, if not such potent factionalism. Behind these attacks on the pledge stood the rising tide of work stoppages and wildcat strikes, now often led by well respected local union officials committed to a broad political and economic offensive against the National War Labor Board and other agencies of economic regimentation. The strikes they led were now better organized and more tenacious than in previous years. In 1944, work stoppages involving more than 1,000 workers each were more frequent, and disputes over working conditions and management policies increased markedly. Although these stoppages were still of considerably shorter duration than in prewar years, the total number of strikes and lockouts – almost 5,000 – was higher than that of any other twelve-month period.[22]

With their authority so severely threatened, top CIO union officers feared that unless they could restore labor peace – or at least demonstrate a firm effort to do so – they would be ground mercilessly between the millstone of government intervention and regimentation on the one hand and the militancy of a rebellious rank and file on the other. In the United Steelworkers, where the president held great power, effective international union control merely demanded the more efficient application of existing executive power. But in those CIO unions with a more democratic tradition and a relatively well-organized oppositional faction, the leadership's ability to crack down on wildcat strikes required a strengthening of the international's power over that of the locals. In the UAW, both major executive board factions agreed upon the constitutional steps necessary to discipline wildcat strikers. In the URW, where a strong and unified opposition to the union's president existed, the control of rebellious rank-and-file elements took an unconstitutional and illegal form, ultimately resulting in the intervention of the CIO national office and resignation of the union's president to stabilize the situation.

Executive power in the USW

The Pittsburgh bureaucracy of the United Steelworkers had sufficient institutional power during the war to prevent wildcat strikes or local union dissidents from getting out of hand. Although there were hundreds of unauthorized strikes in the steel industry and scores of locals that opposed the no-strike pledge, this sentiment remained generally inchoate because of the power of the international, the prestige of its president, and the failure of oppositional elements to build a union-wide organization.

By mid-1944, the union's maintenance-of-membership contract provisions enabled the USW national office to build a $3.5 million treasury. But the local unions remained impoverished, with 75 percent of their funds going directly to the international coffers. Their financial plight made these locals dependent upon the district director and his agents for many of their day-to-day services. International representatives, under close supervision by the district offices, took on much of this work.[23]

At the same time, local unions were sharply limited in the extent to which they could influence even the negotiation of their own local contract. During the war, Murray and Pressman moved toward industrywide bargaining by ensuring the relative uniformity of all NWLB-approved contracts. With officers of the labor board, they reached agreement that the NWLB would refuse to review a local union contract dispute unless it was first channeled through the USW's Washington office. The USW later extended this principle to the National Labor Relations Board after the passage of the Smith–Connally Act. All local union requests for an NLRB strike vote were handed over to the USW national office. Murray then put pressure on the local involved to rescind its petition. Usually, the local complied without further compulsion.[24]

Leaders of the international also kept a tight political check on their regional directors and staff representatives. They feared, resisted, and successfully avoided the factionalism that flourished in the UAW and the URW. Clinton Golden and David McDonald, who supervised the internal life of the union while Philip Murray tended to CIO business, carefully suppressed the open advertisement of political differences within their organization. Regional directors were not permitted to publish their own newspapers; *Steel Labor* and its various editions remained the sole news organ of the international. Golden admonished staff members not to exhibit their political differences before the union rank and file. Such arguments "set a bad example which cannot be condoned and [are] an invitation and incitement to factionalism which can easily disrupt, if not destroy, an organization."[25] Golden and McDonald also intervened directly in district electoral contests to ensure the selection of loyal directors. On at least one occasion, McDonald defeated an oppositionist by packing a delegated election caucus with administration supporters from outside the region.[26]

Such institutional muscle enabled Murray to apply the no-strike policy in the USW with a free hand. In February 1944, the USW held a special 500-member Policy Committee meeting in Pittsburgh, where Murray emphasized the leadership's renewed opposition to unauthorized work stoppages or slowdowns. The need to reassert the USW's no-strike pledge may have been prompted not only by the threat of national service legislation but also by the semiofficial Christmas eve strike of

150,000 steelworkers, which undoubtedly gave some in the union the idea that the no-strike prohibition had been unofficially relaxed. Murray therefore declared that the union would not use its grievance procedure to defend "any individual or group which participates in a work stoppage as a means towards getting an adjustment of a grievance."[27]

Murray's announcement was but an emphatic restatement of the provision in standard USW contracts that all employee complaints must be settled through the use of the grievance procedure, a doctrine that Harold Ruttenberg and Clinton Golden considered central to the establishment of responsible unionism. Of course, many locals continued to defend those who engaged in short work stoppages on the grounds that extenuating circumstances prompted such formal violations of the contract. However, a rigid application of the USW policy would leave these strikers completely at the mercy of their employer. This situation enhanced management power; company foremen and supervisors could now alter working conditions, transfer employees, and speed up production, safe in the knowledge that the union's only recourse was to an often cumbersome grievance procedure. Should employees strike, management had the right to discharge or discipline them in any way it saw fit, and the union would stand aside. Many local unionists held that this policy was an open invitation to company provocation, for it could now use wildcat strikes as a means of eliminating those union militants it could not dispose of through outright discharge.[28]

Where local union leaders condoned or actually led such wildcat strikes, the international empowered district directors to intervene. If necessary, local officers could be removed and a staff representative assigned to administer the affairs of the union for an indefinite period. Usually, such drastic action was unnecessary; a telegram from Philip Murray to the offending local was sufficiently impressive to persuade the union to return to work.[29]

Throughout the war, Murray's remarkable prestige in the USW remained undiminished. There was considerable grumbling because of his devotion to the no-strike pledge and his continuing faith in the NWLB, but the steelworker president never faced a serious internal challenge to his control. In the 1945 elections, a few district directors were defeated by a restive membership, but their replacements were as loyal to Murray as their predecessors. Only after David McDonald assumed command in the early 1950s did the presidential mystique shatter and a series of challenges arise to autocratic control of the union.[30]

Wildcat strikes and wartime discipline in the UAW

In the UAW, the wildcat strike problem proved more serious than in the USW because many of these work stoppages were now defended by important secondary leaders of the union. And because of the UAW's tradition of factionalism and democracy, union leaders had far less effective power than their counterparts in the USW when it came to imposing internal discipline. Hence, the move toward greater international control required both a relative suspension of factional conflict at the top and a diminution of local autonomy at the union base.

When the UAW's executive board met in February 1944, the wildcat strike issue dominated its agenda. In the wake of the president's endorsement of national service legislation, the CIO demanded that constituent unions take effective steps to halt the spreading work stoppages. In Detroit the auto corporations had begun a new drive to convince the NWLB that the UAW contracts should be stripped of maintenance of membership because union officials seemed unwilling or unable to prevent unauthorized strikes. In fact, Chrysler had already won this point in August 1943, when the corporation convinced the NWLB to deny the UAW a company-wide union security clause for a six-month trial period. Now, Briggs and Ford were pressing similar claims before the labor board.[31]

The problem seemed particularly serious at Ford's giant factories in or near Detroit. Ford Director Richard Leonard informed the union executive board that at the Willow Run, Highland Park, and River Rouge facilities, the number of wildcat strikes was increasing rapidly. Some 256 had already taken place in 1943, far more than at General Motors or Chrysler. At the Rouge, where some 85,000 labored in America's single largest production complex, some UAW staffers feared that Local 600 might disintegrate if some control were not imposed from without. Moreover, Ford's management had finally begun to professionalize its labor relations policies and personnel, and Leonard warned that "unless we take some constructive position there is a possibility that the company will have a good case in the public eye to deny many of the demands of the union."[32]

Leonard's problem, and that of the entire UAW bureaucracy, stemmed from the fact that elected union officers and their local trial committees could not be relied upon to discipline those groups or individuals who advocated or participated in unauthorized strikes. When such work stoppages occurred, plant managers usually attempted to penalize the strikers through disciplinary layoffs or outright firings. But all too often, a local union's leadership – its stewards, committeemen, even elected plant-wide officials – had actively led these wildcat strikes. When the company attempted to discipline these ringleaders, most local officials resisted and fought for those penalized through the established grievance machinery, even though they were formally bound to uphold the no-strike pledge by personally disciplining or expelling strikers from the union. Ad hoc efforts by UAW regional directors to impose their own discipline on these recalcitrant locals were often checked by the renewed wartime factionalism that made top officers of the union ultra-sensitive to the exercise of such unilateral power.[33]

Faced with this difficulty, UAW leaders adopted a systematic method of enforcing their authority at the February executive board meeting in Los Angeles. Under the new policy, locals were instructed to report immediately all work stoppages to the international. The executive board, not the local, would conduct an investigation to determine the cause of the strike and those responsible. If union members were in fact at fault, then all officials from president to shop steward would be "instructed to withhold all services to such members and all intervention in their behalf, in the event of disciplinary action against them by management." In addition, the locals were instructed to try those members indicted by the international and expel them if necessary. Should the local refuse to cooperate with the top UAW leadership, its elected officials could be removed from office and an administrator installed.[34]

These steps decisively shifted formal power in the union from the locals to the international bureaucracy. Committeemen, stewards, and local officers were made responsible for the suppression of wildcat strikes even if they themselves were not involved. The elementary links of solidarity that put shop-floor leaders on the side of the rank and file during unauthorized stoppages were now declared, in the words of the Ford Motor Company umpire, "a romantic expression of a perverse and debasing view of the committeeman's obligations."[35] Under this Los Angeles policy, the UAW finally adopted the disciplinary posture that General Motors had unsuccessfully sought to impose since the corporation's abortive negotiations with Homer Martin in the summer of 1937. When work stoppages now took place, secondary union leaders could be penalized at will by the company while the international stood aside.

The new policy moved the UAW one step closer to the bureaucratic regime and conservative spirit typified by the United Steelworkers union.

Within a month of its adoption, Richard T. Leonard found an opportunity to apply forcefully the Los Angeles resolution against wildcat strikers and politically dissident unionists at the mammoth Rouge complex. On the evening of March 7, 1944, word reached workers in the Pratt and Whitney aircraft engine building that two of their number, both veterans, had been caught smoking and fired. Thereupon, several hundred aircraft workers surged into the building's personnel office to demand an explanation. In the ensuing "riot," workers disrupted the labor relations office, destroyed work records, and roughed up management personnel. [36] Implementing its new get-tough labor policy, Ford's management soon announced the discharge or suspension of twenty of the participants, including eleven UAW committeemen, whose involvement in the affair was at best tangential but whom Ford considered responsible for the maintenance of order among their fellow workers. "Who are these [fired] members?" asked *Ford Facts*, the organ of Local 600. "Militant union leaders, district and building committeemen, the backbone of the UAW–CIO." [37]

The penalties of those disciplined were routinely taken to the grievance procedure and soon began working their way to arbitration under the Ford–UAW umpire agreement. Even though a coalition of Communists and conservatives held top leadership posts in the local, they intended to defend those fired by Ford. Before the incident, local officials had conducted a campaign against Ford's provocative personnel policies, and local President Joseph Twyman characterized the recent wildcat as a "spontaneous reaction of the rank and file against inhuman and dictatorial treatment." [38]

But now, the international entered the affair. R. J. Thomas called for "drastic and effective action" against those responsible for the riot. Thomas and Leonard condoned Ford's harsh discipline: "Our union can not and will not tolerate rowdyism as a means of adjusting its problems," they announced to the *Detroit Free Press*. Thomas and Leonard ordered the leadership of Local 600 to deprive those fired by Ford of any further use of the grievance procedure. The international executive board began its own investigation into the causes of the strike and those the union itself should penalize. The *Free Press*, which had long headlined news of

UAW wildcat strikes, now applauded Thomas and his executive board for taking a "long stride towards a new era of responsibility among war-working unionists."[39]

But within the Rouge, union militants grew alarmed at the international's willingness to sacrifice twenty workers to the new no-strike policy. This concern centered in the Rouge aircraft unit, where radical opposition to both the international and the local Ford leadership had strong influence. Led by the charismatic Lawrence Yost, this group in the Pratt and Whitney building became a strong base for the union-wide Rank and File caucus that challenged the no-strike pledge at the UAW's 1944 convention. During the second week in March, they laid plans for a plant-wide strike to demand restoration of the rights of those whom Ford had disciplined the week before. On the night of March 14, aircraft unit militants attempted to close the Rouge complex with auto barricades and picket lines reminiscent of the great strike in April 1941. Initially, thousands respected the new strike call, but their audacious gambit failed the next day after the leadership of Local 600 and the UAW Ford department mobilized its forces against the work stoppage.[40]

To those in control of the international and Local 600, this second strike was even more serious than the first, for it represented a politically inspired attempt to challenge enforcement of the no-strike pledge. Now, leaders of the Ford local announced that they would stand aside if Ford chose to discipline those who had instigated the stoppage; eventually 121 were suspended or fired. Leonard defended the new policy at tumultuous meetings of the Ford local and promised even more international union intervention in the event that "irresponsible stoppages" failed to subside. When dissident strikers demanded a trial by their peers in the aircraft unit, Leonard and Addes realized that they might well be exonerated. Consequently, the UAW executive board hurriedly abrogated that section of the Los Angeles policy calling for a trial by a local union committee. Instead, union disciplinary measures could rest entirely in the hands of the executive board itself. Concluded *Ford Facts* on the whole affair: "The adamant position of our leadership on the violation of the no-strike pledge by irresponsible union representatives is a stern warning that the kid glove tactics of yesteryear have definitely been discarded."[41]

During the Ford incident, the UAW top leadership did not find it necessary to bring the full weight of the union's disciplinary apparatus to bear because the international dealt with cooperative local officers and a rebellious department. But not all local leaders could be relied upon to carry out the Los Angeles policy resolution. Caught between the demands of the international and the pressures generated by their rank and file, a substantial proportion chose to defy the international in order to maintain a semblance of credibility with their shop-floor constituency. The tension inherent in this decision is captured in the minutes of a meeting between a UAW regional director and a Cleveland local president who had just led his union on a wildcat strike in defense of two members fired by the company.

UAW Regional Director Paul Miley: Do you understand clearly that I instructed you to get the plant back in operation?

Local 91 President Lawrence Wilkey: You told me, Brother Miley, that if this committee and myself did not change our mind and order those people back into the plant immediately that you were going to kick us out of office.

Miley: Do you understand that the production of some four or five hundred aircraft engines has been lost already . . . doesn't [that] affect your judgment in this case at all?

Wilkey: I wouldn't say, Paul, that it doesn't affect my judgment, but I wasn't elected by those people to win the war. I was elected to lead those people and to represent them. I have tried my best to abide by the Constitution [of the UAW], but at this time my conscience will not let me because of my duty to those people.[42]

By the summer of 1944, many local officials found themselves in much the same dilemma. In such cases, the UAW executive board closed ranks and placed the offending local unions under appointed administrators. When in May 1944 the leadership of Chrysler Local 490 organized a week-long strike in defiance of the international, all fourteen members of its executive board were suspended. They were replaced by Administrator Leo LaMotte, an Addes–Frankensteen caucus partisan who never hesitated to accept an unpopular assignment.[43] Walter Reuther also took disciplinary measures within his own department. When in August a Chevrolet local struck for eleven days in defense of two unionists fired by GM, Reuther put his prestige on the line to end the embarrassing strike in his own jurisdiction. After the leaders of the local could not be persuaded to order a return to work, they were suspended from office and a regional director loyal to Reuther was made administrator, although only a year before, he had questioned the usefulness of such receiverships when his factional opponents had proposed them. Now, Reuther found himself in tactical agreement with his erstwhile rivals on the executive board, and his work on behalf of the no-strike pledge did much to erode his support among those in the left wing of his caucus who had heretofore given the GM director at least critical backing.[44]

Debate over the no-strike pledge

The UAW's crackdown on wildcat strikes generated widespread resentment in union ranks during the spring and summer of 1944. Key locals in Detroit, Flint, Chicago, and Cleveland adopted resolutions against the no-strike pledge, and dissident aircraft unit leaders at the Rouge called a citywide conference in April to protest the tough new international policy. Organizing into a new Rank and File caucus, these mavericks began a union-wide campaign to revoke outright the no-strike pledge at the next UAW convention.

Independent of and opposed to the older "power caucuses" in the UAW, the new group took its character from two types of unionists: the veteran secondary leaders in Michigan, who through their practical wartime experience had grown opposed to the pledge, and a few score ideological radicals who worked hard to advance the program of the caucus as part of a larger effort to move the UAW decisively to the left. The small anti-Stalinist Worker's party provided much of the caucus's organizational backbone. It denounced the world war as one of interimperialist rivalry and counterposed the fight for socialism and the interests of the working class to the victory of either side in the conflict. Thus, the movement against the no-strike pledge was a concrete step that a key sector of the American working class could take to begin to declare its independence and assert the democratic rights of labor against the growing tendency in the capitalist West toward an authoritarian and statist solution of the current crisis.[45]

Of course, most of those who were attracted to the Rank and File caucus, including the bulk of its leadership, did not hold such radical views. They found little contradiction between their patriotic support of the war effort and their opposition to the no-strike pledge. They fought the pledge from a strictly trade union point of view, insisting that continued enforcement of the no-strike policy weakened and fragmented their locals. They saw the movement primarily as a means of reintegrating the unions. A Chicago local's broadside against the pledge emphasized this viewpoint: "Wildcat strikes develop only when the rank and file members lose confidence in their elected leader's ability to settle their problems without long delay . . . This same elected leadership in such a situation is forced to line up with management against the workers under the no-strike pledge and order the workers back to work without a solution to their problems. A union cannot survive under such conditions. The gap between the rank and file and their elected leaders will grow so wide that our whole structure will collapse. Vote against the no-strike pledge and save your union."[46]

When the UAW assembled for its annual convention in Grand Rapids in September 1944, the no-strike pledge held center stage as the only real item on the union's agenda save, of course, the annual contest for office. Three resolutions on the pledge confronted the 2,400 delegates: a majority position, backed by most of the leadership and the Communists, reaffirming the pledge for the duration; a separate Reuther caucus resolution proposing that after the defeat of Germany, strikes might be selectively authorized in factories converted to civilian production; and a "superminority" plank sponsored by the Rank and File group that simply revoked the pledge immediately, subject to later ratification by a union-wide referendum.

In a two-day debate that captured the attention of the nation, Reuther's effort once again to straddle the fence between left and right utterly collapsed. Both conservatives and radicals easily slashed away at his proposal, for it rested on the false distinction between civilian and military production, long recognized by labor as invalid in a total war, and on the mistaken belief that a smooth and early conversion to civilian production was about to begin. With many of his usual supporters deserting him, Reuther found his plan hooted down by the convention in a voice vote. At the nadir of his fortunes in the wartime UAW, Reuther lost the first vice-presidency to Richard Frankensteen two days later. He barely retained a top post in the union by defeating one-time ally Richard Leonard in another vice-presidential ballot, and then only with the help of the CIO's Allen Haywood and Sidney Hillman, who intervened directly at the convention to maintain the status quo in the UAW hierarchy.[47]

The real debate lay between those who favored and those who opposed outright revocation of the no-strike pledge. Just back from the war front in France, R. J. Thomas once more justified the pledge on patriotic grounds, whereas Philip Murray, in an extraordinary appeal to UAW delegates, laid special emphasis upon the need to retain the strike prohibition in order to ensure Roosevelt's reelection. But the unreflective call to support patriotically the commander-in-chief had worn thin by late

1944. When some UAW officers made ready to bring wounded war veterans to the microphones in their support, leaders of the Rank and File caucus threatened to bring their own recently hospitalized servicemen to the convention floor. Both sides agreed to forego this macabre confrontation.[48]

When the votes were counted, the superminority resolution revoking the pledge took 37 percent of the vote, chiefly from the older locals in Detroit, Flint, and Chicago. But backers of the pledge also failed to win a majority, so the UAW now found itself with no formal position on this crucial issue. In the ensuing confusion, Victor Reuther and the leaders of the Rank and File caucus worked out an interim compromise. The strike pledge would be reaffirmed, but only until a union-wide referendum after the national elections resolved the issue. In the meantime, UAW officers were barred from the use of union funds, facilities, or personnel to campaign for their point of view.[49]

Threatened from within, leaders of the UAW instinctively turned to Washington and the rest of the CIO for help. Thomas worked to secure FDR's personal intervention during the referendum, and officers of sharply divided Local 600 solicited the propledge views of popular front liberals such as Claude Pepper and Helen Gahagan Douglas in support of a large affirmative vote at the Rouge. Meanwhile, elements close to the Communist Party set up a "Committee to Uphold the No-Strike Pledge," which gained financial backing from several CIO unions. Joseph Curran's National Maritime Union was particularly active, donating money and manpower to help get out the propledge vote in the Detroit area. On the other side, the Rank and File caucus held city-wide meetings and published a widely distributed newssheet.[50]

Despite all this activity, the referendum failed to excite union ranks. Delays in the actual balloting proved frustrating, and the final turnout disappointed both sides in the contest. When the postcard ballots were finally tallied in March 1945, less than 300,000 had voted, about 30 percent of the union membership. Supporters of the pledge took a two-to-one lead over their opponents, although the contest was closer in Flint and Detroit, where antipledge votes reached almost 45 percent of all those cast.[51]

The referendum lost, but the wildcat strikes continued. In UAW region 1 on Detroit's East Side, for example, only about 12 percent of the almost 200,000 workers had cast a vote against the no-strike pledge. But their region remained a hotbed of wartime strike activity, and numerous stoppages swept through the Briggs, Packard, Hudson, and Chrysler plants early in 1945. Even as they reaffirmed the pledge in March, the government reported more Detroit workers on strike than at any other time during the war.[52]

If there is an explanation for this dichotomous behavior, it lies in the contradictory nature of twentieth-century working-class consciousness. Since at least the 1920s, and never more so than during the war itself, virtually every form of American culture and politics has urged workers to consider themselves part of the mainstream of national life. And like the flag and the uniform, the no-strike pledge had a powerfully symbolic content, representing an unquestionable affirmation of working-class patriotism and participation in the American consensus. Thus, most workers who bothered to return their postcard ballots cast affirmative votes in the referendum. Yet, consciousness represents concrete activity as much as verbalized expression or symbolic politics. The harsh reality of factory life enclosed these same workers in a social environment that reduced to an icon their abstract patriotism. In their continuing wildcat strikes, auto workers put an evaluation on the conduct of the home front and served notice that the meaning of their daily struggle contained more social reality than the sloganized war aims that bombarded them from the press and the radio.[53]

Order and disorder in the URW

Although measures of discipline and control adopted by the UAW's leadership proved increasingly ineffective as the war neared its end, the union's top officers maintained their posts and enforced their policies as best they could. The Rubber Workers offer a contrary example of a union whose executive officers took extreme measures to maintain their authority but who ultimately failed to enforce the no-strike pledge in the most important sections of their industry. By the summer of 1945, URW President Sherman Dalrymple admitted defeat and resigned from office, although power in the union did not shift to the dissident locals that had done so much to cause his downfall.

The URW's wartime membership had swollen to almost 180,000, but the heart of the union remained concentrated in the Big Four rubber locals in Akron: Goodyear Local 2, Goodrich 5, Firestone 7, and General Tire 9. By mid-1943, these locals had become consistent opponents of President Dalrymple and his bloc of Communist–conservative backers on the URW's executive board. Although Dalrymple and his vice-president, L. S. Buckmaster, had risen from the ranks of the Akron rubber workers, they now based their control of the international upon the many war-born locals outside of Akron. These locals had benefited greatly from the NWLB's wage equalization decisions and its union security policy.

Following the big Akron wildcat in May 1943, an open break took place between the Big Four locals and the Dalrymple administration. The URW's executive board relied upon increasingly bureaucratic measures of discipline, backed by NWLB authority, to enforce the union's no-strike pledge. When the URW met in the fall of 1943, Dalrymple vowed to be a "damned sight tougher" in the coming year against unauthorized strikes. "Too much local autonomy," he told the Akron Big Four, "is liable to engulf us in a stream of disaster."54 In Akron the wildcat strike had long served as a substitute for or adjunct to the formal grievance procedure, but the companies, the international union, and the NWLB were determined to put an end to this practice. The labor board specifically awarded the URW maintenance of membership so that the international leadership would have additional disciplinary powers to curb these quickie strikes. But most of the local union leadership in the Akron Big Four either stood aside or supported their memberships when wildcat strikes flared.55 Therefore, Dalrymple and his executive board felt it necessary to intervene directly to curb these strikes and exercise what they took to be their constitutional responsibility.

When in January 1944 a strike of General Tire band builders protested company reductions in the piecerate, Dalrymple moved quickly. He expelled seventy strikers from the local, invoked the union's maintenance-of-membership clause to have them fired by the company, and put an executive board administrator in charge of URW Local 9. Later, when two past presidents of the local championed the cause of those expelled, Dalrymple had them fired by the company as well.56 This brutal crackdown aroused the entire Akron labor movement, and many considered Dalrymple's exercise of discipline a direct violation of the URW constitution. The Akron industrial union council, dominated by the Big Four, condemned both General Tire and President Dalrymple for the firing and expulsion of the seventy-two Local 9 unionists. But an even more embarrassing blow soon fell on the URW president. Dalrymple held formal membership in Goodrich Local 5, one of the most militant and oppositional locals in the URW. This local now expelled him from its ranks for "dictatorial violation" of the URW constitution. In turn, the URW executive board reinstated Dalrymple and directed Local 5 to do likewise.[57]

This controversy fused the issues of local union autonomy, executive board power, and the no-strike pledge at the URW's 1944 convention in September. Akron locals, united in their opposition to the pledge, wanted to overturn the General Tire expulsions, curb the power of the URW executive board, and oust Dalrymple from office. But in an early test vote on these issues, the Akron progressives were defeated by a vote of about two to one, and this figure became typical for the remainder of the contests at the convention. Although Akron held a solid 35 percent of the vote, the majority remained firmly in the hands of the war-swollen outlying locals, which were dependent upon the international for much of their routine bargaining and all of their political guidance.[58]

The URW's 1944 convention demonstrated the extent to which Dalrymple's control of the union remained formal and tenuous. He reached a compromise with Akron dissidents over those expelled in the General Tire incident, but used his majority power to push through new amendments to the URW constitution giving the executive board a more explicit right to intervene in local affairs when they broke the no-strike pledge or when local unions acted counter to top union policy.[59] A prudent union executive would have acted more cautiously. Although the URW opposition was not always as sophisticated or politically radical as that in the UAW, it had become by far the most solid and unified of any in the CIO. Hence Dalrymple's ability to enforce his program remained limited by his popular repudiation in the union's oldest and most important center of strength.

But Dalrymple remained inflexible in his determination to use the formal power at his command to discipline those who defied his authority. Immediately following the convention, a strike at U.S. Rubber in Detroit gave Dalrymple the opportunity to assert international authority on a massive scale. Local 101 was a medium-sized rubber local with a Communist leadership that normally supported the Dalrymple administration. The strike seemed to undermine the local's loyal leadership, and Dalrymple retaliated by fining 1,000 members $12.50 each for their part in the walkout. Most workers refused to pay, and Dalrymple formally expelled 572 of them from the union. He demanded that the company fire them, as provided by the union security clause in its contract with the URW. However, U.S. Rubber refused, citing the shortage of skilled labor in the industry and the disruption that such a mass expulsion would surely cause.[60]

With this impasse, Dalrymple appealed to the NWLB for help, and the board acted promptly to restore the URW president's power. U.S. Rubber did not have to fire all those whom the union had expelled, but the NWLB did instruct the company to check off the fines and reinstatement fees of the several hundred who refused to pay. The board also assigned one of its own representatives to supervise labor relations at the U.S. Rubber plant and report on any subsequent unauthorized work stoppages. This bureaucratic crackdown fired the intense hostility of Local 101 dissidents. The fines were imposed in January 1945. Shortly thereafter, about 2,000 members of the local accepted an offer by the maverick Mechanics Educational Society of America to disaffiliate from the URW and join that Detroit-based organization. Over the next six months, Dalrymple frustrated this movement, but only after he had again expelled leaders of the local and sustained a seventeen-day strike directed at the URW and finally broken by army seizure of the plant.[61]

In Akron, Dalrymple had even less success in maintaining URW authority over the dissident Big Four locals. In each issue of the *United Rubber Worker*, Dalrymple appealed for observance of the no-strike pledge. But by the spring of 1945, Akron locals had ceased to regard the international as a serious factor in their growing fight with the rubber companies to return the six-hour day and maintain union power in the reconversion period. By June and July, Goodyear and Firestone locals were engaged in lengthy strikes organized and led by their local union leadership. Akron's CIO council formally endorsed these work stoppages despite the national CIO policy to continue the no-strike pledge at least until the defeat of Japan. Meanwhile, Dalrymple remained a virtual bystander as the NWLB threatened to deprive these locals of their union security, vacation pay, and night shift bonuses. Even these threats proved ineffective, and in July the army seized both the Goodyear and Firestone facilities in Akron to halt the strikes.[62]

Despite the formal constitutional power at his command, Dalrymple had lost control of his union by the summer of 1945. Three unauthorized strikes in important URW locals were ended only with the intervention of the military. In July, Dalrymple announced his resignation, probably under pressure from Philip Murray himself, who certainly feared that unless the URW was put in more capable hands, the Akron dissidents might win control at the next constitutional convention. Vice-president L. S. Buckmaster, who had backed all of Dalrymple's wartime policies, assumed the URW presidency.[63]

Buckmaster stabilized the situation through a combination of good luck and political intelligence. It was his good fortune to assume command just as the war ended and the CIO's no-strike pledge became a moot issue. He accommodated the Akron Big Four by incorporating many of their aggressive economic demands into the URW's reconversion wage program. During the ensuing negotiations with the rubber industry, Buckmaster worked closely with leaders of the Akron locals and included their representatives on the URW top bargaining committee. The URW did not call a strike in the industry, but nevertheless it succeeded in obtaining perhaps the best overall contract of any CIO union during the first postwar round of negotiations. The URW resisted industry demands for greater discipline over the workforce, reestablished the six-hour day, and got a better than average wage deal. These measures reestablished much of the international's credibility and enabled Buckmaster's administration to retain control of the union during the early postwar years.[64]

Conclusion

Most CIO leaders did not relish the disciplinary tasks they carried out in defense of the no-strike pledge. Quite the contrary; they recognized the opposition their policy generated within their organizations and the unpopular burden it thrust upon top union leaders. By 1944, even Philip Murray and other Roosevelt loyalists realized that the unions had become policemen for the National War Labor Board. As Murray complained, "a very substantial portion of the monies collected by each of the international organizations is now being used to enforce the WLB directives . . . which in the first instance we do not believe in. The services of our countless field workers, who ordinarily should be engaging themselves in the administrative duties of an organization – settling disputes and so forth – their duties are now substantially confined to keeping people at work."[65]

Despite misgivings such as these, CIO unionists still felt they had no alternative but to enforce the no-strike pledge, maintain their alliance with FDR, and abide by unsatisfactory NWLB directives. On the right, powerful forces in the military and in Congress encouraged popular antilabor sentiment while they made steady progress, with FDR's help, toward enactment of crippling national service legislation. More subtly, the NWLB promised union leaders institutional security and personal support if they maintained their house in order, and retribution if they did not.

Linked to these concrete pressures was the commitment of the CIO to a policy of social peace that contained no place for class division or struggle: what the German Social Democratic party of World War I called their *burgfrieden*, or truce of classes. In this context, wildcat strikes were important not for the production losses incurred, which were minor and easily recouped, but because of their explosive social implications within the national polity itself. Most participants in unauthorized strikes did not dissent from overall support of the war or even of the no-strike pledge, but when they downed their tools, they struck a blow at the myth of a common national interest and undivided purpose so important to the ideology of the existing union leadership and the effective prosecution of total war. Many CIO unionists recognized the shortcomings of the home front as well, but they nevertheless thought it imperative to suppress these work stoppages to make credible their own larger commitment to the war effort and the Roosevelt government. In so doing, they hoped merely to preserve their organizations to fight on more favorable terms in the postwar era. But the maintenance of labor peace in an era when grievances were rife required the permanent weakening of those elements in the union structure upon which trade union power ultimately rested. After the war the additional authority garnered by the international apparatus, by corporate management, and by government bureaucracy would not automatically return to the hands of the local union and the rank and file.

11. Reconversion politics

With the end of the war in sight, all sections of the body politic began to prepare for the new wave of conflict that would accompany the reconversion to peacetime production and the diminution of the state's capacity directly to shape economic life. Although the CIO had helped reelect the president and blunt the wildcat strike movement's direct assault, its leaders felt far from secure as they entered the postwar round of conflict with adversaries in the government apparatus or in corporate executive suites. The CIO had doubled in size during the previous four years, but the war had increasingly become a political holding action in terms of the CIO's ability to accommodate those hostile external forces that sought to recast the entire structure of the political economy on a basis more suitable to the renewed hegemony of the corporate sector. In the year or so before the final military victory over Japan, the shape of reconversion politics became clear, first in terms of a far-reaching conflict over the pace of reconversion, second in terms of the renewed self-confidence and aggressiveness that characterized the outlook of many manufacturing firms in the South and Midwest, and third in terms of the erosion of internal CIO discipline at the highest levels of decision making.

The reconversion controversy

The difficult terrain that the CIO would have to cross in the reconversion era became apparent in the course of two disputes that took place within the government's economic stabilization apparatus. The first involved the fate of the War Production Board's reconversion program; the second the integrity of the National War Labor Board, an institution to which the leaders of the CIO clung as one of the few agencies in which they had direct participation. By the end of 1943, military production and war-related employment had reached their wartime peak; thereafter, arms expenditures were expected to decline precipitously until victory came in Europe and the Far East. Military spending in 1945 would be half the $74 billion spent in 1943. Consequently, the reconversion of manpower and production facilities to civilian work became an important political issue long before the first American soldier crossed the shoreline at Normandy.

At the War Production Board, Donald Nelson fought his last battle over this issue. With backing from the trade unions, advocates of postwar planning, and small business champions such as Maury Maverick, Nelson announced in late 1943 that he would permit an increase in civilian production as materials, facilities, and manpower became available. He argued that as the military cut back arms procurement, idle production facilities could be reconverted to civilian manufacturing without hindering the overall war effort. His plans were particularly advantageous to small businesses and were strongly endorsed by those opposed to the increasing military–corporate domination of the economy. Because the major war production contracts were concentrated in the hands of the large corporations, cutbacks would first affect the small manufacturers who held subcontracts from these giants. As production orders were canceled, the prime contractors would begin to pull in their subcontracts to maintain full production in their own facilities. Thus, smaller firms would be free to reconvert to the civilian market, thereby gaining a jump on their giant competitors in the postwar field.[1]

The labor movement expected to gain much from a smooth and continuous reconversion process as well. With civilian production taking up the slack when military cutbacks were announced, labor hoped to avoid a massive employment slump or the disruptive shift of large numbers of employees and union members from one plant or community to another. Unionists resented the army's tendency to cancel orders without advance warning and to lay off workers in areas where there was a surplus rather than a shortage of labor. The United Steelworkers of America campaigned to save the jobs of some 27,000 unionized steelworkers by the allocation of nonessential pig iron to twenty small, semiintegrated producers in early 1944.[2] More dramatically, thousands of militant workers at the Long Island City plant of the Brewster Aeronautical Corporation highlighted the reconversion problem in May 1944, when the navy abruptly canceled their contract. UAW Local 365 called a sit-down strike in response and unfurled banners on the outside walls of the building that announced, "We have the tools, we have the workers, give us the work!" The strike lasted little more than a day but made newspaper headlines across the country. UAW and CIO officials rushed to

Washington for well-publicized but fruitless discussions with Navy Department personnel.[3] Concluded Donald Nelson, "What gives workers and others 'cutback jitters' is the fear that they will find themselves thrust into a planless and chaotic economic state of affairs as soon as war orders fall off on a large scale, becoming worse when peace comes."[4]

Wartime conversion of some plants to civilian production (under conditions of high employment) would help ensure that the relatively high wartime wage scales would continue into the postwar era. Instead of a simultaneous battle with the giant corporations in the immediate postwar months, organized labor could renegotiate new civilian contracts piecemeal with a divided employer opposition. This perspective underlay Walter Reuther's abortive 1944 proposal to rescind the no-strike pledge in those plants that were to be converted to civilian production. He naively assumed that military victory over Germany would come before Christmas and that a gradual plan for reconversion would proceed without hindrance.[5]

Although Donald Nelson did begin to authorize an expanded reconversion program in mid-1944, his plans soon met with decisive resistance from a coalition of corporate and military interests. As a consequence of the Brewster incident and the successful landings in France, Nelson established a system of "spot authorizations" under which WPB regional directors could allow manufacturers to resume civilian production as long as adequate raw materials, manpower, and facilities existed and were not needed to fill military orders. Such a plan would have threatened the oligopolistic structure of the giant consumer durable manufacturers; not unexpectedly, therefore, the opposition to the Nelson program came from men such as General Electric President Charles E. Wilson, then serving as chairman of the WPB's Production Executive Committee. On the military side, the attack was led by Under Secretary of War Robert Patterson and Army Supply Chief Brehon Somervell, who insisted that any substantial increase in civilian production would lead to widespread demands from all manufacturers, including the large prime contractors, for equal access to the nonmilitary market. This would downgrade arms production and the war effort. The military also feared that once civilian employment became available, workers would flock to these new and presumably permanent jobs, secure in the belief that they were no longer needed in temporary military production work. The armed services therefore favored maintaining America's wartime psychology at a high level. Patterson and Somervell warned that casualties would be high in 1944, that there was little likelihood of an internal German collapse, and that the war was far from over. They complained that production "slippages" and materials shortages were already threatening to lengthen the war. When the Germans counterattacked in the Ardennes during December 1944, many in the military accepted the blow with some relief; their attack upon Nelson's reconversion plan had found a vindication in battle.[6]

By then, the decisive conflict over reconversion had already taken place. Late in June 1944, Nelson fell ill, and in his absence Wilson delayed promulgating the spot authorization orders that were to have gone into effect on July 1. Clinton Golden and Joseph Keenan, labor vice chairmen of the WPB, denounced the postponement, and Senator Harry Truman, then courting liberal and labor support for the vice-presidential nomination, charged that reconversion was being delayed by "some selfish business groups that want to see their competition kept idle . . . [and] by Army and Navy representatives who want to create a surplus of manpower." Nelson threatened to denounce big business opponents of his program as well.[7] But the real bureaucratic power lay out of his hands, and on July 11 Office of War Mobilization Director James Byrnes intervened to end the squabble by delaying full implementation of Nelson's program for at least forty-five days. The military thereupon stepped up its propaganda against civilian production. Somervell, for example, implied that manpower problems had created a shortage of large artillery shells, requiring substitution of smaller weapons, "which inevitably mean closer fighting and greater loss of American lives." Early in August, Byrnes again yielded to the military when he removed certification for spot authorization from the WPB and placed it under control of the War Manpower Commission.[8]

By this point, Nelson had obviously outlived his usefulness, and in mid-August Roosevelt exiled him to China as special emissary to Chiang Kai-shek. In his place, the president turned to Julius A. Krug, a thirty-six-year-old former WPB vice-chairman then serving in the navy. Krug actually favored many of Nelson's policies, but he also proved to be a good deal more amenable to the military–industrial viewpoint. Spot authorization went into effect in only a few areas, so that until March 1945, reconversion planning virtually ceased at the WPB. Barton Bernstein, the foremost historian of this episode, concluded that the year-long delay "guaranteed that the wartime growth of the industrial giants would not be endangered by new competition in the postwar period."[9]

Assault from the right

The government's failure to plan for an overall reconversion program promised the industrial unions an unpredictable postwar economic environment, but the reemergence of an aggressive brand of right-wing business sentiment in 1944 and 1945 represented an immediate threat that could not be ignored. The conservative turn in domestic politics symbolized by the passage of the Smith–Connally Act and the agitation for national service legislation ended much of the political truce over labor issues that the Roosevelt administration had imposed in the first two years of the war. At the same time, the very success the industrial unions had enjoyed in penetrating sectors of the economy heretofore nonunion had awakened and politicized elements of the business community that had not been active on the national scene before the war. An intransigent anti-union mood spread rapidly in labor-intensive industries such as the retail, textile, and service sectors and in middle-sized manufacturing firms in the South and Midwest that had long resisted the organizing efforts of the CIO and the directive orders of the NLRB and the NWLB. Among the most visible representatives of this movement were Sewell Avery, the bitterly anti-New Deal chairman of Montgomery Ward, and Fred Crawford of Cleveland's Thompson Products, elected president of the National Association of Manufacturers in 1943. Others included entrepreneurs of a similar type at Hughes Tool, Kohler Industries, and Humble Oil. All these companies had fought, often successfully, CIO organizing efforts and violated federal labor laws during the war.[10]

In the last eighteen months of the conflict, this sector of the business community led a general attack on the NWLB's maintenance-of-membership policy. Although corporate liberal NWLB members such as Roger Lapham and Cyrus Ching had endorsed the policy as a step toward stable labor relations and conservative trade unionism, many of the large corporations had only reluctantly accepted the union security policy as a war emergency measure. By 1944, moreover, it was clear that despite the NWLB's best efforts, union security per se had done nothing to temper shop-floor militancy or slow the union impulse that threatened to erode managerial prerogatives. And in industries such as textiles and retail trade, where unionism had made little headway, the NWLB maintenance-of-membership policy spelled the difference between capitulation to a union and continuation of a de facto open shop. As a consequence, men such as Ching and Lapham lost much of their influence; by 1944, they had been replaced on the NWLB by anti-union conservatives, among the most prominent of which were Lee H. Hill, vice-president of Allis-Chalmers, and Reuben B. Robertson, executive vice-president of the Champion Fiber and Paper Company of Canton, North Carolina. Industry members of the NWLB signaled the new mood in April 1944, when for the first time in two years they vigorously denounced the usual grant of maintenance of membership in the Humble Oil and Refining Company case. Echoing prewar attacks on the Wagner Act, the dissenting industry members condemned union maintenance because "its application contemplates widespread undemocratic restriction of the rights of workers and of employers; . . . and because it would constitute a potent threat to harmonious industrial relations so necessary now and in the post-war period."[11]

For many CIO unions, especially those in textiles and retail trade, the NWLB's maintenance policy had been essential to the growth they had enjoyed during the war. The fledgling United Retail, Wholesale, and Department Store Employees (URWDSE) enrolled only 60,000 in 1944, but they had begun to penetrate the large mail order houses for the first time. The Textile Workers Union of America doubled its membership during the war to almost 300,000; more importantly, it had finally begun to put down roots in the southern cotton mills, where the bulk of its potential membership now toiled. Industry resistance to NWLB policies undercut these gains and would certainly threaten the very existence of these unions in the inhospitable postwar era.

The dispute over union security at Montgomery Ward had the effect of weakening the CIO's commitment to the no-strike pledge itself. Under pressure from the NWLB and a direct order from the president, Ward chairman Sewell Avery had signed a union security contract with the URWDSE late in 1942. But the next year, Avery defied NWLB orders and refused to renew the contract. Management at the company's central Chicago warehouse cut wages, fired, and transferred employees, and Avery demanded a new NLRB election to determine if the union still held the allegiance of the majority of his employees. In this crisis, the Chicago URWDSE local struck early in April 1944 to force government seizure of Montgomery Ward and implementation of the NWLB directives. URWDSE National President Samuel Wolchok, a social democratic right winger in the CIO hierarchy, immediately sanctioned the strike and appealed for help throughout the labor movement. Soon money and organizers poured in, not only from the CIO but from the railroad brotherhoods and the AFL as well, all anxious to aid the struggle against an intransigent symbol of business arrogance. The CIO officially endorsed the work stoppage, although Philip Murray emphasized that the strike came in support, not defiance, of NWLB authority.[12]

As expected, the strike failed to bring Avery to terms, forcing FDR to order government seizure of the Ward facilities. When the army marched in on April 26, Avery played out his self-appointed role as martyr to a militaristic New Deal. As two battle-dressed soldiers removed him bodily from his office, a photographer captured a portrait of Avery's passive resistance in one of the most memorable and widely distributed pictures of the war. Meanwhile, Ward's management remained loyal and refused to recognize the union or abide by NWLB directives setting grievance procedures, seniority standards, and wages. Backed by resurgent business sentiment, Avery fought the seizure in the courts and took back direct control of his company when normal production resumed.

Despite the government's show of raw power, the URWDSE failed to gain a secure foothold at Ward. Even with massive support from the rest of the labor movement, the Chicago local lost members and strength. In desperation, URWDSE leaders called another Ward strike in December 1944. This time the work stoppage was centered in Detroit, where militant secondary leaders of the UAW used the strike as a means of building sentiment for a city-wide sympathy walkout. Again FDR seized company properties, and again Avery remained defiant. With the help of a favorable court ruling, he succeeded in breaking for the duration of the war the unionization campaign among his 60,000 employees. Only after the war was the URWDSE able to call a sustained strike and organize the Ward system.[13]

Another incident that pointed to an erosion of CIO support for the no-strike pledge came in the winter of 1945, when officials of the Textile Workers Union of America resigned from the NWLB and rescinded the no-strike pledge for a large proportion of their membership. During the war, the TWUA had become the dominant union in the textile field, completing the organization of northern mills and signing contracts covering 42,500 workers in the South. By 1945, its membership in that crucial region numbered over 70,000, or about one-sixth of the total southern textile mill labor force. The union had its greatest strength there in Virginia and North Carolina and had inaugurated organizing campaigns in Georgia, South Carolina, and Alabama. With the help of the NWLB, which issued frequent directives against recalcitrant mill owners, the TWUA seemed to stand on the verge of a historic break-through that would raise wages throughout the region and make the union a real power in the industry.[14]

But the textile industry tenaciously resisted such a possibility. Mill managers in the South had often violated or dragged their feet on implementation of NWLB directives, but in 1944 and 1945 the industry virtually repudiated the board, especially the hated maintenance-of-membership orders that gave the TWUA a foothold in their plants. By January 1945, forty-four textile mills in the South were boldly violating labor board directives; the industry represented the greatest non-compliance problem faced by the NWLB. Because this defiance excited none of the national furor surrounding the Montgomery Ward case, and because of the powerful influence the southern congressional delegation exerted, the NWLB did little to force southern mill owners to comply with its orders. As a consequence, TWUA organization in the South remained in a "continuous state of siege." By early 1945, the union had ceased active organizing work in Georgia because of the determined employer resistance there and the futility of appeal to the NWLB.[15]

Stymied in its organizing activity, the TWUA hoped to demonstrate its strength indirectly by securing from the NWLB a general wage increase in the southern textile industry that would help to equalize labor costs with northern unionized mills. In 1944 a large proportion of southern textile workers still earned only fifty cents an hour, the minimum established by the NWLB's regional office in Atlanta. As a consequence, the cotton textile industry ranked 132nd out of 135 industries surveyed in 1944 in terms of average hourly earnings. Workers in the mills earned about twenty-five dollars per week, whereas the Bureau of Labor Statistics estimated that almost nine dollars more were necessary to sustain an "emergency level budget" in southern mill towns. In a series of board hearings dating from mid-1942, the TWUA repeatedly urged the NWLB to eliminate the North–South wage differential and raise southern cotton mill wages to a minimum of sixty and, later, sixty-five cents per hour.[16]

By late 1944, the plight of the southern textile worker came to national attention when a labor shortage in the mills cut cotton cloth production. Employment in southern mills had dropped from about 500,000 to 420,000 between early 1942 and late 1944 even as the demand for military and civilian fabric grew. Voting with their feet against low wages, autocratic management, and nonunion conditions, textile workers flocked to northern industrial centers or the South's newly built aircraft plants and shipyards. Because the differential between cotton mill and other wage rates had widened dramatically during the war, a War Production Board report on the crisis concluded: "Only a direct attack on the basic cause of the cotton textile industry's manpower difficulties will enable it to maintain and expand production. Its wage structure must be brought back into line with wage trends in industry generally."[17]

This situation provides the background to an NWLB administrative crisis that came to a head during the winter of 1944–5. At this time, the TWUA had a major case before the NWLB, seeking to raise textile wages to a minimum of sixty cents per hour and to secure for the industry a series of fringe benefits, including vacation pay, night shift differentials, and interplant wage adjustments. In November 1944, many of these same fringes had been won by the United Steelworkers when the NWLB issued an interim directive in the USW's year-long assault on the Little Steel formula. For more than a year, the NWLB had encouraged labor to seek these fringe benefits as a means of releasing some of the steam in labor's wage demands, but this view was not shared by the new director of the Office of Economic Stabilization (OES), Fred Vinson, who took over from fellow southerner James Byrnes in June 1943. Vinson favored a hard line on the wage front and supported the armed services' renewed efforts to win a national service law. A month after the steel decision, in December 1944, he ordered the NWLB not to issue any directive order involving fringe wage issues until the board had first obtained assurances from the Office of Price Administration that new directives would not result in new price increases. As yet another in a long series of executive decisions limiting the NWLB's powers, the Vinson order forced the board to postpone work on the textile case and begin negotiations with the OES director to recapture some of its administrative authority, if only to maintain a minimal level of credibility with leaders of the labor movement.[18]

In the meantime, the OPA and OES came under intense pressure from textile industry lobbyists to block NWLB-approved wage increases. In February the liberal newspaper *PM* uncovered evidence that Fred Vinson and OPA chief Chester Bowles had met privately with industry spokesmen, who also worked closely with the southern congressional delegation to pressure the OPA by threatening to cut its appropriation and investigate its internal affairs. Bowles and Vinson denied that they had in any way accommodated the textile lobby, but the revelation that OPA and OES decisions were subject to such influence finally snapped the already fragile confidence of TWUA leaders in the fairness of the government's wage stabilization machinery. On February 21, the NWLB released a directive order in its textile case that increased the southern textile minimum wage to fifty-five cents and granted the TWUA many of the fringe benefits that the union had requested. But this order came too late. On the same day, the TWUA executive board voted to withdraw its representatives from the NWLB and release over 100,000 of its members in the cotton and rayon textile industries from their no-strike pledge.[19] In his letter of resignation, TWUA President Emil Rieve pointed out that even the NWLB's most recent wage order was but a "paper directive," inoperative until put into effect by Vinson and the OPA. Rieve, once one of the NWLB's staunchest defenders in the CIO, now denounced the board as little more than a "hollow echo of the opinion and authority of other federal agencies."[20]

Immediately after the TWUA announcement, southern locals deluged the national office with requests for strike sanctions. Under provisions of the Smith–Connally Act, TWUA leaders called on the NLRB to hold a series of strike ballots in March. With tens of thousands voting overwhelmingly to cease work, the union finally made its weight felt in Washington. Vinson modified his harsh directive limiting NWLB-approved fringe benefits, but labor and public members of the board remained distrustful, and in this tense situation Vinson resigned as director of the Office of Economic Stabilization. In his place, FDR appointed longtime NWLB Chairman William Davis as a means of shoring up labor's confidence in the government's faltering wage stabilization program. Within a month, Davis had "reinterpreted" Vinson's fringe benefit guidelines out of existence and restored NWLB authority in this limited sphere to the level existing in late 1944. Although TWUA leaders still boycotted the NWLB, the textile union got its raise.[21]

Factionalism at the top

The Ward strike and the textile fight were notable for several reasons. These protracted conflicts recorded the declining prestige of the National War Labor Board and the rising strength of conservative elements in the business community. They demonstrated that even when Roosevelt's wartime agencies were favorably disposed toward labor, determined business resistance could checkmate the weaker unions and erode their strength. Sewell Avery emerged from the Ward seizure a hero among those characteristically middle-sized midwestern and southern business interests that would later play so prominent a role in the agitation for new legal curbs on the unions in the immediate postwar era. On the other side of the ledger, the Ward strikes and the TWUA resignation from the labor board revealed a widespread impatience with the wartime administrative setup among even top union officials. Backed by the obvious rank-and-file sentiment for a fight manifest in Chicago, Detroit, and southern textile mills, many now looked forward to a direct confrontation with management power unmediated by the NWLB and the wartime strike prohibition.

Finally, these incidents opened, for the first time in the war, a small but widening breach between the national CIO and those union leaders identified with a Communist-oriented strategy for labor. Actually, this division within the ranks had appeared as early as January 1944, when several left-wing CIO leaders, including Bridges, Curran, and Emspak, publicly endorsed national service legislation at the same time that CIO policy called for its denunciation in the strongest terms.[22] The Ward strikes revealed another split along the same lines. Although their work stoppage was sanctioned by the CIO, Communists characteristically attacked the Ward strikers as "generally irresponsible elements, who like Avery also want to embarrass the Roosevelt administration and smear the war effort and national unity."[23] Bridges's International Longshoremen's and Warehousemen's Union, which had often clashed with the URWDSE in warehouse jurisdictional disputes, added substance to these sentiments by undercutting the strikes' overall effectiveness. To the alarm of even conservative CIO partisans, Bridges ordered the ILWU-organized Montgomery Ward distribution center local in St. Paul to work overtime during the strike to fill mail orders diverted from Chicago.[24]

As a sort of ideological point man for the Communist-oriented wing of the CIO, Bridges followed up his opposition to the Ward strikes with a well-advertised campaign for a permanent no-strike pledge to ensure industrial peace and "Big Three Unity" in the postwar world. Under this plan, actually adopted by some ILWU locals, all disputes would be settled through compulsory arbitration in return for an employer guarantee of union security for the indefinite future. Bridges publicized the idea as the domestic version of the Teheran agreements and linked it with the CIO's own proposal for 5 million new jobs in foreign trade in a stable postwar world dominated by a powerful Soviet–American detente. [25]

Bridges's advocacy of a postwar no-strike pledge, like his support of national service legislation, infuriated even conservatives in the CIO's hierarchy. R. J. Thomas, struggling to hold down work stoppages in the UAW, denounced the idea because it tarnished, and hence made more difficult, enforcement of the wartime no-strike pledge itself. Social democratic CIO unionists such as Samuel Wolchok, the Newspaper Guild's Milton Murray, and the TWUA's Irving Abramson and George Baldanzi feared that the Bridges proposals were the beginning of a Communist campaign to fetter the CIO with far-reaching postwar limitations on the right to strike. If such a program encouraged conservatives to mobilize behind new antilabor initiatives, their relatively weak unions would be the first to suffer. However, when Wolchok and others brought the matter to a CIO executive board meeting in June 1944, Philip Murray characteristically deflected attempts to condemn the Bridges postwar proposals or discuss his attitude toward the Ward strike. Although Murray himself did not favor such a carte blanche no-strike plan, he had already adopted a posture on the Communist issue in the CIO that regarded an open split as something to be avoided at almost any cost. [26]

As in the weaker unions with social democratic leadership, so too in the powerful United Auto Workers did second thoughts arise over the wisdom of the no-strike pledge and continued CIO participation in the NWLB. Although the rank-and-file insurgents who challenged the no-strike pledge at the 1944 UAW convention did not win a permanent organizational base in the union, their campaign and the wildcat strike movement that stood behind it helped shatter the stalemate in the union's internal life. The Rank and File caucus undermined the power of the Reuther faction, in particular, because the new group vied with the General Motors Department director for the allegiance of non-Communist progressives in the union, who had heretofore given political cohesion to his caucus. As we have seen, Reuther's vacillation on the no-strike pledge at the 1944 convention represented a nearly fatal miscalculation that almost lost him his union office.

His close call proved a turning point in Reuther's wartime career. Thereafter he sought an accommodation with the militant and rebellious sentiment in the ranks, if only to retain his own power in the union hierarchy. Although he formally backed an affirmative vote in the referendum, Reuther refused to serve with other top UAW officers on a committee to uphold the pledge, and he offered strong support to the Detroit Ward strikers in December.[27] Early in 1945, he urged that the CIO withdraw from the NWLB until that government agency was reorganized and adopted a more liberal wage policy. "The International Union would be irresponsible to its trust and to our members," argued Reuther, "if we were to constantly denounce unauthorized strikes without doing something basic to correct the situation out of which they grow."[28] In March he reversed his position on enforcement of the pledge and insisted that the UAW executive board not impose the usual disciplinary measures against two Detroit locals then on strike. His supporters carried the day on this issue, and as a result these work stoppages continued unabated, forcing the NWLB to consider the grievances of these locals even while they maintained their picket lines. With the fall of Germany, those insurgent elements in the union that had long fought for an end to the pledge now insisted upon an immediate industry-wide strike vote to back CIO demands for an upward revision of the Little Steel formula. Alone among prominent members of the UAW leadership, Reuther backed this proposal, and in July he called for a new referendum on the no-strike pledge itself. By shifting to the left, he sought to win back the support he had lost the year before.[29]

The pressures that had grown all year in the auto, textile, and retail service unions were sharply defined for the entire CIO in March 1945, when Emil Rieve and Walter Reuther formally proposed that the organization withdraw its representatives from the NWLB until Roosevelt reorganized the board and gave it substantially more liberal wage guidelines. To Rieve and Reuther, the time seemed ripe: FDR had won the 1944 election, military victory in Europe was only weeks away, and the postwar layoffs had already begun. The CIO needed to adopt an aggressive posture, both to accommodate the growing restlessness in the ranks and to prepare for the inevitable contest of the reconversion era.[30]

The CIO convened a special executive board meeting in New York to decide the issue. There it became clear that almost every major industrial union officer thought withdrawal from the NWLB untenable under almost any circumstances. Talk of this sort, warned Philip Murray, had already generated "confusion in the ranks"; a formal withdrawal would open the floodgates to rank-and-file insurgency and "thrust into jeopardy the life of almost every [CIO] organization."[31] Such a move would end the government's sponsorship of maintenance of membership covering over 2 million CIO workers and turn the president against the unions. In the ensuing chaos, Murray doubted whether many CIO leaders could survive. Backed by the votes of union leaders from conservative and Communist-influenced internationals, Murray's decision to continue CIO participation on the NWLB, along with enforcement of the no-strike pledge, easily carried the day against the Reuther–Rieve proposals.[32]

"It's industrial peace for the postwar period"

This attitude – fear of the rank and file, dependency on the government – lay at the root of the bureaucracy's conservatism and foreshadowed the cautious economic and political strategy that the CIO would follow as the unpredictable reconversion era unfolded. Backed by the estimates of many economists and some government officials, CIO experts feared that once large-scale military cutbacks began after the fall of Germany, unemployment would rise as high as 6 to 10 million. Layoffs would strike particularly hard at the industrial unions in shipbuilding, aircraft, and munitions, which had ballooned during the war. Union membership, dues income, and bargaining power were sure to fall and internal conflict to increase as veteran and war worker, black and white, women and men, competed for jobs and income. Meanwhile, corporate strength was never greater. The remarkable advance in productive efficiency and new plant construction during the war made possible a profitable level of output at about 50 percent of capacity in many mass production industries. And as a result of the refunds due them under the carry-back provisions of wartime excess profits tax legislation, many companies would actually make money in the last quarter of 1945 by shutting down completely. The bleak economic forecast prompted Murray and those in the CIO who followed his lead to try to avoid, at almost any cost, a trial of strength with either big business or the government after the war.[33]

The CIO reconversion strategy forecast the continuation of a strong labor board that would impose a government-backed accommodation with industry, along with a somewhat more liberal wage–price formula. As Philip Murray told the 1944 CIO convention, "Only chaos and destruction of our industrial life will result if employers look to the war's end as an opportunity for a union-breaking, wage-cutting, open-shop drive, and if labor unions have to resort to widespread strikes to defend their very existence and the living standards of their members."[34] To forestall such a prospect, the CIO in March 1945 helped sponsor a "Labor–Management Charter" with William Green of the AFL and Eric Johnston, the corporate liberal president of the U.S. Chamber of Commerce. Consisting of a list of often irreconcilable platitudes hailing the virtues of unfettered free enterprise and the rights of labor, the charter nevertheless symbolized the CIO's hope for cooperation with the liberal wing of American capitalism in stabilizing postwar industrial relations along roughly the lines established during the war. "It's Industrial Peace for the Postwar Period," headlined the *CIO News*. In return for management support of the unamended Wagner Act and a high-wage, high-employment postwar strategy, the unions pledged to defend "a system of private competitive capitalism" including "the inherent right and responsibility of management to direct the operations of an enterprise."[35]

Of course, the CIO insisted upon a quick upward revision of the Little Steel formula – an across-the-board 20 percent wage increase to compensate for the loss of most overtime pay after victory came in Europe. But Murray and other CIO leaders were willing to extend a de facto no-strike pledge for an indefinite period after the fall of Japan in return for such a government wage policy. With the help of the CIO's old friend, William Davis, now head of the Office of Economic Stabilization, Green, Murray, and Johnston reached an interim agreement in August 1945 that provided for a continuation of OPA price controls, an immediate 10 percent wage increase, and a promise of labor peace.[36] In the policy vacuum that existed immediately after the Japanese surrender (V-J Day) this proposal failed to win general government approval, but the CIO kept trying throughout the fall to work out some new wage–price arrangement. Murray therefore told affiliated unions to resist industry "provocation" and await the negotiation of a new pact that would hold the price line and permit a pattern wage increase for 1946.[37]

CIO leadership enthusiasm for the charter, and the accommodationist policy that flowed out of it, derived from several sources that had developed during the war. Ideologically, the charter reflected a revival of the strong Catholic corporativist sentiment that had earlier been implicit in the Industrial Council Plan of 1941 and that the CIO now revived to ameliorate competition in what it feared were the postwar industries of excess capacity: steel, aluminum, copper, and aircraft. In parallel fashion, the charter derived its support from the Browder-era Communist groups in the CIO who foresaw the postwar period as one of peaceful coexistence abroad and muted class conflict, gradualist social advance, and progressive capitalism at home. This viewpoint was not too different from the mainstream CIO perspective of men such as Clinton Golden and Sidney Hillman. Not unexpectedly, therefore, CIO staffers influenced by the Communists had in fact played a central role in drafting the charter's original text.[38]

Finally, the charter represented the general CIO belief that the trade unions could secure an accord with progressive industrialists that might institutionalize some of the cooperative arrangements worked out on government boards and agencies during the war. These businessmen were not only collective bargaining progressives such as Ching and Lapham, but moderate Keynesians who favored a countercyclical fiscal policy and a degree of structural reform as the minimum program necessary to stabilize postwar capitalism. Often influenced by the Committee for Economic Development and the Twentieth Century Fund, they also supported the 1946 Full Employment Act in something like its original liberal Keynesian form. Among these progressive industrialists with whom the CIO sought an alliance were not only the Chamber of Commerce's Eric Johnston, who called for a "people's capitalism" in the postwar era, but also Paul Hoffman of the Studebaker Corporation and J. D. Zellerbach of Crown Zellerbach, both of whom supported the charter. Also included were numerous executives of the garment and smaller steelmaking and fabricating companies with which the CIO had long cooperated to increase productivity and stabilize employment. The most famous of these progressives was undoubtedly Henry J. Kaiser, whose innovative shipyards had broken the steel monopoly on the west coast and forged a bridge of ships to Europe and Asia. Kaiser had built his empire on New Deal construction projects and wartime contracts, so he was no opponent of government planning or public works spending. In addition to his good relations with the unions, extensive child- and health-care facilities at his shipyards and mills gave Kaiser a reputation as a social liberal. In 1945 he won strong UAW cooperation in his well-publicized effort to convert the giant Willow Run bomber plant to civilian car production.[39]

Implementation of a new wage–price policy was one of the key elements in such an accord with the liberal wing of the business community, so state action was essential. Many of the administrative liberals who had staffed the wartime stabilization bodies now thought a new wage–price formula essential to maintain living standards at their current level and avoid the long-feared postwar downturn. Because of the productivity gains of the war and the decline in postwar corporate tax rates, they estimated that profits would not suffer even if wages were increased substantially while prices were held at their current levels. Thus Secretary of Commerce Henry Wallace favored a 10 to 15 percent wage increase in 1945, and Robert Nathan of the Office of War Mobilization and Reconversion projected a 24 percent increase as essential to maintain aggregate demand. In mid-September, William Davis stated at a press conference that living standards would have to rise by 40 to 50 percent over the next five years to avoid a crisis of underconsumption.[40]

Such forecasts were music to CIO ears, but the political and social base for such a liberal postwar prospect had already eroded. President Franklin Roosevelt died suddenly on April 12, 1945. Under his administrations, the CIO had been born and had won its greatest victories. His passing did not fundamentally alter the framework of domestic politics, but it undermined the self-confidence of those who identified with the labor movement and the New Deal. The new chief executive, Harry Truman, had often supported CIO initiatives while a senator, but as president he came under an even more aggressive set of conservative pressures than those that had contained the liberalism of his predecessor. Moreover, Truman had won none of the enormous respect or loyalty FDR could command, so the necessary contradictions of his statecraft were far more damaging. For example, in an important blunder, Truman allowed a jurisdictional fight between William Davis and Lewis Schwellanbach, the new secretary of labor, to end prematurely the NWLB's usefulness as a wage-setting instrument. Along with other liberals of long Roosevelt-era experience, Davis soon left the government. These old New Dealers were replaced by a series of generally second-rate and maladroit figures who surrounded the new president.[41]

More importantly, the CIO had profoundly misjudged the tenor of the postwar business community. The progressive industrialists with whom the industrial union federation hoped to achieve an accord were in fact a relatively uninfluential minority. Although business did not follow the intransigent anti-union program of the Averys, Crawfords, and their vocal congressional supporters, it took its leadership from men far more conservative than Henry Kaiser or Eric Johnston. The latter's identification with the Labor–Management Charter had hardly proven popular within the Chamber of Commerce, eroding still further the support he had enjoyed there when he revived the institution in the early war years. Johnston was viewed by most members as an impractical idealist, and the chamber was relieved by his announcement in September 1945 that he would soon resign.[42]

Key business spokesmen were those practical conservatives who presided over the core manufacturing firms in the unionized steel, electrical, auto, rubber, and transport industries. Led by men such as John A. Stephens of U.S. Steel, Ira Mosher of the National Association of Manufacturers, and the Charles E. Wilsons of GM and GE, these industrialists had emerged from the war with a sophistication and self-confidence that the Avery–Kohler–southern textile wing of the business community sorely lacked. Unlike the southern mill owners, they recognized the usefulness of the new industrial unions as stabilizers of the labor force and moderators of industrial conflict. And they put a relatively low priority on enactment of antilabor legislation of the sort many nonunion manufacturers hoped Congress would pass.[43] But these individuals also shared several points of agreement with the extreme conservatives. In no uncertain terms, they sought the restoration of managerial prerogatives that wartime conditions had eroded in the areas of product pricing, market allocation, and shop-floor work environment. Until the character of postwar economic conditions became clear, they wanted to be free of government or union interference in determining the wage–price relationship in each industry. Thus, the first round of "free" collective bargaining in steel, autos, and rubber ended in stalemate in the fall of 1945 because industry leaders were determined to resist any new wage package until they knew the fate of price control and the general shape of the government's postwar economic program. On the question of restoring management power at the point of production, the key companies were those in the auto, electrical manufacturing, and rubber industries, where plant supervisors battled daily with militant stewards and well-organized work groups. Executives in these industries were determined that "management must manage" the actual work that went on in the factory. They sought to regain the initiative in this arena in 1945 and 1946, even if they suspected that success would entail an effort of many years' duration.[44]

These fundamental issues remained unresolved at the month-long Labor–Management Conference that President Truman convoked on November 5. Although management and labor could agree that collective bargaining would continue as a bedrock institution of American democracy, no accord proved possible on either the prerogatives of management or the scope of legitimate union demands. Neither could the two sides find an area of agreement on possible remedies, legislative or otherwise, for jurisdictional disputes, the "threat" of supervisory unionism, or strikes creating a "national emergency."[45] On the crucial issue of a general wage policy, the CIO got nowhere. At the first session, Philip Murray offered industry a de facto policy of labor peace in return for a pattern wage increase, which in his speech of October 30 even the president had endorsed. So great was the opposition, however, that the issue never secured a place on the formal conference agenda. In fact, the CIO faced resistance not only from industry but from within the labor movement itself. AFL unions, especially those in the booming construction industry, felt themselves strong enough to weather even a turbulent reconversion era and come out ahead. Never as committed as the CIO's mass production unions to the tripartite arrangements of the war era, these unions demanded a rapid return to free and unrestrained collective bargaining.[46] And of course, John L. Lewis, who played a prominent role at the conference, anxiously sought to exercise the United Mine Workers' power unfettered by a new set of government regulations or guidelines. "What Murray and the CIO are asking for," Lewis declared, "is a corporate state, wherein the activities of the people are regulated and constrained by a dictatorial government. We are opposed to the corporate state."[47]

The GM strike

Even if the Labor–Management Conference had not ended in an impasse, the CIO's blueprint for the postwar future would have run into major opposition from the industrial union rank and file, who were no longer to be controlled through imposition of a new wage stabilization formula worked out among top labor leaders, government administrators, and business spokesmen. To most workers V-J Day in mid-August signaled the end of what was left of the wartime truce. Overnight cancellation of some $24 billion in war contracts triggered massive layoffs and downgrading throughout industry. Real income dropped an average of 15 percent in three months, and unemployment reached almost two million by October 1. Eight million veterans were on their way home.[48] All unions formally canceled their no-strike pledge, and many called in the NLRB for morale-boosting strike votes. Given these unsettled conditions, a wave of strikes swept unionized industry. In September the number of man-days lost to strikes doubled, and doubled again in October, when the government listed 750,000 out, more than in any similar period since 1941. Although a number of these strikes – in oil, glass, lumber, textiles, and trucking – were formally authorized, the majority were not. Some local conflicts were of an exceptionally bitter nature, and two, at Yale and Towne in Stamford, Connecticut, and at the Conestoga Transportation Company in Lancaster, Pennsylvania, led to city-wide general strikes in the winter. To many workers in the fall of 1945, the distinction between wildcat and official stoppages had begun to blur. The postwar strike wave had begun, even if many union leaders failed to acknowledge it.[49]

Philip Murray's hope of trading a reconversion no-strike policy for a new higher wage formula received its most shattering blow from the ranks of the CIO's largest and most important affiliate. As early as the summer of 1945, internal discipline in the UAW had reached an advanced stage of disintegration. Widespread layoffs in the Detroit area after the defeat of Germany sent a surge of panic through auto worker ranks. UAW-organized maintenance men struck to protect their jurisdiction against AFL craftsmen in the shrinking job market. The newly organized foremen's union contributed to a confusing situation by picketing many plants where the UAW held bargaining rights for production workers. In nearby Canada, where victory over Germany signaled the return of open industrial conflict, the Ford Motor Company canceled its contract with the UAW at its key Windsor Assembly plant. When workers struck, the Canadian government used police to keep the factory open and break mass picket lines. The strike dragged on through the summer.[50]

The end of the war released a wave of pent-up frustration among Detroit area unionists. Upward of 300,000 Michigan war workers lost their jobs in the weeks immediately following the surrender of Japan, but UAW local leaders were not intimidated by this massive reduction in union ranks. R. J. Thomas declared the situation "chaotic" as local after local struck to reassert its power in the shops. One observer estimated that there were some ninety unauthorized strikes in the Detroit area during August and September.[51]

Although the UAW rescinded its no-strike pledge on August 25, union officials resisted the clamorous local union requests for strike sanction. With Murray and other CIO conservatives, they feared that a rash of bitter strikes would utterly deplete the union treasury, fragment the union, and wreck the CIO's larger chances of securing a strike-free across-the-board wage package later in the fall. Their sense of mingled fear, hope, and confusion is preserved in the minutes of the UAW's executive board's first postwar meeting in Flint early in September. A beleaguered R. J. Thomas assessed the deteriorating situation:

The unemployment situation certainly is not abating the temperament of the workers but rather is causing considerable agitation among the membership and what the workers actually believe is a militant and progressive stand is in reality a move designed to destroy the Union. Pending labor legislation in Congress and the present unplanned reconversion situation places the union today in a much weaker position than it has ever been in its history. The conference of management and labor soon to be called by President Truman will place a great responsibility upon the shoulders of the conferees . . . Discipline and order within the ranks of labor must be regained; otherwise, if the present unruly condition is permitted to increase, the Union will be destroyed.[52]

But in the absence of a patriotic wartime ideology or a formal no-strike pledge, order in the UAW could not be restored by appeals to follow national CIO policy. Of the many strikes that flared in the early weeks of reconversion, the tenacious six-week-long stoppage at the Kelsey-Hayes Wheel Company on Detroit's West Side graphically demonstrated the new impotence of the union hierarchy. In typical fashion, the strike originated in a series of unresolved wartime grievances, the most important of which stemmed from the company's dismissal after an earlier wildcat of thirteen union activists. The NWLB reinstated nine in the summer but failed to put four others back to work, including popular militant Chester "Moon" Mullins. After V-J Day, leaders of the 4,500-member local unanimously agreed that the time had come to "revert to prewar methods" to reassert union power in their plant, teach recalcitrant management a lesson, and return Mullins and the others to work. On August 25 they closed the factory.[53]

The stoppage soon made its weight felt in the wider circle of reconversion politics. Kelsey–Hayes supplied Ford's Highland Park and River Rouge facilities, and by the middle of September about 30,000 were idled there for lack of parts. By the end of the month, an estimated 75,000 were laid off throughout Detroit. Emphasizing that the union could not hope to win against Ford or GM or to influence the government if it could not maintain order within its own ranks, the UAW refused strike sanction on September 13 and ordered Kelsey–Hayes workers back. When local officers refused to cooperate, they were quick-ly removed and an administrator placed in their stead.

For more than a month, the Kelsey–Hayes unit voted time and again to defy the international and maintain mass picket lines. As the number of other workers idled by the strike mounted, the UAW took out adver-tisements in the Detroit papers urging a return to work. Later, the international stood by while the company secured an injunction against 200 of the most active strikers and used a police line to reopen the factory. Meanwhile, national publications such as *Time* and the *New York Times* carried a blow-by-blow account of the UAW's embarrassing impo-tence in the dispute with its rebellious local. Combined manage-ment–international pressure finally secured a return of most Kel-sey–Hayes workers in mid-October, but by then the toll was extraordinarily heavy. The company no longer recognized the UAW as its bargaining agent, and the four discharged men remained off the payroll. More than 100,000 workers lost almost $27 million in wages. Confusion and demoralization spread through UAW ranks.[54]

In this crisis, Walter Reuther came forward with his plan for an early company-wide strike against General Motors, a proposal that provides a classic example of the characterization C. Wright Mills once gave to the labor leader as a "manager of discontent." Reuther's GM strike program would harness the restless energy of the auto workers, restore legitimacy to top union authority, and advance his own fortunes in the internal union scramble for office. The key GM strike demand – for a 30 percent wage boost without an increase in the price of cars – was but a militant restatement of the current, but soon to be abandoned, CIO postwar wage policy.[55] Yet the demand excited the union rank and file because it was made directly to the corporation and backed by union strike power, rather than offered to a government agency for tripartite negotiation and compromise. Thus Victor Reuther, in a thinly veiled attack on Murray's reconversion program, argued, "It is time to debunk the notion that labor can meet in parlays with government and management and by some miracle, fashion a compromise that will keep all parties happy and contented."[56]

The Reuther brothers recognized that such conferences could at best rearrange the status quo, leaving the essential power of monopoly capital untouched. Although Murray still hoped that Truman could put to-gether a suitable wage–price package, the Reuthers had little faith in the president's ability to resist big business pressure. In fact, Victor Reuther, who always stood slightly to the left of his brother, came out squarely for the immediate formation of a labor-based third party that would campaign for the social ownership of monopolistic industries. Paralleling the aggressive demands of the GM strike program, this advanced political perspective climaxed the Reuthers' accommodation to the radical forces within the UAW that the wildcat strike movement and campaign against the no-strike pledge had set in motion. In 1946, Walter Reuther would capture the UAW presidency by luring the wartime militants back into his caucus.[57]

The GM strike began on November 21, 1945, in the midst of the long-awaited but unproductive Labor–Management Conference. More than 200,000 stayed out for 113 days, returning to work in the middle of March 1946. As the strike dragged on, Communist and conservative critics of Reuther's leadership attacked the GM director for calling the walkout too early and closing GM plants before reconversion had been far advanced, at a time when wartime excess profit taxes ensured that the company had already earned the maximum possible during 1945.[58] But the victory in the GM strike – and in the other massive walkouts called by CIO unions during the winter of 1946 – hardly depended upon the dent that such strikes might put in current corporate balance statements. Instead these strikes, and the GM walkout above all, were ultimately political, designed to exert sufficient pressure upon the Truman administration to keep its price control apparatus intact while substantial wage increases were taken from swollen wartime profits. A GM strike in November not only appeased a restive rank and file but forcefully projected the issue on the national scene while the administration's wage–price policy might still be turned to labor's advantage.

Reuther and his supporters consciously politicized the GM strike by challenging managerial control of product pricing and by emphasizing the stake the consuming public had in the victory of the auto workers. The neo-Trotskyist demand that the corporation "open the books" to demonstrate its "ability to pay" boldly asserted the social character of business enterprise and questioned management's prerogatives in determining the relative distribution of its profits. A wholesale effort to raise working-class purchasing power in order to take advantage of the enormous increase in the industry's wartime productive capacity, the GM strike represented the powerful cutting edge of the advanced program of Keynesian social planning that the CIO had advocated since the early years of the war.[59] Although not directly anticapitalist, the UAW demand raised, if only implicitly, fundamental issues of capitalist social relations. Certainly, General Motors recognized the potentially far-reaching thrust of the UAW strike. In a nation-wide newspaper advertisement of December 31, GM warned: "America is at the crossroads! It must preserve the freedom of each unit of American business to determine its own destiny . . . The idea of ability to pay, whatever its validity may be, is not applicable to an individual business within an industry as a basis for raising its wages beyond the going rate."[60]

Although Reuther's bold strike plan accommodated the radical temper of the UAW rank and file, it simultaneously defused much of the insurgent impulse that had kept the union in turmoil for the last two years. "The GM strike was designed to take the ball out of the hands of the stewards and committeemen," recalled Victor Reuther, "and put it back in the hands of the national leadership."[61] During the war, auto workers had fought management directly over the most basic and chronic issues of factory life – shop discipline and production standards – but this widespread movement never achieved programmatic articulation from any significant part of the union leadership. In contrast, General Motors gave as much priority to fighting the UAW at the shop-floor level as it did in turning aside the union's innovative wage proposals; GM executives were determined to restore to full effectiveness those management prerogatives they thought had been eroded during the high-employment years of the war. In the 1945–6 contract negotiations, GM made a long list of counterdemands, of which only the most important were the end of maintenance of membership, a reduction in the number and power of union committeemen, and a dilution of the seniority principle as applied to plant promotion and transfers. The corporation sought a guarantee of no official union opposition to any management effort to speed up production, as well as an absolute no-strike pledge for the life of the contract. At the same time, GM plant managers pressed UAW locals for numerous contract changes specific to each factory.[62]

Many of these shop-control issues were fought with considerable bitterness during the course of the strike, and the UAW resisted most of what General Motors wanted. (However, the union did lose maintenance of membership.) But Reuther's conduct of the GM strike inaugurated a postwar bargaining pattern that would relegate to secondary importance these often difficult shop-floor issues, and in their stead focus union and national attention on across-the-board wage and fringe benefit increases. Unlike the local conflicts over working conditions and management authority, the national wage package had a unifying effect on the whole workforce; it provided a readily available channel into which the pent-up wartime grievances could be poured, as well as cutting off opportunities for their direct local expression. It was an issue on which top union leadership could effectively negotiate at the national level, and it promised benefits in which all workers could equally share.[63]

At the same time, the General Motors strike plan served to legitimize executive board control over the locals. Reuther's one-at-a-time strike tactic meant that Ford, Chrysler, and other auto makers were to be encouraged by the union to continue their reconversion plans in order to put competitive pressure on the big auto maker. In addition, the continuation of work at these other corporations would ensure the UAW of a reduced but steady flow of dues income during the difficult strike period. Thus the GM strike program gave the UAW bureaucracy a fresh rationale for opposing shop-floor militancy and unauthorized strikes at those companies whose successful operation was necessary to keep market pressure on GM. Reuther supported suppression of the Kelsey–Hayes strike because it hindered Ford's production work. Likewise, strikes at Ford and Chrysler themselves were to be prevented at all costs.[64]

It was not surprising, therefore, that in December UAW negotiators with Ford and Chrysler acceded to long-standing management demands that "company security" clauses penalizing wildcat strikers be inserted into the new postwar contracts. In the pacesetting negotiations with Ford, management demanded the unqualified right to set production standards and receive contractual assurance against unauthorized strikes. Bargaining for the UAW, Richard Leonard agreed that a modified version of the UAW's wartime Los Angeles policy on wildcat strikes be incorporated into the new contract. Ford would have the right to discipline those it considered guilty of unauthorized work stoppages. In turn, the union would deny these individuals the use of the grievance machinery unless the entire local undertook a special investigation and decided to defend those accused by the company of participating in the strike. In return for this company security, Ford continued the union shop and the dues checkoff and offered the UAW a pay package of about eighteen and a half cents an hour.[65]

The company security clauses incorporated into the Ford, Chrysler, and Kaiser-Frazer contracts in January 1946 were designed to assure these GM competitors of union cooperation in the continuous operation of their plants while the giant auto maker was shut. Although Reuther's factional opponents took the spotlight in negotiating these contract provisions, neither the GM director nor his more conservative supporters voiced real objections to these onerous new contract terms. They were an integral part of the one-at-a-time strike strategy and, in a larger sense, of the capitulation to management's definition of industrial order in the postwar era. Such management prerogatives and industrial discipline contract language spread rapidly to most of the collective-bargaining agreements negotiated between unions and management in basic industry.[66]

Pyrrhic victory: the strike settlement of 1946

While the UAW–GM strike stretched on into the early months of 1946, conflict in the steel industry created the postwar wage–price pattern settlement for most CIO organized workers. Here, a tug-of-war among the Office of Price Administration, the United Steelworkers union, and the steel industry management reached a climax in February 1946. Like GM, U.S. Steel and other large corporations in the industry were determined that ability to pay would not become an issue subject to collective bargaining negotiations. The USW demanded twenty-five cents an hour, little less than in the auto industry, but the steel corporations refused to negotiate. In mid-November the American Iron and Steel Institute had flatly announced that "until OPA authorizes fair prices, nothing can be settled through collective bargaining."[67] Later, U.S. Steel's Benjamin Fairless made it clear to Truman and OPA chief Chester Bowles that the industry's dispute with the USW could only be settled by a price increase of four dollars and, later, five dollars a ton. While the government fought a rearguard action with the steel industry on price relief, Truman's fact-finding panel in the auto dispute recommended a wage increase of nineteen and a half cents per hour, which Truman later reduced by a penny in steel in the hopes of facilitating a prestrike settlement. These wage increases in both industries were held in abeyance so long as government and industry could not agree on a price level acceptable to corporate management.[68]

At this critical juncture Philip Murray, as USW president and CIO chief, failed to fight for the maintenance of OPA controls. "Unlike the union in the General Motors case," he told the government, "the steel union . . . has not coupled its demand for wage increases with a flat demand that present basic steel prices be maintained."[69] Historians of this episode have charged that the USW officers did not follow Reuther's lead because their brand of conservative leadership subordinated larger social issues – such as those implicit in the UAW's GM strike program – to the immediate need for a highly visible wage hike.[70] However, the difficulty was not one of economic analysis but of political fortitude. The CIO's inability to secure a new wage–price formula at the November Labor–Management Conference convinced Murray that any attempt to increase wages and maintain a ceiling on prices would require a major showdown with industry and a probable political confrontation with the Truman administration. From this the CIO leader characteristically shrank back. In early December, Murray held a secret Pittsburgh meeting with Walter Reuther and GM negotiators. There Murray counseled the auto leader to "go easy on the price issue" because continuing UAW intransigence on this question might jeopardize the forthcoming round of USW talks with the steel industry.[71]

Hence, in January 1946, when steel company pressure against the OPA reached a climax, the USW and other CIO unions that followed Murray's lead did little to defend the Truman administration's crumbling price control policy. By the third week in January, General Motors workers already on strike were joined by hundreds of thousands of steel, electrical equipment, and meatpacking workers in the largest strike wave in American history. But this massive and generally uncontested demonstration of union strength merely accelerated the removal of price controls. Without a firm determination to back OPA price regulations, these CIO strikes were simply used as an industry battering ram to break the administration's price stabilization program. By the second week in February, the battle was over. The OPA agreed to an increase of about five dollars in the price of a ton of steel, over twice what it had hoped to allow only a few weeks earlier. Furthermore, Truman issued a new executive order that permitted those industries confronted by union wage demands to use their higher labor costs as the basis for immediate price relief from the OPA.[72]

The eighteen-and-a-half-cent-an-hour steel settlement set the pattern. UAW wage agreements at this level were reached with Ford and Chrysler in late January. On February 9 the United Electrical, Radio, and Machine Workers, bargaining for 30,000 of their members employed in GM's electrical and appliance division, also agreed to the eighteen-and-a-half-cent formula, and these workers returned to work.

A city-wide UAW strike committee condemned the UE settlement as a Communist stab in the back, and Reuther attacked it as a politically inspired move to undercut his direction of the GM strike. Of course, the separate agreement with GM was a breach of interunion solidarity against a common foe, but in a larger sense, UE leaders merely followed the pattern already set by the steelworkers and by UAW leaders at Ford and Chrysler.[73] By the end of February, settlements in meatpacking, oil, rubber, and the rest of the electrical industry all conformed to the eighteen-and-a-half-cent pattern established in steel. Although Reuther held out for a penny more at GM, he finally capitulated on March 13 and accepted eighteen-and-a-half-cents plus contract changes and fringe benefits that, the UAW claimed, increased the settlement to more than nineteen and a half cents.[74]

Conclusion

The wage increases of early 1946 soon evaporated under the galloping inflation let loose when government price controls were drastically weakened during the summer. In the fall, therefore, all the major CIO unions returned to the bargaining table for another round of wage negotiations. Exhausted by the great strikes of early 1946, most of the CIO unions settled without a stoppage for a pattern fifteen-cent wage advance. Repeated annual or biannual pay boosts of this sort, which were used by industry to "administer" higher prices, were at least partially responsible for creating the conservative, antilabor political environment characteristic of the immediate postwar years. Unions that sought to break such postwar wage patterns, such as the Railway Brotherhoods and the UMW, found that "free" collective bargaining of the kind advocated by John L. Lewis was now ruled incompatible with the national welfare. In 1946, both of these unions were involved in major confrontations with the Truman administration or the federal courts when they shut down their respective industries in a vain effort to improve the original 1946 wage bargain. Combined with the CIO strikes of the winter, the coal and rail shutdowns helped make 1946 the greatest year of strike activity since 1919. And like the strikes of that other postwar year, the failure of the 1946 stoppages helped generate the conservative political climate that sustained the drive for the kind of antilabor legislation that culminated in the passage of the Taft–Hartley Act in 1947.[75]

In fact, the memories of 1919 and the postwar repression of that era had prompted Philip Murray and other mainstream CIO leaders to seek an extension of the corporativist arrangements of World War II as a bridge that might span the difficult reconversion era. This was the meaning of the CIO-sponsored Labor–Management Charter of early 1945 and of Murray's desperate efforts to achieve a new wage–price formula after the demise of the National War Labor Board in the fall. But the political and economic basis for such a tripartite accommodation had been so eroded by the decay of the New Deal that the effort could hardly have succeeded. Within the business community, those elements that might have been partners to such a social contract had been eclipsed during the war by executives of the core industrial firms, whose self-confidence had been renewed by their effective control of the mobilization apparatus. Their power was such that those who still advocated a postwar New Deal planning perspective were easily outmaneuvered in the War Production Board and the Office of Price Administration. In turn, this success meant that representatives of large corporate capital could proceed with the dismantling of most government price and production controls, certain that the enormous market power of their key firms would remain intact. Companies such as General Motors and General Electric therefore had an immeasurably stronger strategic position when they confronted labor's battalions in the political and economic battles waged during the fall and winter of 1945–6.

Corporativism also failed because it encountered opposition from within the CIO itself. Communist-influenced unionists retained their ideological commitment to the no-strike pledge and a new accommodation with capital until late in the spring of 1945, but thereafter their repudiation of Browderism turned the Communist party and its union circle away from the more extreme forms of labor–management cooperation advocated between 1942 and 1945. Meanwhile, the social democratic wing of the CIO's leadership found the continuation of the no-strike pledge a burden that it could no longer afford. In industries such as retail trade and textiles, National War Labor Board authority became valueless even before the defeat of Germany, and in other sectors, including steel, electrical, rubber, and especially autos, union leaders found themselves under enormous pressure from their own rank and file.

Earlier than most, the Reuther group in the UAW recognized both the tenuousness of the Murray program and the necessity of harnessing the forces unleashed by the collapse of the no-strike pledge. The GM strike program provided a vehicle to both reintegrate the UAW and erect a platform for a progessive realignment of the political economy as a whole. The genuine popularity of the strike against GM enabled Reuther to accomplish the first task, but success in the second proved out of reach. To force through the kinds of social controls implicit in the GM demands would require not only the maintenance of interunion solidarity on the picket line but also a political confrontation with the Truman administration itself. The CIO attempted neither, and its failure laid the basis for the pyrrhic victory won by labor in the winter of 1946. The outcome of this conflict with a phalanx of major corporations demonstrated the permanence and the tremendous potential power of industrial unionism, but it also doomed American labor to a Sisyphean struggle against the inflationary spiral and political harassment of the immediate postwar years.

12. Epilogue: Labor in postwar America

The experience of the CIO industrial unions during World War II formed a crucial stage in the transition from their institutionally fluid, socially aggressive character in the 1930s to the relative accommodation and bureaucratic stability of the postwar years. During the war, the unions completed the organization of basic industry, more than doubled their dues-paying membership, and fortified themselves with such an array of contractual and administrative defenses that few contemplated their postwar disintegration. The CIO remained numerically smaller than the AFL, but the strategic location of its major affiliates in the heart of basic industry assured the federation of industry-wide economic influence almost unthinkable a decade before. Building upon the framework established by the National War Labor Board, the big industrial unions settled into a postwar collective-bargaining routine that increased real weekly wages some 50 percent in the next two decades and greatly expanded their fringe benefit welfare packages. By the late 1940s, the trade union movement, paced by the CIO, had organized at least 80 percent of all workers in basic industry. As a proportion of the nonfarm workforce, total union membership was more than 35 percent in 1954, and for the first time, American unions enrolled a section of the working class that approached northern European levels. [1]

This institutional growth was real, but the consolidation of the new unions coincided with a generation-long decline in the power of the reformist wing of the New Deal coalition and a turn toward management of the political economy increasingly in the interests of an effective prosecution of the Cold War. The program of military Keynesianism inaugurated with the defense buildup of 1940 ensured that the growth and relative stability of American capitalism would continue for the next quarter of a century, but the new political regime also required the maintenance of an ideological consensus and the moderation of social and economic conflict throughout the realm of industrial relations. The support that most trade union leaders gave to government policy in this era limited the impact that the labor movement could have on the society

233

as a whole and eroded the union movement's internal strength by damp-
ening class consciousness and stifling internal debate. The accommodation of the major CIO unions, which began under wartime conditions,
proceeded equally rapidly in the late 1940s, especially after the passage
of the Taft–Hartley Act in 1947 and the expulsion or defeat of the
Communists in the following two years. At the same time, the dependent relationship the CIO had built with the Democratic party with-
stood the trauma of the reconversion crisis and the Henry Wallace presidential candidacy, even as the political and economic payoff from this
alliance declined with the recomposition of Democratic party politics in
the postwar years. Finally, the increasingly conservative political environment generated a set of conditions under which shop-floor activism
atrophied, union bureaucracy flourished, and the power of management
renewed itself, even in the narrow field of contract collective bargaining.

The Cold War and the anti-Communist purge

Despite the tensions engendered during the reconversion crisis, the
CIO's wartime pattern of both fear and dependency upon the national
Democratic administration continued into the postwar era. The Cold
War replicated many of the political and economic pressures under
which the industrial unions had functioned during World War II. Although neither Philip Murray nor any other industrial union leader ever
again offered a no-strike pledge, even during the Korean War, they
continued to enforce a tight political discipline within the CIO, keyed
more than ever to the policy requirements of the national administration
and its foreign policy.

The expulsion of the Communists from the industrial union federation exemplified this continuing pattern. Communist influence in the
CIO had reached its apogee in the second half of the war, but the
seeming legitimacy that the party and its followers enjoyed during those
years was based almost entirely upon the temporary political support
they offered leaders such as Murray and Roosevelt and the ultrapatriotic
mantle that the Communists wore. As the Cold War intensified in 1946
and 1947 and the domestic political scene shifted to the right, the leadership of the CIO moved against the union Communists, not at first to
expel them but rather to enforce at least a paper CIO unity on the crucial
Cold War issues that now dominated national life. The vocal opposition
of unions such as the UE, the ILWU, and the National Maritime Union

to the government's foreign policy threatened to turn a section of the CIO into the core of an opposition political movement that would be strong enough to spread disquiet in Washington but weak enough to invite massive retaliation by a government armed with extensive formal and informal power over the labor movement. As Philip Murray put it in the fall of 1946, the problem with such dissent was that it built "targets, targets that can be easily hit" by anti-union forces. At its 1946 convention, held immediately after the sweeping Republican election victories of that year, the CIO took two important steps to implement this defensive policy. By resolution, the convention declared that its delegates "resent and reject efforts of the Communist Party or other political parties and their adherents to interfere in the affairs of the CIO." At the same time, the CIO executive board took administrative steps to ensure that state and local CIO councils, many heavily influenced by Communist-led union officials, would adopt no policy resolutions counter to those of the national CIO itself. [2]

The CIO effort to maintain internal political orthodoxy without an organizational break with the Communists collapsed in late 1947. There were two major reasons for this. First, the strength of the aggressive anti-Communist elements increased dramatically within the organization. The smashing victory that the Reuther caucus achieved in the UAW late in 1947 wiped out the power of union opponents, such as George Addes and R. J. Thomas, who had formed a cautious alliance with the UAW Communists. Meanwhile, the political realignment of Mike Quill, Joseph Curran, and other leaders of the CIO's transport and maritime unions further cut the strength of the organizations influenced by the Communists. Reduced to about 15 percent of the CIO membership and subject to raiding by anti-Communist unions in both the AFL and the CIO, these unions could now be expelled with considerably less internal damage than was possible a year or two before. [3]

The presidential candidacy of Henry Wallace proved the crucial turning point in the CIO's decision to purge the Communist-dominated unions. Sacked from Truman's cabinet after he had attacked the administration's hard line on U.S. relations with Russia, Wallace thereafter moved gradually toward an independent presidential candidacy, appealing strongly to blacks, Jews, and those who considered themselves faithful adherents of the war era's Rooseveltian popular front. Wallace had a genuine appeal to the CIO rank and file, and his critique of the Truman administration was not dissimilar to that of the national CIO leadership.

After some hesitancy, based on their indecision about the viability of a third party candidacy, the Communists endorsed Wallace in December 1947 and urged like-minded trade unionists to do likewise.

Wallace's candidacy posed an acute dilemma for the CIO. On the one hand, dissatisfaction with Truman's domestic policies and the Democratic party reconversion plans ran high in non-Communist CIO circles. The social democratic wing of the CIO, represented by figures such as Emil Rieve, James Carey, and Walter Reuther, had long adopted at least an arms-length attitude toward the intimate wartime alliance that the popular-front wing of the CIO had sought with FDR and the Democrats. Their disenchantment grew during the immediate postwar era, when President Truman's maladroit handling of the reconversion crisis and the collapse of pro-union sentiment within his party set off a frantic search for a new alignment of political forces. In the spring of 1946, for example, John Dewey, Norman Thomas, and Walter Reuther, all identified with the anti-Communist wing of American liberalism, issued a call for a National Education Committee for a New Party. A year later, the UAW's secretary–treasurer, Emil Mazey, told local union presidents to take "concrete action in building an independent labor party of workers and farmers." The newly formed Americans for Democratic Action were less radical, but these liberals were soon engaged in a frantic search for an attractive candidate – William O. Douglas and General Dwight D. Eisenhower were often mentioned – to replace Truman on the Democratic ticket in 1948.[4]

Despite the appeal of a third party, the Wallace candidacy proved anathema to CIO liberals because it represented a break with what was fundamental in postwar America: alignment with the government in the battalions of the new Cold War. This was the implicit message Secretary of State George Marshall offered the CIO convention when he addressed that body in the fall of 1947, and it was made explicit in the January 1948 CIO executive council resolution rejecting the Wallace candidacy and endorsing the Marshall Plan. A powerful Wallace movement threatened to taint the CIO with the badge of disloyalty in much the same way that opposition to the no-strike pledge represented an intolerable deviation druing the war. President Truman's veto of Taft–Hartley in 1947 and his "Give 'm Hell, Harry" pseudopopulist shift to the left during the 1948 campaign made CIO endorsement of the president again feasible. And of course, this supplied leaders of the liberal–labor community with the usual argument that a vote for the third party was a vote for the

Republicans and reaction. Although the CIO trade unions might still differ radically on their bargaining strategy and their approach to Taft–Hartley, any divergence from the CIO position on the election was tantamount to organizational treason. The president's unexpected success in November sealed the fate of the Communist-influenced unions within the CIO. With the Wallace supporters routed and the Republicans at least temporarily subdued, the industrial union federation could clean house with the least possible institutional damage.[5]

The elimination of the Communists proved an important event in CIO history, not so much because party-influenced unionists themselves represented a viable alternative leadership within the organization but because of the devastating impact their bureaucratic expulsion would have on the structure and politics of the CIO itself. By casting several hundred thousand workers into organizational exile, the purge weakened and split the industrial union movement, fragmented organization in the electrical and farm equipment industries, and foreclosed the possibility of a militant organizing drive in the South. Perhaps even more important, the expulsion of the Communist unions narrowed drastically the limits of internal political life within the union movement. As we have seen, the institutional pressures creating a bureaucratic style of union leadership had been powerfully advanced by support from the state's labor relations apparatus during the war. By accepting the discipline of the Cold War mobilization, the industrial unions themselves advanced this process by identifying industrial radicalism with political subversion. Even in the UAW, where the Reuther caucus had defeated a Communist-supported opposition in a relatively open and democratic fashion, the purge of the Communists undermined the legitimacy of all opposition groups, Communist and anti-Stalinist alike, and inaugurated the reign of a one-party regime that coopted or suppressed potential rivals.[6]

Official anti-Communism powerfully reinforced the recrudescence of antiradical chauvinism that was simultaneously at work within popular working-class consciousness. The decline in the importance of ethnic divisions within the white working class meant that in the 1940s, American patriotism enjoyed a broader cultural base than at any time in the twentieth century. A homogeneous blue-collar Americanism was reforged out of the more insular sense of self-identity that had long characterized so many immigrant and second-generation workers from Southern and Eastern Europe. The pluralist propaganda of the American government, the experience of service in the military, and the influence of a patriotic and officially recognized industrial union movement proved important in this transformation. But the defeat in the 1940s of oppositional currents, such as those embodied in the wildcat strikes and the Wallace candidacy, also ensured that the mainstream working-class patriotism emerging in this decade would be transmuted into a nationalistic Cold War posture. Ironically, the popular-front wing of the CIO had contained some of the most zealous missionaries of this new patriotism, and during the war, the Communists had outdone themselves in twisting antifascism into a raison d'être for promoting official chauvinism. The Soviet army's conquest of East European homelands, which proved grist for the propaganda organs of the right wing and the Catholic Church, helped further to recast working-class ethnic culture into a hard, anti-Communist, anti-radical mold.[7]

The Taft–Hartley Act

The passage of the Taft–Hartley Act in June 1947 was a milestone, not only for the actual legal restrictions it imposed on the trade unions but as a climax to and a symbol of the shifting relationship between government and unions during the 1940s. Although passed under the leadership of congressional conservatives, Taft–Hartley proved less of a break with the past than a rigid codification of many of the key policy goals toward which sophisticated business leaders and state industrial relations managers had been moving since the early 1940s. Many of the most important provisions of the act – legal restrictions imposed on the unions during national emergency disputes, the certification of political orthodoxy required for use of the federal labor relations apparatus, and the prohibition of sympathy boycotts and other forms of industrial solidarity – had not been the program of the anti-union right alone. During the war, the federal government had sought implementation of much of this program, not through direct legislative enactment, which threatened a dangerous labor backlash, but through the progress of tripartite negotiations, most notably in the National War Labor Board. This approach reached its apogee during the years of the no-strike pledge when, as we have seen, the leaders of the major industrial unions cooperated closely with the government to maintain industrial and political discipline within their organizations.

However, with the breakdown of the tripartite negotiation of wages and union status in the reconversion crisis, the program of the congressional right became more compelling. Six months before the sweeping Republican victory in the 1946 congressional elections, the same Democratic legislature elected with FDR in 1944 overwhelmingly passed legislation introduced by Representative Francis Case, Republican of South Dakota, that would have established strike postponement and regulation procedures similar to those eventually enacted under Taft–Hartley a year later. President Truman, who had favored legislative restrictions of an equally draconian character during the rail strike of May 1946, successfully vetoed the Case bill when it became clear that such action would be the minimum necessary to avoid an open break with the trade unions. For similar reasons, he vetoed Taft–Hartley a year later, but this time the swollen Republican–conservative Democratic majority in both houses easily mustered the two-thirds necessary to override him and sweep the bill into law.[8]

The Taft–Hartley Act codified the decade-long effort of those who sought to contain the CIO. The anti-Communist affidavits now demanded of union leaders who would use the NLRB could not alone have destroyed radical politics within the union movement. But in conjunction with the anti-Communist currents then sweeping the working class and stiffening the backs of employers, the anti-Communist clause represented state action of a sort that opened the door to interunion raiding and gave the defenders of union political orthodoxy a new and powerful weapon that decimated their opponents and weakened the idea of interunion solidarity.

Equally significant, the Taft–Hartley Act helped restrict American industrial unionism to roughly the same social and regional terrain that it had won in the previous decade. The CIO effort to penetrate textile, furniture, food processing, and chemical plants in the South was severely hampered by Section 14b of the Taft–Hartley Act, which permitted individual states to outlaw the union shop. At the same time, the prohibition of secondary boycotts and mass picketing contained in the act made it much more difficult for strong unions to use their organizational muscle to aid the unionization effort of weaker groups in the retail and agricultural sectors, even in highly unionized regions of the North and West. Moreover, this containment of the union impulse also proved effective within already organized factories and offices. The Taft–Hartley Act defined as managers many supervisory workers who had been strongly attracted to unionism in the 1940s, and it prohibited their use of NLRB procedures when they sought union recognition. This legislative edict allowed employers to smash the promising foremen's organizations in the auto, steel, rubber, and shipbuilding industries and gave managers a powerful anti-union weapon in bureaucratically structured workplaces such as insurance and telephone offices, where a large number of supervisory personnel could be used as a bulwark against effective union organization.[9]

The anti-Communist purge and the passage of Taft–Hartley contributed to the relative depoliticization of the CIO and that organization's characteristic postwar emphasis on collective bargaining as the most important method by which the unions could improve the lot of their members. With the New Deal impulse exhausted and their influence on the Democratic party in decline, unionists such as Walter Reuther and the new USW president, David J. McDonald, hoped that an American version of the European welfare state might be negotiated bit by bit during annual or biannual bargaining sessions with corporate management. The National War Labor Board had put fringe benefits such as vacation pay, shift bonuses, and sick leave on the bargaining table, initially as a tactic to stem the assault on the Little Steel formula. Then, in each round of postwar contract renewals, the big unions in the auto, steel, rubber, trucking, and coal mining industries vied with each other to push back this collective bargaining frontier. In 1946 came the first health and welfare benefits, in 1948 an automatic wage escalator clause, in 1949 the first pensions, and in 1955 supplemental unemployment benefits. By the end of the postwar boom in the early 1970s, about 90 percent of all unionized workers were covered by some health and welfare plan, and many workers employed in large nonunion firms also received a fringe benefit package.[10]

Welfare privatization of this sort ultimately proved a dead end for the union movement and the social groups it had championed in its formative years. By winning such benefits for those workers most capable of effective political action, the unions and the large corporations had diffused the pressure for increased social benefits for all workers. Of course, CIO unions continued to favor an expansion of the welfare state, but their ability to mobilize rank-and-file workers on behalf of this goal rapidly diminished. Thus, even during the boom years of the postwar era, state-financed unemployment compensation, social security payments, and other health and welfare benefits remained substantially below those of most other industrialized countries. This helped engender among the old CIO unions an increasingly narrow business union outlook. And perhaps even more significantly, the growth of wage and social benefit inequalities within the workforce accentuated the deep racial, sexual, and occupational divisions that have come to characterize postwar labor.[11]

The postwar factory regime

The external pressures generated by World War II, the Cold War, and the Taft–Hartley Act reinforced the tropism toward an internally stolid union regime that arose out of the demands imposed by the postwar collective-bargaining system itself. The bargaining routine generated its own requirements: for discipline and solidarity among the locals, for a centralized technical staff, and for a measure of freewheeling latitude among those actually conducting the negotiations. In unions such as the UAW and the URW, the elimination of organized oppositional groups substantially reduced the relative freedom local union officials had enjoyed when two factions competed for their allegiance. Although auto locals would still hold the formal right to bargain and strike on work standards disputes, the Reuther leadership of the UAW approved stoppages over such issues only with the greatest reluctance, especially when they threatened to upset the union's national bargaining strategy or drain its limited resources. By the early 1950s, local contract issues were increasingly subordinated to the national negotiations. And when local strikes did take place, they were often allowed merely to give the boys "a chance to let off steam."[12]

The elaborate UAW–GM contract of 1950 proved a model for the sort of agreement that emerged under these new circumstances. In return for an unprecedented five-year contract that would make predictable GM's labor costs during its mammoth expansion program of the early 1950s, the union secured a wage escalator clause and an annual productivity increase that guaranteed year-by-year growth in real pay. The UAW finally won a de facto union shop, but in return, it virtually accepted the principle that advances in real wages would be pegged to increased productivity, thus acquiring a stake in the maintenance of stable, efficient industrial relations with the giant corporation. "This kind of collective bargaining," observed the respected labor economist Frederick Harbinson, "calls for intelligent trading rather than table-pounding, for diplomacy rather than belligerency, and for internal union discipline rather than grass roots rank and file activity." *Fortune* magazine declared the billion-dollar package "The Treaty of Detroit."[13]

The stable, almost harmonious relationships established between the negotiators for the industrial unions and their corporate counterparts did not extend far beneath the top ranks of the respective union and management hierarchies. On the contrary, corporate leaders had emerged from World War II with new strength, determined to curb the informal, localistic power unionized workers had won during the previous decade. Above all, managers sought to delimit firmly union power over production and reestablish their right to "manage" the work process on the factory floor.[14] Varying erratically with the particularities of the industry, general economic conditions, and the rate of technological and social change, this counteroffensive kept unionists on the defensive during almost the entire era of the postwar boom. In the late 1940s, managers of most large firms followed Ford's lead and included company security antistrike clauses in their collective bargaining contracts. During the early 1950s, much of the debate over automation and featherbedding armed supervisors with a new rationale to eliminate or weaken production bottlenecks that had traditionally provided workers with a measure of shop control. Then, under the relatively favorable circumstances created by the sharp recession of 1957–8, many companies adopted an increasingly aggressive bargaining strategy, climaxed by the 116-day 1959 steel strike, fought largely over the industry demand to win more control of work rules.[15] As *New York Times* labor reporter A. H. Raskin observed, "It is the employers who are on the march this year, taking the offensive after a quarter of a century of what they consider undue subservience to 'monopolistic' unions . . . The aim of the corporate rebellion is to restore management's initiative at the bargaining table and in the plant."[16]

In this conflict, the steel strike proved exceptional chiefly because of its dramatic visibility; most struggles of this sort took place out of the spotlight, on the local and department levels, where strikes and job actions over shop conditions, work loads, and job security accounted for about a quarter of all stoppages in manufacturing industries. In autos, long delayed grievances over these issues often turned into local work stoppages that spread like wildfire immediately following UAW ratification of each national contract with one of the Big Three auto makers. By the early 1960s, Walter Reuther was spending almost as much energy after each contract settlement cajoling and threatening these locals back to work as he had negotiating with the company beforehand. In steel, unauthorized strikes over working conditions accounted for about half of the industry's work stoppages in the 1950s. Such conflicts also proliferated in rubber and aircraft. By 1960, 60 percent of a sample of 150 major employers listed wildcat strikes over local issues as one of their most serious labor relations problems.[17]

From a structural perspective, the unions could do little to resist the managerial offensive. At the top, trade union leaders in the mass production industries usually found it advantageous to ignore the seemingly parochial, often divisive complaints of the individual locals in order to concede managers additional, incremental control over shop conditions in exchange for a larger monetary package for all.[18] In the locals, union activists found their efforts to fight back hampered by the gradual debilitation of the grievance procedure. Following passage of the Taft–Hartley Act, the transformation of the foreman into a simple disciplinarian and grievance buck passer necessarily diminished the independent leadership role of his counterpart, the union steward, who became at best a referral agent frequently bypassed in the actual working of the grievance procedure. Once shop disputes were reduced to written form and began to make their way up the grievance ladder, they were out of the steward's control and subject to a lockstep body of umpire-made "law" that defended managerial prerogatives regarding the work process and harshly penalized extracontractual pressure tactics by the union. And when stewards or shop activists took action not covered by the contract, they found themselves subject to increasingly severe managerial retaliation. Under the so-called negative leadership doctrine developed by grievance umpires in the auto industry after 1944, local officers were held directly responsible for work stoppages or slowdowns even when they played no role in the contract violation itself. The systematic application of this doctrine in the early postwar era did much to accelerate the decline of the workshop-based steward system and transformed plant committeemen and other local officers into contract policemen.[19]

The demise of an effective union presence on the local level helped advance the general depoliticization that characterized the working class in the first postwar decades. In contrast to Great Britain, where the postwar prosperity and growth of unionism gave rise to an increasingly confident stratum of shop steward militants, in America the rigidity of the collective bargaining process thwarted the emergence of an independent cadre that could give continuous leadership to the episodic conflict that still unfolded in the workplace. Combined with the conservative ethos of the era – the antiradical hysteria of the early 1950s and the consumption ethic of the entire period – this vacuum necessarily helped generate a passive and atomized consciousness among large sections of the industrial working class. Sharp conflicts with the employer still took place, but no tradition of struggle emerged from them. There was little outright rejection of unionism, but most workers came to expect little more from the institution than a periodic readjustment of their wage bargain with the employer.

Atrophy at the base unquestionably played a large role in the stagnation of the union movement in the larger society. The efficacy with which the unions mobilized their own ranks and appealed to the unorganized declined proportionately as they became mere wage-fixing mechanisms. From the end of the Korean War, their membership, especially that of the old CIO unions, grew more slowly than the working population. Despite the 1955 merger of the AFL and the CIO, the unions proved unable to organize the South, to penetrate effectively the burgeoning white-collar occupations, or to adjust their traditional collective-bargaining goals and procedures to meet the needs of a rapidly changing workforce. Although trade unions increased their organizational presence within the Democratic party during the 1960s, they lost their status as the preeminent left–liberal force in American society when they stood apart from or opposed the new movements of that decade challenging the social and political status quo.[20]

By the early 1970s, the postwar boom was over, and with it the cycle of trade unionism that began with the consolidation of the mass industrial unions of the late 1930s and early 1940s. Weakened by stagflation and increasingly outflanked by the multinational conglomerates with which they bargained, even the largest unions found it difficult to prevent a fall in the real wages of their members or to protect those in older industries from periodic bouts of unemployment. As the economic crisis became one of chronic instability, the government eviscerated the idea of free collective bargaining with an on-again, off-again set of wage guidelines that seemed reminiscent of the wartime controls a third of a century earlier. Unlike the late New Deal era, however, the influence of the government apparatus was often overtly hostile and the attacks by the business community more intense. With the union movement at its lowest ebb since the early years of the Great Depression, the whole shape of the political economy and the structure of postwar labor relations have been brought into question. Unions have again become an arena for political debate, and the issues with which the early CIO grappled – the quality of daily work life, union democracy, and the political independence of the labor movement – have again been brought forward on the social agenda.

Notes

1. Introduction

1 For accounts of this episode, see William Serrin, *The Company and the Union* (New York, 1974), 323–6; Jack Weinberg, *Detroit Auto Uprising 1973* (Detroit, n.d.).

2 See, for example, Seymour Martin Lipset, *Political Man* (New York, 1959), 387–436; Richard Lester, *As Unions Mature* (New York, 1958); Daniel Bell, *The End of Ideology* (New York, 1961), 211–26; and Clark Kerr, Frederick Harbison, John Dunlop, and Charles A. Myers, *Industrialism and Industrial Man* (Cambridge, Mass., 1960).

3 Much of this analysis is taken from Michael Paul Rogin, *The Intellectuals and McCarthy: The Radical Specter* (Cambridge, Mass., 1967), 23–6; see also Alvin W. Gouldner, "Metaphysical Pathos and the Theory of Bureaucracy," *American Political Science Review*, 67 (1955), 506.

4 Irving Bernstein, *Turbulent Years, A History of the American Worker, 1933–41* (Boston, 1969); Sidney Fine, *Sit-Down, The General Motors Strike of 1936–1937* (Ann Arbor, Mich., 1969). Fine's volume, perhaps the finest example of this genre, details the events of only a few weeks in the winter of 1937, but the methodology is identical to that of Bernstein's more comprehensive survey. See also David Brody, "The Expansion of the American Labor Movement: Institutional Sources of Stimulus and Restraint," in Stephen E. Ambrose, ed., *Institutions in Modern America: Innovation in Structure and Response* (Baltimore, 1967), 11–36, and "The Emergence of Mass Production Unionism," in David Brody, *Workers in Industrial America: Essays on the 20th Century Struggle* (New York, 1980), 82–119.

5 Joel Seidman, *American Labor from Defense to Reconversion* (Chicago, 1953), especially 276–82.

6 The early New Left took much of its inspiration from C. Wright Mills, whose book *The New Men of Power* (New York, 1948) explains the rise of union bureaucracy in terms of the growing influence of a new stratum of labor leaders linked to the section of the capitalist class that sought to integrate the unions through the state apparatus. In the late 1960s, Ronald Radosh put forward this view most explicitly in *American Labor and United States Foreign Policy* (New York, 1969) and "The Corporate Ideology of American Labor Leaders from Gompers to Hillman" in James Weinstein and David Eakins, eds., *For a New America: Essays in History and Politics from "Studies on the Left," 1959–1967* (New York, 1970), 125–51.

7 Kim McQuaid, "Corporate Liberalism in the American Business Community, 1920–1940," *Business History Review*, 52 (1978), 354–64. David Vogel, "Why Businessmen Distrust Their State: The Political Consciousness of American Corporate Executives," *British Journal of Political Science*, 8 (1978),

246

45–78, passim, provides an excellent discussion of the historical circumstances that have generated antistatism among American businessmen. My understanding of both the corporate liberal and structuralist theories of the state has been substantially advanced by Theda Skocpol, "Political Response to Capitalist Crisis: Neo-Marxist Theories of the State and the Case of the New Deal," *Politics and Society*, 10 (1980), 155–201.

8 Two of the basic texts here are Nicos Poulantzas, *Political Power and Social Classes* (London, 1975), and Claus Offe, "Structural Problems of the Capitalist State," *German Political Studies*, 1 (1974), 31–57.

9 Skocpol, "Political Response to Capitalist Crisis," 178–91; David A. Gold, Clarence Y. H. Lo, and Erik Olin Wright, "Recent Developments in Marxist Theories of the Capitalist State," *Monthly Review*, 27 (1975), 35–40.

10 Jeremy Brecher, *Strike!* (San Francisco, 1972), 181–266, and "Uncovering the Hidden History of the American Workplace," *Review of Radical Political Economics*, 10 (1978), 1–23; Staughton Lynd, *Rank and File: Personal Histories by Working-Class Organizers* (Boston, 1973) and "The Possibility of Radicalism in the Early 1930s: The Case of Steel," *Radical America*, 6 (1972), 37–64; Peter Friedlander, *The Emergence of a UAW Local, 1936–1939: A Study in Class and Culture* (Pittsburgh, 1975); Robert Zieger, *Madison's Battery Workers* (Ithaca, N.Y., 1977).

2. The unfinished struggle

1 The complex character of working-class solidarity and the difficulties in maintaining a permanent organization have been made apparent in Herbert Gutman, *Work, Culture and Society in Industrializing America* (New York, 1976); Daniel Walkowitz, *Worker City, Company Town: Iron and Cotton-Worker Protest in Troy and Cohoes, New York, 1855–84* (Urbana, Ill., 1978); and Alan Dawley, *Class and Community: The Industrial Revolution in Lynn* (Cambridge, Mass., 1976).

2 The power of the government and national corporations to resist even the strongest efforts to achieve industrial unionism is reflected in Melvyn Dubofsky, *We Shall Be All, The Story of the IWW* (New York, 1970); Leon Wolff, *Lockout, The Story of the Homestead Strike of 1892: A Study of Violence, Unionism and the Carnegie Steel Empire* (New York, 1965); Almont Lindsay, *The Pullman Strike* (Chicago, 1964); and David Brody, *Labor in Crisis, The Steel Strike of 1919* (New York, 1965).

3 As quoted in J. Raymond Walsh, *CIO: Industrial Unionism in Action* (New York, 1937), 56.

4 This NRA era insurgency is surveyed in Irving Bernstein, *Turbulent Years, A History of the American Worker, 1933–41* (Boston, 1969), 217–317; Jeremy Brecher, *Strike!* (San Francisco, 1972), 189–219; and Farrell Dobbs, *Teamster Rebellion* (New York, 1972); Charles P. Larrowe, *Harry Bridges: The Rise and Fall of Radical Labor* (New York, 1971), 32–94; Robert Zieger, "The Limits of Militancy: Organized Paper Workers, 1933–1935," *Journal of American History*, 63 (1976), 646–56; and the provocative Frances Fox Piven and Richard A. Cloward, *Poor People's Movements: Why They Succeed, How They Fail* (New York, 1977), 41–76, 96–107.

5 See the important article by Staughton Lynd, "The Possibility of Radicalism in the Early 1930s: The Case of Steel," *Radical America*, 6 (1972), 37–64.

6 Melvyn Dubofsky and Warren Van Tine, *John L. Lewis: A Biography* (New York, 1970), 203–47, passim; David Brody, "The Emergence of Mass Production Unionism," in Brody, *Workers in Industrial America: Essays on the 20th Century Struggle* (New York, 1980), 82–94; Lloyd Ulman, *The Government of the Steel Workers' Union* (New York, 1962), 15; and "The U.S. Steel Corporation III," *Fortune*, 13 (1936), 144.

7 Saul Alinsky, *John L. Lewis: An Unauthorized Biography* (New York, 1949), 149; David J. McDonald, *Union Man* (New York, 1969), 101.

8 This process is aptly described in Peter Friedlander's *The Emergence of a UAW Local, 1936–1939: A Study in Class and Culture* (Pittsburgh, 1975), 3–53. Roger Keeran highlights the role played by the Communist cadre in *"The Communist Party and the Auto Workers Unions* (Bloomington, 1980) 28–59, 77–95.

9 Accounts of the rapid early growth of the new CIO unions are found in Bernstein, *Turbulent Years*, 473–4, 554, 600, 615; James J. Matles and James Higgins, *Them and Us, The Struggle of a Rank and File Union* (Englewood Cliffs, N.J., 1974), 61–88; and Raymond Boryczka, "Militancy and Factionalism in the United Auto Workers, 1937–1941," *Maryland Historian*, 8 (1977), 13–25. See also Robert Travis, "Report on Flint," September 1937, Henry Kraus Collection, Box 12, Archives of Labor History, Wayne State University (ALHWSU).

10 Extracontractual activity of this sort in the auto industry is described in Frank Marquart Oral History, 26; Carl Hassler Oral History, 22; John Anderson Oral History, 56, all in ALHWSU. See also Sidney Fine, *Sit-Down, The General Motors Strike of 1936–1937* (Ann Arbor, Mich., 1969), 323–5, and Irving Howe and B. J. Widick, *The UAW and Walter Reuther* (New York, 1949), 68–9. A fine description of this phenomenon in the rubber industry is found in Daniel Nelson, "The Origins of the Sit-down Era: Worker Militancy and Innovation in the Rubber Industry, 1934–38," *Labor History*, 23 (1982), 198–225.

11 This phenomenon is discussed in Boryczka, "Militancy and Factionalism," 15–18, and Zieger, "The Limits of Militancy," 646–56.

12 Report of John O'Leary and Allan S. Haywood to Philip Murray and Sidney Hillman, November 7, 1938, Hillman Papers, United Textile Workers of America Headquarters, New York; Sherman Dalrymple to Allen S. Haywood, November 30, 1940, John Brophy Papers, Box A7-32, Catholic University, Washington, D.C.

13 McDonald, *Union Man*, 90–8; 120–8; *Steel Labor*, September 10, October 15, 1937, February 20, 1938; Steel Workers Organizing Committee, *Proceedings of the First International Wage and Policy Convention*, Pittsburgh, December 1937, 133–49; interview with Tom Murray, assistant to the secretary-treasurer, United Steelworkers of America, March 9, 1972; the quotation is from Robert R. R. Brooks, *As Steel Goes* (New Haven, Conn., 1940), 162–3.

14 Jack Skeels, "The Development of Political Stability within the United Auto Workers Union," unpublished Ph.D. diss., University of Wisconsin, Madison, 1957, 1–30, 102–39; Skeels, "Background of UAW Factionalism," *Labor History*, 2 (1961), 158–81; Wyndham Mortimer, *Organize! My Life as a Union Man* (Boston, 1971), 69–102; Raymond Boryczka, "Seasons of Discontent: Auto Union Factionalism and the Motor Products Strike of 1935–1936," *Michigan History*, 61 (1977), 3–31.

15 Descriptions of such strikes are found in Nelson, "Worker Militancy in the Rubber Industry," 205–20; Henry Kraus, *The Many and the Few* (Los Angeles, 1947), 48–52; Fine, *Sit-Down*, 321–3.

16 See, for example, "Address by John L. Lewis to Officers and Members of the UAW," April 7, 1937, and Letter, Homer Martin to UAW General Motors Locals, May 18, 1937, Kraus Collection, Box 11; and "Auto Workers Don't Be Provoked," leaflet by Flint City Committee of the Communist party, early 1938, in Kraus Collection, Box 16; for Philip Murray's attack on wildcat strikes see *Steel Labor*, February 18, 1938. For the Communist party's attitude toward such strikes, see Roger Keeran, "The Communists and UAW Factionalism, 1937–1939," *Michigan History*, 60 (1976), 120–4, and Bert Cochran, *Labor and Communism, the Conflict that Shaped American Unions* (Princeton, N.J., 1977), 127–43.

17 Homer Martin to William S. Knudsen, September 16, 1937, Kraus Collection, Box 11; and Bernstein, *Turbulent Years*, 559–63; Hassler Oral History, 29.

18 General Motors Delegate Conference Transcript, November 7, 1937, 44–57, in Pre-Presidential Papers, Walter Reuther Collection, Box 6, ALHWSU; see also Skeels, "The Development of Political Stability," 41–70; Cochran, *Labor and Communism*, 134–6; Frank Cormier and William J. Eaton, *Reuther* (Englewood Cliffs, N.J., 1970), 125.

19 Marquart Oral History, 65; Harry Ross Oral History, 6–20; UAW Executive Board Minutes, May 9–25, 1938, 14–18, in UAW International Executive Board Collection, all ALHWSU. See also Skeels, "The Development of Political Stability," 102–28, and Clayton W. Fountain, *Union Guy* (New York, 1949), 101–3, for an account of the decentralizing impulse at the 1939 convention. The extent to which the powerful locals held effective political power in the union became manifest in the winter of 1938–9. Harry Ross, treasurer of Dodge Local 3, refused to transmit the union's $27,000 dues check to the UAW's national office until the faction fight was resolved. "They [both factions] would look at this Dodge local check," recalled Ross, "and they would drool." Ross Oral History, 6.

20 *United Auto Worker*, May 15, 30, December 13, 1939, January 10, 1940; Joseph Ferris Oral History, 25–30; John Anderson Oral History, 60; UAW Executive Board Minutes, December 4, 1939, all ALHWSU; Michael Devereaux Whitty, "Emil Mazey, Radical as Liberal," unpublished Ph.D. diss., Syracuse University, 1969, 77–8; the Thomas quotation is from Hassler Oral History, 92.

21 Lorin Lee Cary describes the CIO's only partially successful effort to establish tight control of the new unions in his "Institutionalized Conservatism in the Early CIO: Adolph Germer, a Case Study," *Labor History*, 13 (1972), 475–504; see also David Brody, *The Butcher Workmen: A Study of Unionization* (Cambridge, Mass., 1964), 182–6; Matthew Josephson, *Sidney Hillman, Statesman of American Labor* (Garden City, N.Y., 1952), 458–560; Nelson, "Worker Militancy in the Rubber Industry," 220–5; Ronald L. Filippelli, "UE: The Formative Years, 1933–1937," *Labor History*, 17 (1976), 351–71.

22 Harry A. Millis, ed., *How Collective Bargaining Works* (New York, 1942), 641–4, 801–5; Keith Sward, *The Legend of Henry Ford* (New York, 1949), 370–400; Harold S. Roberts, *The Rubber Workers*, (New York, 1944), 192–254; Bernstein, *Turbulent Years*, 478–98; see also Brody, "The

Emergence of Mass Production Unionism," in *Workers in Industrial America*, 107–12, and Ronald Schatz, "The End of Corporate Liberalism: Class Struggle in the Electrical Manufacturing Industry, 1933–1950," *Radical America*, 9 (1975), 192–3. Schatz reports that "IWW style" unionism, local bargaining without a signed contract, prevailed at many Westinghouse plants. But most union cadres considered this situation far from satisfactory and looked forward to a formal collective bargaining contract.

23 Robert Ozanne, *A Century of Labor–Management Relations at McCormick and International Harvester* (Madison, Wis., 1967), 174–6; Brody, *The Butcher Workmen*, 177–8; Harvey Schwartz, *The March Inland: Origins of the ILWU Warehouse Division, 1934–1938* (Los Angeles, 1978), 106–75; Bernstein, *Turbulent Years*, 616–23. For an account of the adaptive ability and striking success enjoyed by rival AFL unions in the 1930s, see Christopher L. Tomlins, "AFL Unions in the 1930s: Their Performance in Historical Perspective," *Journal of American History*, 65 (1979), 1021–42.

24 Robert Aaron Gordon, *Economic Instability and Growth, the American Record* (New York, 1974), 66–70; Dubofsky and Van Tine, *John L. Lewis*, 316–17. In 1938, UE leaders were delighted to adopt wholesale General Electric's employee rules booklet and call it their contract. Matles and Higgins, *Them and Us*, 83–5. Murray considered the renewal of the 1938 contract with U.S. Steel a victory because wages were not reduced, although he was forced to agree to a ten-day reopener should the steel corporation feel that competitive conditions warranted a wage reduction; *Steel Labor*, February 20, 1938; Edward R. Livernash, *Collective Bargaining in the Basic Steel Industry* (Washington, D.C., 1961), 237–8.

25 CIO Executive Board Minutes, June 1939, 15–36; microfilm at ALHWSU, November 20, 1940, 197; McDonald, *Union Man*, 90–8. According to Christopher Tomlins, who has compiled the most recent estimates, the total dues-paying membership of the CIO stood at 1,837,700 in 1939, less than half that of the AFL at 3,878,000. If one excludes the CIO unions in coal mining and the needle trades, which were almost fully organized when they joined the industrial union federation, then the CIO's permanent gains were quite modest by 1940. As Philip Murray told an executive board meeting, "So with all our wind and with all our puffing and blowing we had increased our dues paying membership by about 500,000 in five years, or perhaps 600,000 members." Tomlins, "AFL Unions in the 1930s," 1023; CIO Executive Board Minutes, June 5, 1942, 532–3.

26 Richard Polenberg, "The Decline of the New Deal, 1937–1940," in John Braeman, Robert Bremner, and David Brody, eds., *The New Deal: The National Level* (Columbus, Ohio, 1975), 246–66; James Patterson, *Congressional Conservatism and the New Deal* (Lexington, Ky., 1967), 211–87, passim; Earl Latham, *The Communist Controversy in Washington: From the New Deal to McCarthy* (Cambridge, Mass., 1966), 124–50.

27 The relative weakness of New Deal labor–liberalism has begun to attract much historical attention. See James T. Patterson, *The New Deal and the States: Federalism in Transition* (Princeton, N.J., 1969); and John Braeman, Robert Bremner, and David Brody, eds., *The New Deal: The State and Local Levels* (Columbus, Ohio, 1975), especially the chapters on Pennsylvania, Ohio, Pittsburgh and Kansas City, 45–102, 376–419. For the defeat of the

UAW slate in the Detroit municipal elections, see Cormier and Eaton, *Reuther*, 123–4.

28 This perspective is most admirably advanced by James MacGregor Burns, *Roosevelt: The Lion and the Fox* (New York, 1956); Dubofsky and Van Tine, *John L. Lewis*, 323–9; and C. K. McFarland, "Coalition of Convenience: Lewis and Roosevelt, 1933–1940," *Labor History*, 13 (1972), 409–13.

29 Karl E. Klare, "Judicial Deradicalization of the Wagner Act and the Origins of Modern Legal Consciousness, 1937–1941," *Minnesota Law Review*, 62 (1978), 291. Klare's essay should be read in tandem with Christopher L. Tomlins, "The State and the Unions: Federal Labor Relations Policy and the Organized Labor Movement in America, 1935–55," unpublished Ph.D. diss., Johns Hopkins University, 1980. In contrast to Klare, Tomlins emphasizes the extent to which the Wagner Act was designed to limit the AFL's traditional "autonomous rights of labor" and turn the unions into heavily regulated public institutions. Indeed, New Dealers such as Robert Wagner did favor a sort of statification of the unions, and Tomlins describes well the legal and administrative process that restricted the unions over the next decade and a half. But Tomlins errs in failing to see the politically contingent nature of these developments and in tracing the stages of this process with little regard for the social and institutional life of the unions themselves.

30 Ulman, *Government of the Steel Workers' Union*, 1–39; as late as 1940, two-thirds of SWOC's district directors, plus its chairman, secretary-treasurer, and three of its four regional directors, remained on the United Mine Workers' payroll. SWOC, *Proceedings of the Second International Wage and Policy Convention*, Pittsburgh, May 14–17, 1940, 28; McDonald, *Union Man*, 145–55; *Steel Labor*, March 20, 1937; Frederick H. Harbison, "Steel," in Harry A. Millis, *How Collective Bargaining Works* (New York, 1942), 527–31.

31 The most complete account of the Little Steel strike is still Donald G. Sofchalk, "The Little Steel Strike of 1937," unpublished Ph.D. diss., Ohio State University, 1961; see also SWOC, *Proceedings of the First International Wage and Policy Convention*, Pittsburgh, December 1937, 8; McDonald, *Union Man*, 108–20; and James L. Baughman, "Classes and Company Towns: Legends of the 1937 Little Steel Strike," *Ohio History*, 87 (1978), 175–92. The Adamic quotation is from p. 189.

32 Clinton Golden and Harold Ruttenberg, *The Dynamics of Industrial Democracy* (New York, 1942), 48–57; Harold Ruttenberg, "Strategy of Industrial Peace," *Harvard Business Review*, 17 (1939), 172–3.

33 Golden and Ruttenberg, *Dynamics*, 67.

34 Ruttenberg, "Strategy of Industrial Peace," 164; Golden and Ruttenberg, *Dynamics*, 62.

35 Golden and Ruttenberg, *Dynamics*, 60–1.

36 Philip Murray and Morris Cooke, *Organized Labor and Production* (New York, 1940). The very second handbook that the SWOC published outlined the procedure that local union officers should use to aid management in rationalizing and increasing production. But the guide cautioned the reader, "Do not try anything described in this handbook until the position of the union is secure and it has permanent and satisfactory contractual relations with the employer." SWOC, "Production Problems" (Pittsburgh, 1938), 4. In later years, Clinton Golden and others in the steel union leadership strong-

ly backed the National Planning Association's "Causes of Industrial Peace under Collective Bargaining" series. See, for example, J. Wade Miller, Jr., *Sharon Steel Corporation and United Steelworkers of America: A Case Study* (Washington, D.C., 1949), On Cooke, see Kenneth E. Trombley, *The Life and Times of a Happy Liberal* (New York, 1954), 87–190, passim.

37 Harbison, "Steel," 530, 550.

38 Ulman, *Government of the Steel Workers' Union*, 27–39; Livernash, *Collective Bargaining in the Basic Steel Industry*, 78–83; USW, *Proceedings of the First Constitutional Convention*, Pittsburgh, May 19–22, 1942, 210–21 (Murray's quotation is on p. 224); see also the perspective of the rank-and-file leader in Staughton Lynd, *Rank and File: Personal Histories of Working-Class Organizers* (Boston, 1973), 91–110, 163–75. An excellent critique of the grievance procedure is found in Sidney Lens, "Meaning of the Grievance Procedure," *Harvard Business Review*, 26 (1948), 713–21.

3. CIO politics on the eve of war

1 Harold Ruttenberg, "Steel: Economic Barometer," June 1938, Brophy Collection, Box A7-33, 7.

2 For the postwar union decline in meatpacking, see David Brody, *The Butcher Workmen: A Study of Unionization* (Cambridge, Mass., 1964), 74–105; for coal, Irving Bernstein, *The Lean Years* (Boston, 1966), 358–90; and Melvyn Dubofsky and Warren Van Tine, *John L. Lewis: A Biography* (New York, 1970), 132–50; for the needle trades, Matthew Josephson, *Sidney Hillman, Statesman of American Labor* (Garden City, N.Y., 1952), 213–41, and Benjamin Stolberg, *Tailor's Progress* (Garden City, N.Y., 1944); see also Lewis L. Lorwin, *The American Federation of Labor* (Washington, D.C., 1933), 201–29.

3 CIO, *Proceedings of the Third Constitutional Convention*, Atlantic City, N.J., November 21, 1940, 64; see also Ralph Herzel, Jr., "Report of the CIO Unemployment Division," in CIO Convention, Reports and Resolutions of the Executive Board, June 4, 1940, CIO Secretary-Treasurer's Office Collection, Box 91, Archives of Labor History, Wayne State University (ALHWSU).

4 This Lewis portrait is taken chiefly from the nearly definitive biography of Dubofsky and Van Tine, *John L. Lewis*, but one should also consult the lively although sometimes mistaken Saul Alinsky, *John L. Lewis: An Unauthorized Biography* (New York, 1949), and McAlister Coleman, *Men and Coal* (New York, 1943).

5 As quoted in Alinsky, *John L. Lewis*, 159–60.

6 A summary of these criticisms is found in CIO, *Proceedings of the Third Constitutional Convention*, 22–5, 37–41; and Hertzel, "Report of the CIO Unemployment Division," Box 91.

7 *UMW Journal*, September 15, 1939, 5.

8 Henry W. Berger, "Union Diplomacy: American Labor's Foreign Policy in Latin America, 1932–1955," unpublished Ph.D. diss., University of Wisconsin, Madison, 1966, 160–82. Lewis's ideas on hemispheric defense and trade are put forward in his 1940 Labor Day Address, reprinted in the *UMW Journal*, September 15, 1940; James Carey, then secretary-treasurer of the CIO, emphasized Lewis's Latin American interest in his interview with the author on March 22, 1972.

9 CIO, *Proceedings of the Second Constitutional Convention*, San Francisco, October 1939, 6.

10 Richard J. Purcell, *Labor Policies of the National Defense Advisory Commission and the Office of Production Management, May 1940–April 1942* (Washington, D.C., 1942), 34–45; *CIO Economic Outlook*, March 1941, 2. Conservatives argued that the Nazi victory in Western Europe was due to short working hours, strikes that limited defense production, and social reforms that pampered the workers, especially in France after the victory of the popular front in 1936. See, for example, the full-page editorial in the *Saturday Evening Post*, August 10, 1940, 26.

11 See the extensive correspondence, Lewis to FDR, January 18, 1939; FDR to Lewis, January 30, 1939; Lewis to FDR, February 21, 1939; Lewis to FDR, March 16, 1939; FDR to Lewis, March 20, 1939; Sidney Hillman to Lewis, July 30, 1940; Lewis to Hillman, August 27, 1940; Hillman to Lewis, September 13, 1940; Lewis to Hillman, July 15, 1940, all in John L. Lewis and Executive Order File, Hillman Collection. See also Josephson, *Sidney Hillman*, 518–24.

12 Dubofsky and Van Tine, *John L. Lewis*, 241–364, passim. Lewis closed the door to support of the president only after he became convinced that the minimal demands of the labor movement could not be met in the context of normal Democratic party politics. As late as January 1940, Lewis continued to propose a formal "accord" between organized labor and the Democratic party. Its elements were rather modest and somewhat mechanical: labor representation in the cabinet, a role in writing the Democratic platform, and closer contact between the White House and the leadership of the trade unions. *UMW Journal*, January 15, April 15, 1940.

13 Josephson, *Sidney Hillman*, 488–9; Dubofsky and Van Tine, *John L. Lewis*, 360; Lewis's full endorsement of Wendell Willkie is found in *UMW Journal*, November 1, 1940; Irving Bernstein, "John L. Lewis and the Voting Behavior of the CIO," *Public Opinion Quarterly*, 5 (1941), 233–49. For a detailed account of Lewis's political activities during 1940, and the argument that he knowingly accepted financial support from Nazi sources when he endorsed Willkie, see Hugh Ross, "John L. Lewis and the Election of 1940," *Labor History*, 17 (1976), 160–89.

14 Accounts of the tumultuous 1940 CIO convention are found in Irving Bernstein, *Turbulent Years: A History of the American Worker, 1933–41* (Boston, 1969), 721–6; Josephson, *Sidney Hillman*, 490–502; and Dubofsky and Van Tine, *John L. Lewis*, 364–70.

15 See the discussion of labor politics in J. David Greenstone, *Labor in American Politics* (New York, 1969), 39–52; and Vivian Vale, *Labour in American Politics* (New York, 1971), 51–75.

16 Milton Derber, "The New Deal and Labor," in John Braeman, Robert Bremner, and David Brody, eds., *The New Deal: The State and Local Levels* (Columbus, Ohio, 1975), 110–32.

17 See Bernstein, *Turbulent Years*, 646–63; James A. Gross, *The Making of the National Labor Relations Board*, vol. 1 (Albany, N.Y., 1976), 2–3; Christopher L. Tomlins, "The State and the Unions: Federal Labor Relations Policy and the Organized Labor Movement in America, 1935–55," unpublished Ph.D. diss., Johns Hopkins University, 1980, 195–220. During the recession of 1937–8, industrial union reliance on the NLRB became so great that CIO

council Lee Pressman felt constrained to warn his fellow unionists, "Unless excellent judgment is exercised in this connection, there is danger that organizing work may be seriously impeded by placing too much reliance on the board. All officers and organizers must understand that primary reliance must not be placed upon the board for organizing work." As quoted in Tomlins, "The State and the Unions," 208.

18 Jerold S. Auerbach, *Labor and Liberty: The LaFollette Committee and the New Deal* (New York, 1966), 151–75; Earl Latham, *The Communist Controversy in Washington: From the New Deal to McCarthy* (Cambridge, Mass., 1966), 137–50; Pressman Oral History, 219.

19 Ellis Hawley, *The New Deal and the Problem of Monopoly* (Princeton, N.J., 1966), 205–12; Dubofsky and Van Tine, *John L. Lewis*, 372–4; James P. Johnson, *The Politics of Soft Coal: The Bituminous Industry from World War I through the New Deal* (Urbana, Ill., 1979), 217–38.

20 SWOC, *Proceedings of the Second International Wage and Policy Convention*, Pittsburgh, May 14–17, 1940, 60; Robert R. R. Brooks, *As Steel Goes* (New Haven, Conn., 1940), 217–40; Philip Murray and Morris Cooke, *Organized Labor and Production* (New York, 1940), 159–72.

21 CIO, *Proceedings of the First Constitutional Convention*, Pittsburgh, October 1938, 59.

22 Josephson, *Sidney Hillman*, 160–212, 340–80, 431–60, passim; Steve Fraser's "Dress Rehearsal for the New Deal," in Daniel Walkowitz and Michael Frisch, eds., *Working Class History: Toward an Integrated View of Labor in American Life* (Urbana, Ill., 1982), provides an excellent reinterpretation of the social and ideological framework within which Hillman constructed the "new unionism" of the 1920s.

23 Irving Howe, *World of Our Fathers* (New York, 1976), 391–3.

24 As quoted in Josephson, *Sidney Hillman*, 328; for an account of the formation of the American Labor party that emphasizes its roots in the Jewish community, see Kenneth Waltzer, "The American Labor Party: Third Party Politics in New Deal–Cold War New York, 1936–1954," unpublished Ph.D. diss., Harvard University, 1977, 2–105.

25 See, for example, the comments of J. B. S. Hardman in the ACWA *Advance*, March 1940; see also Josephson, *Sidney Hillman*, 440–56. For an occasionally insightful portrait of Hillman and his circle, see Len DeCaux, *Labor Radical: From the Wobblies to the CIO* (Boston, 1970), 328–344.

26 News release, "Radio Speech by Sidney Hillman," January 28, 1940, in ACWA Political Action File, 1940–1943, Hillman Collection; Josephson, *Sidney Hillman*, 468–70, 481–6; Pressman Oral History, 120. For an indication of the close personal meaning Hillman gained from FDR's friendship, see David K. Niles to Grace Tully, May 19, 1942, President's Personal File (PPF) 3585, Roosevelt Library, Hyde Park, N.Y.

27 A pro-interventionist, pro-Roosevelt history that nevertheless takes account of widespread opposition to the war is Robert A. Divine, *The Reluctant Belligerent: American Entry into World War II* (New York, 1965), 75–158. The CIO attack on the draft is taken from Donald J. Murphy, "The CIO and the Origins of Peacetime Military Conscription, 1940–1941," unpublished M.S. thesis, University of Wisconsin, 1959, 44.

28 Right-wing opposition to the war is thoroughly discussed in Geoffrey S. Smith, *To Save a Nation: American Countersubversives, the New Deal, and the*

Coming of World War II (New York, 1973), 139–81; Ronald Radosh's *Prophets on the Right* (New York, 1975) contains fine profiles of Charles A. Beard, Oswald Garrison Villard, and Robert A. Taft.

29 James MacGregor Burns, *Roosevelt: The Soldier of Freedom, 1940–1945* (New York, 1970), 33–63; Murphy, "Origins of Peacetime Military Conscription," 90–110.

30 John M. Blum, *V Was for Victory: Politics and American Culture during World War II* (New York, 1976), 120; Lewis may have been particularly enraged by Stimson's appointment as secretary of war. In 1923 this Brahmin lawyer had served as counsel for the bituminous coal operators at the U.S. Coal Commission hearings. Stimson then placed the blame for coalfield violence on the UMW and proposed the drastic weakening of the union as a solution to the chaotic conditions then prevailing in the industry. Elting E. Morison, *Turmoil and Tradition, the Life and Times of Henry L. Stimson* (New York, 1960), 214–18.

31 A considerable literature records the complex administrative arrangements Roosevelt constructed and reconstructed to mobilize the economy. Contemporary studies include Eliott Janeway, *The Struggle for Survival* (New Haven, Conn., 1950); Bruce Catton, *The War Lords of Washington* (New York, 1948); I. F. Stone, *Business as Usual: The First Year of Defense* (New York, 1941); and Civilian Production Administration, *Industrial Mobilization for War* (Washington, D.C., 1947), 17–85. The foremost contemporary student of the subject is Paul A. C. Koistinen. See his "The Hammer and the Sword: Labor and the Military during World War II," unpublished Ph.D. diss., University of California, Berkeley, 1964, 554–73, and "Mobilizing the World War II Economy: Labor and the Military–Industrial Alliance," *Pacific Historical Review*, 42 (1973), 443–78.

32 In addition to Hillman, the other members of the NDAC were Chester C. Davis, in charge of agriculture, and Harriet Elliott, adviser on consumer protection. For a good understanding of the several different managerial approaches to the labor problem in the late 1930s and early 1940s, I am indebted to Howell John Harris, *The Right to Manage: Industrial Relations Policies of American Business in the 1940s* (Madison, Wisc., 1982), especially Chap. 1.

33 As quoted in Richard Polenberg, *War and Society: The United States, 1941–1945* (New York, 1972), 12.

34 *CIO Economic Outlook*, March 1941, 2.

35 Stone, *Business as Usual*, 157–84.

36 "Leon Henderson," *Current Biography*, 1 (1940), 377–79; Barton Bernstein, "The Automobile Industry and the Coming of the Second World War," *Southwestern Social Science Quarterly*, 47 (1966), 22–33.

37 Josephson, *Sidney Hillman*, 506–8, 529–34; Civilian Production Administration, *Industrial Mobilization for War*, 81–5.

38 The decade-long history of the Murray Industrial Council Plan is recorded in Merton W. Ertell, "The CIO Industry Council Plan: Its Background and Implications," unpublished Ph.D. diss., University of Chicago, 1955. For surveys of Reuther's proposal and its demise, see George R. Clark, "Strange Story of the Reuther Plan," *Harpers*, 184 (1942), 645–54; Janeway, *Struggle for Survival*, 221–5; Walter P. Reuther, "500 Planes a Day – A Program for the Utilization of the Automobile Industry for Mass Production of Defense

Planes," in Reuther, *Selected Papers* (New York, 1961), 1–12; David Brody, "The New Deal in World War II," in Braeman et al., *The New Deal*, 281–5. For industry resistance to the Reuther Plan, see Bernstein, "The Automobile Industry," 24–7, and Koistinen, "The Hammer and the Sword," 602–6.

39 Reuther's statement is taken from CIO, *Proceedings of the Third Constitutional Convention*, Atlantic City, N.J., November 21, 1940, 25. A sympathetic interpretation of Wallace's wartime role is offered in Norman D. Markowitz, *The Rise and Fall of the People's Century: Henry A. Wallace and American Liberalism, 1941–1948* (New York, 1973), 36–74. An incisive attack upon Wallace, Willkie, and the prowar liberals is found in Dwight MacDonald, *Memoirs of a Revolutionist* (New York, 1957), 107–97, 285–98. For the perspective of a disillusioned liberal, see Blum, *V Was for Victory*, 15–52.

40 As quoted in Burns, *Roosevelt*, 130.

4. "Responsible unionism"

1 CIO plans for a massive organizing drive in 1941 are reported in the *New York Times*, November 20, 1940; in CIO, *Proceedings of the Third Constitutional Convention*, Atlantic City, N.J., November 1940, 20–8, 41–59; and in the CIO Executive Board Minutes, November 22, 1940, 201, from which Murray's statements are taken.

2 No biography exists of Philip Murray. For an outline of his life, see "Philip Murray," *Current Biography*, 2 (1941), 600–2; and Philip Taft, "Philip Murray" in John A. Garraty, ed., *Dictionary of American Biography, Supplement Five* (New York, 1977), 509–11; personality portraits are found in Saul Alinsky, *John L. Lewis: An Unauthorized Biography* (New York, 1949), 220–2, and Len DeCaux, *Labor Radical: From the Wobblies to the CIO* (Boston, 1970), 391–5. One should also consult Murray's rambling, lengthy monologues recorded in the minutes of the CIO executive board. These are often exceptionally revealing in times of stress.

3 For brief surveys of economic conditions during this period, see *CIO Economic Outlook*, March 1941, 1–3; Richard J. Purcell, *Labor Policies of the National Defense Advisory Commission and the Office of Production Management, May 1940–April 1942* (Washington, D.C., 1942), 66–94; Ross M. Robertson, *History of the American Economy* (New York, 1973), 709–11; John Morton Blum, *From the Morgenthau Diaries, Years of Urgency, 1938–41* (Boston, 1965), 198–234; and U.S. Bureau of the Budget, *The United States at War* (Washington, D.C., 1946), 21.

4 Lloyd Ulman, *The Government of the Steelworkers' Union* (New York, 1962), 11; Frank Cormier and William J. Eaton, *Reuther* (Englewood Cliffs, N.J., 1970), 156; and Walter Galenson, *The CIO Challenge to the AFL: A History of the American Labor Movement, 1935–1941* (Ithaca, N.Y., 1960), 112. In the coal industry, Lewis traded a general wage increase for the union shop in negotiations with independent operators in 1939, reports McAlister Coleman, *Men and Coal* (New York, 1943), 188–90.

5 U.S. Department of Labor, *Handbook of Labor Statistics* (Washington, D.C., 1974), 367; "Strikes in 1941," *Monthly Labor Review*, 54 (1942), 1107–10, 1123; Howell John Harris, *The Right to Manage: Industrial Relations Policies of American Business in the 1940s* (Madison, Wis., 1982), chap. 1.

6 Surveys of the labor movement's renewed activity during 1941 are found in Irving Bernstein, *Turbulent Years: A History of the American Worker, 1933–41* (Boston, 1969), 734–52; Joel Seidman, *American Labor from Defense to Reconversion* (Chicago, 1953), 41–52; and Art Preis, *Labor's Giant Step* (New York, 1964), 99–110. For studies of union activity in individual industries, see Robert Ozanne, *A Century of Labor–Management Relations at McCormick and International Harvester* (Madison, Wis., 1967), 195–209; Edward R. Livernash, *Collective Bargaining in the Basic Steel Industry* (Washington, D.C., 1961), 239; and David Brody, *The Butcher Workmen: A Study of Unionization* (Cambridge, Mass., 1964), 203–6.

7 Henry L. Stimson and Frank Knox to FDR, May 29, 1941, Roosevelt Papers, OF 10-B, Box 21.

8 By the end of April 1941, at the latest, top War Department officials wanted to use the FBI and other government agencies to investigate, and if possible discredit, certain trade union leaders. According to Attorney General Robert Jackson, Patterson and McCloy complained in a meeting of April 28 that the FBI has "confined its investigations *within the limits of the law*, whereas they believe that normal methods should be abandoned and that investigators should be unrestrained in wire tapping, in stealing of evidence, breaking in to obtain evidence, in conducting unlimited search and seizures, use of dictaphones, etc. etc." Jackson reported that they favored establishment of what one of them termed a "suicide squad" to conduct these irregular investigations. Jackson reported and opposed these suggestions in a "Memorandum to the President," April 29, 1941, File Labor–1941, Robert Patterson Papers, Box 141, Library of Congress.

9 Seidman, *American Labor from Defense to Reconversion*, 67–73; see also the exhaustive study by James A. Gross, *The Making of the National Labor Relations Board*, vol. 2, especially chaps. 10–14 (forthcoming by the State University of New York Press).

10 William Knudsen to Harry Hopkins, February 21, 1941, in File 242, Record Group 179, Box 1024, National Archives, Washington, D.C.

11 Matthew Josephson, *Sidney Hillman, Statesman of American Labor* (Garden City, N.Y., 1952), 527–8; *Facts on File Yearbook 1941*, 1 (New York, 1942), 76. For a broad sampling of cooperative labor opinion from a leadership perspective, see U.S. Senate, Subcommittee on Education and Labor, *Hearings, Conciliation Act of 1941*, 77th Congress, 1st Sess., 1941, 69–77, 98–109, 167–89, 225–45.

12 Preis, *Labor's Giant Step*, 95–112. The SWOC leadership favored cooperation with Hillman's efforts to curb defense strikes, but lengthy work stoppages nevertheless took place at Universal Cyclops, Vanadium Corporation, John A. Roebling and Sons, and American Car and Foundry in the winter and spring of 1941. Frances Perkins to FDR, January 9, 1941, President's Personal File 3585, Roosevelt Papers; Bureau of Labor Statistics, *Report on the Work of the National Defense Mediation Board*, Bulletin No. 174 (Washington, D.C., 1942), 91, 103, 106–7.

13 The best account of the Allis-Chalmers strike is found in Bert Cochran, *Labor and Communism, the Conflict that Shaped American Unions* (Princeton, N.J., 1977), 166–76; Murray's public query is taken from UAW Press Release, March 27, 1941; see also George Addes to Frank Knox, March 27, 1941, both

in UAW War Policies and Practices File, Joe Brown Collection, Archives of Labor History, Wayne State University (ALHWSU).
14 On the formation of the National Defense Mediation Board, see Sidney Hillman's testimony in U.S. Senate, Special Committee Investigating the National Defense Program, *Hearings*, 77th Congress, 1st Sess., April 21, 1941, 125–8; see also William H. Davis, "A plan to minimize interruptions in the production of defense materials by mutual agreement between managements and workers," November 9, 1940, in File NDMB, Hillman Collection, and Davis's testimony in U.S. House, Committee Investigating the Seizure of Montgomery Wards, *Hearings*, 78th Congress, 2nd Sess., May 22, 1944, 5. Murray's initial opposition to the mediation board was expressed privately in "Re: Defense Industries Labor Board" (March 1941), File NDMB, and publicly in *CIO News*, March 10, 1941. Murray thought implementation of the CIO Industry Council Plan a more advantageous and equitable method to curb defense strikes.
15 "The Right to Strike – Keystone of Liberty," CIO Publication No. 57 (Washington, D.C., 1941). After a private conference with FDR on March 16, Philip Murray agreed to serve on the board he had earlier opposed; *The New York Times*, March 16, 17, 1941.
16 The basic government texts for a study of both the NDMB and the NWLB are: Bureau of Labor Statistics, *Report on the Work of the National Defense Mediation Board* (Washington, D.C., 1942); Department of Labor, *The Termination Report of the National War Labor Board*, vol. 1 (Washington, D.C., 1947); and Bureau of Labor Statistics, *Problems and Policies of Dispute Settlement and Wage Stabilization during World War II* Bulletin 1009 (Washington, D.C., 1950).
17 Harris, *The Right to Manage*, chap. 1; Kim McQuaid, "Corporate Liberalism in the American Business Community, 1920–1940," *Business History Review*, 52 (1978), 356–68; "Eugene Meyer," *Current Biography*, 2 (1941), 575–8; "Walter C. Teagle," *Current Biography*, 2 (1941), 818–21.
18 William H. Davis Oral History, COHC, passim; Nelson Lichtenstein, "William Hammatt Davis," in John Garraty, ed., *Dictionary of American Biography*, Supplement Seven (New York, 1981), 171–3; Warren Ashby, *Frank Porter Graham: A Southern Liberal* (Winston-Salem, N.C., 1980), 141–91; A. Robert Smith, *Tiger in the Senate: The Biography of Wayne Morse* (Garden City, N.Y., 1962), 15–45; Charles P. Larrowe, *Harry Bridges: The Rise and Fall of Radical Labor in the U.S.* (New York, 1972), 204–6.
19 The growth of NDMB power is discussed in *Report on the Work of the NDMB*, 5; Davis Oral History, 107–9, 115–21; and Davis, "Influence of the NDMB's Experience on the National War Labor Board," in *Termination Report of the NWLB*, vol. 1, xii–xv.
20 The literature on Reuther's career is considerable, but most of it consists of either apologia or polemic. The most important accounts of UAW factional politics in the defense era include James R. Prickett, "Communism and Factionalism in the United Automobile Workers, 1939–1947," *Science and Society*, 32 (1968), 257–77; Roger Keeran, *The Communist Party and the Auto Workers Unions* (Bloomington, 1980), 205–25; Jack Skeels, "The Development of Political Stability within the United Auto Workers Union," unpublished Ph.D. diss., University of Wisconsin, Madison, 1957, 129–57; and Cochran, *Labor and Communism*, 162–75 passim. Much evidence exists

that Reuther worked closely with Sidney Hillman to negotiate and then administer the highly controversial grievance umpire system at General Motors. See George Heliker, "Grievance Arbitration in the Automobile Industry: A Comparative Analysis of Its History and Results in the Big Three," unpublished Ph.D. diss., University of Michigan, 1954, 97; George Heliker, interview with Percy Llewellyn, February 24, 1954, Frank Hill Collection, Ford Motor Company Archives, Henry Ford Museum, Dearborn, Mich.; Walter Reuther, "Report of International GM Executive Committee," December 7, 1940, in GM department, 1941, Walter P. Reuther Pre-Presidential Papers Collection, Box 1, ALHWSU; see also Frederick H. Harbison and Robert Dubin, *Patterns of Union–Management Relations* (Chicago, 1947), 22–9, 60–1, for a brief discussion of Reuther's administration of the UAW's GM department in the defense era.

21 Promulgation of this new strike sanction policy late in 1939 came on the heels of a lengthy, complicated dispute at Chrysler that began as a series of unauthorized stoppages over line speed, degenerated into a company lockout, and eventually required Philip Murray's personal intervention to settle. Moreover, this embarrassing situation arose just as the UAW began to feel the first defense era pressure against "irresponsible" union conduct. A brief account of the Chrysler strike is found in *Business Week*, November 27, 1939. The UAW strike policy was outlined in Report of R. J. Thomas to UAW Executive Board, December 4, 1939, George Addes Collection, Box 1, and in *United Auto Worker*, January 10, 1940.

22 The controversy this incident aroused was reported by Thomas A. Johnstone, assistant GM director, in his interview with Heliker, February 19, 1954, in Hill Collection, FMC Archives. A full discussion of the strike is found in UAW Executive Board Minutes, October 7–8, 1940. Addes's statement is found on p. 150; see, as well, George Addes to C. E. Wilson (GM president), October 10, 1940, UAW–GM Collection, Box 1; and "Flint Wildcat Strike Settlement, Fisher 581," in GM department, 1941, WPR-PPM Collection, Box 1.

23 *United Auto Worker*, January 15, April 1, 1941; Irving Howe and B. J. Widick, *The UAW and Walter Reuther* (New York, 1949), 101. Even in Canada, where a state of outright belligerency existed, the UAW defended the right of its locals to strike. See Report of George Burt, Canadian regional director, to UAW Executive Board, December 16, 1940; UAW Executive Board Minutes, December 18, 1940; *United Automobile Worker*, December 15, 1940.

24 *Daily Worker*, January 22, February 8, 11, 1941; UAW Executive Board Minutes, December 18, 1940, 23–5, 48–51; April 27, 1941. Reuther had earlier tried to maneuver out of his difficulties by proposing that if a strike developed, the union would call out only those workers not engaged in defense production, approximately 95 percent of those employed. GM's president, C. E. Wilson, protested this tactic, arguing quite correctly that no effective distinction could be made between defense and civilian output in the early mobilization era. See *West Side Conveyer*, UAW Local 174, May 1, 1941; Cormier and Eaton, *Reuther*, 170.

25 Arthur P. Allen and Betty V. Schneider, *Industrial Relations in the California Aircraft Industry* (Berkeley, 1956), 1–18; Richard Felse, "Aircraft – A Mass Production Industry," in Colston E. Warne, ed., *Yearbook of American Labor* (New York, 1945), 251–60; "Half a Million Workers," *Fortune*, 23 (1941),

97–8, 163–5. The quotation is taken from Wyndham Mortimer, *Organize! My Life as a Union Man* (Boston, 1971), 167. Lew Michener Oral History, 40, ALHWSU.

26 Mortimer, *Organize!*, 166–77; Cochran, *Labor and Communism*, 176–7. Important figures in the California CIO believed to be close to or actually members of the Communist party included Harry Bridges and Louis Goldblatt of the ILWU and Philip Connery of the Los Angeles CIO Council. Smaller unions such as the Screen Actors Guild, the Newspaper Guild, and the Cannery and Agricultural Workers Union were also influenced by the Communist party in California during the early 1940s.

27 L. H. Michener, "Report of Activities of Region Six, July through December 1939," and "Report . . . January through February 1940," in Addes Collection, Box 2; "Half a Million Workers," 165; Mortimer, *Organize!*, 170–3; *The New York Times*, November 9, 15, 23, 24, 26, 27.

28 Michener, "Report of Activities for Region Six," in UAW Executive Board Minutes, December 16, 1940.

29 UAW Executive Board Minutes, December 16, 1940, 7-15. UAW regional directors grumbled at this challenge to their local power. With the curtailment of auto production in the offing and the opening of several huge aircraft plants in the hinterland, many feared the wholesale erosion of their power. Certainly, part of the popularity of Reuther's 500-planes-a-day proposal, announced virtually at the same moment as the joint UAW–CIO California aircraft drive, derived from its effort to stem the relative decline of the Detroit and Flint locals in the internal life of the UAW. Immediate conversion of Michigan auto plants to fighter production would go a long way toward maintaining the jobs and political influence of the midwestern heart of the union. See Eliott Janeway, *The Struggle for Survival* (New Haven, Conn., 1950), 220–5; and Victor G. Reuther, *The Brothers Reuther and the Story of the UAW: A Memoir* (Boston, 1976), 226–9.

30 Mortimer, *Organize!*, 174–80; UAW, *American Aircraft Builder*, "Day by Day Account of North American Strike," July 12, 1941; The NLRB election at North American Aviation, the largest ever held in the Southwest, was characterized by one observer as a "desperate campaign" by both unions. *Los Angeles Times*, February 21, 1941; see also *The CIO Voice* (preelection campaign sheet) February 3, 6, 7, 10, 11, 13, in A. C. McGraw Collection, Box 4, ALHWSU.

31 Mortimer's Letter to President Murray and Answers in Miscellaneous Correspondence, 1942, Thomas Collection, Box 9; *People's Daily World*, May 17, 23, 1941; Letter, Henry Kraus to author, November 1, 1978.

32 *Report on the Work of the NDMB*, 156–7; UAW, *Proceedings of the Sixth Annual Convention*, Buffalo, August 4–16, 1941, 422; *People's Daily World*, June 2, 1941.

33 Mortimer, *Organize!*, 181; Lew Michener Oral History, 26; "Dear Brother" (Local 683 pamphlet) and Letter, David N. Simpson, North American Aviation negotiating committee, to UAW Executive Board, July 7, both in Addes Collection, Box 19; *American Aircraft Builder*, July 12, 1941.

34 Henry Kraus to author, November 1, 1978; however, some strike preparations were obviously underway, as reflected in a series of leaflets issued under the heading "North American News," June 2 and 3, 1941, which set picket line schedules and all but announced commencement of the strike should

negotiations in Washington not prove quickly productive. See A. C. McGraw Collection, Box 4.

35 *People's Daily World*, June 6; *Los Angeles Times*, June 5, 6; "Reply Brief of UAW Local 887," 19–22, in UAW Local 887 Collection, Box 11, ALHWSU. A recent history of 'the strike that downplays the role of the Communists is James R. Prickett's "Communist Conspiracy or Wage Dispute?: The 1941 Strike at North American Aviation," *Pacific Historical Review*, 50 (1981), 215–33.

36 Paul A. C. Koistinen, "The Hammer and the Sword: Labor and the Military during World War II," unpublished Ph.D. diss., University of California, Berkeley, 1964, 113–15; *The New York Times*, June 4, 1941; Samuel I. Rosenman, ed., *The Public Papers and Addresses of Franklin D. Roosevelt, 1942* (New York, 1943), 192–3.

37 Henry Stimson and McGeorge Bundy, *On Active Service in Peace and War* (New York, 1948), 488–90; Elting E. Morison, *Turmoil and Tradition, the Life and Times of Henry L. Stimson* (New York, 1960), 426–7; William H. Davis Oral History, 115–21, COHC.

38 Davis Oral History, 114; Mortimer's Letter, 4–5; *UAW American Aircraft Builder*, July 12, 1944. Frankensteen had the legal–administrative right to take such disciplinary action because of the large-powers he had assumed when he took over direction of the aircraft drive in November 1940. However, as an elected director, Lew Michener was beyond Frankensteen's immediate reach and could be penalized only by the UAW executive board, sustained by the full union convention.

As part of the debate over Michener's fate, the North American Aviation strike and the entire issue of Communist participation in union affairs became key issues when the UAW assembled for a tumultuous two-week convention in August 1941. In a seemingly paradoxical turn of events, Frankensteen now favored only mild disciplinary measures against Michener. With George Addes and his supporters, Frankensteen sought to prevent the Reutherites from using the issue of "Communist-inspired strikes" to sweep the convention. Moreover, by August, German armies were rolling across the Ukraine and the Communists in the UAW had shifted to a tactically conservative stance, which now coincided with Frankensteen's more cautious instincts. Winning additional support from those non-Communist militants in the union who were appalled at the use of troops to break the strike, Frankensteen, Addes, and the Communists narrowly defeated the Reutherites on the Michener penalty issue, thus perpetuating the delicate balance of power that would characterize the UAW throughout most of the wartime era. Removed from office for a year, Michener was reelected west coast regional director in 1942 and 1943. Preis, *Labor's Giant Step*, 123–4; Cormier and Eaton, *Reuther*, 176–80; UAW, *Proceedings of the Sixth Annual Convention*, 243–68, 400–50.

39 Frankensteen, quoted in *Los Angeles Times*, June 8, 1941; see also *UAW American Aircraft Builder*, "Where the CIO Stands," July 12, 1941; Mortimer's Letter, 8; *People's World*, June 10, 1941.

40 Stimson and Bundy, *On Active Service*, 498; Mortimer, *Organize!* 185. When army troops marched in, they were cheered by many of the pickets, probably because most still viewed the federal government as a more friendly force than the local police. The army was certainly more efficient. It cleared a mile-square area around the plant, shut down the union headquarters across from

the factory entrance, and patrolled nearby neighborhoods in jeeps and trucks. Scores of unionists were illegally picked up by the military and held for several hours. Clinton J. Taft, American Civil Liberties Union Southern California Director, to FDR, June 10, 1941, Official File 407-B, Roosevelt Papers, Box 23.

41 Melvyn Dubofsky and Warren Van Time, *John L. Lewis: A Biography* (New York, 1978), 390–3; Preis, *Labor's Giant Step*, 116; UAW, *Proceedings of the Sixth Annual Convention*, 410–11. At the time of the North American Aviation strike, two important local work stoppages with some Communist leadership continued despite NDMB demands that they cease. These included the month-long wildcat strike by machinist locals in the San Francisco Bay Area and the bitter International Woodworkers of America strike in the Northwest. *People's Daily World*, June 6, 1941; Vernon H. Jensen, *Lumber and Labor* (New York, 1945), 261–7.

42 Mortimer's Letter, 3. Frankensteen later denied that he ever made such a statement, but the author has found at least two other accounts of the strike asserting that he did. In any event, Frankensteen freely admitted that until late May he encouraged militancy and the expectation of a strike at North American Aviation. Simpson to UAW, July 7, 1941; Hassler Oral History, 90–2; UAW, *Proceedings of the Sixth Annual Convention*, 430.

43 Michener Oral History, 27; for Mortimer's retrospective comments, see UAW, *Proceedings of the Sixth Annual Convention*, 423; Henry Kraus has this to say about the mind set of the Southern California union leadership: "I myself never thought FDR would send in the troops and break the strike, even though I was troubled by some of the actions and works of the Administration's people. I just couldn't associate Roosevelt with such an act. But then I could not imagine that the UAW and CIO leaders would provide the needed background to this action. Even when I heard that troops had arrived, I didn't think they would be used but were merely to serve as an intimidating purpose by their presence. I was stunned when they arrived on the scene." Kraus to author, November 1, 1978.

44 As quoted in Leonard Baker, *Roosevelt and Pearl Harbor* (New York, 1970), 160; *CIO News*, June 16, 1941; *The New York Times*, July 7, 1941. John L. Lewis was a good deal more strident when he called the second week in June the "blackest in American labor history"; *UMW Journal*, June 15, 1941.

45 *The New York Times*, June 7, 1941; Bernstein, *Turbulent Years*, 631; *Report on the Work of the NDMB*, 150–4; "Strikes in 1941," *Monthly Labor Review*, 54 (1942), 1111–25. Except for the mine strike in November, the last two months of 1941 were marked by extremely few strikes authorized by international union officials.

46 Ralph C. James, "Purge of the Trotskyites from the Teamsters," *Western Political Science Quarterly*, 19 (1966), 5–15; Preis, *Labor's Giant Step*, 133–43.

47 Report of telephone conversation between Colonel Charles Bradshaw and Edward S. Greenbaum, Ordnance Department, June 15, 1941, Entry L. Record Group 202, National Archives, Box 13; Memorandum, Robert F. Patterson to FDR, June 12, 1941, Roosevelt Papers, OF 407-B, Box 20; Josephson, *Hillman*, 546. Eight elected leaders of Local 683 were barred from the plant; see Elmer Freitag to Ralph Seward, Secretary of NDMB, June 15, 1941, Entry 1, RG 202, Box 13.

48 Mortimer's Letter, 10. Soldiers with fixed bayonets were stationed every sixty feet within the plant; telephone interview with Earl Frebert, May 12, 1978. The strike also weakened the UAW aircraft organization at Vultee and Ryan, where membership dropped to a few hundred out of a potential of several thousand. "Partial Report of the Grievance Committee of the UAW–CIO in Re Grievance of the North American Situation," August 4, 1941, in UAW, *Proceedings of the Sixth Annual Convention*, 246.

49 Memorandum of phone call from Bradshaw to Patterson (undated but clearly sometime between June 12 and June 19), Entry 1, RG 202, Box 13. Bradshaw worked closely with Smethurst in the reorganization of the local. In one report to Patterson, Bradshaw suggested that Frankensteen send six more representatives to the area to do some "progressive work." Eventually, Hillman and the CIO sent about twenty-five organizers to the scene. Among these were Eric A. Nichol, Hillman's administrative assistant at OPM, Leo Krzyski, vice-president of the Amalgamated Clothing Workers, and organizers from the UAW, the SWOC, and the URW. Memorandum, Patterson to Hillman, June 20, 1941, Entry 1 RG 202, Box 13; *People's Daily World*, June 14, 16, 1941; *Los Angeles Times*, June 19, 1941.

50 Undated memorandum, Bradshaw to Patterson. Public members of the NDMB were also acutely sensitive to the decline in prestige suffered by their board when the military intervened in the labor dispute. For example, when John J. McCoy and Attorney General Robert Jackson first drafted the executive order seizing the plant, they included a provision stating that the NDMB would fix wages, hours, and other working conditions there. William H. Davis insisted that this clause be dropped because "[we] thought that . . . where the War Department . . . was to operate the plant it would be inadvisable from the standpoint of the general work of the Board in its overall relations with labor that it be associated in the order with the armed forces." Robert Jackson to FDR, June 7, 1941, Roosevelt Papers, OF 407-B, Box 20.

51 Memorandum, Patterson to Hillman, June 20, 1941, Entry 1, RG 202, Box 13.

52 *Report on the Work of the NDMB*, 27, 159–60; *UAW American Aircraft Builder*, July 12, 1941. Bradshaw proved a liberal administrator as well. At Hillman's behest, he reestablished the grievance procedure and, after the contract was signed, held a large meeting where, for the first time, workers saw in one place the military aircraft they were building. He was considered a good guy by many. Earl Frebert, telephone interview.

5. Union security and the Little Steel formula

1 These fears were enunciated by a high steelworkers union official in "Testimony of Clinton Golden before House Committee on Education and Labor," *Hearings on the Conciliation Act of 1941*, 77th Congress, 1st Sess., 178–81. A recent account of the rank-and-file movement in Great Britain during World War I is found in James Hinton, *The First Shop Stewards' Movement* (London, 1973). One important CIO leader in 1941, John Green of the International Union of Marine and Shipyard Workers of America, had been a leader of the insurgent Clydeside stewards a quarter of a century before.

2 James MacGregor Burns, "Maintenance of Membership: A Study in Administrative Statesmanship," *Journal of Politics*, 10 (1948) 101–5.

3 Bureau of Labor Statistics, *Report on the Work of the National Defense Mediation Board* (Washington, D.C., 1942), 26, 156–7.

4 *Report on the Work of the NDMB*, 27. The North American Aviation incident was also important because of the major impact it had on the UAW–Ford negotiations then in progress. Despite the successful strike the UAW conducted at the River Rouge in April and the overwhelming electoral victory the union won in the NLRB election in May, Ford executives still considered the UAW an alien and subversive force with which they negotiated only under great duress. Suppression of the North American Aviation strike had a strong impact on their thinking. Ford boss Harry Bennett and legal counsel I. A. Capizzi now found Philip Murray an eminently "responsible labor leader," and they quickly agreed to sign a collective bargaining contract covering all Ford plants that included a virtually unprecedented union shop and a dues checkoff provision. "People are asking why Ford Motor Company made such an abrupt change in its labor policy," announced Capizzi the next day. "The company never would have any dealings with Communist leadership but it felt it could write a contract with the type of union officials who are on the top of the CIO and UAW–CIO at the present time. The UAW–CIO officials also proved recently that they believe in keeping the contracts and the union constitutional provisions against outlaw strikes." Somewhat contradictorily, Ford officials such as Bennett also thought they might use the several thousand servicemen and the remnants of the AFL in the Ford organization to infiltrate the new union; hence their decision to recognize the UAW in all Ford plants, even those where the union was still weak. Keith Sward, *The Legend of Henry Ford* (New York, 1949), 404–22; Frank Marquart Oral History, 40, ALHWSU; Capizzi statement from *Detroit News*, June 22, 1941.

5 Joel Seidman, *American Labor from Defense to Reconversion* (Chicago, 1953), 63; *NDMB Transcript*, July 8, 1941, in RG 78, NA; *Report on the Work of the NDMB*, 186–7; William H. Davis to FDR, August 15, 1941; Davis to Frank Knox, August 13, 1941; both in Federal Shipbuilding and Drydock Company File, Hillman Collection.

6 McAlister Coleman, *Men and Coal* (New York, 1943), 202; column by Louis Stark, *The New York Times*, November 2, 1941; *UMW Journal*, September 1, October 1, 1941. Steel industry opposition to the drive for the union shop in both its mines and its mills is reported in *Iron Age*, October 9, 16, 30, 1941, and *The New York Times*, October 11, 1941; see also *NDMB Transcript*, "Bituminous Coal Operators," November 3, 1941. Complete accounts of the captive mine strikes and negotiations are found in Irving Bernstein, *The Turbulent Years, A History of the American Worker, 1933–41* (Boston, 1969), 752–67, and UMW, *Proceedings of the 37th Constitutional Convention*, Cincinnati, October 6–14, 1942, 37–88.

7 *NDMB Transcript*, November 4, 1941.

8 *Report on the Work of the NDMB*, 127–8. Next to Davis, Graham was the most influential public member of both the NDMB and its successor, the National War Labor Board.

9 FDR quoted in Bernstein, *Turbulent Years*, 763–4.

10 *Ibid.*, 766–7. See also Melvyn Dubofsky and Warren Van Tine, *John L. Lewis: A Biography* (New York, 1978), 402.

11 Memorandum, Wayne Coy to FDR, November 24, 1941, OF 407; Memorandum, Hillman to FDR, November 24, Perkins to FDR, November 24, both in Roosevelt Papers, OF 4684; Memorandum, Davis to FDR, November 18, 1941, Entry 35, RG 78, NA; Dubofsky and Van Tine, *John L. Lewis*, 404.

12 Hillman to FDR, December 12, 1941, OF 407-B, Box 13; William H. Davis and Elbert D. Thomas, Memorandum Report of the Deliberations of the War Labor Conference Convened by the President in the City of Washington, December 17, 1941, both in Roosevelt Papers, OF 4684; Department of Labor, *The Termination Report of the National War Labor Board* (Washington, D.C., 1947), 5–7. Industry and labor representatives on the NDMB were carried over to the new NWLB. Two new and influential public members were added to the board – Wayne Morse, a dean of the University of Oregon Law School and an arbitrator in the west coast lumber and longshore industries, and George W. Taylor, a University of Pennyslvania economist then serving as full-time umpire under the UAW–GM contract.

13 *CIO News*, January 30, 1942; Bernard Siegal, "Some Comments on Wages in the Little Steel Case," July 10, 1942, in Miscellaneous File, Entry 53, RG 202; see also Bureau of the Budget, *United States at War* (Washington, D.C., 1946), 235–48.

14 *United States at War*, 250–1; Leon Henderson to FDR, February 4, 1942, OF 98; John Morton Blum, *From the Morgenthau Diaries: Years of War* (New York, 1967), 34–9; Carroll R. Daugherty and Milton Derber, "Wage Stabilization," in Colston E. Warne, ed., *Yearbook of American Labor* (New York, 1944), 162–9.

15 William H. Davis to FDR, March 30, 1942; Davis to FDR, April 14, 1942; OF 98, Box 2.

16 *The New York Times*, July 1, 1942. The ten-cent wage increase won in April 1941 represented an average 11.8 percent boost in hourly wages. Subtracting this from the 15 percent overall rate of inflation since January 1 yields a 3.2 percent wage increase under the Little Steel formula. Labor charged that the government's policy of maintaining real wages at the January 1, 1941, level effectively put working-class wages back where they had been during the recession of 1937–8. See Audrey Mack and Broadus Mitchell, "Labor Looks at the National Income Distribution," in Warne, *Yearbook*, 453–64. Government policymakers agreed. See Davis to Judge Samuel Rosenman, July 30, 1942, Entry 5, RG 78, NA; Wayne Coy to FDR, July 23, 1942, public members of the NWLB to FDR, July 28, 1942; both in OF 98, Box 2.

17 In the Detroit area, where a careful study of employment problems was made, the proportion of women in the workforce increased by about 50 percent between 1940 and 1944, whereas the proportion of nonwhites increased by almost 140 percent over the same period. In some aircraft plants, well over half of all employees were women, whereas in foundry work most were black. Between March 1940 and November 1943, when Detroit's war employment reached its peak, an additional 735,000 workers were added to the employment rolls. At the same time, the War Manpower Commission estimated that about 200,000 mainly white male workers left the Detroit labor force in the same period, most of whom probably entered the military. U.S. Congress, Special Committee to Investigate the National Defense Program, Part 28: *Manpower Problems in Detroit*, 79th Congress, 1st Sess., 13523,

1 3530–41. See also War Production Board Report, "Maintaining Production in the Cotton Textile Industry," August 5, 1944, in Entry 53, RG 202, NA; West Coast Airframe Companies, *6 War Labor Reports* (March 3, 1943), 581–639, passim. Richard Frankensteen worried aloud about "superpatriots" in UAW, *Proceedings of the War Emergency Conference*, Detroit, April 7–8, 1942, 33. An excellent firsthand account of the union attitudes of the new heterogeneous wartime workforce is found in Katherine Archibald, *Wartime Shipyard: A Study in Social Disunity* (Berkeley, 1947) 15–99, 128–84.

18 "What's Itching Labor," *Fortune*, 15 (1942), 101–2, 218–20; Office of Facts and Figures, "Labor Morale in Detroit and Pittsburgh, Survey of Intelligence Materials," No. 22 (marked secret), May 6, 1942, in Entry 35, RG 202, NA.

19 Victor E. Reuther, *The Brothers Reuther and the Story of the UAW: A Memoir* (Boston, 1976), 232; *National War Labor Board Transcript*, July 3, 1942, 42–3, RG 202, NA.

20 Walker-Turner Company, *1 War Labor Reports* (April 10, 1942), 108–9; Telegram, Patrick S. Dillon, president, UE Local 435, to William H. Davis, March 3, 1942, in Walker–Turner Case File 2135-ACS-D, RG 202, NA.

21 *NDMB Transcript*, July 8, 1941; *Report on the Work of the NDMB*, 186–7; Federal Shipbuilding and Drydock Company, *1 War Labor Reports* (April 25, 1942), 142–3; see also Wayne Coy to FDR, December 28, FDR to Coy, December 30, 1941, in Coy Papers, Box 18, Hyde Park, N.Y.; Coy to FDR, December 30, 1941, OF 407-B, Box 30; NWLB *Transcript*, March 26, 1942; IUMSWA Local 16 leaders also promised that if the NWLB acted quickly in the union's favor, the leadership of the local would be prepared to take joint disciplinary action with the company against those who were "not contributing their quota in this period of emergency."

22 Roger Lapham, "Thinking Aloud, or the Present Thoughts of One Employer" (March 1942), reprinted in U.S. House, Committee Investigating the Seizure of Montgomery Wards, 78th Congress, 2nd Sess., *Hearings*, May 22–June 8, 1944, 627.

23 The Steel Workers Organizing Committee (SWOC) transformed itself into the United Steel Workers of America (USW) in May 1942. To avoid confusion, "USW" is used hereafter. Frederick H. Harbison, "Steel," in Harry A. Millis, ed., *How Collective Bargaining Works* (New York, 1942), 527–31; David J. McDonald, *Union Man* (New York, 1969), 146.

24 "Memorandum report to Frank Graham" in Miscellaneous File, Entry 53, RG 202, NA. The cost of living index stood at 101.9 in April 1941; by March 1942 it had reached 114.3. Richard H. Lewis, "Effect of War on Employment in the Iron and Steel Industry," *Monthly Labor Review*, 56 (1943), 258–67; SWOC, *Brief Submitted by SWOC to National War Labor Board Panel in the Matter of SWOC vs. Bethlehem, Republic, Youngstown Sheet and Tube, and Inland Steel Companies* (Washington, D.C., 1942), 256–60; "What's Itching Labor," 102; USW, *Proceedings of the First Constitutional Convention*, Pittsburgh, May 19–22, 1942, 292.

25 Bethlehem Steel Corporation et al., *1 War Labor Reports* (July 16, 1942), 387; McDonald, *Union Man*, 120–5; USW, *Proceedings*, 41, 46.

26 Sympathetic accounts of Lewis's wartime stance are found in McAlister Coleman, *Men and Coal* (New York, 1943), 217–78, and Dubofsky and Van Tine, *John L. Lewis*, 389–444, passim. A harsh criticism of the mine leader

will be found in almost every relevant newspaper editorial of the period and in James A. Wechsler, *Labor Baron* (New York, 1944), 207–53, a work perfectly reflective of Rooseveltian liberalism's wartime confusion.

27 Saul Alinsky, *John L. Lewis: An Unauthorized Biography* (New York, 1949), 249–54; E. M. Watson to FDR, January 20, 1942; Gardner Jackson to FDR, January 20, 1942; Wayne Coy to FDR, January 22, 1942, OF 4747; UAW Executive Board Minutes, January 22, 1942.

28 *UMW Journal*, March 1, 15, April 1, May 15, 1942; *The New York Times*, March 29, 1942; *Steel Labor*, April 24, 1942; Harry W. Clifford, United Rubber Workers field representative, to S. H. Dalrymple, URW president, April 16, 1942, Thomas Papers, Box 9; "CIO United for Victory – Against Disruption, Against Disunity," CIO Publication No. 69 (Washington, D.C., 1942), 24; Alinsky, *John L. Lewis*, 256–79.

29 Lauchlin Currie to FDR, "Re: Conversation with Philip Murray on Wage Rate Policy," April 16, 1942, OF 98, Box 2; Wayne Coy to FDR, April 28, 1942; Gardner Jackson to FDR, May 1, 1942; Jackson to Marvin McIntyre, May 13, 1942, OF 2546, Box 3.

30 Administration concern about the USW wage award is found in FDR to McIntyre, May 5, 1942, OF 2546, Box 3; Anna Rosenberg to McIntyre, July 14, 1942, OF 4025, Box 1; McIntyre to FDR, July 13, 1942, OF 407-B, Box 13. For modification of the Little Steel formula see Bethlehem Steel et al., 334–7, and "Comments and Suggestions by Arthur Meyer," July 9, 1942, in Entry 35, RG 202, NA; Davis's confidential assurances to Murray are recorded in "Telephone Conversation between Wayne Morse and Frank Graham," August 21, 1942, in Wayne Morse Papers, Box 55, University of Oregon.

31 See Marshall Field and Co. (February 25, 1942), 47–53; Walker-Turner Company (April 10, 1942), 108–9; International Harvester Company (April 25, 1942), 118–26; for Frank Graham's statement, see Federal Shipbuilding and Drydock Company (April 25, 1942), 143, all in *1 War Labor Reports*; *The New York Times*, April 29, June 19, 1942.

32 Joseph R. Starobin, *American Communism in Crisis, 1943–1957* (Berkeley, 1972), 54–9; Pressman's remarks are found in Bethlehem Steel et al. (July 16, 1942), 397–8.

33 Seidman, *American Labor*, 99. Earlier, in the spring of 1942, public members of the NWLB had insisted that individual employees agree to work under a maintenance-of-membership clause through either voluntary card checkoff or a majority vote in a special plant-wide election. Murray and Pressman objected to this idea on the grounds that it would amount to a referendum on a union's wartime leadership. Public members of the NWLB dropped the idea in favor of the fifteen-day escape clause when it became apparent that wage controls could seriously erode union loyalty. See confidential memorandum, Davis to Murray and Pressman, April 14, 1942, in NWLB Headquarters Non-Case Record, Series 2, Administrative Policy and Processes, RG 202, NA; *The New York Times*, April 29, 1942. War workers rarely used the fifteen-day escape clause and the NWLB's maintenance-of-membership formula amounted to a virtual union shop. "Maintenance of Membership Awards of the National War Labor Board," *Monthly Labor Review*, 57 (1943), 524–33. For contemporary accounts that emphasize the employee rights issue in the development of the NWLB's union security policy, see Burns,

"Maintenance of Membership," 101–16; and Lloyd G. Reynolds and Charles C. Killingsworth, "The Union Security Issue," *Annals of the American Political Science Association*, 224 (1942), 32–9. Both essays seem overly idealistic and formal in their analysis of this social problem.

34 Lee Pressman, Oral History, Columbia University, 308; USW, *Proceedings of the First Constitutional Convention*, 490; interview with Tom Murray, Pittsburgh, March 9, 1972; letter, David J. McDonald to author, October 26, 1972; CIO Executive Board Minutes, March 11, 1945, 104–18; U.S. Bureau of the Census, *Statistical Abstract of the United States* (Washington, 1958), 236.

35 *Voice of Local 212*, May 15, 1944, in ALHWSU; William H. Davis Oral History, 186; *NWLB Termination Report*, 484–8; Wayne Morse thought the executive order of October 1942 under which the NWLB assumed authority over the entire range of labor–management relations an "administrative nightmare." Not surprisingly, Lee Pressman urged CIO unions to set up high-powered offices in Washington. Morse to Warren D. Smith, October 28, 1942, in Morse Papers, Box 55; Pressman's advice is recorded in CIO, *Proceedings of the Fifth Constitutional Convention*, Philadelphia, November 9–12, 1942, 383–7.

6. "Equality of Sacrifice"

1 Paul A. C. Koistinen, "Mobilizing the World War II Economy: Labor and the Military–Industrial Alliance," *Pacific Historical Review*, 42 (1973), 443–78; J. H. Wishart, "Labor Looks at the Production Effort," in Colston E. Warne, ed., *Yearbook of American Labor*, vol. 1 (New York, 1945), 473–81; CIO, *Proceedings of the Fourth Constitutional Convention*, Detroit, November 1941, 40–57.

2 Paul A. C. Koistinen, "The Hammer and the Sword: Labor and the Military during World War II," unpublished Ph.D. diss., Berkeley, 1964, 610–14; the quotation is on p. 676.

3 Address of President Philip Murray on CIO Defense Industry Council Plan, July 7, 1941, in CIO Trade Union File, 1941, ILWU Library, San Francisco.

4 Matthew Josephson, *Sidney Hillman, Statesman of American Labor* (Garden City, N.Y., 1952), 518–28; Koistinen, "Hammer and Sword," 85–164, passim.

5 Neil Betten, *Catholic Activism and the Industrial Worker* (Gainesville, Fla., 1976), 22–4, 113–15. Intellectual origins of the Industrial Council Plan are also found in the depression era attempts of both the UMW and the SWOC to stabilize production in their respective industries. See, for example, *Steel Labor*, July 1938, and John Chamberlain, "The Steelworkers," *Fortune* 14 (1944), 165–220; Address of President Philip Murray to CIO Defense Industry Council Plan; *CIO News*, November 17, 1941.

6 "500 Planes a Day – A Program for the Utilization of the Automobile Industry for Mass Production of Defense Planes," in Walter P. Reuther, *Selected Papers* (New York, 1961), 1–12; George R. Clark, "Strange Story of the Reuther Plan," *Harpers*, 184 (1942), 645–54.

7 Victor G. Reuther, *The Brothers Reuther and the Story of the UAW: A Memoir* (Boston, 1976), 32–111, passim; see also Irving Howe and B. J. Widick, *The UAW and Walter Reuther* (New York, 1949), 187–204.

8 Frank Marquart, *An Auto Worker's Journal*, (University Park, Pa., 1975), 82;
   Frank Cormier and William J. Eaton, *Reuther* (Englewood Cliffs, N.J., 1970),
   124–5, 165; Frank Warren, *An Alternative Vision: The Socialist Party in the
   1930s* (Bloomington, Ind. 1974), 106–7. Martin Glaberman claims that immediately upon his return from the Soviet Union, and during the mid-1930s,
   the era of greatest Socialist party–Communist collaboration, Walter Reuther
   actually paid dues to the Communist party. "A Note on Walter Reuther,"
   Radical America, 7 (1973), 113–17.
9 "500 Planes a Day," 9–12; Reuther developed the plan with the help of I. F.
   Stone, then an interventionist-minded, left-of-center journalist from the *Nation*. Stone composed the final draft of the plan in Washington in the fall of
   1940. Interview with I. F. Stone, Washington, D.C., February 2, 1979; see
   also Stone's laudatory commentary on the plan in his *Business as Usual: The
   First Year of Defense* (New York, 1941), 264–6.
10 Barton Bernstein, "The Automobile Industry and the Coming of the Second
   World War," *Southwestern Social Science Quarterly*, 47 (1966), 24–7; Clark,
   "Strange Story of the Reuther Plan," 646–50.
11 Stone, *Business as Usual*, 221.
12 See, for example, "Booming Aircraft Firms Fear Reuther Plan May Curb
   Profits," *PM*, January 13, 1941; see also David Brody, "The New Deal and
   World War II," in John Braeman, Robert Bremner, and David Brody, eds.,
   The New Deal: The National Level (Columbus, Ohio, 1975), 281–5.
13 As quoted in Clark, "Strange Story of the Reuther Plan," 649–50.
14 Reuther, *The Brothers Reuther*, 230; Reuther quotation taken from Transcript,
   "Joint Meeting of Labor and Industry Subcommittees on General Automo-
   tive Problems," Hillman Collection, January 6, 1942, 29. Brody, "The New
   Deal and World War II," 285.
15 Richard Polenberg, *War and Society: The United States, 1941–1945* (New
   York, 1972), 7–9; Eliot Janeway, *The Struggle for Survival* (New Haven,
   Conn., 1950), 285–96; Donald M. Nelson, *Arsenal of Democracy: The Story of
   American War Production* (New York, 1946), 1–178, passim; "Donald M.
   Nelson," *Current Biography*, 2 (1941), 608–10.
16 Nelson quoted in Bruce Catton, *The War Lords of Washington* (New York,
   1948), 149; Civilian Production Administration, *Industrial Mobilization for
   War* (Washington, D.C., 1947), 207–14, 969–70; *CIO News*, March 15, 1942;
   Nelson, *Arsenal of Democracy*, 318–22. Many unionists were suspicious of the
   work of these labor–management committees because trade union officials
   were disqualified from service. For a local union attack on the committee
   idea, see UAW, *Proceedings of the War Emergency Conference*, Detroit, April
   1942, 47–61. Although it was the largest union, the UAW ranked well below
   the SWOC and the UE in the number of labor–management production
   committees set up. *The New York Times*, July 9, 1942.
17 As quoted in CPA, *Industrial Mobilization*, 246.
18 Nelson, *Arsenal of Democracy*, 332–5; CPA, *Industrial Mobilization for War*,
   212–16.
19 Koistinen, "Hammer and Sword," 630–44; CPA, *Industrial Mobilization for
   War*, 282–90, 324–34.
20 Koistinen, "Mobilizing the World War II Economy," 449.
21 Catton, *War Lords*, 121.

22 George Q. Flynn, *The Mess in Washington: Manpower Mobilization in World War II* (Westport, Conn., 1979), 24–54, 106, 187; Koistinen, "Mobilizing the World War II Economy," 450–60.
23 CIO, *Proceedings of the Fifth Constitutional Convention*, Boston, November 9–13, 1942, 235.
24 Donald H. Riddle, *The Truman Committee* (New Brunswick, N.J., 1964), 128; interview with Irving Richter, former UAW legislative representative, February 9, 1981, Washington, D.C.
25 CIO, *Proceedings of the Fifth Constitutional Convention*, 42–3; Koistinen, "Hammer and Sword," 464–5, 691–9.
26 Herman Somers, *Presidential Agency: The Office of War Mobilization and Reconversion* (Cambridge, Mass., 1950), 35–66; Polenberg, *War and Society*, 167–8, 232–6.
27 *CIO News*, March 9, 1942.
28 As quoted in Polenberg, *War and Society*, 76; *Business Week*, April 4, 1942.
29 Joel Seidman, *American Labor from Defense to Reconversion* (Chicago, 1953), 67–73.
30 Samuel I. Rosenman, *Public Papers and Addresses of Franklin D. Roosevelt* (New York, 1950), 527; Koistinen, "Hammer and Sword," 185–6; *Chester Wright's Labor Letter*, March 28, 1942; CIO Maritime Committee, *Washington Newsletter*, March 3, 23, 1942, in ILWU Library Files, San Francisco.
31 "Statement of UAW before WLB Concerning Question of Premium Payment for Sunday Work," February 20, 1942, 1–2, Addes Collection, Box 99; Hillman to Murray, December 11, 1941; James Carey circular letter to CIO international unions, December 22, 1941, Box 38; and David J. McDonald to Carey, December 26, 1941, Box 59, all in CIO Secretary-Treasurer's Office Collection, Archives of Labor History, Wayne State University, (ALH-WSU). See also James Carey's report in the CIO Executive Board Minutes, January 24, 1942, 370–4. Although most union leaders closely associated with the Communists hewed to the CIO line, they often acquiesced more readily in the new demands of the WPB and the administration. In early 1942, for example, leaders of the National Maritime Union proposed the virtual abolition of the three-watch system on oceangoing ships and its replacement with a system of two twelve-hour turns; Frederick J. Lang, *Maritime: A Historical Sketch and Worker's Program* (New York, 1945), 146–56.
32 Ronald Young, *Congressional Politics in the Second World War* (New York, 1956), 60.
33 Murray reported Roosevelt's understanding in CIO Executive Board Minutes, March 24, 1942, 8–9; *PM* quoted in Art Preis, *Labor's Giant Step* (New York, 1964), 152.
34 CIO Executive Board Minutes, March 24, 1942, 121–5; *Militant*, March 28, 1942; *The New York Times*, March 18, 25, 1942; *CIO News*, February 2, March 23, 1942.
35 *CIO News*, March 30, 1942.
36 United Steelworkers of America, *Proceedings of the First Constitutional Convention*, Pittsburgh, May 19–22, 1942, 31–32, 86–91. *UE News*, March 28, 1942; Wayne W. Hield, "Democracy and Oligarchy in the ILWU," unpublished master's thesis, University of California, Berkeley, 1950, 88–92.
37 UAW Executive Board Minutes, January 22, 1942, 18–20; Richard J. Purcell, *Labor Policies of the National Defense Advisory Commission and the Office of*

Production Management, May 1940–April 1942 (Washington, D.C., 1942), 156–8; *The New York Times*, March 14, 1942.

38 Discussion of the Victory through Equality of Sacrifice Program related to the elimination of premium pay is found in UAW Executive Board Minutes, March 24, 1942, and in UAW, *Proceedings of the War Emergency Conference*, Detroit, April 7–8, 1942, 6–10.

39 Memorandum, Wayne Coy to FDR, April 4, 1942; FDR to R. J. Thomas, April 4, 1942, PPF 4816. The impact of the presidential letter is recorded in UAW, *Proceedings of the War Emergency Conference*, 16–17, 38–39.

40 UAW, *Proceedings of the War Emergency Conference*, 24–32, 51–8; *Militant*, April 18, 1942.

41 UAW, *Proceedings of the War Emergency Conference*, 34, 37.

42 *Ibid.*, 35–6, 41; *United Auto Worker*, April 15, May 1, May 15, 1942; Cormier and Eaton, *Reuther*, 200.

43 UAW, *Proceedings of the War Emergency Conference*, 33, 37.

44 See leaflets, radio script (April 7, 1942), and letters, Los Angeles CIO Council to Allen Haywood, April 9, 1942, Haywood to Slim Connelly, April 24, 1942, all in Brophy Collection, Box A7-23. The Communist-led Los Angeles CIO council played a major part in the Southern California aircraft drive. In the process, they attacked Frankensteen's non-Communist assistant, Walter Smethurst (who had directed the reorganization of the North American Aviation local), for not taking a sufficiently win-the-war attitude in the preparation of CIO organizational literature.

45 "Report of International Executive Board Hearing into Region Six Affairs," May 1944, Thomas Collection, Box 9; see also UAW, *Proceedings of the Ninth Annual Convention*, Grand Rapids, Mich., September 17, 1944, 419–41.

46 Young, *Congressional Politics*, 90–122; Polenberg, *War and Society*, 89, 137.

47 *NWLB Transcript*, July 24, 1942, 444.

48 "Report on CIO Aviation Drive Since February 1941," Brophy Collection, Box A7-23; *Militant*, August 1, 1942; Nicholas Dragon to FDR, July 27, 1942; IAM quotations taken from special Curtiss edition, *American Aircraft Builder* (UAW–CIO), July 24, 1942, all in Roosevelt Papers, OF 142.

49 *American Aircraft Builder*, July 24, 1942; *NWLB Transcript*, July 24, 1942, 437–40; excerpts from the letter were reprinted in *CIO News*, July 27, 1942.

50 Memorandum of telephone call, Philip Murray to Marvin McIntyre, August 1, 1942, OF 407-B, Box 28.

51 UAW, *Proceedings of the Seventh Annual Convention*, Chicago, August 3–9, 1942, 62–6, 96–105, 209–30, 273–91, 296–304, 317–33, 416–28, 453–6.

52 Frances Perkins to Marvin McIntyre, August 8, 1942, OF 407-B, Box 28; UAW, *Proceedings of the Seventh Annual Convention*, 86–111.

53 UAW, *Proceedings of the Seventh Annual Convention*, 126–32.

54 UAW Executive Board Minutes, August 24–31, 1942; George Addes circular letter to all UAW locals, September 3, 1942, Addes Collection, Box 27; Thomas to FDR, OF 98, Box 2; Perkins to McIntyre, August 8, 1942, OF 407-B, Box 28; Koistinen, "Hammer and Sword," 188–9.

55 Memorandum, McIntyre to FDR, September 8, 1942, OF 98, Box 2; George Addes circular letter to UAW locals, September 11, 1942, copy of executive order attached, Addes Collection, Box 27.

56 Bureau of Labor Statistics, Working Conditions and Industrial Relations Branch, "Saturday and Sunday Pay Provisions of Union Agreements in

Twelve War Industries," in *Industrial Relations Problem Arising under War Production* (Washington, D.C., 1942), 10; "Executive Order 9240" (excerpts from USW Executive Board Meeting, November 17–18, 1942), USW Publication No. 10; Lee Pressman Memorandum, September 18, 1942, in CIO Circular File, ILWU Library; Wayne Coy to FDR, September 17, 1942, OF 98, Box 2; Perkins to Murray, February 4, 1943, OF 98, Box 3.

57 UAW Executive Board Minutes, December 7–11, 1942; OWI Intelligence Report, 207, Richard Deverall Notebooks, Catholic University. Deverall served as education director of the UAW until the summer of 1942, when his strongly anti-Communist views made him dispensable in the wartime era of popular front unity. He thereupon joined the Office of War Information (OWI) and for the next year generated for his superiors there a series of almost daily field reports on the internal politics of the labor movement. In August 1943 he joined the army.

58 Murray to FDR, October 21, 1942, FDR to Murray, November 6, 1942, Coy Memorandum to FDR, September 17, 1942, OF 98, Box 2; "Executive Order 9240," USW Publication No. 10.

59 OWI Intelligence Report, 211, Deverall Notebooks; CIO circular letter, January 29, 1943 in CIO program and policies file, ILWU Library; Koistinen, "Hammer and Sword," 190–1.

60 Murray to FDR, January 28, 1943; Murray to FDR, February 5, 1943; Memorandum, Byrnes to FDR, February 10, 1943; Memorandum, Bureau of the Budget to Anna Rosenberg, February 3, 1943, all in OF 98, Box 3; Murray to Perkins, January 28, 1943, CIO Secretary-Treasurer's Collection, Box 38; *CIO News*, February 6, 1943.

61 Ben Segal, "CIO WLB Letter," No. 13, January 15, 1944, Entry 53, RG 202, Box 189; Department of Labor, *The Termination Report of the National War Labor Board*, vol. 1 (Washington, D.C., 1947), 319–21.

7. The social ecology of shop-floor conflict

1 H. M. Douty, "Review of Basic American Labor Conditions," in Colston E. Warne, ed., *Yearbook of American Labor* (New York, 1945), 1–11; Carroll R. Daugherty and George H. Hildebrand, Jr., *Labor Problems in American Industry* (Boston, 1948), 1007–19.

2 Douty, "Review of Basic American Labor Conditions," 48–9.

3 Summer H. Slichter, "The Labor Crisis," *The Atlantic Monthly*, 173 (1944), 37–40; "Money and Real Weekly Earnings during Defense, War and Reconversion Periods," *Monthly Labor Review*, 64 (1947), 987–9.

4 Slichter, "Labor Crisis," 38.

5 F. D. Newbury, "Wages and Productivity – the Problems Involved," American Management Association, *Personnel Series*, no. 105 (1946), 5–6; see also the extensive testimony in U.S. Senate, Special Committee to Investigate the National Defense Program, Part 28, *Manpower Problems in Detroit*, 79th Congress, 1st Sess., 13332–4, 13251–5.

6 See, for example, Katherine Archibald, *Wartime Shipyard: A Study in Social Disunity* (Berkeley, 1947), 46–50; "What's Itching Labor?," *Fortune*, 15 (1942), 102, 232–3.

7 Harriette Arnow, *The Dollmaker* (New York, 1962), 160. See also Mary Heaton Vorse, "And the Workers Say . . .," *Public Opinion Quarterly*, 7 (1943), 447–50.

8 A good discussion of defense migration is found in Philip J. Funigiello, *The Challenge to Urban Liberalism: Federal–City Relations during World War II* (Knoxville, Tenn., 1978), 3–38. See also Richard Polenberg, *War and Society: The United States, 1941–1945* (New York, 1972), 137–42, and John Dos Passos, *State of the Nation* (New York, 1944), for a panoramic survey of the social disruption generated by the mobilization effort. Two fine studies of Willow Run, the quintessential war boom community, are Lowell J. Carr and James E. Stermer, *Willow Run: A Study of Industrialization and Cultural Inadequacy* (New York, 1952), and Judy Rosen, "Women in the Plant, the Community and the Union at Willow Run," unpublished master's thesis, University of Pittsburgh, 1978.

9 Boris Shishkin, "Labor Looks at Wartime Wage Problems," in Warne, ed. *Yearbook*, 440–3; see also Arnold Tolls, "Spendable Earnings of Factory Workers," *Monthly Labor Review*, 58 (1944), 477–9.

10 "What's Itching Labor?," 230.

11 Vorse, "And the Workers Say . . . ," 446.

12 U.S. Department of Labor, *Problems and Policies of Dispute Settlement and Wage Stabilization during World War II*, Bulletin 1009 (Washington, D.C., 1950), 129–37; Department of Labor, *The Termination Report of the National War Labor Board*, vol. 1 (Washington, D.C., 1947), 150–5, 211–21, 290–7.

13 Taylor quoted in Chrysler Corporation, *3 War Labor Reports* (October 2, 1942), 451; Fifty-Nine Cotton Textile Companies, *2 War Labor Reports* (August 20, 1942), 349–50; Four Meat Packing Companies, *6 War Labor Reports* (February 8, 1943), 410–20; West Coast Airframe Companies, *6 War Labor Reports* (March 4, 1943), 581–639, passim. The NWLB decision in the aircraft case created immense difficulties for the board because it used the predominantly nonunion prewar Southern California regional wage average as a benchmark for setting war era aircraft pay.

14 Byron Fairchild and Jonathan Grossman, *The Army and Industrial Manpower: The United States Army in World War II* (Washington, D.C., 1959), 129–46, passim; George Q. Flynn, *The Mess in Washington: Manpower Mobilization in World War II* (Westport, Conn., 1979), 67–9.

15 The development of the extraordinarily complicated preunion wage scale is insightfully recorded by Katherine Stone in her "Origins of Job Structures in the Steel Industry" in Richard C. Edwards, Michael Reich, and David Gorden, eds., *Labor Market Segmentation* (Lexington, Mass., 1975); see also Jack W. Stieber, *The Steel Industry Wage Structure* (Cambridge, Mass., 1959), 4–11, for an account of the problems the new steel union encountered as a result of the Byzantine industry wage structure. Stieber reports that wage matters represented 65 percent of all grievances under the USW's 1942 contract at U.S. Steel. Individual pay inequities caused three-quarters of these wage grievances and generated half of the work stoppages during the two-year contract. USW district official quoted in "What's Itching Labor?" 228.

16 NWLB quotation taken from Four Meat Packing Companies, 404; Allen R. Richard, "War Labor Boards in the Field," in *James Sprunt Studies in History and Political Science*, 25 (Chapel Hill, N.C., 1953), 39–62, passim. See also Bureau of the Budget, *The United States at War* (Washington, D.C., 1946), 195–202 for an overview of the NWLB's "elastic" defense of the Little Steel formula in 1942 and 1943.

17 Joel Seidman, *American Labor from Defense to Reconversion* (Chicago, 1953), 120–1; Bureau of the Budget, *United States at War* (Washington, D.C., 1946),

388–9; Department of Labor, *Problems and Policies of Dispute Settlement*, 136–8; also "The Roosevelt Edict," *New International*, 9 (1943), 99–101.

18 *The New York Times*, April 14, May 13, 1943; *NWLB Transcript*, May 11, 1943, 212–26; Department of Labor, *Problems and Policies of Dispute Settlement*, 137; CIO Circular Letters, April 24, 28, 1943, in Circular Letter File, ILWU Library. In general, AFL representatives on the board took a considerably harder tactical stance in opposition to the hold-the-line order than did those of the CIO. See, for example, the dialogue between the IAM's Fred Hewitt and Van Bittner of the CIO in *NWLB Transcript*, May 11, 228–30; see also Joseph C. Goulden, *Meany: The Unchallenged Strong Man of American Labor* (New York, 1972), 104–5.

19 *NWLB Termination Report*, 229–33; Walter Reuther, "Contributing Factors Leading to Dissatisfaction and Unrest in the Automobile Industry," June 22, 1944, in Walter P. Reuther World War II Collection, Box 1; Robert M. MacDonald, *Collective Bargaining in the Automobile Industry: A Study of Wage Structure and Competitive Relations* (New Haven, Conn., 1963), 208–10.

20 Daniel Nelson, *Managers and Workers: The Origins of the New Factory System* (Madison, Wis., 1975), 34–54, provides the best description of the vast powers of the foreman before the rise of scientific management. The declining status of the foreman in the late 1930s and early 1940s is recounted in Foremen's Cases, *26 War Labor Reports* (July 23, 1945), 666–7; F. J. Roethlisberger, "The Foreman: Master and Victim of Double Talk," *Harvard Business Review*, 23 (1945), 283–98, and Donald E. Wray, "Marginal Men of Industry: The Foremen," *American Journal of Sociology*, 54 (1949), 298–301.

21 U.S. House of Representatives, Committee on Military Affairs, Part 68, *Full Utilization of Manpower*, 78th Congress, 1st Sess., 375–8.

22 Ernest Dale, "The Development of Foremen in Management," *AMA Research Report*, no. 7 (1945), 9–59; Herbert R. Northrup, "The Foreman's Association of America," *Harvard Business Review*, 23 (1945), 187–91; Packard supervisor quoted in *Manpower Problems in Detroit*, 13730.

23 Charles P. Larrowe, "A Meteor on the Industrial Relations Horizon: The Foreman's Association of America," *Labor History*, 2 (1961), 259–87; Foreman's Cases, *26 War Labor Reports*, 655–66.

24 Testimony of Edward Butler, *Full Utilization of Manpower*, 91. For an excellent analysis of management's fear of supervisory unionism, see Howell John Harris, *The Right to Manage: Industrial Relations Policies of American Business in the 1940s* (Madison, Wis., 1982), 74–89.

25 *Manpower Problems in Detroit*, 13576–609, passim, for these and several other examples; Ronald Schatz, "American Electrical Workers: Work, Struggles, Aspirations, 1930–1950," unpublished Ph.D. diss., University of Pittsburgh, 1977, 188.

26 *Manpower Problems in Detroit*, 13320, 13540. The index records the ratio of employment to unit production as measured by the consumption of electrical power. Although crude, it illustrates the general trend. An internal Ford memorandum comparing prewar and postwar labor input for the manufacture of virtually the same motor vehicle also indicates a decline in the level of work intensity. See File No. 204, Accession 157, in Harold Martindale Collection, FMC Archives.

27 Harris, *Right to Manage*, chap. 2. The quotation is taken from H. W. Anderson to Walter Reuther, August 31, 1943, UAW–GM Collection, Box 1, Archives of Labor History, Wayne State University (ALHWSU).

28 Frank Marquart in *Ford Facts*, February 15, 1943; Dos Passos, *State of the Nation*, 48.
29 Jess Ferrazza Oral History, 15, ALHWSU.
30 After October 1942, when the NWLB took on the responsibility for changes in wage rates and working conditions, the board found itself swamped. "It's not an expansion of the work we're doing," asserted Chairman Davis, "it's an explosion." In 1943, the average interval between certification of a dispute to the NWLB and its final resolution was four and a half months. But this figure understates by far the delays experienced by CIO unions because their cases usually involved more employees than those of the AFL and were often first contracts in which difficult nonwage issues involving union security, seniority, and grievance procedures were thrashed out before the board. Even after the NWLB had rendered its decision, a trade union might still find a wage increase held in abeyance if an employer could prove that government price relief was necessary. Davis Oral History, 186–7, COHC; NWLB Internal Memoranda, "Overall Case Load" and "Time Elapsed in Processing of Cases," in Wayne Morse Papers, Box AX 73-41, University of Oregon; *Problems and Policies of Dispute Settlement*, 140; *NWLB Termination Report*, 486–8; Aaron Levenstein, *Labor, Today and Tomorrow* (New York, 1946), 109–10.
31 Clarence M. Bolds, Labor Production Division, NWLB, to George Addes, January 2, 1943, in Victor Reuther Collection, Box 13, ALHWSU; editorial in *Wage Earner*, October 16, 1942; Frank Marquart's column in *Ford Facts*, January 15, 1943; see also Richard Deverall's 1943 series of Office of War Information reports on Chrysler labor relations in Deverall Notebooks, 102–47; see also Chrysler Corporation, *10 War Labor Reports* (August 27, 1943), 554–6.
32 Malcolm Denise, "Labor Relations and Implementation of Policy – 1943, 1944, 1945," as quoted in George Heliker, "Report," in Frank Hill Papers, FMC Archives, 303; *Ford Facts*, November 15, December 15, 1943, March 1, 1944; *PM*, March 3, 4, 1944; S. Evans, Labor Relations Department, to all building superintendents, Rouge Plant, April 4, 1944, in Thomas Collection, Box 13. For a general overview of the stormy wartime labor relations at Ford, see Heliker, "Report," and Allan Nevins and Frank Ernest Hill, *Ford: Decline and Rebirth, 1933–1962* (New York, 1962), 228–51; and Keith Sward, *The Legend of Henry Ford* (New York, 1949), 422–50.
33 *Manpower Problems in Detroit*, 13558.
34 Data compiled from "Strikes in 1942," *Monthly Labor Review*, 56 (1943), 964; "Strikes in 1943," *Monthly Labor Review*, 58 (1944), 934; "Strikes and Lockouts in 1944," *Monthly Labor Review*, 60 (1945), 961; "Work Stoppages Caused by Labor–Management Disputes in 1945," *Monthly Labor Review*, 62 (1946), 726. In 1945, about 75 percent of all auto industry workers were involved in a strike, but this figure includes the official GM work stoppage as well.
35 *Manpower Problems in Detroit*, 13619, 13624.
36 Ibid., 13563.
37 "Strikes and Lockouts in 1944," 961. All statistics on such unauthorized strikes are necessarily imprecise because of the lack of a uniform and consistent means to measure their frequency and duration. See also Jerome F. Scott and George C. Homans, "Reflections on the Wildcat Strikes," *American Sociological Review*, 54 (1947), 278–87.
38 *Monthly Labor Review*, 58 (1944), 917–29; Clark Kerr and Lloyd H. Fisher,

"Effect of Environment and Administration on Job Evaluation," *Harvard Business Review*, 27 (1949), 77–96; *Labor Action*, June 21, 1943; telephone interview with Tom Whelan, editor, UAW Local 887 *Propeller*, February 12, 1978.

39 *NWLB Termination Report*, 1134–6; Detroit Tool and Die Shops, *4 War Labor Reports* (October 24, 1942), 33–7. For a more extensive discussion, see Nelson Lichtenstein, "Industrial Unionism Under the No-Strike Pledge: A Study of the CIO During the Second World War," unpublished Ph.D. diss., University of California, Berkeley, 1974, 309–16.

40 *Manpower Problems in Detroit*, 13525–32; Joshua Freeman, "Delivering the Goods: Industrial Unionism during World War II," *Labor History*, 19 (1978), 574–91, provides a critique of the union movement and of worker consciousness that rests heavily on the consequences of this social transformation of the workforce.

41 Report of William McAulay, administrator of Local 50 (Willow Run), June 3, 1942, Thomas Collection, Box 7. A detailed statistical survey of the social and geographical origins of the Willow Run workforce is found in Carr and Stermer, *Willow Run*, 359.

42 Increasing female participation in the wartime labor force has received much recent attention. Among the better books and articles are Leila Rupp, *Mobilizing Women for War; German and American Propaganda, 1939–1945* (Princeton, N.J., 1978), 74–114; Karen Anderson, *Wartime Women: Sex Roles, Family Relations, and the Status of Women during World War II* (Westport, Conn., 1981). For the Detroit scene, see Ruth Milkman, "Redefining the Sexual Division of Labor: the Automobile Industry in World War II," *Feminist Studies* 8 (1982), forthcoming; and Alan Clive, *State of War: Michigan in World War II* (Ann Arbor, Mich., 1979), 185–203.

43 Judy Rosen, "Women in the Plant, the Community, and the Union at Willow Run," unpublished master's diss., University of Pittsburgh, 1979, 4–6, 34–7; Martin Glaberman, *Wartime Strikes: the Struggle against the No-Strike Pledge in the UAW during World War II* (Detroit, 1980), 21–4. See also Milkman, "Redefining the Sexual Division of Labor," for a penetrating analysis of sex typing in war work.

44 August Meier and Elliott Rudwick, *Black Detroit and the Rise of the UAW* (New York, 1979), 108–74, passim; Clive, *State of War*, 130–7.

45 Meier and Rudwick, *Black Detroit*, 112–26; Clive, *State of War*, 141.

46 Meier and Rudwick, *Black Detroit*, 162–74.

47 *Manpower Problems in Detroit*, 13795–6; Clive, *State of War*, 142; see also the excellent first-person account of Charles Denby, *Indignant Heart: A Black Worker's Journal* (Boston, 1978), 87–109.

48 Glaberman, *Wartime Strikes*, 34, 123–5; Freeman, "Delivering the Goods," 584–9; Ed Jennings, "Wildcat! The Wartime Strike Wave in Auto," *Radical America*, 9 (1975), 83–97. Although they differ in their evaluation of the social and political character of these strikes, all three writers emphasize the extent to which the influx of new workers, untutored in the meaning of union solidarity, may have been responsible for the increased number of stoppages. In doing so, they ignore much of the empirical evidence to the contrary and reject most of what we know about the consciousness of workers who engage in strike actions.

49 Scott and Homans, "Reflections on the Wildcat Strikes," 281.

50 Interview with Erwin Baur; interview with Jack T. Conway, June 19, 1980, Washington, D.C.; Scott and Homans, "Reflections on the Wildcat Strikes," 283–4. For an example of Ford management's use of a wildcat to weaken a union, see "Complete Report of March 7 and March 14 Incidents," in UAW International Executive Board Minutes, September 7–8, 1944, UAW–IEB Collection, Box 5, ALHWSU; "Council Upholds Aircraft Dismissals," *Ford Facts*, April 1, 1944.

51 James W. Kuhn, *Bargaining in Grievance Settlement: The Power of Industrial Work Groups* (New York, 1961), 111–43, 167–90, provides an excellent analysis of the problems inherent in what he calls "fractional bargaining" of this sort.

52 As quoted in Glaberman, *Wartime Strikes*, 44.

53 Jess Ferrazza, "Radio Address on No-Strike Pledge," *Voice of Local 212*, February 1, 1945.

54 *Wage Earner*, May 28, 1943.

55 "Revoke the No-Strike Pledge," *The Hi-Flyer* (UAW Local 6), November 1944.

56 Quoted in "Meeting of the International Executive Board, UAW–CIO, for the Purpose of Requiring Officers of Local 91 to Show Cause Why They Should Not Comply with the Provisions of Article 12 of the Constitution," Cleveland, July 14–15, 14, UAW–IEB Collection, Box 3. The strike began after management fired a popular inspector who refused a work reassignment.

57 Brewster Aeronautical Corporation, *5 War Labor Reports* (December 30, 1942), 386–8; *Labor Action*, December 21, 1942; Richard Deverall to Phillo Nash, January 11, 1942, Deverall Notebooks.

58 Al Nash, "A Unionist Remembers," *Dissent*, 24 (1977), 181–9; Deverall to Nash, March 1, 1943; Deverall to Clarence Glick, June 1, 1943, Deverall Notebooks. *Labor Action*, January 18, 1943.

59 The tense background of the Chrysler situation is reported in Chrysler Corporation, *3 War Labor Reports* (October 2, 1942), 451–64, and Chrysler Corporation, *10 War Labor Reports* (August 27, 1943), 552–6. Between December 1941 and January 1943, some sixty-six work stoppages took place in corporation plants. See also Deverall to Nash, December 23, 1942, and Nash to A. H. Feller, January 26, 1943, Deverall Notebooks. The strike incident on May 20 is reported in *Labor Action*, June 1, 1943, 2.

60 The Chrysler strike became a major factional issue in the UAW when the more extreme partisans of the Addes–Frankensteen caucus accused the Reutherites of instigating the strike. UAW Executive Board Minutes, June 7–11, 1943, 60–9; Deverall to Glick, May 24, 1943, Deverall Notebooks.

61 These conclusions are based on an analysis of 157 Chrysler Corporation strikes between July 18, 1944, and March 22, 1945. Robert W. Conder, Director of Labor Relations to R. J. Thomas, December 13, 1944, April 16, 1946, in Thomas Collection, Box 5.

62 Paul R. Porter, "Labor in the Shipbuilding Industry," in Colston E. Warne, ed., *Yearbook of American Labor* (New York, 1945), 345–60; Foremen's Cases, *26 War Labor Reports* (July 23, 1945), 702.

63 Victor H. Johnson, "Why War Workers Strike: The Case History of a Shipyard 'Wildcat,'" *The Nation*, 158 (January 15, 1944), 68–71.

64 Ibid., 70; "Federal Yards Demand Militant Action," *Labor Action* (August 2, 1943).

65 Johnson, "Why War Workers Strike," 70–1; Federal Shipbuilding and Drydock Company, *11 War Labor Reports* (September 15, 1943), 226–37; Federal
   Shipbuilding and Drydock Company, *12 War Labor Reports* (October 28,
   1943), 39–40.
66 "Local 16 Rank and File Wins Large Vote," *Labor Action* (January 22, 1945);
   Federal Shipbuilding and Drydock Company, *21 War Labor Reports* (January
   10, 1945), 121–36. The Shipbuilding Commission increased average pay by
   less than two cents an hour.
67 "Strikes and Lockouts in 1944," 961–4; Work Stoppages Caused by Labor–Management Disputes in 1945," 726–8.
68 Ibid.
69 Deverall to Nash, "Analysis of Certain Strikes Affecting War Department
   Procurement during the Period March 15 to April 3, 1943," April 7, 1943,
   Deverall Notebooks.

8. Incentive pay politics

1 General Motors, *3 War Labor Reports* (September 26, 1942), 383–4.
2 Walter Weiss, "What Is Incentive Pay?" *New International*, 9 (1943), 168;
   Department of Labor, *The Termination Report of the National War Labor Board*,
   vol. 1 (Washington, D.C., 1947), 322–7; "Wage Incentives in the War,"
   Business Week (August 14, 1943), 82–8; and E. J. Lever, "Incentive Plans as a
   Stimulus to War Production," RG 202, Box 47.
3 Bureau of Labor Statistics, Working Conditions and Industrial Relations
   Branch, "Wage Incentives and Collective Bargaining," 2–5, unpublished
   Memorandum no. 2 (April 1942), in *Industrial Relations Problems Arising under
   War Production* in files, Tenth Regional NWLB, Institute of Industrial Relations, University of California, Berkeley; see also Donald Roy, "Efficiency
   and the 'Fix': Informal Intergroup Relations in a Piecework Machine Shop,"
   The American Journal of Sociology, 60 (1954), 255–65; and Ronald Schatz's
   excellent discussion of work consciousness, union program and incentive pay
   in "American Electrical Workers: Work, Struggles, Aspirations,
   1930–1950," unpublished Ph.D. diss., University of Pittsburgh, 1977,
   45–56, 174–97.
4 Milton Nadworny, *Scientific Management and the Unions, 1900–1932*
   (Cambridge, Mass., 1955), 48–96; "Wage Incentives and Collective Bargaining," 5–11. In autos, incentive pay systems were for the most part eliminated
   before the UAW became a power in the industry. Resistance by workers,
   combined with a growing reliance on the assembly line itself as a labor control
   device, led to management's gradual abandonment of the pay scheme in the
   early and mid-1930s.
5 Significantly, the referendum lost in the home locals of the UAW's top four
   officers: Local 7 (Thomas), 12 (Addes), 3 (Frankensteen), and 174 (Reuther);
   Nash to Feller, January 26, 1943, Deverall Notebooks; UAW Executive
   Board Minutes, March 1–10, 1943.
6 West Coast Airframe Companies, *6 War Labor Reports* (March 3, 1943),
   614–15.
7 Deverall to Nash, "Unrest in West Coast Aircraft Plants Due to Lack of
   Wage Increases," March 1, 1943; also Deverall to Nash, March 3, March 5,
   1943, Deverall Notebooks.

8 Elizabeth Hawes, *Hurry Up, Please, It's Time* (New York, 1949), 83–4; UAW Executive Board Minutes, December 7–11, 1943. By November 1943, women comprised 42.5 percent of the airframe workforce in California. For a statistical overview, see Leonard G. Levenson, "Wartime Expansion of the California Airframe Industry," *Monthly Labor Review*, 61 (1945), 721–7. Extraordinary labor turnover also materially affected aircraft production, especially at Boeing in Seattle; George Flynn, *The Mess in Washington: Manpower Mobilization in World War II* (Westport, Conn., 1979), 66–8.

9 UAW, *Proceedings of the Ninth Annual Convention*, Grand Rapids, Mich., September 17, 1944, 423; *Business Week*, April 3, 1943; *Labor Action*, April 19, 1943.

10 CIO, *Proceedings of the Fifth Constitutional Convention*, Boston, November 9–13, 1942, 336–7.

11 UAW Executive Board Minutes, April 20, 1943, 16–20; Deverall to Glick, "A Study of the Incentive Pay Issue as It Has Developed in the CIO during the Past Year," July 10, 1943; Deverall Notebooks; UAW, *Proceedings of the Eighth Annual Convention*, Buffalo, October 4–10, 1943, 183. For the extraordinary rise in aircraft worker productivity, see Leonard G. Levenson, "Wartime Development of the Aircraft Industry," *Monthly Labor Review*, 59, (1944), 930.

12 UAW Executive Board Minutes, March 10, 1943.

13 Roger Keeran, *The Communist Party and the Auto Workers Unions* (Bloomington, Ind., 1980), 77–185, passim; Bert Cochran, *Labor and Communism: The Conflict that Shaped American Unions* (Princeton, N.J., 1977), 43–126, passim. See also Nelson Lichtenstein, "The Communist Experience in American Trade Unions," *Industrial Relations*, 19 (1980), 119–30.

14 Brian Peterson, "Working Class Communism: A Review of the Literature," *Radical America*, 5 (1971), 37–61; Ronald Schatz, "Union Pioneers: The Founders of Local Unions at General Electric and Westinghouse, 1933–1937," *Journal of American History*, 64 (1979), 586–602; Schatz, "American Electrical Workers," 227–35; Cochran, *Labor and Communism*, 68–71; Keeran, *The Communist Party and the Auto Workers*, 103–7.

15 Nathan Glazer, *The Social Basis of American Communism* (New York, 1961), 114–16; the quotation is taken from Joseph Starobin, *American Communism in Crisis, 1943–1957* (Berkeley, 1975), 23–4.

16 Maurice Isserman, "Peat Bog Soldiers: The American Communist Party during World War II, 1939–1945," unpublished Ph.D. diss., University of Rochester, 1979, 356.

17 A critical perspective on the Communist popular front strategy and its relationship to New Deal liberalism is found in George P. Rawick, "The New Deal and Youth: The Civilian Conservation Corps, the National Youth Administration and the American Youth Congress," unpublished Ph.D. diss., University of Wisconsin, 1957, 274–377; Hal Draper, "The Student Movement of the Thirties: A Political History," in Rita J. Simon, ed., *As We Saw the Thirties* (Urbana, Ill., 1967), 151–89; and Irving Howe and Lewis Coser, *The American Communist Party, a Critical History* (New York, 1962), 319–85, 500–44.

18 Interview with James Carey, March 24, 1972, Washington, D.C.

19 Isserman, "Peat Bog Soldiers," 284; interview with Erwin Baur, August 12, 1978, Berkeley, California. On the public presence of the Communists dur-

ing World War II see Howe and Coser, *American Communist Party*, 419–24, and Starobin, *American Communism*, 24–6.

20 For studies of factionalism in the UE see Ronald Filippelli, "The United Electrical, Radio and Machine Workers of America, 1933–1949: The Struggle for Control," unpublished Ph.D. diss., Pennsylvania State University, 1970, 48–132, passim; for Mine, Mill, the only full-length study is Vernon H. Jenson, *Nonferrous Metal Industry Unionism* (Ithaca, N.Y., 1954).

21 Colston E. Warne, ed., *Yearbook of American Labor* (New York, 1945), 543. The strategic power of the union possibly exceeded even its giant size, for in the auto industry alone the UAW represented workers who produced 25 percent of all war material made of metal; Dwight Macdonald, "The World's Biggest Union," *Common Sense* (1943), 411.

22 Irving Howe and B. J. Widick, *The UAW and Walter Reuther* (New York, 1949), 70–80; Wyndham Mortimer, *Organize! My Life as a Union Man* (Boston, 1971), 150–65; Keeran, *The Communist Party and the Auto Workers*, 205–12, 227, 247; Roy Hudson, "The Auto Workers' Convention," *Communist*, 22 (1943), 1006–9; Deverall to FBI, August 3, 1943, 183–91, Deverall Notebooks.

23 Browder quoted in Howe and Coser, *American Communist Party*, 426.

24 CIO Executive Board Minutes, March 24, 1942, 64.

25 *California Labor Herald*, April 9, 23, 1943; Nat Ganley, "Our Wages and the War," *United Auto Worker* (Local 155), March 1, 1943; C. G. "Pop" Edelen, "Production with Incentive Pay" pamphlet published by UAW Local 51, April 25, 1943, in Ganley Collection, Archives of Labor History, Wayne State University (ALHWSU).

26 As quoted in Deverall to Glick, "A Study of the Incentive Pay Issue."

27 Circular letter, Philip Murray to all CIO affiliates, April 13, 1943, in CIO trade union programs and policies file, ILWU Library. In an April 14 interview with the OWI's Richard Deverall, Murray recorded his personal opposition to incentive pay but still asserted that "it is up to the various international unions to decide whether or not they want incentive pay." Deverall to Nash, April 14, 1943, Deverall Notebooks.

28 See, for example, Jessica Rhine to Reid Robinson, May 4, 1943, in which a Mine, Mill staffer found in the hold-the-line order an obvious inducement for her union to begin immediate preparations of incentive pay plans for the copper industry, in RG 179, Box 1028. The quotation is from "Preliminary Memorandum on Incentive Wages," April 30, 1943 in Incentive Wage File, Tenth Regional NWLB.

29 Quoted in Deverall to Glick, "A Study of the Incentive Pay Issue."

30 Cochran, *Labor and Communism*, 217.

31 Quoted in Howe and Widick, *The UAW and Walter Reuther*, 117.

32 See, for example, Jack Butler, vice-chairman, UAW Local 50, to George Addes, April 14, 1943, Addes Collection, Box 42; *Detroit Free Press*, April 20, 1943. The membership of the Mazey lobbying effort was a roll call of the UAW's militant secondary leaders in the Detroit area, many informally associated with the Socialist party. Included were Matt Hammond (Local 157), Ben Garrison (400), Lloyd Jones (2), Edwin Carey (7), Ed Cote (174), Al Germain (154), and Mike Lacey (235). On the Ford election, see Deverall to Glick, "A Study of the Incentive Pay Issue."

33 Charles P. Larrowe, *Harry Bridges: The Rise and Fall of Radical Labor in the U.S.* (New York, 1972), 254–7; Isserman, "Peat Bog Soldiers," 285.

34 An account of the Camp Atterbury trip is found in Frank Cormier and William J. Eaton, *Reuther* (Englewood Cliffs, N.J., 1970), 205–6.

35 "SWP and the UAW," *New International*, 13 (1947), 231–2; interview with John Zupan, Local 50 committeeman during the war, August 22, 1972, Detroit; Howe and Widick, *UAW and Walter Reuther*, 122. See also Chapter 10 of this text.

36 See Reuther's remarks at the UAW War Problems Conference, May 1–3, Detroit, in *Labor Action*, May 17, 1943.

37 *United Auto Worker*, May 15, 1943.

38 UAW Executive Board Minutes, April 19, 1943, 16–20; Deverall to Nash, April 22, 1943, Deverall Notebooks. Deverall estimated that the Addes–Frankensteen caucus held about 45 percent of the voting strength on the UAW board, with Reuther and his allies commanding a somewhat smaller percentage. Normally, Thomas voted with Addes and Frankensteen, giving them a working majority, but this time he voted with Reuther.

39 UAW Executive Board Minutes, April 20, 1943, 15–16; Victor Reuther to All Regional Directors and International Staff Members, "Establishment of Area Management–Labor War Manpower Committees," November 23, 1942; V. Reuther to Richard Leonard, March 30, 1943; Press Release on UAW Resignations, War Manpower Commission, April 21, 1943; Walter Reuther, "Report on the Home Front," April 16, 1943; Walter Reuther to John Baggott, Local 46, IUMSWA, April 28; Press Release, "Manpower," June 1943; Robert Goodwin, regional director, WMC, to August Scholle, CIO, June 4, all in Victor Reuther War Policy Division Collection, Box 13, ALHWSU.

40 As quoted in Howe and Widick, *UAW and Walter Reuther*, 117.

41 *Labor Action*, May 17; *Aero Notes*, May 17; UAW, *Proceedings of the Eighth Annual Convention*, Buffalo, October 4–10, 1943, 170–240, passim. Addes nearly lost his secretary-treasurership of the union to a Reuther-backed opponent in the uproar; Nat Ganley Oral History, 40, ALHWSU.

42 *The New York Times*, May 2, 6, 1943; see also Reuther's speech attacking both Lewis and the Communists at the CIO executive board meeting, May 14–15, 1943, in "Excerpts from the Proceedings," Walter P. Reuther–World War II Collection, Box 1.

43 Browder quoted in Deverall to Glick, "A Study of the Incentive Pay Issue." Lucas quoted in *Labor Action*, May 17, 1943. See also Earl Browder, "The Strike Wave Conspiracy," *Communist*, 22 (1943), 489–92. An effort to apply the Communist "strike conspiracy" theory within the UAW backfired, however. During the city-wide Chrysler wildcat strike in late May, Chrysler Department Director Leo LaMotte claimed that among Reuther's supporters on the incentive pay issue were individuals such as Emil Mazey, who condoned the work stoppage and agitated for repudiation of the no-strike pledge. Said LaMotte of Reuther, "His weak and irresponsible position gave encouragement and comfort to those who wanted to avoid their responsibilities against strikes in this war period." After a mass meeting of Chrysler workers called for LaMotte's replacement, Reuther demanded that the UAW executive board censure LaMotte and repudiate his divisive attack on a fellow

board member. Following a close vote on factional lines, the board supported Reuther, but then, to assure that no one interpreted the vote as a repudiation of the no-strike pledge, they endorsed LaMotte's "forthright position in the affairs of the Chrysler strike." UAW Executive Board Minutes, June 7–11, 1943; *Wage Earner*, May 28, 1943; *Dodge Main News*, June 1, 1943.

44 Michigan CIO Council, *Proceedings of the Sixth Annual Convention*, Detroit, June 28–July 1, 1943, 210–11. For evidence of the leading role that Mazey played in crystallizing a left wing in the Reuther caucus, see "Socialist Party Statement on Wage Freeze Order," Local 212 Collection, ALHWSU; also Michael Devereaux Whitty, "Emil Mazey, Radical as Liberal," unpublished Ph.D. diss., Syracuse University, 1969, 104–10. No good study of the ACTU exists, but much of its character can be understood through its excellent weekly, *The Wage Earner*, published in Detroit throughout the war.

45 Analysis of the factional lineup and voting strength is found in Deverall to Glick, July 12, 1943, as well as in Michigan CIO Council, *Proceedings of the Sixth Annual Convention*, 227–8.

46 See Chapter 9 for a full discussion of these developments.

47 Michigan CIO Council, *Proceedings of the Sixth Annual Convention*, 68–72.

48 *Ibid.*, 137.

49 *Ibid.*, 138. Despite its militancy, Reynolds's Dodge Local 3 steadfastly supported Frankensteen for office in UAW elections. See voting tables, Michigan CIO Council, *Proceedings of the Sixth Annual Convention*, 229–30, and UAW, *Proceedings of the Eighth Annual Convention*, 468.

50 Quoted in Richard R. Lingerman, *Don't You Know There's a War On?* (New York, 1970), 139.

51 Michigan CIO Council, *Proceedings of the Sixth Annual Convention*, 144–5. See also Victor Reuther, "Labor in the War and After," *Antioch Review*, 3 (1943), 311–27, for an elaboration of Reutherite national political strategy.

52 Thomas Shane to Philip Murray, July 6, 1943, Murray Collection, Box A4-6.

53 Deverall to Glick, "A Summary: The Michigan CIO Council Convention," July 7, 1943; Michigan CIO Council, *Proceedings of the Sixth Annual Convention*, 169–76, 212–14. The Labor party resolution precipitated a bitter fight in the Scholle–Reuther–Mazey caucus. Eventually, a pro-Roosevelt third party resolution passed by a vote of 2,195 to 1,909, but the national CIO squelched the idea.

54 UAW, *Proceedings of the Eighth Annual Convention*, 236–40; Victor Reuther, "Labor in the War and After," *Antioch Review*, 3 (1943), 324–7.

9. Holding the line

1 McAlister Coleman, *Men and Coal* (New York, 1943), 224–6; Deverall to Nash, January 14, 1943, Deverall Notebooks; *UMW Journal*, January 15, 1943; Transcript, *NWLB Hearing in the Matter of Five Anthracite Coal Companies*, January 15, 1943, 22–8.

2 Nash to Feller, January 25, 1943, Deverall Notebooks; *UMW Journal*, January 15; *NWLB Hearing*, 133–40; *NWLB Transcript*, January 20, 1943, 270–4.

3 *UMW Journal*, February 15, 1943.

4 Arthur Suffern, "The National War Labor Board and Coal," in Department of Labor, *The Termination Report of the National War Labor Board*, vol. 1 (Wash-

ington, D.C., 1947), 1084–6. Actually, few miners worked a six-day week even as late as the spring of 1943.

5 *UMW Journal*, March 15, 1943.

6 *UMW Journal*, February 15, 1943.

7 Melvyn Dubofsky and Warren Van Tine, *John L. Lewis: A Biography* (New York, 1970), 416–20; *UMW Journal*, March 15, 1943.

8 *UMW Journal*, February 15, 1943.

9 See Harold Ickes, "Crisis in Coal," *Colliers*, September 4, 1943, 56–8, and Ickes's remarks in "Minutes of the War Production Board," *Historical Reports on War Administration*, Documentary Publication No. 4 (Washington, D.C., 1946), 286–7.

10 Saul Alinsky, *John L. Lewis: An Unauthorized Biography* (New York, 1949), 308–9; Joseph C. Goulden, *Meany: The Unchallenged Strong Man of American Labor* (New York), 1972, 104–7.

11 On the IAM, see Deverall to Glick, July 29, 1943, Deverall Notebooks. On the threat of a strike by the railroad brotherhoods late in 1943, see *Chester Wright's Labor Letter*, December 18, 25, 1943, and Malcolm Keir, "Railways – The Question of Labor's Share," in Colston E. Warne, ed., *Yearbook of American Labor* (New York, 1945), 324–31. John Frey, head of the AFL metal trades department and certainly one of the more reactionary craft union leaders, threatened a strike by west coast shipyard workers if the NLRB tampered with the sweetheart contracts he had negotiated with Kaiser in Portland, Oregon, and Richmond, California; reported in Tacoma, Washington, *Labor Advocate*, January 29, 1943. For more on the AFL's brand of conservative voluntarism, see Joshua Freeman, "Delivering the Goods: Industrial Unionism during World War II," *Labor History*, 19 (1978), 580–1.

12 Alinsky, *John L. Lewis*, 254–7; Deverall to Nash, December 15, 1942, March 1, 1943, Deverall Notebooks.

13 Telegrams, Irving Abramson to William H. Davis, February 17, March 16, 1943; to W. A. Waldron, February 19, 1943; Howard Gill (District 50) to NWLB, March 17, all in Celanese Corporation File, RG 202; Deverall to Nash, April 22, 1943, Deverall Notebooks; Morse to FDR, April 23, 1943, Roosevelt Papers, OF-407-B. For background on the TWUA's dispute with the corporation, see Celanese Corporation, *7 War Labor Reports* (March 16, 1943), 97–9.

14 Celanese Corporation, *7 War Labor Reports*, 96; Deverall to Nash, April 15, 1943, Deverall Notebooks; Memorandum, Philip Marshall to Wayne Morse, April 21, 1943, in Wayne Morse Papers, Box AX 73-41.

15 Deverall to Nash, April 15, 21, 23, 1943, Deverall Notebooks; Edward Heckelbeck (District 50) to Philip Marshall (NWLB), April 15, 1943; Carl Schedler (NWLB) to Heckelbeck, Michael Widman, John L. Lewis, April 14, 1943; Heckelbeck to Morse, no date; Morse to Heckelbeck, Lewis, Widman, April 21, 1943; Heckelbeck to Morse, April 23, 1943, all in Wayne Morse Papers, Box AX 73-41; *NWLB Transcript*, April 16, 1943, 41–3; *The New York Times*, April 21, 1943.

16 Morse to FDR, April 23, 1943; Francis Biddle to FDR, April 23, 1943, in Wayne Morse Papers, Box AX 73-41; Deverall to Nash, April 27, Deverall Notebooks.

17 Interview with Clayton W. Fountain, July 1, 1973, Half Moon Bay, California; Deverall to Nash, April 16, 20, 1943; Vorse quoted in Deverall to Glick,

May 17, 1943, Deverall Notebooks; Thomas quoted in CIO Executive Board Minutes, May 14–15, 1943, 62–3. See also UAW Executive Board Minutes, July 16–23, 1943, for a general discussion of the Lewis problem. The NWLB was not unaware of the Lewis influence in the UAW. For a brief assessment, see Osgood Nichols (NWLB) to John Chamberlain (*Fortune*), July 29, 1943, Wayne Morse Papers, Box 55.

18 Memorandum, Isador Lubin to Harry Hopkins, May 27, 1943, in President's Personal File (PSF), Roosevelt Papers, Box 145.

19 Harold S. Roberts, *The Rubber Workers* (New York, 1944), 318–58, passim; *Business Week*, April 16, 1943; Deverall to Glick, May 24, 1943, Deverall Notebooks; Big Four Rubber Companies, *8 War Labor Reports* (May 21, 1943), 540–4.

20 *Labor Action*, May 31, June 7; Telegram, George Bass to FDR, May 27, 1943, in Wayne Morse Papers, Box AX 73–41.

21 Nichols to Chamberlain, July 29; Deverall to Glick, May 25, 1943, Deverall Notebooks; *NWLB Transcript*, May 22; NWLB Press Release, May 26, 1943, in Wayne Morse Papers, Box AX 73-41.

22 Morse to FDR, May 26, 1943; FDR to Dalrymple, Bass, Harley Treen (president URW Local 7), and G. L. Lewis (president, URW Local 2) May 26, 1943, in Roosevelt Papers: OF 407-B, Box 32. Undated draft of executive order seizing four Akron rubber companies, Wayne Morse Papers, Box AX 73-41. The order was never put into effect.

23 *Labor Action*, June 7; NWLB Press Release, June 30, 1943, Wayne Morse Papers, Box AX 73-41; United Rubber Workers, *Proceedings of the Ninth Annual Convention*, New York City, September 18–23, 1943, 72–138, passim; Mary Bell, "Progressives at the Rubber Convention," *New International*, 10 (1944), 318–20.

24 See, for example, Emil Rieve's comments in CIO, *Proceedings of the Fifth Constitutional Convention*, Boston, November 9–13, 1942, 294; and Sidney Hillman's Speech to the Amalgamated Clothing Workers, May 13, 1943, in Hillman Scrapbooks, Hillman Collection.

25 *CIO News*, May 24, 1943.

26 Malcolm Ross and Richard Deverall to Harold Ickes, "CIO–AFL–RR Strategy on Wage and Price Policy and Its Relation to the John L. Lewis Situation," May 11, 1943, Deverall Notebooks; Paul A. C. Koistinen, "The Hammer and the Sword: Labor and the Military during World War II," unpublished Ph.D. diss., Berkeley, 1964, 268.

27 As quoted in Aaron Levenstein, *Labor Today and Tomorrow* (New York, 1946), 92.

28 *Business Week*, May 22, 1943; Ickes, "Crisis in Coal," 58.

29 *NWLB Transcript*, June 2, 1943, 260–6; June 5, 628–9.

30 Morse to Byrnes, June 2, 1943, Wayne Morse Papers, Box AX 73-41; Morse to "Paul and Ruth," June 9, 1943, Wayne Morse Papers, Box 55; *The New York Times*, June 5, 1943. For an indication of the enormous hostility between Ickes, his assistant Abe Fortas, and Morse, see the correspondence reprinted in A. Robert Smith, *Tiger in the Senate: The Biography of Wayne Morse* (Garden City, N.Y., 1962), 58–69.

31 Oscar Cox (assistant solicitor general) to Warner Gardner (solicitor, Interior Department), "A Bill to prevent the interruption of work in wartime (draft)," May 3, 1943, in File Coal, Warner Gardner Papers, Truman Library, Inde-

pendence, Missouri; also Cox telephone conversation with Harry Hopkins, June 3, 1943, Cox Papers, Hyde Park, N.Y.

32 Joel Seidman, *American Labor from Defense to Reconversion* (Chicago, 1953), 188; Roland Young, *Congressional Politics in the Second World War*, (New York, 1956), 63–67.

33 Ickes to Harold Smith (Bureau of the Budget), June 17, 1943; Davis to Byrnes, June 18, 1943, in Roosevelt Papers OF 407-B, Box 34.

34 Wayne Coy to FDR, June 21, Roosevelt Papers, OF 407-B, Box 34.

35 Dubofsky and Van Tine, *John L. Lewis*, 434–7; *UMW Journal*, July 1, 15, 1943; *Chester Wright's Labor Letter*, June 26, 1943.

36 Morse to Clarence E. Luckey, July 26, Wayne Morse Papers, Box 55; *NWLB Transcript*, July 16, 1943, 652–8; Richard Polenberg, *War and Society: The United States, 1941–1945* (New York, 1972), 164, *Chester Wright's Labor Letter*, August 28, 1943.

37 *NWLB Transcript*, July 16, 1943, 660–1; Ickes to Davis, July 27, in File Coal, Gardner Papers; *NWLB Termination Report*, 422–4. Ickes opposed the new executive order on the grounds that a union could never recapture dues lost during a plant or mine seizure, but management profits would continue. See Ickes to FDR, July 28, 1943, in File Coal.

38 *NWLB Transcript*, July 31, 1943, 940–1; Morse was strongly backed by the CIO representatives on the NWLB in this instance.

39 Colston E. Warne, "Coal – The First Major Test of the Little Steel Formula," in Warne, ed., *Yearbook*, 293–6.

40 Dubofsky and Van Tine, *John L. Lewis*, 438.

41 Dubofsky and Van Tine rely upon the work of economist Colston E. Warne to assert that for all of the UMW's efforts, the final wage package amounted to a weekly increase of but two dollars and fifty-six cents over a work week of 48 hours under the old contract. However, Warne's calculations rested upon a hypothetical pre-1943 work week that overestimated the number of hours of underground work for which miners were actually paid. The final 1943 contract assured miners of overtime and portal-to-portal pay, thereby increasing the average weekly wage from about forty-five to fifty-seven dollars. The political wisdom of Lewis's policy of confrontation may still arouse debate, but it put undeniable dividends in mineworkers' pocketbooks. The weekly pay of bituminous coal miners increased by 92 percent between January 1941 and August 1945, more than for any other major industry group. Suffern, "The WLB and Coal," in *NWLB Termination Report*, 1102–5; see Carroll R. Daugherty, *Labor Problems in American Industry* (New York, 1948), 1014, for miners' wage figures. A final note: When the Ickes–Lewis agreement was submitted to the board for its final approval, all public members of the NWLB save one voted for it. Only Wayne Morse dissented, and he would not serve on a board that buckled under pressure. Morse resigned early in 1944 and ran a successful Republican campaign for the Senate from Oregon. See *NWLB Transcript*, November 12, 1943, 695–702.

42 Seidman, *American Labor*, 123; Murray to FDR, July 10, 1943, in OF 98, Box 10; CIO, "Report of President Philip Murray," *Proceedings of the Sixth Constitutional Convention*, Philadelphia, November 1–15, 1943, 1–26.

43 CIO Executive Board Minutes, October 28, 1943, 96–7.

44 CIO, *Proceedings of the Sixth Constitutional Convention*, November 2, 1943, 27.

45 *NWLB Termination Report*, 443–67.

46 *NWLB Public Hearing: Carnegie-Illinois Steel Corporation*, December 21, 1943, 12–15.
47 *NWLB Transcript*, December 22, 1943; *The New York Times*, December 23–27, 1943; Steel Case Research Committee, *The Steel Case: Industry Statements Presented to the Steel Panel of the National War Labor Board* (Washington, D.C., 1944), 878–86.
48 *The New York Times*, December 28; *NWLB Termination Report*, 192–4.
49 Norman D. Markowitz, *The Rise and Fall of the People's Century: Henry A. Wallace and American Liberalism, 1941–1948* (New York, 1973), 81–5; Polenberg, *War and Society*, 73–98. An analysis of the disastrous 1942 elections is offered by CIO congressional lobbyist Nathen E. Cowan to the CIO Legislative Conference, January 8, 1943, in CIO Maritime Committee Files, ILWU Library. Cowan estimated that only 25 percent of the new Congress could be considered solidly prolabor; for a trenchant analysis of the rightward drift in American politics, see Dwight Macdonald's wartime essays in his *Memoirs of a Revolutionist* (New York, 1957), especially "The Unconscious War," 107–12.
50 Robert F. Carter, "Pressure from the Left: The American Labor Party, 1936–1954," unpublished Ph.D. diss., Syracuse University, 1965, 156–8. *The New York Times*, May 23, 24, 1943; *PM*, July 7, 8, 10–12, 1943; *United Auto Worker* (Local 174 edition), July 1, 1943; *Justice*, July 1, 1943; Matthew Josephson, *Sidney Hillman, Statesman of American Labor* (Garden City, N.Y., 1952), 590–2. The Dubinsky faction of the American Labor party, which controlled the New York State apparatus, scored an impressive moral victory in 1942 when they nominated and ran for governor Dean Alfange against a regular Democratic candidate endorsed by FDR himself. The rather colorless Alfange garnered over 400,000 votes, the largest total of any American Labor party candidate and enough to swing the election to Republican Thomas E. Dewey. Bitterly opposed by the Communists and disavowed by Sidney Hillman, who favored the regular Democrat, the Alfange campaign proved, as David Dubinsky later put it, "that no party has a mortgage on our allegiance and politics, and that no individual leader or set of leaders carry our votes tucked away in their vest pocket." *Justice*, June 1, 1943.
51 Interview with James Carey, March 22, 1972; *The New York Times*, March 31, 1943; *Labor Action*, March 21, 1943; *Daily Worker*, March 30, 1943; *Justice*, July 15, 1943, February 15, 1944; Deverall to Nash, March 31, April 7, April 15, 1943, Deverall Notebooks. See also John P. Windmuller, *American Labor and the International Labor Movement, 1940–1953* (Ithaca, N.Y., 1954), 16–35.
52 For the Reuther brothers' perspective, see "Excerpts from CIO Executive Board Meeting," May 14–15, 1943, and Victor Reuther, "Labor in the War and After," *Antioch Review*, 3 (1943), 311–27. The CIO engaged in one of its few open debates on the no-strike pledge during its July 7–8, 1943, meeting. For the contrasting views of Wolchok, Rieve, Hillman, and Murray, see *CIO Executive Board Minutes*, July 7–8, 1943, 18–77, passim. For the Communist perspective see Earl Browder, "The Strike Wave Conspiracy," *Communist*, 22 (1943), 474–83.
53 CIO Executive Board Minutes, July 7–8, 1943, 79–81.
54 David J. McDonald, *Union Man* (New York, 1969), 169. *Aero Notes*, organ of UAW Local 365, commented upon this development from the point of view of those who supported formation of a third party. "One is startled by the CIO Executive Board attempting to knock off in its infancy a regenerative

spontaneous movement for labor action instituted by the rank and file. Murray and Hillman would rather substitute an impotent program for political action than have a genuine independent mass movement because they fear that they will be unable to control the direction of this movement." *Aero Notes*, October 6, 1943.

55 *CIO News*, July 19, 1943; see also Deverall to Glick, July 19, 1943, Deverall Notebooks.

56 Joseph Gaer, *The First Round, The Story of the CIO–PAC* (New York, 1944), 60–1, 161–3; Len DeCaux, *Labor Radical: From the Wobblies to the CIO* (Boston, 1970), 441–3; Bert Cochran, *Labor and Communism: The Conflict that Shaped American Unions* (Princeton, N.J., 1977), 232–4.

57 The PAC also played a large role in helping to defeat two other conservative HUAC members: Joe Starnes of Alabama and John M. Costello of California, Gaer, *First Round*, 101–2, 266.

58 *Ibid.*, 60, 109. A generally sympathetic account of the PAC, which nevertheless reaches some of the same conclusions put forward here, is found in James C. Foster's *The Union Politic: The CIO Political Action Committee* (Columbia, Mo., 1975), 3–48, passim.

59 Josephson, *Sidney Hillman*, 600–2; *Labor Action*, February 14, 1944; Carter, "Pressure from the Left," 193–4. After their defeat, the Dubinsky faction withdrew from the American Labor party to form the new Liberal party. The American Labor party thereupon fell under increasing Communist control, despite Hillman's titular leadership.

60 Foster, *Union Politic*, 34, 41. In Michigan, a substantial group continued to press for some form of independent political action, and in March 1944 they founded the Michigan Commonwealth Federation (MCF), a third-party formation pledged to support FDR on the national level. At the same time, many of these UAW radicals, led by Paul Silver (UAW Local 351) and Matthew Hammond (UAW Local 157) sought to give the PAC itself a more radical, programmatic flavor. Although most leaders of the MCF were Reutherites, Reuther himself eventually backed national CIO policy, sealing the fate of even the most tentative independent political movement in the state. Deverall to Glick, August 4, 1943, Deverall Notebooks; *United Auto Worker*, August 15, 1943, March 1, 15, 1944; *Labor Action*, May 8, 1944; L. Smith, "Michigan Commonwealth Federation," *New International*, 10 (1944), 172–8.

61 J. David Greenstone, *Labor in American Politics* (New York, 1969), 49–52; Foster, *Union Politic*, 25–7. For an excellent nuts-and-bolts account of PAC activity in the industrial cities of upstate New York, see Charlotte Carr, "The 1944 PAC Campaign in Up-State New York" (mimeo), December 19, 1944, in ALP–1944 folder, Hillman Papers.

62 The CIO also contributed about 20 percent ($1.57 million) of the Democratic party's campaign fund. William H. Riker, "The CIO in Politics, 1936–1948," unpublished Ph.D. diss., Harvard University, 1948, 132, 179. Philip Murray and Sidney Hillman to all International Unions, April 3, 1944; Leo C. Bonner (area director, CIO–PAC) to Howard T. Curtiss (District 3, USW), November 15, 1944, both in Murray Papers, Box A-4; Carr, "The 1944 PAC Campaign," 10.

63 Foster, *Union Politic*, 27; Gaer, *The First Round*, provides a handy collection of many of the CIO's most widely distributed pamphlets and posters. See also

Cochran, *Labor and Communism*, 237, and Richard Rovere, "Labor's Political Machine," *Harper's Magazine*, 190 (1945), 592–601.

64 McDonald, *Union Man*, 169; Riker, "The CIO in Politics," 139–43: Dominating the executive board of the NC–PAC were liberals such as Freda Kirschway (*The Nation*), James Loeb (Union for Democratic Action), Ralph McGill (Atlanta *Constitution*), and Robert Weaver (Urban League), but the rank and file of the NC–PAC were predominantly popular front liberals on the periphery of the Communist party. The organization was one of the first to fracture under the impact of the Cold War, with its right wing regrouping as the Americans for Democratic Action and its left wing as the pro-Wallace Progressive Citizens of America. Memo., Anthony Wayne Smith, November 4, 1944, Murray Papers, Box A4-13; Gaer, *First Round*, 215; Mary Sperling McAuliffe, *Crisis on the Left: Cold War Politics and American Liberals, 1947–1954* (Amherst, Mass., 1978), 17–18.

65 Foster, *Union Politic*, 44.

66 On Hillman's role at the 1944 Democratic party convention, see Markowitz, *Wallace*, 81–117; Josephson, *Hillman*, 612–25; Foster, *Union Politic*, 45–8; Cochran, *Labor and Communism*, 238–42; and James Byrnes, *All in One Lifetime* (New York, 1958), 216–37. Virtually all these sources agree that Hillman had known for several days prior to the convention that FDR favored Truman for the vice-presidency. Hillman's great service to the Democratic party during and immediately following the convention was to smooth the way for CIO acceptance of FDR's choice over that of the popular Henry Wallace. Even James Byrnes admitted that it was FDR, not Hillman, who spiked his vice-presidential ambitions.

67 *Labor Action*, October 9, 1944; *NWLB Termination Report*, 192.

10. The bureaucratic imperative

1 Data compiled from "Strikes and Lockouts in 1944," *Monthly Labor Review*, 60 (1945), 960–7; "Work Stoppages Caused by Labor–Management Disputes in 1945," *Monthly Labor Review*, 62 (1946), 723–30; and from Department of Labor, *Handbook of Labor Statistics* (Washington, D.C., 1974), 367.

2 Taken from Ford Umpire Opinion A-2, June 17, 1943, as quoted in Neil Chamberlain, ed., *Sourcebook on Labor* (New York, 1958), 641.

3 Department of Labor, *The Termination Report of the National War Labor Board*, vol. 2 (Washington, D.C., 1947), 539.

4 Sidney Lens, "The Meaning of the Grievance Procedure," *Harvard Business Review*, 26 (1948), 713–2; Leonard R. Sayles and George Strauss, *The Local Union: Its Place in the Industrial Plant* (New York, 1953), 27–33.

5 Clinton Golden and Harold Ruttenberg, *The Dynamics of Industrial Democracy* (New York, 1942), CIO, *Proceedings of the Fifth Constitutional Convention*, Philadelphia, November 9–12, 1942, 288, 293–4.

6 This perspective draws upon material in the unpublished manuscript by Michael Urquhart, "The Grievance Procedure and the Challenge to Management's Control of Production," Department of Economics, New School for Social Research, 1980, 1–20.

7 *NWLB Termination Report*, 93–8; Chrysler Corporation, *10 War Labor Reports* (August 27, 1943), 553–55; *NWLB Transcript*, July 28, 1943, 25–9; Ben Segal, "CIO Weekly Letter," August 14, 1943, in Entry 53, RG 202.

8 *NWLB Transcript*, July 31, 1943, 940–1; James MacGregor Burns, "Maintenance of Membership: A Study in Administrative Statesmanship," *Journal of Politics*, 10 (1948), 113.

9 Roger Baldwin and Arthur Garfield Hays to William Davis, August 21, 1943, Entry 31, RG 202; see also Roger Baldwin, "Union Administration and Civil Liberties," *Annals of the American Academy of Political and Social Science*, 248 (1946), 54–61.

10 Worcester Pressed Steel, *3 War Labor Reports* (September 30, 1942), 504, 509.

11 Harold S. Roberts, *The Rubber Workers* (New York, 1944), 362–4; Big Four Rubber Companies, *8 War Labor Reports* (May 21, 1943), 598.

12 UAW Local 904 Statement, in Consolidated Vultee Corporation Case Files, Tenth Regional NWLB.

13 For criticism of labor "conscripts," see the column by UAW Local 212 Secretary-Treasurer P. P. McManus in *Voice of Local 212*, May 11, 1944; "Report of President Philip Murray" in CIO, *Proceedings of the Seventh Constitutional Convention*, Chicago, November 20–4, 1944, 56–9; and CIO Executive Board Minutes, March 11, 1944, 123–4. Murray reported CIO membership at 5 million in March 1945, but this figure is probably exaggerated.

14 Donald M. Nelson, *Arsenal of Democracy: The Story of American War Production* (New York, 1946), 391–416; U.S. Congress, Special Committee to Investigate the National Defense Program, Part 28: *Manpower Problems in Detroit*, 79th Congress, 1st Sess., 13240–67. See Chapter 11 for a larger discussion of the reconversion controversy.

15 FDR to Grenville Clark, December 30, 1942; Memorandum, Henry Stimson to FDR, July 1, 1943; Memorandum, Stimson, Patterson, Knox, Forrestal, Land, and Vickey to FDR, December 27, 1943, in Samuel I. Rosenman Papers, Box 15, 1413–F, Hyde Park, N.Y. Roosevelt's change of heart is recorded in Samuel I. Rosenman, *Working with Roosevelt* (New York, 1952), 420–5, and George Q. Flynn, *The Mess in Washington: Manpower Mobilization in World War II* (Westport, Conn., 1979), 82–91.

16 Henry Stimson and McGeorge Bundy, *On Active Service* (New York, 1947), 483–4.

17 Joel Seidman, *American Labor from Defense to Reconversion* (Chicago, 1953), 163; CIO Executive Board Minutes, January 27, 1944, 89–91.

18 Circular letter, Philip Murray to all CIO national and international unions, February 1, 1944, in Murray Papers, Box A4-3.

19 Paul A. C. Koistinen, "Hammer and Sword: Labor and the Military during World War II," unpublished Ph.D. diss., Berkeley, 1964, 476–83, 527–32; CIO Executive Board Minutes, January 27, 1944, 103.

20 USW, *Proceedings of the Second Constitutional Convention*, Cleveland, May 9–13, 1944, 135.

21 *United Auto Worker*, June 1, 1944.

22 "Strikes and Lockouts in 1944," 963–4. *Handbook of Labor Statistics*, 1974, 367.

23 John Chamberlain, "The Steelworkers," *Fortune*, 10 (1944), 166; Lloyd Ulman, *The Government of the Steel Workers' Union* (New York, 1962), 21–33, 40–65; Philip Taft, *The Structure and Government of Labor Unions* (Cambridge, Mass., 1954), 222–4; USW, *Proceedings of the Second Constitutional Convention*, 49. By contrast, UAW locals kept almost 60 percent of their dues income in the local and sent only about 40 percent on to the international. As a result of

this division and the repeated defeat of dues increase proposals, the UAW treasury never held more than about $2 million despite the fact that the auto union was at least one-third larger than the USW. "Financial Report," UAW Executive Board Minutes, July 16–23, 1945, 12.

24 Philip Murray to William H. Davis, September 28, 1943, Murray Papers, Box A4-6; Memorandum, Lee Pressman to Van Bittner, January 18, 1943, Entry 406, RG 202. For examples of Murray's pressure to stop strike ballots under the Smith–Connally Law, see David Sneddon (USW Local 1743) to Murray, August 12, 1943; Murray to Sneddon, August 13, 1943; Lee Pressman to Murray, June 21, 1944; Thomas E. Dunn (USW Local 3180) to Murray, November 4, 1944; Murray to Dunn, November 7, 1944; Howard T. Curtiss, district director, to Daniel P. Sheehan, staff representative, June 27, 1944, all in Murray Papers, Box A4-6.

25 A. F. Kojetinsky, district director, to Murray, April 5, 1944; Clinton Golden to Daniel P. Sheehan, October 18, in Murray Papers, Box A4-6.

26 David J. McDonald, *Union Man* (New York, 1969), 150; see also McDonald to Murray, May 28, 1943, in Murray Papers, Box A4-6.

27 "Work Stoppages and Slowdowns," Report of Policy Committee Meeting, February 11, 1944, by Howard T. Curtiss, in Murray Papers, Box A4-6. Industry sources reported 993 strikes in 1943, triple the number in 1942, and more than double the number of work stoppages in 1941. Steel Case Research Committee, *Industry Statements*, 869.

28 See, for example, Leo Levinson (USW Local 2054) to Murray, May 17, 1945, in Murray Papers, Box A4-6; also Frank Marquart Oral History, 50–4.

29 Telegrams, Murray to Kojetinsky, November 22, 1943; Roy Constine to Murray, August 21, 1944; Murray to Constine, August 22, 1944, in Murray Papers, Box A4-6.

30 Edward Heppenstall, "Internal Government and Politics of the United Steelworkers," unpublished senior thesis, Williams College, 1955), 113–16; John Herling, *Right to Challenge: People and Power in the Steelworkers Union* (New York, 1972), 1–41; Ulman, *Government of the Steel Workers' Union*, 129.

31 *NWLB Transcript*, January 10, 1944, 105–12; January 18, 1944, 231–41; W. D. Robinson (Briggs Manufacturing) to Emil Mazey, December 19, 1943, Local 212 Collection, Box 7, ALHWSU.

32 Strike data taken from appendix, Harry Elmer Barnes manuscript; Monroe Lake (assistant director, Ford department) interview with George Heliker, March 12, 1954, as quoted in Heliker, "Report," 310, both FMC archives; *Ford Facts*, November 15, December 15, 1943; March 1, 1944; UAW Executive Board Minutes, February 7–16, 1944, 83–4.

33 Frank Marquart Oral History, 53. For example, when Chrysler Director Leo LaMotte bypassed an uncooperative local executive board to discipline a tank arsenal steward for instigating a strike, the officers of Local 833 there protested loudly to the international executive board. The issue raised a factional dispute, with George Addes defending LaMotte and Walter Reuther supporting the local in the name of its constitutional autonomy. UAW Executive Board Minutes, March 1–10, 1943, 33–4, 50–4.

34 *United Auto Worker*, March 1, 1944.

35 Marquart Oral History, 55; Harry Shulman and Neil W. Chamberlain, *Cases on Labor Relations* (Brooklyn, N.Y., 1949), 434. Umpire systems at Ford, Chrysler, and other large firms were set up in the second half of the war

largely at the behest of the NWLB, which sought to regularize grievance handling and to routinize in-plant collective bargaining. By the mid-1950s, these grievance umpire systems had created an enormous body of quasilegal precedents that largely defined and guarded management's disciplinary power. See Orme W. Phelps, *Discipline and Discharge in the Unionized Firm* (Berkeley, 1959), especially chap. 6, "Grounds for Discipline: Violation of the Agreement," 115–35.

36 "Complete Report of March 7 and March 14, 1944, Incidents," in UAW Executive Board Minutes, September 7–8, 1944, 52–62.

37 *Ford Facts*, March 15, 1944.

38 *Ford Facts*, May 15, June 1, 1943; *Detroit Free Press*, March 9, 1944. See also "Complete Report" and debate over Ford wildcat incidents in UAW, *Proceedings of the Ninth Annual Convention*, Grand Rapids, Mich., September 11–17, 1944, 447–66.

39 *Detroit Free Press*, March 10, 1944; *Labor Action*, March 17, 1944.

40 "Complete Report,"; *Ford Facts*, April 1, 1944; *Labor Action*, April 3, 1944.

41 *Ford Facts*, April 1, 1944; *United Auto Worker*, April 15, 1944.

42 "Meeting of the International Executive Board, UAW–CIO, for the Purpose of Requiring Officers of Local 91 to Show Cause Why They Should Not Comply with the Provisions of Article 12 of the Constitution," Cleveland, July 27, 1944, 16–18.

43 *Detroit Free Press*, May 22, 25, 27, 1944; *Labor Action*, June 5, 1944.

44 On Reuther's initial opposition to administratorships, see UAW Executive Board Minutes, September 8–13, 1943, 19–20; on his handling of the Chevrolet situation, see UAW Executive Board Minutes, August 1, 1944, 18–19; *Labor Action*, August 28, September 25, 1944. Subsequently, GM fired these officers, whose only offense was to stand aside when their membership struck. Reuther cried "double-cross" and took their case to the NWLB. They were reinstated by the board after a second strike in their support at Chevrolet's Local 235.

45 Locals formally on record against the no-strike pledge included: Fleetwood 15, Briggs 212, Flint 599, Dodge Aircraft 6 (Chicago), Chrysler 7, Willow Run 50, and Brewster 365. The growth and ideology of the Rank and File caucus are discussed in the pages of *Labor Action* and *The New International* for the year 1944 and in Irving Howe and B. J. Widick, *The UAW and Walter Reuther* (New York, 1949), 120–23. See also its organ, *Rank and Filer*, January–March 1945.

46 "Revoke the No-Strike Pledge," *The Hi-Flyer* (UAW Local 6), November 1944. Although the caucus won most of its strength in the older UAW strongholds in the Detroit–Flint area, the new group also gained support in such "war baby" locals as Brewster 365, Willow Run 50, Bell Aircraft 501 (Buffalo), and Dodge 6 (Chicago). In some of these new locals, young ideological radicals who had "industrialized" during the war were able to win a good deal of political influence in the fluid political climate of these explosive locals. See, for example, Jack T. Conway Oral History, 6–8, in ALHWSU; Al Nash, "A Unionist Remembers," *Dissent*, 24 (1977), 182, 186; and interview with John Zupan, August 28, 1972, Detroit.

47 UAW, *Proceedings of the Ninth Annual Convention*, 147–225, passim; Conway Oral History, 16–18. See also coverage of internal UAW politics in *Wage Earner*, various issues, August–September 1945. The convention fight over

the pledge has been recounted in numerous published sources. Among the best are Art Preis, *Labor's Giant Step* (New York, 1964), 231–5, and Frank Cormier and William J. Eaton, *Reuther* (Englewood Cliffs, N.J., 1970), 211–15. The Rank and File caucus ran John McGill, president of Flint Local 599, against both Reuther and Leonard on the second vice-presidential ballot. McGill received but 4 percent of all the votes cast. Conway reported that most Rank and File caucus members, himself included, now voted to keep Reuther as UAW vice-president.

48 UAW, *Proceedings of the Ninth Annual Convention*, 105–7, 177–9.

49 *Ibid.*, 193–225, passim; see also Max Shachtman, "Politics Among the Auto Workers," *New International*, 10 (1944), 310–12, and *Labor Action*, September 25, 1944.

50 R. J. Thomas to FDR, November 15, 1944, in PPF 4816; "Straight Talk about Our No-Strike Pledge" and Roy Hudson, "The Plot Against the No-Strike Pledge" in Nat Ganley Collection, Box 2; *Ford Facts*, January 15, 1945; *Rank and Filer*, April 1945; Thomas asked Murray to put out a special edition of the *CIO News* backing the pledge. Murray, alarmed about the possibility of defeat in the UAW, readily assented. See CIO Executive Board Minutes, November 25, 1944, 314–24.

51 "UAW Referendum Committee Final Report," in Ganley Collection, Box 2.

52 Ibid.; *United Auto Worker*, April 15, 1945; Preis, *Labor's Giant Step*, 236.

53 The relationship between worker consciousness and action is a problem central to Marxist thought. For a contemporary discussion of the wildcat strike phenomenon, see Sidney Hertzberg, "Strikes Can Prolong the Peace," *Common Sense*, 13 (1944), 60–2; and for a latter-day defense, see Martin Glaberman, *Wartime Strikes: The Struggle against the No-Strike Pledge in the UAW during World War II* (Detroit, 1980), 98–134. Richard Hyman offers an excellent theoretical analysis in his *Strikes* (London, 1972), especially "Strikes and Society," 140–72.

54 URW, *Proceedings of the Eighth Annual Convention*, Toronto, September 20–4, 1943, 58.

55 Big Four Rubber Companies, *8 War Labor Reports*, 594–8.

56 *United Rubber Worker*, February, March 1944; *Labor Action*, January 17, 31, 1944.

57 *United Rubber Worker*, May 1944; *Labor Action*, March 13, April 24, 1944.

58 Mary Bell, "Progressives at the Rubber Convention," *New International*, 10 (1944), 318–20; URW, *Proceedings of the Ninth Annual Convention*, New York, September 18–23, 1944, 90–154; *United Rubber Worker*, September 1944.

59 URW, *Proceedings of the Ninth Annual Convention*, 184–200.

60 *United Rubber Worker*, February 1945; U.S. Rubber Company, *21 War Labor Reports* (January 16, 1945), 182–3. Garth L. Mangum later considered this incident "the classic example of a union attempt to control wildcat strikes in the absence of strong company discipline." See his "Taming Wildcat Strikes," *Harvard Business Review*, 38 (1960), 94–5.

61 *Labor Action*, July 30, August 6, November 26, 1945; *United Rubber Worker*, July 1945. Significantly, Communist party influence in the local was eliminated when new elections were held in late 1945.

62 *United Rubber Worker*, May, June, July 1945; *Labor Action*, July 2, 9, 16, 1945; *The New York Times*, July 6, 13, 1945. For the step-by-step development of this enforcement policy, see *NWLB Termination Report*, 419.

63 *United Rubber Worker*, October 1945; *The New York Times*, July 13, 1945.
64 *United Rubber Worker*, December 1945; *Labor Action*, December 31, 1945; Preis, *Labor's Giant Step*, 280. Led by Goodrich Local President George Bass, the Akron Progressives nevertheless remained a powerful force. In 1948 they temporarily unseated Buckmaster from the URW presidency. More importantly, their influence provided a relatively favorable political–institutional framework for a tradition of shop-floor militancy in the rubber industry that continued for at least a decade after the war. Taft, *Structure and Government of Labor Unions*, 48–50; James W. Kuhn, *Bargaining in Grievance Settlement: The Power of Industrial Work Groups* (New York, 1961), 145–90, passim.
65 CIO Executive Board Minutes, June 18, 1944, 166–8.

.11. Reconversion politics

1 The reconversion controversy has been described in a number of accounts. Participant memoirs include Donald M. Nelson, *Arsenal of Democracy: The Story of American War Production* (New York, 1946), 391–416, and Bruce Catton, *The War Lords of Washington* (New York, 1948), 196–313. Official histories include: Bureau of the Budget, *United States at War* (Washington, D.C., 1946), 459–501; Civilian Production Administration, *Industrial Mobilization for War* (Washington, D.C., 1947), 789–814; and J. Carlyle Sitterson, *Development of the Reconversion Policies of the War Production Board* (Washington, D.C., 1946). Good scholarly accounts are Paul A. C. Koistinen, "The Hammer and the Sword: Labor and the Military during World War II," unpublished Ph.D. diss., Berkeley, 1964, 700–802; and Barton J. Bernstein, "The Debate on Industrial Reconversion: The Protection of Oligopoly and Military Control of the Economy," *American Journal of Economics and Sociology*, 26 (1967), 159–72. David Brody, "The New Deal and World War II," in John Braeman et al., eds., *The New Deal: The National Level* (Columbus, Ohio, 1975), 292–7, and Richard Polenberg, *War and Society: The United States, 1941–1945* (New York, 1972), 227–37, put the reconversion debate in a larger context.
2 "Save Small Steel," March, 1944, pamphlet in Murray Papers, Box A-4.
3 *United Auto Worker*, June 3, 1944; *PM*, June 3, 1944; *Chester Wright's Labor Letter*, June 3, 1944; quotation taken from Al Nash, "A Unionist Remembers," *Dissent*, 24 (1977), 188–9.
4 As quoted in Polenberg, *War and Society*, 229.
5 Aaron Levenstein, *Labor Today and Tomorrow* (New York, 1946), 201–6; UAW, *Proceedings of the Ninth Annual Convention*, Grand Rapids, Mich., September 10–17, 1944, 176–7.
6 Civilian Production Administration, *Minutes of the War Production Board* (Washington, 1946), 299, 342, 392; Catton, *War Lords*, 211–41; George Q. Flynn, *The Mess in Washington: Manpower Mobilization in World War II* (Westport, Conn., 1979), 234–40; Koistinen, "Hammer and Sword," 712–27.
7 Bernstein, "Debate on Industrial Reconversion," 166–7.
8 *Ibid.*, 168; Polenberg, *War and Society*, 232–3.
9 Koistinen, "Hammer and Sword," 740–4; Bernstein, "Debate on Industrial Reconversion," 172.
10 Howell John Harris, *The Right to Manage: Industrial Relations Policies of American Business in the 1940s* (Madison, Wis., 1982), chap. 4. See also Ronald

Schatz, "The End of Corporate Liberalism: Class Struggle in the Electrical Manufacturing Industry, 1933–1950," *Radical America*, 9 (1975), 187–205. Schatz provides an excellent explanation for the increasingly hard-line labor policy pursued by the major electrical manufacturers during and after the great strike of 1945–6.

11 Harris, *The Right to Manage*, chap. 4. quotation taken from Department of Labor, *The Termination. Report of the National War Labor Board*, vol. 2 (Washington, D.C., 1947), 368.

12 Sidney Lens, *Left, Right and Center: Conflicting Forces in American Labor* (Hinsdale, Ill., 1949), 360–1; Levenstein, *Labor, Today and Tomorrow*, 1–12, 98–9; *CIO News*, April 24, 1944. The URWDSE remained a relatively weak international because of the opposition of tens of thousands of scattered employers and the competition of rival unions such as the Teamsters and the Retail Clerks International Association. Wolchok also faced internal opposition, chiefly from New York District 65, controlled by Communist elements hostile to his leadership. See Constance Williams, "Developments in Union Agreements," in Colston E. Warne, ed., *Yearbook of American Labor* (New York, 1945), 112–13; Max Kampelman, *The Communist Party vs. the CIO* (New York, 1957), 33.

13 Art Preis, *Labor's Giant Step* (New York, 1964), 220; *CIO News*, December 18, 1944.

14 Paul D. Richards, "The History of the Textile Workers Union of America, CIO, in the South, 1937–1945," unpublished Ph.D. diss., University of Wisconsin, Madison, 1978, 150–76.

15 Testimony, Solomon Barkin and Horace White, in U.S. Senate, Special Committee Investigating the National Defense Program, 79th Congress, 1st Sess., *Hearings*, January 19, 1945, 12342, 12383–4; NWLB, *Termination Report*, 424; Fourth Regional War Labor Board Press Release, February 17, 1945, in RG 202, Box 25; Richards, "Textile Workers," 175.

16 TWUA, *Proceedings, Third Biennial Convention*, New York, May 10–14, 1943, 103–5; "Statement of the Textile Workers Union of America in the Matter of 23 Southern Cotton Textile Mills," in U.S. Senate, *Hearings*, January 19, 1945, 12881–98.

17 War Production Board Report, "Maintaining Production in the Cotton Textile Industry," in RG 202, Box 25.

18 George W. Taylor, *Government Regulation of Industrial Relations* (New York, 1948), 190–2; *The New York Times*, December 12–14, 1944; *Chester Wright's Labor Letter*, January 27, February 10, 1945; Labor Members of NWLB to William H. Davis, April 13, 1945, in CIO National and International Trade Union File, ILWU Library.

19 *PM*, February 10, 16, 21, 1945; *Textile Labor*, February, March 1945.

20 *PM*, February 22, 1945.

21 *Labor Action*, March 26, 1945; Allen R. Richard, "War Labor Boards in the Field," in *James Sprunt Studies in History and Political Science*, 25 (Chapel Hill, N.C., 1953), 151–4.

22 Bert Cochran, *Labor and Communism, the Conflict That Shaped American Unions* (Princeton, N.J., 1977) 244; CIO Executive Board Minutes, January 27, 1944, 99–100. Murray thought that the public division within CIO ranks made him the "laughingstock of the nation."

23 As quoted in Preis, *Labor's Giant Step*, 222.

24 *PM*, May 17, 1944; Levenstein, *Labor Today and Tomorrow*, 163–5.

25 Richard P. Boyden, "The West Coast Longshoremen, the Communist Party and the Second World War," unpublished manuscript, 1967, in author's possession, 38–9; Joseph R. Starobin, *American Communism in Crisis, 1943–1957* (Berkeley, 1972), 59, 77. The most vociferous advocates of government-regulated international trade were the maritime unions, Communist and non-Communist alike, who feared the collapse of their swollen membership base if shipbuilding and trade were cut back after the war. See "What's Ahead" in *CIO News*, January 24, 1944, and "Five Million Jobs in Foreign Trade," CIO Publication No. 194, 1944. For a critique, see Daniel Bell, "Danger Ahead for the Unions," *Common Sense*, 14 (February 1945), 7–9. Bell called the CIO maritime program "an endorsement of imperialist expansion without regard to the economies of other nations and to the needs of world trade."

26 *PM*, May 29, 31, June 19, 1944. The idea of a postwar no-strike pledge also proved unpopular among many in the Communist rank and file, who found the proposal confusing at best. Roger Keeran, *The Communist Party and the Auto Workers Unions* (Bloomington, Ind., 1980), 246–7.

27 *Detroit News*, January 14, 1945; *Wage Earner*, February 2, 1945; *Labor Action*, January 1, 8, 1945; William H. Davis to FDR, December 20, 1944, in Davis Papers, Box 25, Wisconsin State Historical Society. In December, presidents of more than 200 CIO locals in Detroit pledged their "fullest moral, financial and physical support" to the Ward strikers, and Davis thought the work stoppage filled with "epidemic possibilities" in the explosive Detroit cauldron. Later, when the Communist-controlled Wayne County CIO Council refused to back the URWDSE strike, several Detroit area UAW locals under Reutherite leadership withdrew from the council and demanded a national CIO investigation into its affairs.

28 UAW Executive Board Minutes, March 5–8, 1945, 51.

29 *Ibid.*, 61–2; UAW Executive Board Minutes, July 16–23, 1945, 54–8; *Wage Earner*, June 22, 1945; *Labor Action*, March 12, 1945.

30 UAW Executive Board Minutes, January 26, 1945, 90–3; March 5, 1945, 50–4.

31 Reprinted excerpts of CIO Executive Board Minutes, March 11, 1945, 8, in Murray Papers, Box A4-10.

32 *Ibid.*, 9; *PM*, March 14, 1945; *Wage Earner*, March 20, 1945.

33 See the abstract of the proceedings, "Conference of State Industrial Union Councils on Full Production," Washington, D.C., June 18–20, 1945, 7–10, in CIO National and International Union File, ILWU Library; see also *PM*, June 13, 1945. CIO fears of a postwar slump similar to the one that followed World War I were given wide currency in the PAC–CIO pamphlet "Jobs for All After the War," in Joseph Gaer, *The First Round, the Story of the CIO–PAC* (New York, 1944), 77–97. The general fear of a postwar depression is discussed in Frank C. Pierson, "The Employment Act of 1946," in Colston E. Warne, ed., *Labor in Postwar America* (Brooklyn, N.Y., 1949), 284–7, and W. S. Woytinsky, "What Was Wrong in Forecasts of Postwar Depression?" *Journal of Political Economy*, 55 (1947), 142–151.

34 CIO, *Proceedings of the Seventh Constitutional Convention*, Chicago, November 20–4, 1944, 39.

35 *The New York Times*, March 29, 1945; *Chester Wright's Labor Letter*, March 31, 1945; *CIO News*, April 1, 1945.

36 *PM*, May 7, 23, 1945; "Conference of State Industrial Union Councils," 11;

Chester Wright's Labor Letter, July 21, 1945; Eric A. Johnston, "The Wage Crisis," radio address, September 29, 1945, in Davis Collection, Box 26. For a discussion of the first phase of the government's reconversion wage policy, see Barton Bernstein, "The Truman Administration and Its Reconversion Wage Policy," *Labor History*, 4 (1965), 214–31; see also John T. Dunlop, "The Decontrol of Wages and Prices," in Warne, ed., *Labor in Postwar America*, 3–24.

37 CIO Executive Board Minutes, November 1, 1945, 81–4, 110–12, 135–6; *Chester Wright's Labor Letter*, November 10, 1945.

38 Interview with Irving Richter, Washington, D.C., February 20, 1981.

39 Harris, *The Right to Manage*, chap. 4. Robert M. Collins, "Business Response to Keynesian Economics, 1929–1964: An Analysis of the Process by Which the Modern American Political Economy Was Defined," unpublished Ph.D. diss., Johns Hopkins University, 1976, 109. CIO, *Proceedings of the Seventh Constitutional Convention*, 259; and on Henry Kaiser, Janeway, *Struggle for Survival*, 249–253; and "Adventures of Henry and Joe in Autoland," *Fortune*, 38 (1946), 96–103.

40 Bernstein, "The Truman Administration and its Reconversion Wage Policy," 216–25.

41 *Ibid.*, 221.

42 Collins, "Keynesian Economics," 161–3.

43 Harris, *The Right to Manage*, chap. 4.

44 Robert M. C. Littler, "Managers Must Manage," *Harvard Business Review*, 24 (1946), 366–76. Among the best accounts of the managerial offensive of the immediate postwar era are: David Brody, "The Uses of Power I: Industrial Battleground," in Brody, *Workers in Industrial America: Essays on the 20th Century Struggle* (New York, 1980), 173–214, passim; Harris, *The Right to Manage*, 129–58; and Schatz, "The End of Corporate Liberalism," 194–203.

45 Harris, *The Right to Manage*, chap. 4; Brody, *Workers in Industrial America*, 175–6.

46 For Murray's retrospective admission of this hope, see UAW, *Proceedings of the Tenth Constitutional Convention*, Atlantic City, N.J., March 23–31, 1946, 94–5; *The New York Times*, November 9, 1945; *CIO News*, November 26, December 3, 10, 1945; U.S. Department of Labor, *The President's National Labor–Management Conference*, Bulletin 77 (Washington, D.C., 1945), 12–24.

47 As quoted in Melvyn Dubofsky and Warren Van Tine, *John L. Lewis: A Biography* (New York, 1978), 456–7.

48 "Money and Real Weekly Earnings during Defense, War and Reconversion Periods," *Monthly Labor Review*, 64 (1947), 989; H. M. Douty, "Review of Basic American Labor Conditions," in Warne, ed., *Labor in Postwar America*, 109–20.

49 "Work Stoppages Caused by Labor Management Disputes in 1945," *Monthly Labor Review*, 62 (1946), 726–8; *Chester Wright's Labor Letter*, October 5, 1945. For accounts of these general strikes and of those at Rochester, New York, Pittsburgh, Pennsylvania, and Oakland, California, that followed in 1946, see George Lipsitz, *Class and Culture in Cold War America: "A Rainbow at Midnight"* (South Hadley, Mass., 1982), 56–86.

50 *Labor Action*, May 7, 1945; *PM*, May 19, 1945; *Wage Earner*, June 22, 1945; *United Auto Worker*, May 1, July 1, 1945; UAW Executive Board Minutes, July 16–23, 1945, 22–3, 58–61. Widespread uneasiness in Detroit UAW

ranks was also reflected in a large number of defeats for incumbent local union officers. At Willow Run, now threatened with virtual abandonment, candidates close to the Rank and File caucus ousted incumbent officers loyal to R. J. Thomas. In the strategic Ford Local 600, partisans of Walter Reuther gained control of the general council and took several top posts there. *Wage Earner*, March 30, 1945; *Rank and Filer*, April 1945; *Militant*, May 5, 1945.

51 UAW Executive Board Minutes, September 10–18, 1945, 98–106 (Thomas's quotation is on p. 46); *The New York Times*, September 16, 1945; Preis, *Labor's Giant Step*, 262.

52 *United Auto Worker*, September 1, 1945; UAW Executive Board Minutes, September 10–18, 1945, 46, 56–8. Secretary-Treasurer George Addes reported that the dues-paying UAW membership had dropped by 500,000 in the weeks following V-J Day, and he recommended an immediate staff cut of fifty field representatives.

53 Rosa Lee Swafford, *Wartime Record of Strikes and Lockouts, 1940–1945* (Washington, D.C., 1946), 20–1; UAW Executive Board Minutes, September 10–18, 1945, 19–23.

54 *Time*, September 24, 1945; *The New York Times*, September 16, 17, 19, 21, 30, 1945; *Labor Action*, September 24, October 15, 1945; *Militant*, September 29, 1945; Swafford, *Wartime Record*, 21; UAW Executive Board Minutes, September 10–18, 1945, 59–62. At one point during the strike, 100 Detroit unionists threw up a picket line in Flint, where the UAW executive board was meeting to demand that the international authorize rather than suppress the Kelsey–Hayes strike.

55 C. Wright Mills, *The New Men of Power* (New York, 1948), 9; UAW Executive Board Minutes, September 10–18, 1945, 47–8.

56 Victor G. Reuther, "Look Forward Labor," *Common Sense*, 14 (1945), 8–9.

57 Of course, Walter always stood slightly to the right of his brother Victor and was never so bold when writing in *The New York Times Magazine* as Victor could be in *Common Sense* and other left–liberal publications. Nevertheless, Walter Reuther also considered the Labor–Management conference a "phony" and took a very critical attitude toward the Truman administration and the Democratic party during the GM strike period. See *The New York Times Magazine*, September 16, 1945; *Labor Action*, November 12, 1945.

By the winter of 1946, the Mazey group in the UAW and most who identified with the wartime Rank and File caucus backed Reuther for the UAW presidency. Of the seventy largest locals in the union, about three-quarters of their delegates who had voted against the no-strike pledge in 1944 cast their ballots in favor of Reuther in 1946. Conversely, about three-quarters of those who had backed the no-strike pledge in 1944 voted for R. J. Thomas in 1946. The data were derived from vote lists, UAW, *Proceedings*, 1944 and 1946 conventions.

58 Barton Bernstein, "Walter Reuther and the General Motors Strike of 1945–1946," *Michigan History*, 49 (1965), 264–6.

59 Victor Reuther, *The Brothers Reuther and the Story of the UAW: A Memoir* (Boston, 1976), 246–56; Irving Howe and B. J. Widick offer an insightful analysis of the GM strike program in *The UAW and Walter Reuther* (New York, 1949), 136–48. See also the UAW pamphlet, "Purchasing Power for Prosperity," in UAW–GM Collection, Box 3.

60 *The New York Times*, December 30, 1945.

61 Interview with Victor Reuther, Washington, D.C., September 25, 1979.
62 For an excellent discussion of GM's strategy, see Harris, *Right to Manage*, 139–43. See also Bureau of National Affairs, *17 Labor Relations Reference Manual* (Washington, D.C., 1946), 2544–52.
63 Alvin W. Gouldner offers a perceptive interpretation of the function of the wage demand in aggregating localist grievances in *Wildcat Strike: A Study in Worker–Management Relations* (Yellow Springs, Ohio, 1954), 32–7.
64 Reuther first presented this strategy at the Flint meeting of the UAW leadership. *UAW Executive Board Minutes*, September 10–18, 1945, 43–8, 54.
65 The Ford–UAW negotiations are discussed in Harris, *Right to Manage*, 143–6; Bureau of National Affairs, *17 Labor Relations Reference Manual*, 2327–34; in Allan Nevins and Frank Hill, *Ford: Decline and Rebirth, 1933–1962* (New York, 1962), 302–7; and in Benjamin M. Selekman et al., *Problems in Labor Relations* (New York, 1948), 361–80.
66 *Wage Earner*, December 7, 1945; *Militant*, January 12, March 23, 1946; *The New York Times*, March 15, 1945; Fred H. Joiner, "Developments in Union Agreements," in Colston E. Warne, ed., *Labor in Postwar America* (New York, 1949), 25–34. The one-at-a-time strike strategy proved a tactical failure. GM competitors were unable to take advantage of the giant auto maker's 113-day shutdown because shortages of power, raw materials, and components limited their own production. So confident was GM that in early December 1945 it offered to reopen those of its parts plants that supplied competing auto manufacturers. Initially, Reuther and Thomas accepted the offer, but a tide of local union opposition, cognizant of the effect that such a move might have on rank-and-file morale, forced the union leadership to reverse its decision.
67 *Journal of Commerce*, November 13, 1945.
68 Edward W. Livernash, *Collective Bargaining in the Basic Steel Industry* (Washington, D.C., 1961), 242–4; Barton Bernstein, "The Truman Administration and the Steel Strike of 1946," *Journal of American History*, 52 (1966), 793–6.
69 As quoted in Livernash, *Collective Bargaining*, 252.
70 See, for example, the comments of Lens, *Left, Right and Center*, 366; and Bernstein, "The Truman Administration and the Steel Strike," 794.
71 *Wage Earner*, December 21, 1945.
72 Brecher, *Strike!* (San Francisco, 1972), 277; Bernstein, "The Truman Administration and the Steel Strike," 798–800.
73 Bernstein, "Walter Reuther and the General Motors Strike," 273–4; Clayton W. Fountain, *Union Guy* (New York, 1949), 183–4; *Wage Earner*, March 1, 8, 1946. As early as January 20, Reuther knew that Murray had agreed to accept eighteen and a half cents in the steel negotiations. The executive board then authorized Ford and Chrysler negotiators to conclude settlements at this level. UAW Executive Board Minutes, January 12–22, 1946, 134. For the UE's defense of its early contract with GM, see Albert J. Fitzgerald to R. J. Thomas, February 22, 1946, CIO Secretary-Treasurer Collection, Box 62.
74 *Wage Earner*, March 15, 1946; Sidney Lens points out that the eighteen-and-a-half-cent pattern held only for the strongest unions in the largest industries. Workers in retail trade, textiles, the garment industry, and lumber won less in the first postwar round. Lens, *Left, Right and Center*, 367–9.

75 Joel Seidman, *American Labor from Defense to Reconversion* (Chicago, 1953), 233–44.

12. Epilogue: Labor in postwar America

1 Fred H. Joiner, "Developments in Union Agreements," in Colston E. Warne, ed., *Labor in Postwar America* (Brooklyn, N.Y., 1949), 25–34; Ross M. Robertson, *History of the American Economy* (New York, 1973), 672–3; Paul Sultan, *Labor Economics* (New York, 1957), 123, 144–6.

2 Mary Sperling McAuliffe, *Crisis on the Left: Cold War Politics and American Liberals, 1947–1954* (Amherst, Mass., 1978), 14–15; Harvey A. Levenstein, *Communism, Anticommunism, and the CIO* (Westport, Conn., 1981), 208–32.

3 Levenstein, *Communism, Anticommunism*, 253–68, provides a good account of the defection of Curran and Quill.

4 David Brody, "The Uses of Power II: Political Action," in Brody, *Workers in Industrial America: Essays on the Twentieth Century Struggle* (New York, 1980), 222–5; see also Mike Davis, "The Barren Marriage of American Labour and the Democratic Party," *New Left Review*, 124 (1980), 72–4.

5 McAuliffe, *Crisis on the Left*, 41–7; Levenstein, *Communism, Anticommunism*, 280–97; Brody, "The Uses of Power," 226–8.

6 For an elaboration of some of these ideas, see Levenstein, *Communism, Anticommunism*, 330–40. A staunch defense of the Communist-line unions, which nevertheless offers some indication of the tragic consequences the CIO suffered on their expulsion, is found in Frank Emspak, "The Break-up of the Congress of Industrial Organizations (CIO), 1945–1950," unpublished Ph.D. diss., University of Wisconsin, 1972, 135–90, passim.

7 This paragraph relies heavily upon Davis, "The Barren Marriage," 74–5.

8 R. Alton Lee, *Truman and Taft–Hartley* (Lexington, Mass., 1966), 32–43, 94–6; Bert Cochran, *Harry Truman and the Crisis Presidency* (New York, 1973), 215–20.

9 A good summary of Taft–Hartley is provided in Lloyd Ulman, "Unionism and Collective Bargaining in the Modern Period," in Seymour E. Harris, ed., *American Economic History* (New York, 1961), 428–36.

10 Ulman, "Unionism and Collective Bargaining in the Modern Period," 436–48; Sanford Cohen, *Labor in the United States* (Columbus, Ohio, 1966), 215–28; and on the influence of the NWLB, see Sanford M. Jacoby and Daniel J. B. Mitchell, "Development of Contractual Features of the Union–Management Relationship," paper presented at the spring meeting of the Industrial Relations Research Association, Milwaukee, April 30, 1982.

11 For an assessment of the postwar regimentation of the labor movement, see Richard Edwards, *Contested Terrain: The Transformation of the Workplace in the Twentieth Century* (New York, 1979), 163–216, passim.

12 Bureau of National Affairs, "Significant Changes in Local Issue Bargaining Noted in Autos and Steel," *Daily Labor Report*, No. 243 (August 18, 1973), 4; Jack Stieber, *Govering the UAW* (New York, 1962), 131–57; William Serrin, *The Company and the Union* (New York, 1974), 303–33.

13 Frederick H. Harbison, "The General Motors–United Auto Workers Agreement of 1950," *Journal of Political Economy*, 58 (1950), 408; "The Treaty of Detroit," *Fortune*, 42 (1950), 53.

14 See, for example, Robert M. C. Littler, "Managers Must Manage," *Harvard Business Review*, 24 (1946), 366–76; and Clark Kerr, "Employer Policies in Industrial Relations, 1945–1947," in Warne, ed., *Labor in Postwar America*, 43–76.

15 Joiner, "Developments in Union Agreements," 34–5; Julius Rezler, *Automation and Industrial Labor* (New York, 1969), 83–196, passim. For brief discussions of the conflict over automation in specific industries, see George Strauss, "The Shifting Power Balance in the Plant," *Industrial Relations*, 1 (1962), 76–9, and Robert M. MacDonald, *Collective Bargaining in the Automobile Industry: A Study of Wage Structure and Competitive Relations* (New Haven, Conn., 1963), 99–104. A good account of the 1959 steel strike is found in Edward W. Livernash, *Collective Bargaining in the Basic Steel Industry* (Washington, D.C., 1961), 113–17, 300–7.

16 As quoted in Strauss, "Shifting Power Balance in the Plant," 82.

17 Jack Stieber, "Work Rules and Practices in Mass Production Industries," in *Proceedings of the 14th Annual Meeting of the Industrial Relations Research Association* (New York, 1961), 399–412; James W. Kuhn, *Bargaining in Grievance Settlement: The Power of Industrial Work Groups* (New York, 1961), 34–57, 144–66; Garth L. Mangum, "Taming Wildcat Strikes," *Harvard Business Review*, 38 (1960), 88.

18 For an excellent discussion of these developments, see R. Herding, *Job Control and Union Structure* (Rotterdam, 1972), 131–59.

19 This issue is followed more closely in Nelson Lichtenstein, "Conflict over Workers' Control: The Automobile Industry in World War II," in Michael Frisch and Daniel Walkowitz, eds., *Working Class History: Toward an Integrated View of Labor in American Life* (Urbana, Ill., 1982).

20 Two good essays that illuminate several of the ideas mentioned above are Stanley Aronowitz, "The Labor Movement and the Left," *Socialist Review*, 44 (1979), 9–61; and Sumner Rosen, "The United States: A Time for Reassessment," in Soloman Barkin, ed., *Worker Militancy and Its Consequences, 1965–1975* (New York, 1975), 333–63. See also Hyman, *Strikes*, 11–51, for a contrasting survey of the British scene.

Bibliographical essay

Manuscript sources

Manuscript sources for a study of the CIO are located in a variety of depositories. The following collections are only the most important consulted for this book. The papers of Philip Murray and John Brophy are found at the Catholic University of America, along with the official CIO archives. These collections are somewhat disappointing, although they do contain considerable correspondence between the CIO's general office and its affiliates for the years 1937 to 1943. The notebooks of Richard Deverall, onetime director of education for the UAW and later a field representative for the Office of War Information are also at the Catholic University. These notebooks provide much valuable reportage on the internal politics of the various CIO unions during the first half of the war. A multireel microfilm transcript of the CIO's executive board minutes is found at Wayne State University's Walter Reuther Library, along with the rather thin CIO Secretary–Treasurer's Collection.

The Reuther Library holds most of the enormous UAW collection. Among the major manuscript collections found there are those of the principal wartime UAW officers: George Addes, R. J. Thomas, Richard Frankensteen, and Walter Reuther. The UAW–General Motors and the UAW Executive Board Collections proved rich sources in revealing something of the character of the shop-floor struggle as seen by the union leadership. The Victor Reuther–War Policy Committee papers contained much material on the UAW's relationship to the wartime mobilization process. Among the local union manuscript collections, I found the papers of locals 3 (Dodge) and 212 (Briggs) most illuminating on shop-floor issues. These can be supplemented by a careful reading of the *United Automobile Worker* and its numerous independently edited local editions, including those of locals 3 (Dodge), 7 (Chrysler), 190 (Packard), 212 (Briggs), 365 (Brewster), 400 (Ford Lincoln), 599 (GM–Flint), 600 (Ford–Rouge), and 887 (North American Aviation).

Other important manuscript collections used in the preparation of this book include those of the International Longshoremen and Warehousemen's Union and the Amalgamated Clothing Workers Union both housed in their respective union headquarters in San Francisco and New York. The former contains a complete file of all CIO circular letters, plus much material on California labor during the war; the latter is a rich source for understanding the problems faced by the CIO in the late 1930s and for the formation of the CIO–Political Action Committee in 1943 and 1944. Sidney Hillman's career can also be traced quite well. The W. Jett Lauck papers at the University of Virginia offer important insights into the strategy John L. Lewis pursued in the coal strikes of 1941 and 1943. Material on the internal life of the United Steelworkers of America is found in both the Murray papers at the Catholic University and at the Pennslyvania State University, the depository for a much larger collection of USW material.

The most important government archive used in this work was the voluminous records of the National Defense Mediation Board and the National War Labor Board (Record Group 202) in the National Archives. This collection is well organized and contains a generally complete transcript of all the important meetings and hearings of the NDMB and the NWLB. Chairman William Hammett Davis has a useful oral history in the Columbia Oral History Collection, but his papers at the University of Wisconsin proved disappointing in terms of his wartime career. The Wayne Morse Collection at the University of Oregon contains a series of personal letters and memoranda that reveals this maverick administrator and politician at his acerbic best. I also used the still unorganized NWLB files for Region Ten (California) located at the University of California's Institute of Industrial Relations at Berkeley.

Before plunging into these collections, one should consult the Bureau of National Affairs' well-indexed *War Labor Reports*, 1942–6 (26 vols.) and the Department of Labor's *Termination Report of the National War Labor Board* (Washington, 1947). The latter is a topically organized summary of the major policy decisions of the board; the former contains a wealth of information from labor, management, and the government about industrial conditions in specific companies and industries, as well as the directive orders of the NWLB in each case that came before it. Also useful is Allen R. Richards's *War Labor Boards in the Field* (Chapel Hill, N.C., 1953) and the Department of Labor publications *Report on the Work of the National Defense Mediation Board* (Washington, D.C., 1942) and *Problems and Policies of Dispute Settlement and Wage Stabilization during World War II* (Washington, D.C., 1950).

Also in the National Archives are the records of the War Production Board (Record Group 79), which contain much material on the Reuther Plan and the reconversion controversy. Under Secretary of War Robert Patterson's papers are in the Library of Congress and contain a record of the army's decision to suppress the North American Aviation strike and then help rebuild a loyal UAW local in Southern California. The Franklin D. Roosevelt Library at Hyde Park, New York, is an extremely well-organized archive that contains a number of important collections reflecting the national administration's relationship to the union movement. Much of the material upon which FDR acted is preserved in his private and official correspondence, but one should not neglect the very useful papers of Oscar Cox, Wayne Coy, Isador Lubin, Leon Henderson, Harold Smith, and Samuel I. Rosenman also on deposit at Hyde Park.

Industrial unionism

Although a number of excellent studies of CIO affiliates have begun to appear, no integrated history of the industrial union movement now exists. Several of David Brody's essays, now collected in his *Workers in Industrial America: Essays on the 20th Century Struggle* (New York, 1980), constitute the basis for a new cycle of revisionism, but his work must still be supplemented by a number of older studies from the school of institutional labor economics. The two standard overviews of the CIO in the 1930s and 1940s are Irving Bernstein, *Turbulent Years: A History of the American Worker, 1933–1941* (Boston, 1969), and Joel Seidman, *American Labor from Defense to Reconversion* (Chicago, 1953). But the two information-packed volumes edited by Colston E. Warne in the 1940s should not be overlooked. These are *Yearbook of American Labor* (New York, 1944) and *Labor in*

Postwar America (New York, 1949). Art Preis's *Labor's Giant Step* (New York, 1972) offers a Trotskyist interpretation that is often a refreshing challenge to the undaunted Whiggery of many of these other studies. In 1975 *Radical America* published a special issue (August–September) on labor in the 1940s. The journal included a valuable memoir by Stan Weir and essays by a number of younger labor historians, including Jim Green, Nelson Lichtenstein, Ronald Schatz, Ed Jennings, and Patty Quick.

As the largest and most politically significant of all the new CIO unions, the UAW has naturally attracted the most attention. Important older studies of this union include Irving Howe and B. J. Widick, *The UAW and Walter Reuther* (New York, 1949); Jack Skeels, "The Development of Political Stability within the United Auto Workers Union" (unpublished Ph.D. diss., University of Wisconsin, 1957); Jack Stieber, *Governing the UAW* (New York, 1962); and the exhaustive Sidney Fine, *Sitdown: The General Motors Strike of 1936–37* (Ann Arbor, Mich., 1969). Two studies that focus on the character of shop-floor militancy are Peter Friedlander, *The Emergence of a UAW Local, 1936–39: A Study in Class and Culture* (Pittsburgh, 1975), and Martin Glaberman, *Wartime Strikes: The Struggle against the No-Strike Pledge in the UAW* (Detroit, 1980). These should be supplemented by the dense and lengthy record of the U.S. Senate's *Hearings before a Special Committee Investigating the National Defense Program*, Part 28: *Manpower Problems in Detroit* (Washington, D.C., 1945), which closely reviews shop-floor production restrictions and the wildcat strike issue in hundreds of pages of testimony from a variety of witnesses. August Meier and Elliott Rudwick examine the relationship between the UAW and the black community, including the hate strike phenomenon, in their *Black Detroit and the Rise of the UAW* (New York, 1979). Over the years, a number of memoirs by UAW activists have been published. Among the most useful to this study have been Clayton Fountain, *Union Guy* (New York, 1949); Frank Marquart, *An Auto Worker's Journal* (University Park, Pa., 1975); Al Nash, "A Unionist Remembers," *Dissent*, 24 (Spring 1977), 181–9; and Victor Reuther, *The Brothers Reuther and the Story of the UAW: A Memoir* (Boston, 1976).

The United Steelworkers of America have not fared as well as a subject for the historian's interest. Clinton S. Golden and Harold J. Ruttenberg's *The Dynamics of Industrial Democracy* (New York, 1942) is a fascinating portrait of the bureaucratic mentality as revealed in the writings of two of the union's early officers, and Morris Cooke and Philip Murray's *Organized Labor and Production* (New York, 1946) provides important insights into the social ideology of the first USW president. Lloyd Ulman's *Government of the Steelworkers Union* (New York, 1962) is a workmanlike, convention-focused history of the union, and Edward Livernash's *Collective Bargaining in the Basic Steel Industry* (Washington, D.C., 1961) contains a good record of the tripartite bargaining relationship established among the union, the government, and the industry. David J. McDonald's *Union Man* (New York, 1969) is an unexpectedly frank and useful autobiography.

Two good dissertations have been written on the UE. Ronald Filippelli, "The United Electrical, Radio and Machine Workers of America, 1933–1949: The Struggle for Control" (unpublished Ph.D. diss., Pennsylvania State University, 1970), is a balanced account of internal factionalism, and Ronald Schatz, "American Electrical Workers: Work, Struggles, Aspirations, 1930–1950" (unpublished Ph.D. diss., University of Pittsburgh, 1977), is a perceptive social history very much in the tradition of David Montgomery. James J. Matles and

James Higgins's *Them and Us* (Englewood Cliffs, N.J., 1974) is a disappointing memoir by the union's general secretary that virtually ignores the war years. Other union histories that cover the 1940s include Harold S. Roberts, *The Rubber Workers* (New York, 1944), and David Brody, *The Butcher Workmen: A Study of Unionization* (Cambridge, Mass., 1964), the standard account of the two meat-packing unions. Robert Ozanne's *A Century of Labor–Management Relations at McCormick and International Harvester* (Madison, Wis., 1967) contains two good chapters on the farm equipment workers and their struggle to unionize the old-line agriculture implement makers. Paul D. Richards, "The History of the Textile Workers Union of America, CIO, in the South, 1937–1945" (unpublished Ph.D. diss., University of Wisconsin, 1978), makes use of the TWUA's large collection on deposit with the Wisconsin Historical Society.

Biography is usually a poor method by which to examine the texture of a social movement such as the CIO, but historians and journalists have been unable to resist the lure of this genre. Any study of trade union leadership in the 1940s must begin with C. Wright Mills's seminal collective portrait, *The New Men of Power* (New York, 1948). Matthew Josephson's *Sidney Hillman: Statesman of American Labor* (New York, 1952) and Frank Cormier and William J. Eaton's *Reuther* (Englewood Cliffs, N.J., 1970) were both biographies authorized by the unions of which these individuals were once president. These should soon be superseded by new scholarly studies of Hillman by Steve Fraser and of Reuther by John Barnard. Charles P. Larrowe's *Harry Bridges, the Rise and Fall of Radical Labor* (New York, 1971) devotes relatively little space to the Bridges leadership in the 1940s. A model for all labor biographies is Melvyn Dubofsky and Warren Van Tine, *John L. Lewis: A Biography* (New York, 1978), which makes an impor-tant contribution to understanding the relationship between the union move-ment and the state apparatus in the decades after 1935. Joseph C. Goulden's *Meany: The Unchallenged Strong Man of American Labor* (New York, 1972) lacks much historical understanding but nevertheless provides considerable material on the AFL's relationship with both the CIO and the NWLB during the war.

In the decade since I began research on this study, the oral history of the labor movement has come of age, with major projects undertaken and depositories established at The Tamiment Institute, Pennsylvania State University, the Ohio Historical Society, the University of Michigan, University of North Carolina, and Wayne State University. The elite-oriented Columbia Oral History Collec-tion contains transcripts of Lee Pressman, John Brophy, James Carey, and Julius Emspak. Wayne State University has an extensive collection, and there I found useful the interviews with John W. Anderson, Jack Conway, Joseph Ferris, Richard Frankensteen, Nat Ganley, Carl Haessler, Frank Marquart, Leon Pody, and R. J. Thomas. In addition, I conducted several interviews, and these are footnotes throughout the text where appropriate.

Politics and the unions

A discussion of the complex relationship between the new industrial unions and the national political scene is, of course, intrinsic to any study of the labor movement in the 1940s. Works that focus specifically on the CIO's political apparatus include James C. Foster, *The Union Politic: The CIO Political Action Committee* (Columbia, Mo., 1975), and William Riker, "The CIO in Politics, 1936–1948" (unpublished Ph.D. diss., Harvard University, 1948). Joseph

Gaer's *The First Round* (New York, 1944) conveniently compiles a valuable collection of CIO–PAC pamphlets, resolutions, and vote mobilization guides used in the 1944 campaign. Kenneth Waltzer's "The American Labor Party: Third Party Politics in New Deal–Cold War New York, 1936–1954" (unpublished Ph.D. diss., Harvard University, 1977) is an excellent guide to the Byzantine labor politics of the city, and Mike Davis's "The Barren Marriage of American Labor and the Democratic Party," *New Left Review*, 124 (November–December 1980) 43–84, is an insightful indictment of the CIO's failure to adopt an independent political orientation. The fate of popular front liberalism in this era is well recorded in Norman Markowitz's *The Rise and Fall of the People's Century: Henry A. Wallace and American Liberalism, 1941–1948* (New York, 1973) and in Mary Sperling McAuliffe's *Crisis on the Left: Cold War Politics and American Liberals, 1947–1954* (Amherst, Mass., 1978).

In the first quarter century of the Cold War, historical work on the role of the Communists in the trade unions was almost entirely subordinated to the orthodoxies of that conflict. Max Kampelman's *The Communist Party vs. the CIO* (New York, 1952) is the best (or worst) example of this genre. Irving Howe and Lewis Coser, *The American Communist Party: A Critical History* (New York, 1962), reflects a neo-Trotskyist viewpoint. Bert Cochran, *Labor and Communism, the Conflict that Shaped American Unions* (Princeton, N.J., 1977), and Roger Keeran, *The Communist Party and the Auto Workers Unions* (Bloomington, Ind., 1980), offer well-researched but contrasting perspectives on party work in the UAW and other unions. Harvey A. Levenstein's *Communism, Anticommunism and the CIO* (Westport, Conn., 1981) summarizes much recent scholarship, and Maurice Isserman provides a thorough and sympathetic treatment of party work in his *Which Side Were You On? The American Communist Party during the Second World War* (Middletown, Conn., 1982). Ex-Communists have begun to write memoirs of considerable insight. Among the best are Robert Starobin, *American Communism in Crisis, 1943–1957* (Berkeley, 1972), and Al Richmond, *A Long View from the Left* (Boston, 1973).

Any study of the CIO requires the extensive use of newspapers and periodicals. *The CIO News, United Auto Worker, Steel Labor, Advance* (Amalgamated Clothing Workers of America), *UE News, United Mine Workers Journal, United Rubber Worker*, and *Textile Labor* proved useful in following the official line of the trade union leadership especially in regard to the shifting course of government labor policy in the 1940s. The annual or semiannual published proceedings of the various international unions, including those of the CIO and its state industrial union councils (especially in Michigan), often provided a much better guide to the internal politics of these unions. If one takes into account their particular "line," then the publications of several of the radical political groups prove essential in understanding the changing relationship between the various factions of the union leadership and their often heterogeneous constituency. Among these sources were the *Daily Worker* and the *Communist* (Communist party); *Labor Action* and the *New International* (Workers party); *The Militant* and the *Fourth International* (Socialist Workers party); and the *New Leader* (Social Democratic Federation). *The Wage Earner* provided excellent reportage on the Detroit scene from the perspective of the Association of Catholic Trade Unionists. From a broadly popular front viewpoint, *PM*, the New York City daily, offered a close reading of CIO politics and internal affairs. The business-oriented press also offered significant coverage of the industrial union movement. *Business Week* probed the industrial relations scene in virtually every issue, and *Chester Wright's Labor Letter* provided its subscribers with a running commentary on government labor policy. *Fortune's* periodic essays on the working class and their unions were of unusually high caliber during the war years.

Social history of the working class

No adequate social and economic history of the American home front during World War II has yet been written; the subject may be too vast for any definitive study. Two highly readable, yet critical, overviews of the war are Richard Polenberg, *War and Society: The United States, 1941–1945* (New York, 1972), and John Morton Blum, *V was for Victory: Politics and American Culture during World War II* (New York, 1976). Richard R. Lingerman's *Don't You Know There's a War On?* (New York, 1970) and Geoffrey Perrett's *Days of Sadness, Years of Triumph: The American People, 1939–1945* (Baltimore, 1973) are probably the best of a poor lot of popular social histories, but Alan Clive's *State of War: Michigan in World War II* (Ann Arbor, 1979) sets a new standard for state historical studies.

The study of the social history of American workers during World War II is in its infancy. An essential source is the *Monthly Labor Review*, as well as the many occasional bulletins put out by the Bureau of Labor Statistics. Strike statistics are summarized in Rosa L. Swafford, *Wartime Record of Strikes and Lockouts, 1940–1946* (Washington, D.C., 1946). A number of impressionistic surveys appeared during the war or shortly thereafter. Among the best of these are Mary Heaton Vorse's "And the Workers Say . . . ," *Public Opinion Quarterly*, 7 (Fall 1943), 443–56; John Dos Passos, *State of the Nation* (New York, 1944); Katherine Archibald, *Diary of a Wartime Shipyard* (Berkeley, 1947); and Harriette Arnow's brilliant novel of wartime Detroit, *The Dollmaker* (New York, 1962). Charles Denby's *Indignant Heart: A Black Worker's Journal* (Boston, 1978) is a moving account of shop-floor racial tension and accommodation in the motor city.

Sociologists were close contemporary students of American war workers, although their observations were often just as impressionistic as those of novelists such as Dos Passos and Arnow. See, for example, Jerome F. Scott and George C. Homans, "Reflections on the Wildcat Strikes," *American Sociological Review*, 54 (June 1947), 278–87, and Lowell J. Carr and James E. Stermer, *Willow Run: A Study of Industrialization and Cultural Inadequacy* (New York, 1952). Joshua Freeman and Nelson Lichtenstein offer divergent interpretations of the wildcat strike phenomenon in two recent essays: "Delivering the Goods: Industrial Unionism during World War II," *Labor History*, 19 (Fall 1978), 574–91, and "Auto Worker Militancy and the Structure of Factory Life, 1937–1955," *Journal of American History*, 67 (1980), 335–53.

By far the most imaginative work on the social history of American workers during the war has been devoted to understanding the changing status of women. William Chafe's *The American Woman: Her Changing Social, Economic and Political Roles, 1920–1970* (New York, 1970) contains a pioneering evaluation of the war-time experience, but three new studies have refined, and in some cases revised, his summary. These are Leila Rupp, *Mobilizing Women for War, German and American Propaganda, 1939–1945* (Princeton, N.J., 1978); Karen Anderson, *Wartime Women: Sex Roles, Family Relations and the Status of Women during World War II* (Westport, Conn., 1981); and Ruth Milkman's highly sophisticated and densely researched "The Reproduction of Job Segregation by Sex: A Study of the

Changing Sexual Division of Labor in the Auto and Electrical Manufacturing Industries in the 1940s" (unpublished Ph.D. diss., University of California, Berkeley, 1981).

The political economy

The social history of workers and the institutional history of the unions cannot be divorced from the investigation of the war era's political economy. A number of good studies have appeared, written both by contemporaries, usually government officials, and by latter-day historians. The two most useful official publications are the Bureau of the Budget, *The United States at War: Development and Administration of the War Program by the Federal Government* (Washington, D. C., 1946), and the Civilian Production Administration's *Industrial Mobilization for War* (Washington, D.C., 1947), which offers an exhaustive internal history of the War Production Board. Memoirs by Bruce Catton, *The War Lords of Washington* (New York, 1948), and Donald Nelson, *The Arsenal of Democracy* (New York, 1946), are critical of military and big business control of the production program, whereas Eliot Janeway's *Struggle for Survival, A Chronicle of Economic Mobilization in World War II* (New Haven, Conn., 1951) casts most of its arrows at the administrative ineptness of the Roosevelt administration itself. Herman Miles Somers, *Presidential Agency: The Office of War Mobilization and Reconversion* (Cambridge, Mass., 1950), is a colorless administrative history of that important agency.

David Brody's "The New Deal and World War II" in John Braeman et al., *The New Deal: The National Level* (Columbus, Ohio, 1975), is a concise guide to the often complicated disputes that divided government policymakers. Brody argues that the war represented a consolidation of New Deal reformism that at the same time created the economic and political conditions that halted its postwar advance. Paul A. C. Koistinen's "The Hammer and the Sword: Labor, the Military and Industrial Mobilization, 1920–1945" (unpublished Ph.D. diss., University of California, Berkeley, 1965) is an exhaustive indictment of military control of the production effort. It is more readably condensed as "Mobilizing the World War II Economy: Labor and the Industrial Military Alliance," *Pacific Historical Review* 42 (1973), 443–78. Several essays by Barton Bernstein reflect much that was best in New Left scholarship. These include "The Automobile Industry and the Coming of the Second World War," *Southwestern Social Science Quarterly* 47 (1966), 20–32; "The Truman Administration and Its Reconversion Wage Policy," *Labor History* 6 (1965), 214–31; and "The Debate on Industrial Reconversion: The Protection of Oligopoly and Military Control of the Economy," *American Journal of Economics and Sociology* 26 (1967), 159–72. The best study of the national service legislation controversy appears in Bryon Fairchild and Jonathan Grossman, *The Army and Industrial Manpower* (Washington, D.C., 1959). A sympathetic evaluation of Paul McNutt and the War Manpower Commission is offered in George Q. Flynn, *The Mess in Washington: Manpower Mobilization in World War II* (Westport, Conn., 1979). Finally, business ideology and practice are probed in two fine books: Robert M. Collins, *The Business Response to Keynes, 1929–1964* (New York, 1981); and Howell John Harris, *The Right to Manage: Industrial Relations Policies of American Business in the 1940s* (Madison, Wis., 1982).

Index

309